American Association of Collegiate Registrars and Admissions Officers

The AACRAO International Guide

A Resource for International Education Professionals

Edited By

DEANA WILLIAMS | **MARY BAXTON** | **ROBERT WATKINS**

The AACRAO
International Guide

American Association of Collegiate
Registrars and Admissions Officers
One Dupont Circle, NW, Suite 520
Washington, DC 20036–1135

Tel: (202) 293–9161 | Fax: (202) 872–8857 | www.aacrao.org

For a complete listing of AACRAO publications, visit www.aacrao.org/publications.

The American Association of Collegiate Registrars and Admissions Officers, founded in 1910, is a nonprofit, voluntary, professional association of more than 10,000 higher education administrators who represent more than 2,600 institutions and agencies in the United States and in twenty-eight countries around the world. The mission of the Association is to provide leadership in policy initiation, interpretation, and implementation in the global educational community. This is accomplished through the identification and promotion of standards and best practices in enrollment management, information technology, instructional management, and student services.

LIBRARY OF CONGRESS CATALOGING-IN-PUBLICATION DATA

The AACRAO international guide: a resource for international education professionals/edited by Deana Williams, Robert Watkins, Mary Baxton. — 2010 update.

p. cm.

ISBN 978-1-57858-093-4

1. Student exchange programs—United States.
2. Universities and colleges—United States—Admission.

I. Williams, Deana.
II. Watkins, Robert.
III. Baxton, Mary.
IV. American Association of Collegiate Registrars and Admissions Officers
V. Title: American Association of Collegiate Registrars and Admissions Officers international guide.

LB2376.4.G85 2010
370.116'20973—dc22
2010032483

Table of Contents

NINE

The International Aspects of Enrollment Management

TEN

International Undergraduate Admissions Checklist

ELEVEN

Graduate Admissions Issues

TWELVE

Community College Issues

C

THIRTEEN

Student Visa and Immigration Issues

FOURTEEN

Orientation as a Key Component to International Student Success

FIFTEEN

Special International Student Populations: Undocumented Students

SIXTEEN

Special International Student Populations: Students with Disabilities

SEVENTEEN

Special International Student Populations: College Athletes

EIGHTEEN

Financial Aid and Regulatory Considerations

NINETEEN

English Proficiency Tests and University Admissions

TWENTY

The Evolving Field of Education Abroad

Introduction

One of the fastest growing sectors of higher education administration in the United States is the field of international education. Once the preserve of a seeming handful of experts, the field of international education has grown exponentially to include specialists in immigration advising; recruitment and admissions; credential evaluation; international undergraduate and graduate admissions; English language assessment; international athlete evaluation; education abroad advising; and many other aspects of this sometimes arcane field. AACRAO has been involved in providing resources for better understanding this complex arena for much of the second half of the association's first hundred years. In addition to numerous individual country educational system volumes, AACRAO published a guide for international education professionals in 1994, followed by a revised edition in 2001. This current volume, *The 2010 International Guide,* further updates those prior books with a rich array of topics by knowledgeable experts in international education.

We begin the book with an overview that provides a compelling look at the field as it now stands and end it with a tantalizing glimpse of the future of international education. In between these overviews are a series of chapters on an array of issues faced by international education professionals across the country. Some of these issues—such as international recruitment and enrollment management, fraudulent documents, and the continuing saga of the Bologna Process, which has been sweeping Europe for over a decade now—engender much discussion and, indeed, debate throughout U.S. higher education. The *Guide* also addresses vital concerns such as international credential evaluation, office policies and procedures, undergraduate and graduate admissions questions, and English proficiency assessment, often in a how-to format that enables the reader to create or revise institutional policies regarding these important topics.

Most of the authors are established experts in the field whose names will be very familiar to international education practitioners. Some of the authors, on the other hand, will be new to AACRAO members. Yet the expertise of these contributors quickly becomes apparent as they address the specific international subject of their chapters. The wealth of knowledge and expertise represented in the following twenty-three chapters assures the reader of a truly comprehensive review of the entire field of international education. The appendices to the *Guide* represent a fitting epilogue by listing key resources, organizations, and publications, capped off with the AACRAO Bill of Rights and Responsibilities for International Students and Institutions.

No single volume, however wide-ranging, can provide all the answers to the questions that arise in international education. One reason that so many of us have remained in the field for as long as we have is that international education is complex and ever-changing. What was true last year or even last week may not be true today. The *Guide* is a good place to start in grappling with the myriad aspects of international education. It is hoped that it will serve to inspire a desire for more information, information that can be found through networking with other international educators and attending sessions at events such as the AACRAO Annual Meeting and the many state and regional associational conferences. Equally important publications on various international education subjects are also available through AACRAO. The *Guide* will introduce

you to this fascinating field and provide a solid foundation of knowledge, through which you can investigate
further aspects of this dynamic subject.

Robert Watkins
The University of Texas at Austin
AACRAO Vice President for International Education

About the Authors

Teri Albrecht, Ph.D.

Teri is the Director of International Student & Scholar Services at The University of Texas at Austin and has been with the International Office since 1999. Prior to joining UT Austin, she held positions at St. Edward's University in Austin, Texas and Louisiana State University in Baton Rouge, Louisiana. Active in NAFSA, She actively follows regulatory changes that affect institutions of higher education and works closely with colleagues around the nation to create resources for international student and scholar advisors. Teri has also written several articles for NAFSA's monthly publication, *International Educator*. She has a bachelor's in business administration and master's in student affairs administration in higher education from Texas A&M University. She received a Ph.D. in higher education administration from the University of Texas at Austin, where her dissertation research focused on the experiences of undocumented students in institutions of higher education.

Adria L. Baker, Ed.D.

Adria is currently Executive Director in the Office of International Students & Scholars at Rice University, and has held various leadership positions in her 25 years in international education. Her focus on public policy issues in international education allows her to serve on NAFSA's State Whip Network as Texas' key congressional liaison, the Mayor's Task Force for International Visitors, and the Governor's Critical Infrastructure Council. She also led the Committee for an International Education Policy in Texas, which resulted in Texas H.R. 143 and Texas S.R. 532.

Adria has written several articles and presented often on subjects including advocacy in international education, international student and scholar advising, and foreign credentials evaluation. She has worked in Mexico City teaching English, and studied as a Research Fellow at the University of Costa Rica. She received her doctorate from the University of Houston, and M.A. and B.A. from Texas Tech University.

Mary E. Baxton

Mary is the Director of Admissions and Recruitment at The Tseng College of Extended Learning, California State University, Northridge. Her position at CSUN focuses on coordination of international and domestic admission, development of recruitment activities, and special project management. She also participates in the campus policy and planning committee for international enrollment management. Mary has been an active member of AACRAO and NAFSA, serving as AACRAO vice president for international education from 2006 to 2009. She has written numerous publications on international admission and given presentations at regional, national, and international conferences. She is the author of more than 12 country profiles for the AACRAO EDGE project (*Electronic*

Database for Global Education). Mary holds a B.S. and M.S. degree in business administration from CSUN.

Sandra Bloem-Curtis

Sandra Bloem-Curtis is the Senior Associate Director for International Compliance, Systems Management and Administration in Rice University's Office of International Students & Scholars. She has worked in international education for eight years, with a principal focus on compliance issues related to SEVIS (Students & Exchange Visitor Information System). She consults for several universities and assists/trains many international educators regularly on information systems that interface with the U.S. Department of Homeland Security's SEVIS programs and the related laws. She is an expert on compliance of F and J immigration regulations, as well as Brazilian culture. She speaks Portuguese, Spanish, and French fluently, and has taught Portuguese and conversational French. She received her B.A. from Texas A&M University, and while pursuing her degree, she studied abroad in both Caen and Aix-en-Provence, France.

Bridget E. Canty, M.B.A.

Bridget is a student service associate in the Office of International Student Services at Houston Community College. She was the associate director of Office of International Admissions at the University of Houston from 2006–2009 and assistant director from 1996–2006. She has served as chair of the Council on Ethical Practice for NAFSA: Association of International Educators, as subcommittee chair for the mayor of Houston, and on the Task Force for International Visitors.

Patrick Colabucci

Patrick is the Senior Academic Director at the American Language Institute, College of Extended Studies at San Diego State University. He earned his bachelor's in politics and government at the University of Maryland and his master's at the Tokyo branch of Temple University. He has worked in academic and corporate contexts in Japan, Taiwan, China, Saudi Arabia and the United Arab Emirates. Currently, he is also the U.S. outsourcing coordinator for the IELTS through the University of Cambridge. Patrick has been an active member of JALT, TESOL Arabia, CATESOL and TESOL.

Edward Devlin

Ed currently works as a part-time credentials evaluator for AACRAO's International Education Services (IES). He has been in the field of International Education for more than 40 years, directing the International Student Program and teaching English at Monterey Peninsula College for 28 of those years. He has directed intensive English/academic orientation programs at Stanford University, Monterey Peninsula College and the University of California Santa Cruz; has worked as director of the international admissions office at Golden Gate University, and has served as a consultant for many schools and programs in the United States and abroad. Before retiring, he was the director of special projects for AACRAO IES.

Ed contributed the first model for AACRAO EDGE. He is a life member of NAFSA and has served on the International Admissions Committee of AACRAO. He has presented at many AACRAO and NAFSA conferences and workshops, and is the author of *Australia: Training & Education*. He has co-authored and/or edited the AACRAO/NAFSA volumes on Poland, the Czech and Slovak Federated Republics, in addition to articles for NAFSA and AACRAO publications.

Peggy Bell Hendrickson

Peggy is the Director of Transcript Research, a private international credentials evaluation company located in Dallas, Texas. Prior to working in the private sector, she worked for the University of North Texas for nearly a decade where she was assistant director of international admissions. She has written several country profiles for both AACRAO EDGE and NAFSA's *Online Guide to Educational Systems around the World*. Peggy has also presented and written workshops, sessions, and poster fairs at all levels of NAFSA (state, regional, and national).

She is the managing editor of the *NAFSA wRAP-Up Newsletter* which is devoted to international admissions and credentials evaluation. She publishes her own blog on international education and has written a free book titled, *Researching International Education Systems and Institutions*. Peggy holds bachelor's degrees in English and marketing and a master's degree in interdisciplinary studies from the University of North Texas where she also teaches part-time.

Chris J. Foley

Chris is the Director of Undergraduate Admissions at Indiana University-Purdue University Indianapolis. He has presented nationally and internationally on domestic and international admissions, recruitment, enrollment management, transfer credit, urban higher education, and technology issues. An active member of both NAFSA and AACRAO, he is the author of several articles and book chapters on these topics as well as the author and/or editor of AACRAO's books on the educational systems of the Russian Federation and the Kyrgyz Republic. He was a Sturgis Fellow at the University of Arkansas where he completed his undergraduate studies, and he holds master's degrees from Indiana University in English and creative writing.

Van Hillier

Van is Teacher Training Program Coordinator at San Diego State University. He is a graduate of the University of California, San Diego and of Rutgers University. At Rutgers, Van studied linguistics and second-language acquisition. His master's degree is in language education. He has over 20 years of experience teaching English as a second language at several institutions in the United States, including San Diego State University and Harvard University. His overseas experience includes teaching English in Switzerland and Saudi Arabia. He has given many presentations at national conferences on topics ranging from English as an international language to the neurobiology of language acquisition. As a teacher trainer, Van has ten years experience and has taught in the United States, Korea, Japan, Mexico and Jordan.

Marilee Hong

Marilee worked at San Diego State University for over 37 years in the offices of records, admissions, advising and evaluations, and enrollment services. She earned her bachelor's degree from San Diego State University. She has worked in the field of international education as an evaluator of international documents for over 25 years, advising students, and recruiting overseas in Asia.

As a member of both NAFSA and AACRAO, she has served as a presenter of international topics; chaired a NAFSA Regional and National Conference Registration; ADSEC district chair; and trainer in the Professional Development Program (PDP) Trainer Corp. For AACRAO, she served as a member of the International Admissions Committee, chair of the International Admission committee, and as a member of the International Publications Advisory Committee (IPAC). She has authored profiles for the AACRAO *Electronic Database for Global Education* (EDGE).

Melanie Gottlieb

Melanie is Director of Admission Operations and International Campus Liaison at Webster University in St. Louis, Missouri. She has been involved in international education research and credential evaluation for Webster's international campus network for eight years. Melanie has been an active member of NAFSA and AACRAO for more than 12 years, presenting numerous sessions and workshops at the annual regional and national conferences and coordinating the international sessions for the AACRAO annual conference for the past four years. She holds a bachelor's degree in the history of U.S. higher education at Marlboro College in Vermont and a master's degree in information science from the University of Missouri, Columbia.

Veronica Jarek-Prinz

Veronica is the Director of Graduate, Transfer and Adult Admissions at Iona College. While studying psychology at Boston College, Veronica worked the freshmen registration hotline and has been working in higher education ever since. She has over 20 years of admissions experience—undergraduate, graduate and professional—at a variety of institutions, including Harvard University, the University of Virginia, and New York University. She has also worked in enrollment services at Boston College and at NYU. Outside the academy, Veronica has been a fundraiser, a software support technician, and a restaurant reviewer.

Johnny K. Johnson

Johnny's 35 years in international education includes administrative and teaching positions at two-year and four-year colleges and universities, both public and private, in the United States, Asia and the Caribbean. He has been responsible for international, graduate and professional school admissions, academic and foreign student advising, ESL, study abroad and academic exchange programs. Education research, writing, and conference presentations have taken Johnny to 75 countries. He has also done consultations for educational institutions, businesses and the U.S. government. Johnny has served on the board of directors for AACRAO, NAFSA: Association of International Educators, and California Colleges for International Education (CCIE).

Christine Kerlin, Ed.D.

Christine is the Vice President for the University Center of North Puget Sound and Strategic Planning at Everett Community College, WA. Prior to joining the college she served as the director of admissions and records at Central Oregon Community College and as the director of admissions at The Evergreen State College. Christine holds her doctorate from Oregon State University and her bachelor's and master's degrees from Western Washington University. She is active in

AACRAO and serves on several committees. She has also held leadership positions in PACRAO and NAFSA-Region I. Christine has been involved in the field of international admissions and advising for over 20 years.

Ann M. Koenig

Ann is the Southwest Regional Director of AACRAO International Education Services. Her career in international education spans more than 20 years, including foreign credential evaluation with two other foreign credential evaluation services, and campus-based work in international admissions, student records management and academic advising, at Cardinal Stritch University in Milwaukee, at the University of Maryland University College program in Germany, at Golden Gate University in San Francisco, and at the University of California, Berkeley.

Ann has done in-depth research and writing on education in several countries, including Poland and countries in the east/central Europe, Albania and other Balkan countries, Germany, Russia, Ukraine, Uzbekistan (AACRAO EDGE profile) and other countries of Central Asia. She has given numerous workshop and conference presentations for AACRAO, NAFSA, NAGAP, EAIE, and several other organizations in the U.S. and Europe. Ann has served on the AACRAO International Education Committee and the NAFSA National ADSEC Committee.

Sarah Martin

Sarah is Graduate Programs Coordinator at the Duke Global Health Institute. Prior to her position at Duke University, she spent nearly ten years working in the field of education abroad, from both the provider and university side. She was most recently the director of university relations for SIT Study Abroad, where she worked with administrators and students from colleges and universities across the country. She earned a B.A. in international studies from UNC Chapel Hill and a M.Ed. in higher education and student affairs administration from The University of Vermont.

Sarah has served as the chair of the AACRAO Study Abroad committee, was a member of NAFSA: Association of International Educators, and served as a coach for new international education professionals in the 5th NAFSA Academy. She has facilitated workshops and presented sessions on a wide variety of education abroad topics at regional and national NAFSA conferences, AACRAO national conferences, and various other international education meetings.

Darcy E. McGillicuddy

Darcy is the Coordinator of the Sponsored Student Program at The University of Texas at Austin, where she manages the placement of over 350 students from more than 40 countries and 50 sponsoring agencies. As a strategic university partner liaison for several social justice related programs, she works closely with the university's international admissions office and various academic departments to provide opportunities for students from underrepresented countries and marginalized communities. Darcy has worked in the field of international education for nine years. She currently serves as the chair of the Crisis Task Force for NAFSA: Association of International Educators, and serves as an International Issues committee member for AACRAO.

Daniel Obst

Daniel is Deputy Vice President of International Partnerships at the New York headquarters of the Institute of International Education (IIE), one of the largest and oldest not-for-profit organizations in the field of international educational exchange and development training. He provides strategic leadership in the creation and implementation of international academic partnerships, and oversees all the activities of IIE's network of 1,000 member institutions, as well as IIE's print publications, online directories, conference, and seminars. He is the editor of *IIENetworker*, IIE's international education magazine, and executive editor of IIE's *Global Education Research Reports* series. Daniel recently coedited a new book funded by the EU-U.S. Atlantis Program,

Joint and Double Degree Programs: An Emerging Model for Transatlantic Exchange. He received his B.A. in international relations from the George Washington University and holds a master's degree in European studies from the London School of Economics.

William J. Paver, Ph.D.

Bill is the former director of the Graduate and International Admissions Center at The University of Texas at Austin where he worked for over 20 years. He is a past vice president for international education for AACRAO, a former ADSEC chair and NAFSA board member, twice a member of the National Council on the Evaluation of Foreign Educational Credentials and a member of the TOEFL Board. Currently he is one of the creators and contributors to the *Electronic Database for Global Education* (EDGE) project for AACRAO and maintains an active role in that endeavor. Bill is currently Director of Foreign Credentials Service of America. He holds a Ph.D. in higher education from Washington State University.

Linda Tobash

Linda is Director of University Placement Services at the Institute of International Education (IIE) and leads a staff responsible for the placement of over 1,700 students, primarily Fulbright scholarship recipients, in U.S. university programs each year. With over 25 years experience in the areas of admissions and international education, she is a frequent presenter on the U.S. higher education system, U.S. admission practices and trends, and best practices in attracting international students. Linda is active in NAFSA: Association of International Educators, AACRAO, the National Council for the Evaluation of Foreign Educational Credentials, and TESOL (Teachers of English to Speakers of Other Languages). She holds a master's degree from Teachers College, Columbia University. Linda is on the faculty of the New School University where she has taught courses on intercultural communication. Prior to her current position, she worked eighteen years in the City University of New York system, including ten years as director of admissions at LaGuardia Community College. She also served in the Republic of Korea as a U.S. Peace Corps volunteer.

Robert Watkins

Robert is Assistant Director of Admissions in the Graduate and International Admissions Center of The University of Texas at Austin. He has been in admissions at UT-Austin for 33 years, focused mainly on international student admission and credential evaluation. A member of NAFSA: Association of International Educators since 1983, he has served that organization in a number of capacities: ADSEC (Admissions Section) regional representative, ADSEC national team member and chair, NAFSA 1992–2000 (Chair of the Council 1996–2000), and chair of NAFSA Region III, 2000. Robert has served on the NCAA Foreign Student Records Committee since 2000, chairing that committee since 2001. He is also a member of AACRAO and has served on the International Publications Advisory Committee (IPAC) and chaired the International Admissions Committee. Robert is currently AACRAO Vice President for International Education. He holds a B.A. and an M.A. in history from the University of Texas at Austin.

Elizabeth White

Elizabeth White is Assistant Director in the Office of International Admissions at the University at Buffalo, State University of New York. The majority of her 15-year career in admissions has been spent working with international student applications and credentials. She has served on AACRAO's International Admissions Committee and has been the publications editor for NAFSA Region X (NY/NJ). Beth has presented frequently on technology and marketing communication issues at AACRAO annual meetings and NAFSA regional conferences. She holds a bachelor's degree in communications from SUNY Geneseo and a master's degree in college student personnel from University at Buffalo.

Deana Williams, B.M.

Deana Williams is currently Assistant Director of Graduate and International Admissions and the Residency Official at the University of Texas at Austin. She has worked in the field of international education for 15 years and currently serves as the chair of AACRAO's International Publications Advisory Committee (IPAC). She was a participant in the creation of AACRAO's EDGE (*Electronic Database for Global Education*) database. Deana has presented numerous sessions on international topics and residency issues at AACRAO, SACRAO, TACRAO, NAFSA, NACAC, The College Board and the Texas State Bar Association conferences. She serves on the Residency Advisory Committee for the Texas Higher Education Coordinating Board. Deana holds a bachelor's of music from Baylor University.

ONE

Overview of the

State of
International
Higher
Education

2010 AACRAO INTERNATIONAL GUIDE

LINDA TOBASH

Director
University Placement Services Division
Institute of International Education

DANIEL OBST

Deputy Vice President
International Partnerships in Higher Education
Institute of International Education

Overview of the State of International Higher Education

These are exciting times in higher education. In an environment of rapid change driven by increased mobility, wide-ranging internationalization efforts and technological advances, institutions worldwide are witnessing increased demand from both domestic and international students. These conditions have produced a variety of educational delivery modes unthinkable just a generation ago and a student culture technologically accustomed to real-time communications with immediate responses. Volatile fiscal markets, shrinking endowments and drastically reduced levels of state funding in many locales make international students and the funding they bring even more attractive to U.S. institutions. However, these same factors are encouraging overseas institutions to step up their effort towards offering programs at lower costs than their counterparts in the United States.

In this shifting landscape, U.S. higher education institutions have retained the lead in knowledge creation, creativity and innovation, and continue to promote new curricular initiatives that draw faculty, researchers and students from across disciplines to tackle global issues. However, educational reforms outside the U.S. have made the international environment more complex and competitive. Changes abroad affect not only U.S. strategies to attract talented students and scholars, but also approaches to admission and foreign credential review. That said, the U.S. system, accustomed to the idea that high quality is best achieved through competition rather than central planning (Eckel and King 2004), is well positioned to treat increases in competition as fertile ground for advances and greater international collaboration.

The unprecedented changes in higher education worldwide in the last 10 to 15 years can best be understood by examining four key trends. First is the sheer increase in the number of students seeking higher education. Enrollment has increased dramatically throughout the world; the 144 million students enrolled in higher education institutions worldwide as of 2005 represent a 120 percent increase in just one generation (UNESCO 2008). Students and their families understand the need to pursue higher education in order to thrive in the 21st century economy. But capacity to meet this rapidly escalating demand, while growing, still falls short in many countries and regions.

In addition to the growing local demand for higher education, a second trend is a change in the attitudes of companies, governments and higher education institutions. The belief that the workforce of the 21st century needs to be prepared to function and excel in globally interactive and interdependent environments is now widespread throughout public and private sectors. Higher education institutions increasingly see overseas study and research experiences for students as critical to their mission and success, and ensuring that campuses present an environment conducive to meaningful cross-cultural interactions is seen as equally important in many cases. Institutions face more pressure to not only position their programs to attract international students, faculty, researchers and funding, but also to identify and advance transnational linkages that will help advance their missions, add value to curricula and provide greater visibility in targeted countries and regions.

A third closely related trend is the growing economic impact of international education. NAFSA: Association of International Educators' annual analysis of the economic benefits of international education analysis—using tuition data from Wintergreen Orchard House, enrollment figures from *Open Doors 2009* and living expenses based on the two reports and analyzed by Jason Baumgartner at Indiana University—estimates that during the 2008/09 academic year foreign students and their dependents contributed approximately $17.6 billion to the U.S. economy. Similar data have been well documented and publicized for several years, but these data have become even more urgent in the current economic climate. Additionally, there is an apparent increase in business and industry preference for individuals who have studied abroad. A brief survey, conducted by the Institute for International Education (IIE) with the assistance of the Dilenschneider Group and aimed at over 200 senior-level international business leaders, reported that 60 percent of respondents indicated their organization's hiring and promotion strategies pursued and rewarded recruits who had international experience through study abroad. In fact, 30 percent reported that they had studied abroad during their own academic careers (Gutierrez and Bhandari 2009).

Finally, and perhaps most critically, is the rapid pace of globalization in the higher education sector, fueled by economic changes leading to deregulation of educational services, the increasing ease of communication irrespective of time and distance barriers, increased faculty and student mobility, the emergence of global issues such as climate change and terrorism that demand international collaboration and the desire to keep one's institution and national system at the competitive forefront. In such an interactive, global atmosphere, opportunities abound for cooperation and collaboration.

These four factors—worldwide growth in higher education enrollments, the realization that global competence is increasingly a basic necessity of a competitive workforce, the growing recognition of the economic impact of international experiences and the myriad effects of globalization on communications and the economy—have created an opportune moment for rapid expansion in student and scholar mobility. This increase is the subject of the next section.

Increased Student and Scholar Mobility

Nearly three million students were studying and researching outside of their home countries in 2006 (OECD 2008)—a 59 percent increase since 2000—and it is likely that this number will grow to as high as eight million by 2025 (Bohm *et al.* 2002). This rapidly expanding circulation of talent is also leading to a paradigm change in the prevailing theories that describe the outcomes of student mobility. The traditional frameworks of "brain drain" and "brain gain" are being replaced by more multidirectional models, conceived as "brain circulation" and "brain exchange" (Bhandari and Blumenthal 2009).

In this progressively mobile environment, the U.S. has benefited from having more foreign students and scholars pursuing study and research within its borders. *Open Doors 2009*, the most recent report on student and scholar mobility to and from the United States, indicates that 671,616 international students studied in the U.S. during academic year 2008/09, an all-time high. This represents an 8 percent increase over the previous year and, even more significantly, the largest one-year percentage increase since 1980/81 (Bhandari and Chow 2009). This is a noteworthy and welcomed increase, as data since 9/11 have shown fluctuations in international student enrollments. These data help to alleviate fears that the U.S. is no longer seen as a leading or welcoming destination for international students. The good news also extends to international scholars—U.S. higher education institutions attracted 113,494 scholars during the same time frame, reflecting a 6.9 percent increase over the previous year.

Similarly, *Open Doors 2009* reports that in academic year 2007/08, the most recent year for available data, 262,416 U.S. students studied outside of the country, representing an 8.5 percent increase over the previous year and a 143 percent increase in the past decade alone. These striking increases can be attributed to many of the same factors discussed earlier, but certainly the rising emphasis on institutional internationalization, the increased number of higher education institutions establishing ambitious study abroad goals (with some aiming to have all students participate in at least one study abroad experience), the growth in the number of study abroad programs (particularly at the community college level) and the acknowledgement by Congress and business and industry leaders that study abroad advances the U.S. competitive edge in global markets, all help to advance an aggressive study abroad agenda. Another significant development is the rise in the number of students studying in nontraditional destinations, which include most countries outside Western Europe, Australia and New Zealand. Some of the most popular nontraditional destinations in recent years have been China, Costa Rica, Japan, Argentina and South Africa. A trend, both in the U.S. and worldwide, toward shorter study abroad stays, which, while limiting the extent of immersion in different cultures and languages, has made it possible for many more students to participate.

Engaging over a quarter million students in study abroad experiences signals a significant increase in 10 years; however, it still represents less than two percent of the overall U.S. student higher education population. New initiatives to expand access to diverse populations have been supported by the U.S. government. Two examples include the Gilman International Scholarship Program, supported by the U.S. Department of State's Bureau of Educational and Cultural Affairs, which provides scholarships for study abroad to students on federal Pell Grants and has been recognized for its efforts to extend study abroad participation to underrepresented economic, social and ethnic groups and the Boren Scholarships, funded by the National Security Education Program, representing a pioneering effort to expand opportunities for students to study abroad in geographic areas offering less commonly taught languages critical to U.S. national security.

The United States as a Leading Destination

At the beginning of the new millennium, the U.S. has maintained its reputation for unparalleled capacity to absorb additional students. With over 4,000 accredited degree-granting institutions representing a wide range of institutional types and offering a wide array of innovative programs and curricula, the U.S. still attracts more international students than any other country. Significantly, community colleges have emerged in this decade as a fast growing destination for international students.

Maintaining and advancing this lead, however, becomes more challenging as the international education landscape evolves, and competition from both traditional international competitors, like the United Kingdom, Australia and Germany, as well as new ones, such as China, grows at a rapid pace. The U.S. remains the preferred destination for international students, with 21 percent of all international student enrollments in 2008/09. However, the 671,000 international students in 2008/09 studying on U.S. campuses comprise only 3.7 percent of total U.S. higher education enrollments, though within certain fields and degree levels this percentage is much higher, *e.g.*, foreign students comprise 10.5 percent of all graduate enrollments and an even larger percentage of enrollments in science and technology fields. It is noteworthy that other leading systems achieve far higher overall ratios of students who are international: Germany and France with 12 percent, the UK with 16.3 percent and Australia with 22.5 percent. And while international students attend thousands of different programs and institutions across the U.S., not all institutions benefit from the diverse perspectives they bring and the ongoing multiplier effect and international visibility they can provide. Fifty-seven percent of all international students in the U.S. in 2008/09 studied at just 172 institutions; ten states hosted 60 percent of the total population.

Higher Education Reforms Advancing Competition and Collaboration

Higher education in recent years has become a more portable commodity, and countries and regions that once found themselves at the periphery of higher education and research worldwide are now emerging as viable competitors with established centers of learning in economically advanced nations. While internationalization efforts have steadily grown over the last few decades, a number of recent reforms have jumped started what many consider to be the globalization of higher education.

The United States, with its range of institutions, commitment to universal access, decentralized but shared forms of governance and continued advancement through cutting-edge research and creative and innovative approaches, continues to serve as a model for reform, attracting educational visitors from around the world. These visitors come to better understand and explore aspects of this large, decentralized system, seeking to identify aspects that might prove adaptable to their educational environments. Community colleges, seen as unique to the u.s., are of special interest to systems seeking to expand access to higher education and advance schemas for meeting workforce needs, while facilitating greater collaboration with local industry and government actors.

Across the Atlantic, the reforms and outcomes resulting from Europe's decade-long Bologna Process are having a significant impact on higher education systems well beyond its borders. This unique regional initiative currently has 46 signatory countries encompassing all of Europe, with the exception of Belarus. Collectively, these countries represent nearly a quarter of the nations of the world and an even larger portion of the developed world, and they encompass nearly 4,000 higher education institutions. The creation of the European Higher Education Area has had a clear impact on the United States. The growth in courses and degrees offered in English; the expansion of national marketing schemes to keep students in Europe, as well as attract international students worldwide; well-established joint and double degree programs; a growing number of three-year undergraduate degrees and, in many locations, significantly lower tuition and fees—altogether, these initiatives position Europe as a desirable destination for students worldwide.

The ongoing degree reforms also pose major challenges to u.s. admissions and foreign credential professionals, not least of which is the movement to three-year undergraduate degrees in some countries. These professionals must now

* keep abreast of national changes;
* deal with credentials from old, evolving and new systems, which, in the case of applicants who have participated in joint or double degree programs, might contain study from two or more institutions;
* review all three-year degree study in a fair and equitable manner vis-à-vis the requirements of their institutions; and
* educate faculty and administrators about national and regional trends that can impact institutional policies.

But all of this change has provided many opportunities for professionals from diverse backgrounds to join together to identify issues, suggest solutions and exploit potential for stronger collaboration. Examples include:

* A variety of professional organizational collaborations in the Asia-Pacific region (particularly Australia and China), Europe, Latin America, the Middle East and North America advancing dialogue on global directions for the higher education sector, *e.g.*, the graduate global education seminars (of which the Council of Graduate Schools is a major organizer) hosted annually since 2007.
* Collaborations between professional associations in the u.s., in cooperation with European sister organizations, to advance knowledge among their members of reforms and their impact.
* Efforts to include wider perspectives in government forums; at the April 2009 European Ministers of

Education Conference, representatives from the forty-six European Higher Education Area (EHEA) countries hosted a Bologna Policy Forum, inviting representatives from 20 other countries, including the U.S., to join in a stocktaking discussion.

✳ Curricular innovations; in summer 2009, the Lumina Foundation initiated a yearlong Tuning USA pilot project with faculty and administrators from select universities in Minnesota, Indiana and Utah. Modeled after the European Tuning initiatives, which have previously been replicated in Latin America and Asia, "tuning" focuses on the identification of transparent and agreed-upon field of study outcomes at different degree levels.

Another significant trend is the realization of positive results by many countries that have invested heavily over the past decades to build capacity in their higher education systems. China, India, the Asia-Pacific region in general and countries in Latin America such as Brazil, Chile and Colombia stand out in their sustained efforts to improve the quality of their postsecondary institutions. As institutions' capacity-building efforts come to fruition, domestic students have fewer reasons to travel abroad for degree study, and institutions become more attractive to students from neighboring countries. While this trend could potentially result in lower numbers seeking degree study in the U.S., it also opens new opportunities for exchange. Faculty and programs in the U.S., which frequently contributed to the preceding capacity-building efforts, generally maintain strong ties and widely-distributed alumni networks in these countries positioning them to take advantage of emerging exchange opportunities, including:

✳ "sandwich programs" for both undergraduate and graduate students, where students come for an extended period of study during the course of their degree;

✳ increased opportunities for exchange of faculty and other scholars and researchers; and

✳ new prospects for joint programming and degrees—including face-to-face programs, e-learning offerings and blended offerings—and possibly branch campuses.

The creation of "centers of excellence," frequently driven by national and regional efforts to create institutions that can compete globally for the best and brightest students and faculty, is another emerging phenomenon. In the past decade, a number of interesting initiatives have been launched in the Middle East. The King Abdullah University of Science of Technology (KAUST) in Saudi Arabia, a new graduate school opened in fall 2009, has recruited faculty, staff and students worldwide and initiated early identification of students through the provision of competitive undergraduate scholarships. The Qatar Foundation's Education City provides a different model. Engaging in partnerships with select U.S. higher education institutions to offer some of their most reputable degree curricula in Education City, Qatar has replicated world-class degree study within their own country with built-in opportunities for student, faculty and research exchange. New York University's Abu Dhabi campus is an example of a different type of branch campus initiative. Collaboration with the Emirate of Abu Dhabi has resulted in the establishment of the first world-class liberal arts college in the Middle East with a mission to attract students from around the world (http://nyuad.nyu.edu).

International Education Policy in the U.S.

With its historically decentralized and competitive higher education sector, the United States has traditionally not advanced a coordinated international education policy to respond to opportunities and challenges in the higher education sector. However, widespread concern over declining international enrollments after 9/11 and fears about the event's impact on U.S. global competitiveness in key science and technology fields have encouraged U.S. campuses, Congress and several U.S. government agencies and educational nonprofit organizations to take proactive steps to attract new students and scholars from abroad. These mostly decentralized efforts typify the U.S. higher education system and its relation to the federal government, but expanded efforts to ensure that the U.S. maintains its competitive lead have prompted a number of supportive public statements and actions by the U.S. Secretary of State, the Department of Homeland Security and the Department of Education, which have clarified the federal commitment to keeping America's doors open to international students.

In the past decade, the U.S. Department of State has provided significant funding to increase outreach and promote the U.S. as a study destination. In addition to increasing resources for its network of over 400 Educational Advising Centers, it has appreciably enhanced the look and feel of the EducationUSA Web site, incorporating interactive social media technologies attractive to younger students. Other initiatives of the U.S. Department of State include:

* The English Access Microscholarships program reaches out to younger students in the developing world, especially those with limited resources, providing courses to strengthen English language skills and to raise expectations that studying in the U.S. can be a reality.

* Opportunity Grants, provided in select countries and geared to underserved student populations, help defray costs of preparing for undergraduate or graduate study including test preparation courses, standardized testing fees, university application fees and visa application fees.

* The Global Undergraduate Exchange Program (Global UGRAD) provides scholarships to support a semester or academic year of non-degree study and cooperative learning programs to underrepresented students from select countries.

* The International Fulbright Science and Technology Award for Outstanding Foreign Students, launched in 2007 in response to the scientific educational community's call for greater national support in promoting the U.S. as a study and research destination, provides three years of funding for Ph.D. study at world-class U.S. universities.

Changing Recruitment and Marketing Strategies

United States institutions have a long tradition of competing with one another for students, faculty and funding. With the reality of aggressive marketing schemes from abroad, institutions are increasing their international recruitment efforts. Even U.S. graduate programs, not particularly recognized for aggressive international marketing, are establishing a more visible international recruitment presence and expanding efforts to develop strong, sustainable linkages in critical geographic regions.

While recruitment efforts have been mostly decentralized, there is a mounting acknowledgement that national and regional marketing approaches resonate in many cultures and that pooling financial resources can help to expand outreach. Indiana was the first state to advance a coordinated consortium-based approach, pooling resources and tapping into support from state legislatures and departments of trade and commerce. "Destination Indiana," initiated in 2001 by the International Trade Division of the Indiana Department of Commerce and the Indiana Consortium of International Programs (ICIP), is a consortium of public and private, small and large colleges and universities in the state of Indiana. The consortium created a partnership to make education opportunities available in Indiana "known to interested students, their families and their schools and advisors around the world … [and] to increase the diversity of our educational environments for the benefit of all students" (http://fadams.iweb.bsu. edu). The group works extensively with EducationUSA and uses the 12 overseas offices of the Economic Development Corporation of the State of Indiana to promote statewide international education opportunities. California, Illinois, Iowa, Oregon, Washington and, most recently, New York have followed suit, forming similar statewide international education consortia.

International Linkages

The rise of new economic centers in Asia and the Middle East, the recognition that problems such as pandemics, terrorism and climate change transcend country boundaries, the increasing global competition for employment at all levels—these are among the factors that have prompted U.S. institutions to extend international studies and the treatment of global issues beyond specific departments and into institution-wide core objectives and strategic plans. This increasing commitment to internationalization is also reflected in formal, mutually beneficial partnerships that U.S. institutions are establishing with academic institutions around the world. The growth of such partnerships indicates that U.S. faculty and administrators no longer view study abroad and international research collaborations as marginal or the sole responsibility of departments, but rather as central and deliberate. Formal, long-term institutional partnerships are particularly well-suited to this deliberate approach and provide a sustained impact on student learning outcomes.

One of the more prominent recent developments is the emergence of transatlantic degree programs, such as dual diplomas, joint degrees, consortia and other forms of curriculum cooperation arrangements. Among European countries the introduction of joint and double degree programs has long been a vital part of internationalization strategies in higher education, helping to create stronger links and flourishing institutional partnerships, as well as preparing students for a global workplace. In the U.S. context, such programs have been until recently a less common feature of internationalization strategies for institutions. However, the interest in curriculum cooperation is gaining momentum not only in the U.S., but in most countries around the world.

A recent report, "Joint and Double Degree Programs in the Transatlantic Context," released by IIE and the Freie Universität Berlin, finds that universities on both sides of the Atlantic are working to establish more international joint and dual degree programs. One key finding was that 87 percent of respondents said that they wanted to develop more joint and dual degree programs (Obst and Kuder 2009), which clearly attests to the growing importance of this form of academic cooperation.

Institutional partnership arrangements can take many other forms as well—the signing of memoranda of understanding (MoUs) and interdisciplinary joint research initiatives to name just two—but their common link is that they must require formal institutional commitments to be successful. For students and scholars to benefit from such agreements over the long term, U.S. institutions must first identify the overseas institutions with the strategic, geographic and curricular characteristics most likely to result in productive mutual engagement. This initial step proves to be a significant barrier to entry for many U.S. institutions, especially those lacking a history of establishing global partnerships or an infrastructure for doing so. Many well-known U.S. institutions can point to decades-long relationships with elite institutions abroad, but even these institutions often lack knowledge about institutions in non-Western countries such as China and India, where governments have recently made massive investments in higher education and strategically seek international linkages.

For institutions in the U.S. that are relatively new to international activities, the initial fact finding required to identify appropriate partners can be a daunting, opaque process involving many false starts and misunderstandings. Some institutions, including many community colleges, historically black colleges and universities (HBCUs) and tribal colleges, may wish to partner with overseas institutions that serve similar constituencies in their respective countries, but face seemingly insuperable barriers: they are less well-known internationally than other public or private flagship U.S. institutions, have less installed capacity such as international faculty or study abroad offices and very limited funding to pursue international linkages.

Concluding Observations

At the beginning of this new millennium, higher education institutions worldwide increasingly seek commonalities in purpose and greater avenues for collaboration while, at the same time, assertively promoting their global capabilities to attract the growing number of talented and mobile students and faculty. Technological advances, including e-learning and open source materials and courseware and a student population well-versed in social networking, have advanced virtual mobility. In an atmosphere of growing global competition, flexible approaches, cutting edge programming, creative courses and an ability to reduce barriers—whether language, visa or cost related—are all needed to attract and retain top talent among a very fast growing student population.

The following chapters will explore in much greater depth a number of the issues outlined here and will further identify trends, sharing best practices and technological solutions to key challenges in admissions, enrollment management, credential evaluation and study abroad, as well as other areas.

International Student Recruitment:

Framing the Topic

2010 AACRAO INTERNATIONAL GUIDE

Director of Admissions and Recruitment
The Tseng College
California State University, Northridge

MARY E. BAXTON

International Student Recruitment: Framing the Topic

The concept of international recruitment has been a topic of much interest over the past 20 years. The efforts to develop, fine-tune and implement international recruitment throughout universities and colleges has led to multiple approaches, budget adjustments and refinement of philosophy and techniques. Within higher education, we now have conferences devoted to the topic and elevated respect for the classification of international student recruiter. The main driver for this move is the important role that international students have on campuses, as institutions have come to recognize that these students expand the global dimension of the campus, contribute large sums of money to the U.S. economy, enrich the academic experience of U.S. students, become future alumni and promote interchange of values in an interactive global world. This chapter will focus on how international educators can learn the basic concepts of international recruitment and put together the pieces to fulfill international enrollment management goals.

Before we discuss international recruitment, we must mention enrollment management. As a concept, it is a process used by colleges and universities to control the size and composition of the student body. It brings together the functions of recruiting, funding, enrolling, tracking and retaining students. It leads to the determination of how many students to enroll, what kinds of students and what services they need. By adding the word "international" to enrollment management, we quickly sharpen our view of the relationship between the two and of the importance of a key component—international recruitment. A strong recruitment plan will develop from a well thought-out vision of how international students will fit into the institution. Although U.S. colleges and universities are aware of the benefits of including international students on the campus, the dynamics of competing to attract international students include broad enrollment management concepts, such as competition from institutions within a country and in other countries; complications arising out of large educational initiatives and implications of country dynamics, *e.g.*, the rapid development of India and China, among other nations.

The days of having a tried and true marketing strategy and expecting international students simply to arrive at the door of the institution are gone. Thus, U.S. institutions must rely on their own policies and initiatives. Finally, there is a growing trend for countries to concentrate on increasing the capacity and quality of higher education institutions within their own country. As noted in Chapter 9, "The International Aspects of Enrollment Management," running a university is akin to running a mutual fund. The enrollment portfolio should be diversified to guard against exposure to any single negative influence. For example, you want to diversify within your international segment to minimize exposure to enrollment drops from a particular country or a weak dollar. Conversely, spreading your recruitment resources across too many markets may dilute your results.

Developing an international community and building upon it takes time. Institutions cannot enter into the process and expect it to grow overnight. Thus each institution must assess for itself how a population of international students will fit into the mission and enrollment management plan on campus. Goals can range from merely adding numbers to the student body as a whole, to recruiting students with interests in specific academic disciplines, to targeting students from a specific part of the world. Whatever the goal in recruiting students from abroad, your institution must be prepared to muster the resources and the support services necessary to address the special needs of international students.

When a prospective international student initiates contact, whether long distance or in person, you should be prepared to convey what makes your institution different. Your recruiters should have given thought in advance to such a question—as to how they would respond or how they would initiate such a conversation. In short, consider the importance of differentiation and marketing strategy, and identify your key attributes. Display those key attributes on the cover of your recruitment brochures and in the photos you use.

Recruitment Principles

The previous discussion established that it is critical to adopt an international enrollment management plan and good recruitment principles before implementing or expanding an international recruitment program. Also essential is ensuring adequate support facilities to accommodate international students. These include satisfactory housing options; dietary considerations; campus access, remembering that international students do not go home over all holidays; advisors who are culturally aware; knowledgeable staff that understand international admissions for the admissions and credit transfer process; immigration advising and registration access that supports the necessity for international students to maintain status in SEVIS.

Various organizations have developed statements of good principles over the years. AACRAO's "Bill of Rights and Responsibilities for International Students and Institutions" is particularly helpful in establishing the services you should be prepared to provide to your international students. Resources such as this *International Guide* and NAFSA's "Principles for the

Admission of Foreign Students and Principles for Institutions" put forth the following key principles:

✳ Admission goals and policies for foreign students should be directly related to overall institutional goals and policies.

✳ Admission materials should be sensitive to candidates' unfamiliarity with the U.S. education system and lack of fluency in English. You should make clear what the admissions process entails—what documentation is necessary and under what timelines.

✳ It is highly advisable to assess the language abilities of international students, to determine if their skills are sufficient to enable them to benefit from the host institution's academic course offerings.

✳ Information should be presented in a manner in which students can make informed academic judgments. You should make available a clear and complete description of the academic offerings—and the approximate time normally required to complete an academic program.

✳ Applications for admission and transcripts/documents should be evaluated by international admission evaluators or credential evaluation agencies skilled in evaluating international credentials.

✳ Materials should provide a clear and accurate account of all costs for the academic year. This explanation should be included along with the response to an application.

✳ Clear and complete information should be provided as to all legal requirements governing the enrollment of international students, including how to maintain their student status.

✳ A visa is not just a credit card! International students must obtain a visa—regulations which, of course, are not necessary for domestic students. You must become familiar with a completely different vocabulary. Provide visa information in general terms and then link international students to the immigration Web site for more information.

✳ International students have the right to know what personal information is collected about them, why it is being collected and how they may review their files and correct any errors.

Best Practices to Optimize Recruitment Efforts

Those responsible for the development, implementation and assessment of international enrollment strategy should locate and make use of resources that tell them where international students come from, what they study and why they wish to come. *Open Doors*, published by the Institute of International Education (IIE), is a good source for such information. Once you have decided which segments of the international market you wish to target, you need to determine what strategies will prove most effective in reaching those populations. A good place to start is with the international population on your own campus or attending local colleges; why did they select that institution? The information they provide can be valuable in designing effective outreach. Find out what they have heard about U.S. institutions, where they heard it, why they came and how well their expectations have been met.

In order to be effective in countries you want to target, you must become knowledgeable about the educational systems in these countries. A number of excellent resources published by AACRAO provide a wealth of information on educational systems, both specific countries and world regions, such as the *World Education Series*, the *Country Guide Series* and the *AACRAO Electronic Database for Global Education (EDGE)*, a web-based resource for the evaluation of foreign educational credentials. You can find information on these at www.aacrao.org/publications and in Appendix B of this book.

By doing some initial fact-finding you will be better able to anticipate the questions and concerns your target population might have. Also, know your own campus and how to market its assets. Always state in a straightforward manner your location, size, accreditation, reputation, admission requirements, strong majors that will be of interest to international students, costs,

housing, campus organizations, sports programs and ethnic diversity, for example. Anticipate questions about such topics and formulate marketing messages and materials that will attract your target population.

International Recruitment Teamwork

One very large resource is the campus itself, including the people who make up the campus. It makes sense to consider an on-campus team approach, which will provide support to the efforts of the offices charged with international student recruitment. Making those efforts more effective and dynamic provides increased international visibility for the entire campus. The involvement of faculty and staff strengthens the institution's academic reputation. Students and alumni who exhibit that spark of cultural diversity, good communication skills and hold the institution in high regard provide the final component of an on-campus team.

Teamwork offers an economy of scale and budget. Extend recruitment dollars by taking advantage of faculty who are already planning to lecture internationally or the intensive English recruiter arranging an extensive trip who is able to represent individual campus areas as well as the larger institution in general. Planning to attend a recruitment fair in a country where the recruiter may not know the language is the perfect opportunity to contact alumni in the country and ask them to join you at the table. Alumni are often delighted to be called upon to assist; they can represent the institution from the student perspective at a minimal cost. At times an alumnus can be paired with a member of the recruitment team and each can attend separate events in a particular country.

One should not forget that the single most important key to success in an area rests on developing your office's team. Set the example by showing a passion for international students and the work you do for them. Expect others in the area to share that belief. See that they have the training and skills needed to empower them to work with and understand your area's role in international education. Attend local, regional and national conferences. Keep abreast of developments in the field. Know your staff and identify those who welcome a challenge. Finally, if you enjoy what you do and do it well, you will be a model for others, and this will spread throughout the campus community.

Effective marketing and recruitment takes place in a variety of ways, starting in the office and expanding to the targeted countries and areas. It is wise to maximize the institution's reach from the office before expanding to recruitment in the targeted locations. Only then should the discussion shift to travel outside the U.S. and the opportunities as well as the occasional pitfalls in recruiting in other countries. For example, four-year schools could have an on-campus recruiter contact local community colleges in an area containing concentrated populations of international students. A combination of admissions staff and outreach staff skilled in international admission matters can contact the local community college and, with permission, meet with prospective students and even provide pre-admission advisement. Then, you can consider the possible move to overseas travel.

Recruitment Travel Planning

When considering overseas travel, invest a great deal of thought and consideration in advance to take full advantage of this more expensive investment. A few questions should be addressed, such as:

* Who will travel?
* Where does it make the most sense to begin the overseas travel efforts?
* Should the travel be in a group or independent?
* Is there a procedure in place to contact students in your database, alumni and international partners prior to travel, and is there a follow-up procedure in place?

WHO SHOULD TRAVEL

The recruiter will probably travel to many countries, but it is important to keep in mind that the work days are long, work extends into weekends, total travel time may be lengthy and time away extensive. It is definitely not a holiday.

In addition, one must build in extensive planning and debriefing time. An effective international recruiter should possess flexibility and good health with, ideally, experience living or traveling in foreign countries and knowledge of a foreign language. The recruiter should have a good marketing aptitude, ability to communicate and as much knowledge as possible about the campus, the majors, admission requirements, the campus environment and support services. Homework should be done to know the country and anticipate questions concerning the most popular majors, the availability of scholarships and the ranking of your campus. In short, know the key "selling" attributes of your campus.

WHERE TO TRAVEL

This decision requires consideration of the strength of your majors, availability of financial aid, whether English preparation can be offered, diversity vs. filling seats and the potential for assistance from alumni or partners in a country.

GROUP OR INDIVIDUAL TRAVEL

There are college fairs and group tours. Does your institution have the name recognition to travel independently or in a small group? Do you have an experienced recruiter? What financial resources are available for overseas travel? Are the available tours best suited for your institution? The convenience of traveling with a tour group and the contacts the tour may offer can outweigh the benefits of independent travel. It may cost more, however. On the other hand, independent travel allows for tailoring the trip and the contacts to target select groups. One model is to make the first trip with a group, learn the ropes and then begin independent travel.

WHAT TO DO OVERSEAS

College fairs are a quick and easy way to access a large crowd of prospective students. For many years, the Institute of International Education (IIE) has been conducting fairs in many countries and, in some countries, the government offers large fairs. Commercial companies offer fairs as well. Tours benefit institutions with little name recognition or those just beginning to recruit overseas. Receptions and seminars can be arranged for prospective students and parents. Although usually held in hotels, these do not require expensive catering. A PowerPoint presentation followed by a question and answer period over coffee or tea is sufficient. Overseas educational government agencies are well worth the time to visit. In addition make the effort to include a visit to the U.S. embassy or consulate in the targeted cities.

Overseas educational centers are another rich source of information. Over 450 Overseas Educational Advising (OSEAS) Centers exist in over 150 countries. They share a common mission of providing educational advising services on study in the U.S. As noted in the College Board's *Directory of Overseas Educational Advising Centers*, the advisors, funded by the U.S. Department of State, often serve as the first point of contact for prospective overseas students, guiding them through career counseling, lists of U.S. institutions, college searches, testing, admission requirements, financial aid and orientation. They also provide information on educational trends, and they can help you to maximize your networking (www.educationusa.info/centers.php). Commercial consultants and agents provide another overseas connection. Reputable agents earn their fees by matching students to the most appropriate institutions. Commissions are sometimes included. This approach has both pros and cons, and we suggest the following practices when using partners and agents.

Best Practices in the Use of Partners and Agents

The number of U.S. institutions using partners or agents to recruit international students has increased, and a large learning curve is required to understand the playing field and the rules. The use of agent partners is now a growing issue. Colleges follow various practices in

support of ethical standards, to include researching prospective agents and their Web sites, requesting and checking references, citing their agents on the U.S. school Web site, signing campus approved agent agreements and making an effort to monitor agent integrity. As noted in an *Inside Higher Education*, June 10, 2009 article titled "Not So-Secret Agents," American colleges seem increasingly willing to at least try out the use of agents in recruiting international students. Many American college officials are proactively moving in that direction, with a pilot certification process by the American International Recruitment Council scheduled during meetings at the May 2010 NAFSA: Association of International Educators annual conference. The *Inside Higher Education* article notes that the IIE promotes collaboration with the U.S. State Department's network of Education USA centers, which are charged with providing objective advice on U.S. higher education opportunities. While IIE feels the student is best served by having the widest array of choices, they acknowledge that if an individual school wants to find students and does not have the resources, they may make the decision to use agents.

If an institution wants to use agents, knowing how best to identify, contact, vet and conduct business with agents is crucial. The following points highlight the key areas of consideration:

✳ First, contact colleagues in the field to determine if and how they use agents. Then, ask if they are willing to share the names of agents they use. Ask them how they conduct business with the agents.

✳ Review the Web site of a prospective agent.

✳ Ask the prospective agent to provide you with letters of reference from other U.S. institutions with which you are familiar.

✳ Contact the references to vet the prospective agent.

✳ Develop an agent agreement that has been reviewed and approved by the campus legal department. The agreement should list the main points of the agreement, the financial terms, an expectation of results and the start and end date of the agreement. It may be necessary to initiate or modify financial processes to accommodate fulfillment of the agreement.

✳ Be open and transparent about the use of agents and agent agreements.

Communication Skills

Effective recruitment requires a communication plan. And that plan can be as simple as a list of letters, brochures and emails sent to students and when they are sent, or it can be a massive multimedia database that segments out the applicant pool and tracks multiple streams of communications to different types of prospects and applicants. Whatever your mode and level of tracking, be mindful that school budgets fluctuate and that the numbers and origin of international students coming to the U.S. from various countries or regions can shift. Thus communications planning, documentation and assessment of effectiveness is essential.

Start with the development of an informative and effective Web site. Both domestic and international students rely heavily on the information they can access on the Internet. Establish an accessible Web site that uses clear terminology, contains the information in one location and includes the following topics:

✳ Contact information for the admissions and/or recruitment office, with links to other key areas such as housing, major departments and immigration information

✳ Application deadlines, detailed information about documents required and what is considered an official transcript

✳ Exact information about admission requirements at each entry level: first-time freshman, undergraduate transfer, graduate level

✳ English proficiency requirements and/or other entry test requirements

✳ Costs of attendance and what financial documentation is required

✳ International student financial aid policy

✳ Web-housed forms for inquiries to build a prospect file, financial verification forms and other necessary information

✳ Easy links to the application for admission

✳ Simple links to SEVIS

It is important, also, to have an international student link on the homepage or on the second screen of the Web site. Remember that in some countries downloading large images can take time. In terms of type of language used, avoid slang; it may lead to confusion. Similarly, do not use excessively bureaucratic language that might be difficult for nonnative speakers to understand.

Email is often a blessing in dealing with international applicants and yet sometimes a curse. It is by far the best way to maintain contact with international prospects and applicants. Gone are the days of using the postal system as the only means of communication. Give out as much detailed contact information as you can to applicants. It is amazing what several emails to clarify requirements and verify the receipt of documents can accomplish. Email also allows for personalized responses to student needs and even anticipation of them. Response time for inquiries is one of the measures prospective students will often use to gauge the student service quality of an institution. Applicants and their agents constantly demand better and faster service. At times it seems that responding to inquiries can be a full time job, thus making it important to have a system that allows for rapid response.

One must also not forget the advantage of using currently-enrolled international students to dialogue with international student prospects. Some schools are using interactive orientation and registration for out-of-country international students. If at all possible send your paper admission materials and I-20 visa paperwork by express mail. The cost is minor compared to the speed of your admission information reaching the student quickly and increasing the odds of students selecting your school.

Use dual marketing to speak to the students and parents in your outreach and promotional communication. These are two distinctly different audiences, often with very different values, aims and stakes in the process. In addition, there is strength in partnerships, as, for example, an admissions office partners with a strong on-campus or local English as a Second Language (ESL) program by developing an admission process contingent upon success in that ESL program. Finally, international alumni of your school who have returned to their home country become a vital asset when you attend college fairs in the field.

Streamline Admissions

Last, streamline admission processes when possible. Accept faxed financial documents and application forms. Consider providing pre-admission advisement. It will not only help the prospective students understand how their credit might transfer, but it could secure an immeasurable amount of good will should, for example, you establish a strong working relationship with advisors at local community colleges. If feasible, establish an international transfer articulation database with cooperating institutions abroad.

Currently, transfer is one of the most popular topics in higher education. Indeed, with regard to international admissions, so many gaps remain in the process of mapping one course or program to another. One solution to the issue of international transfer credit is to develop a database of your articulations so that you have a standardized process of awarding specific transfer credit from overseas university X to your institution. Such an international transfer articulation database allows for transparency and consistency. AACRAO's *EDGE—Electronic Database for Global Education* is a web-based resource which provides country profiles, including grading systems, sample credentials, glossaries and other means of decoding the educational system of more than 230 countries, with expansions and updates made regularly (www. aacraoedge.aacrao.org).

Successfully recruiting and enrolling students is but the first step of the process. International student retention is the second and equally important step. Establishing or enhancing services will be necessary for an institution planning to increase their international student population. As part of the planning process, assess existing resources on campus. Consider what constitutes an adequate number of personnel available for student services and academic advising and for addressing immigration regulations, the need for an English language placement or bridge program, personal counseling, housing and dietary considerations for students from different cultures who may not leave the campus for holiday breaks.

It has often been observed in recruitment and admissions that professionals who work in international education do so because of a passion for the field. Sometimes, however, the process can seem overwhelming. Overall some basic steps can be learned and cultivated for the benefit of the office and for the overall recruitment process:

* Review all the application data you have accumulated, including the paper application or a database, the educational history of where the applicant attended school and his/her date of birth. Now you are getting a feel for the student's education level—first-time freshman, undergraduate transfer or graduate.

* Verify possession of the required documents and their authenticity. Research the accreditation of the school and the educational level. Is the school recognized by the country's ministry of education?

* Make sure you have the required financial documents and confirm the existence of enough funds to meet your estimate of expenses.

* Determine that English proficiency requirements have been met. This may be through an appropriate TOEFL (Test of English as a Foreign Language) score or through an alternative test or coursework.

* Determine the actual class level of the applicant, eligibility and award transfer credit if appropriate.

✳ Issue the notice of admission and visa documents by express mail.

Conclusion

International enrollment management is increasingly important to the overall success of colleges and universities. Education opportunities in the United States continue to be highly attractive to international students, despite more overseas competition than ever before. Success with international student recruitment starts with a workable, yet flexible enrollment management plan, the application of good recruitment principles and skills, careful preparation, knowing how to find helpful resources and a genuine desire to host international students on your campus.

THREE

The International Admissions Office:
Policies, Procedures and Processes

Director of Graduate, Transfer and Adult Admissions
Iona College

VERONICA JAREK-PRINZ

The International Admissions Office: Policies, Procedures and Processes

It all starts with the admissions office. Achievement of enrollment and revenue goals, as well as strong retention rates are all rooted in the work of admissions. Indeed, a student's experience in being admitted often sets the tone for that student's entire educational career at a particular institution. Therefore, an admissions office must strive to be friendly, responsive, efficient, knowledgeable and accurate—a weighty task compounded by the intense and growing competition between colleges and universities for a shrinking demographic of college-ready applicants.

In addition to these considerations, admissions offices are finding that they must make subtle and sometimes not so subtle adjustments to their office operations to accommodate and assist international applicants. International applicants represent a vast pool of prospective students, many of outstanding quality and promise. In addition, because these students are not usually eligible for financial aid, they represent a way for institutions to increase revenues and enrollments without draining limited scholarship resources. As a result, many admissions officers find themselves navigating, often suddenly and blindly, the unique realm of international admission. However, this realm need not be intimidating.

This chapter will help define the scope and substance of international admissions processing, from inquiry to enrollment. Ideas for policies, procedures and processes will be offered so that an admissions officer faced with international application processing will be able to maintain quality, efficiency and accuracy.

Initial Considerations

Remember the unique requirements of international applicants; they require special handling somewhat different from that necessary for domestic applicants. With this in mind, you can begin to get a sense of the scope of international admissions processing and its place in the admissions office structure. But several important issues must also be considered.

MISSION STATEMENT

The very fact that your office is responsible for international admissions processing proves that your institution values the presence of international students on campus. In order to more fully appreciate the role of the admissions office in bringing these students to campus, review your institution's mission statement, especially as it relates to international education. Then use this during staff training to give the entire office a sense of mission and purpose. (*See* Chapter 1—"Overview of the State of International Higher Education")

EQUALITY

While the admissions process for international applicants may differ in terms of required materials and deadlines, the criteria for reviewing international applicants must compare to that for domestic applicants. That is, the educational standard for admission must be the same for all applicants. Inconsistency with regard to admissions decisions not only does a disservice to the applicant, but also has the very real potential of damaging your institution's reputation abroad.

MARKETING

For most admissions offices, marketing materials include view books, pamphlets, catalogues and the application for admission. Most offices now consider their institution's Web site as part of their marketing effort. You should ask yourself about the appropriateness of these materials for an international audience. A review of your marketing materials will help determine if they need updating for international applicants. It may prove helpful to convene a focus group—a small group of international students already studying at your institution—to review these materials and offer recommendations. If you have sufficient funds, and your enrollment goals require you to make recruiting international students a high priority, you might also consider creating separate marketing materials designed specifically for an international audience.

However, it is arguable that a college's most important marketing tool is its Web site. It is essential, then, to ensure that you communicate appropriately with an international audience—students as well as parents via the Internet. Many colleges find it helpful to create a unique page for international applicants, accessible from their Web site's homepage. This page can feature important information of a particularly relevant nature for international applicants, perhaps in the form of a specially-designed set of frequently asked questions.

TRAINING

The processing of international applications will require a bit of training throughout the office. All staff will benefit from cross-cultural training as they get used to dealing with a more international clientele. Data entry staff will need to learn about international academic credentials in order to properly enter information into the student information database. Evaluating international credentials to determine degree or transfer credit equivalency requires continual training. Any training program should take into consideration the uniqueness of international admissions processing and, therefore, should be thorough and easily digestible.

RESOURCES

The evaluation of international academic credentials requires access to a library of resources with information on educational systems around the world. While many books and articles exist, you can also find a significant amount of information easily available on the Internet. The Appendices at the back of this publication list resources available in international education.

INSTITUTIONAL RESEARCH

Performing some research on your applicant pool can help you better target your resources. Review your application statistics over the past few years in order to identify any trends with regard to international applications. You will get a better sense of the countries and regions from which you receive the most applications, thus helping you plan accordingly. Another research method is to interview current international students on campus. Whether by written survey or in-person interview, canvassing your current international population will allow you to hear the positive and negative experiences, enabling you to adjust the process if necessary.

STAFF DEVELOPMENT

As you and your staff adjust to the unique requirements for processing international applications, do not lose sight of the fact that staff development is essential in maintaining quality and efficiency. Staff should participate in regular training to keep skills sharpened. Local, regional and national conferences of such organizations as the American Association of Collegiate Registrars and Admissions Officers (AACRAO) and NAFSA: Association of International Educators are an excellent way for staff to learn the latest trends in the field of international education. Such conferences offer the opportunity to attend sessions on credentials and trends in individual countries. Knowing which countries or regions send the most applications your way will make it easier to choose which sessions to attend. In addition, networking with colleagues in the field will allow staff to share "war stories" and learn from their peers.

EMPATHY FOR THE EXPERIENCE

International applicants are considering leaving their home and everything they know to study in a foreign country, often in a second or even a third language. Keep this in mind when tempted to give in to impatience or frustration. Taking a moment to consider how difficult it might be for you to comprehend something as complex as an admissions process in Spanish or Mandarin may make it easier for you to work with a student whose communication skills or style may be far from your own experience.

SENSE OF HUMOR

This is a critical component in any undertaking. Without a sense of humor, we may often feel the weight of the world upon our shoulders. While we should approach the processing of international applications with the seriousness it deserves, we should not forget to smile and laugh along the way.

Understanding the Difference: Domestic vs. International Admissions

Before delving into the specifics of processing international applications, let us first consider the basic differences between domestic admissions and international admissions. This brief discussion will help establish a mindset conducive to working with international applications.

If anything is ever the same, it is that nothing is ever the same. This popular statement is appropriate for a discussion on international admissions, which is more complex and diverse than domestic admission. Because the majority of applications come from the U.S., and because most of us have been educated in the American system, domestic admission can be somewhat routine with education in the United States fairly standardized. Transcripts indicate courses with titles that describe the base content of the courses. Math is not listed as just mathematics. Instead courses are entitled in a way that shows the likely material covered—calculus, pre-calculus, trigonometry, algebra or geometry. Syllabi are also

fairly standard, where high school chemistry in New York will educate to the same level and content as high school chemistry in Arizona.

International admissions results in more difficulty with course comparisons as many students will be unable to provide course syllabi because such documents simply do not exist. Also, transcripts may not indicate courses with descriptive titles. A math course may simply say mathematics or history; content may remain a mystery.

Through training, practice and the use of resources, we may gain some understanding of particular foreign educational systems, but departures from educational patterns, varied and confusing transcript formats and exceptions to the rule remain. These exceptions, changes in pattern and revisions in many countries educational systems and structure are why nothing is ever the same and why any new experiences and examples and new educational institutions often challenge the international credential evaluator. And with these new experiences and changes, little background information usually exists to aid in decision making. But this is the nature of a dynamic world. Education variance and reform is part of our world and, in part, what makes international admissions unique, interesting and even exciting. Like learning a new language, processing international applications may seem strange and even uncomfortable at first. But time, practice, a little patience and a sense of humor will soon have you feeling comfortable and more confident.

And, as with any process, the more you do of it, the more comfortable and familiar it becomes. You will likely be processing applications from a small number of countries, as demonstrated by your institutional research. You will begin to develop a familiarity with the documents from that country, its institutions of higher learning, the courses students take and so on. At some point, a transcript from the University of Pune will seem as familiar to you as one from Pomona College. Many admissions personnel find themselves developing an interest and expertise in a particular country's educational system—so much so that they develop into something of a resource for coworkers and colleagues.

Serving the International Prospective Applicant

The distinctiveness of prospective international applicants will require you to modify your current processes and procedures as you incorporate them into your office regimen. From the initial inquiry until the point of enrollment in your institution, you will encounter the specific issues and concerns related to international students. Planning ahead will allow your office to provide quality service with accuracy and efficiency to this group.

INQUIRIES

Response time for inquiries is one of the measures prospective students will often use to gauge the student service quality of an institution. In this age of instant messaging and ubiquitous cell phones, applicants constantly demand better and faster service. Wait times of any length are becoming less and less tolerable. It is therefore important for an admissions office to have a system that allows and encourages rapid response. But doing so can seem like a full-time job, especially when responding to international inquiries. A few simple measures can help assure that responding to inquiries is not all-consuming.

Internet searches have become the primary method used by both domestic and international students to research colleges and universities. With a few clicks, prospective students from nearly every corner of the world can "visit" your institution. The information on your site, therefore, should provide answers to as many questions as possible. In addition, making the application for admission downloadable via your Web site will save your office time and mailing costs. For more information on Web sites and technology, see Chapter 4—"Technology in International Admissions."

Another popular method of inquiry for prospective international students is email. Responding to email inquiries can be rather daunting, especially during peak times. Because of the varying levels of technology around the world, prospective international students may send more than one email inquiry if they do not receive a response fairly quickly. Your email program should allow for an automated response explaining turnaround time and perhaps answering any frequently asked questions. In addition, your email response should instruct prospects to visit your Web site for more immediate information.

At the initial inquiry stage, many applicants need similar information—tuition and fees, application requirements, the availability of financial aid, etc. You may want to take the time to analyze the emails your office receives from international students and prepare an email response that addresses most or all of these issues. It is especially helpful if your email directs students to the appropriate pages of your Web site where they can find the answers and other helpful information. Consider including a link to a virtual tour or campus video, which will allow visitors from abroad to get a sense of how your campus or institution looks and feels.

Colleges and universities increasingly make use of social networking sites on the Internet, such as Facebook and Twitter—popular with both high school and college students, and even with older individuals. Both were initially designed as a way to keep up communication between friends, family members and acquaintances, but more and more have been utilized for marketing everything from celebrities to non-profits to events. Because so many potential students use them, colleges and universities have begun to develop presences here as well.

Whether your institution becomes involved in this trend depends on several factors. The point of Twitter and Facebook is to provide constantly changing, up-to-date information. In order to keep your institutional profile fresh, your office will need to dedicate resources to its upkeep. Text, articles and photos should be refreshed and changed to reflect current happenings on campus and in the world.

You must also make a decision as to how you will allow viewers—or potential students—to access your profile. Once an individual becomes a "friend" or "fan" of your institution, he or she is free to post comments and content to your site. Review these comments frequently, as cases of unflattering or untrue information being posted have occurred. However, these sites do build in a variety of safeguards. Should you decide to involve your institution in social networking, it behooves you and your staff to learn as much as you can about the options available for security and interaction. It is essential to choose the settings that make the most sense given your resources and your commitment.

If these decisions are made carefully and the profile is kept fresh and robust, Facebook, Twitter and other social sites can bring a completely new group of individuals to your institution. Never underestimate the "cool" factor—even students who do not utilize such sites may be impressed that your institution does.

Informational Materials for International Students

Informational materials for international students should address general university information while taking into account the specific needs and requirements pertaining to this population. The goal is to provide pertinent information and gather application data that is unique to international students, while ensuring that the international student receives information that shows all opportunities available for full participation in campus and community life.

The materials must be welcoming and easily understood. They should address the importance of international students and scholars in your institution's academic setting and in the community at large. State the educational institution's mission and goals as they pertain to international students. Ideally, your materials will show how prospective international students can interact with other international students and faculty while becoming an integral part of the college community. Informational materials clearly showing that the college values having international students on campus and in the local community have the potential to generate a significant amount of interest among prospective international students.

Given decreased publication budgets and escalating international mailings costs, most institutions choose to put this information on their Web site. It can be very valuable to have a special section within the admissions pages that provides information targeted to prospective international students, visible from the homepage of your site. This enables international students to go directly to the information they find most valuable.

INFORMATION TO INCLUDE FOR AN INTERNATIONAL AUDIENCE

The following is a brief list of important information of interest to all prospective students that college and university promotional materials should include:

* school specifics, such as mission, history, public or private, size, location
* detailed list of academic programs and degrees offered
* examples of quality programs and nationally recognized faculty
* information about student services, such as housing and meal plans, on-campus and off-campus health services, student activities and organizations, tutoring and learning centers
* community information, such as local popular activities, shopping, entertainment, history, points of local and regional interest
* financial information, such as yearly cost of tuition and living expenses
* application deadlines

In addition to this information, international students will be particularly interested in the following:

* highlights about the school's international focus, *e.g.*, sister institutions, exchange agreements, international and Fulbright scholars on campus
* scholarships for international students, assistantships, on-campus employment

✴ notes on the local climate and weather—seasonal temperature ranges can be quite helpful

✴ a profile or two of an international student who is experiencing success at your institution both inside and outside the classroom

The goal of these informational materials is to turn an inquiry into an application. Therefore the materials should be as clear and concise as possible, while showing the international applicant that the institution values the presence of international students and supports them when they arrive.

Application Requirements: Be Clear, Be Concise, Be Specific

Application requirements can be included in a general brochure or in a separate packet with the application form, as well as made available in an easy to find location on your Web site. Always provide good, detailed definitions so that international students have a clear understanding of the requirements. Clarity will help to prevent numerous communications with students needing more detail. Make students aware of the elements of a complete application. Complete applications reduce processing and evaluation time—particularly important when trying to render and communicate decisions between countries. The information to collect from applicants may vary slightly from institution to institution, but commonly contains the following items:

✴ completed and signed application for admission

✴ application fee (a more appropriate term is processing/evaluation fee)

✴ transcripts, mark sheets, exam results, completion certificates (diploma, degree, etc.) (be sure to specify what constitutes an "official" document)

✴ English translations of all documents listed above (be sure that you define what constitutes an "official" translation)

✴ English language requirements: approved testing vehicles and minimum scores required, *e.g.*, TOEFL, MELAB, etc.

✴ Aptitude test results for undergraduate applicants, *e.g.*, ACT, SAT I, SAT II

✴ Graduate admission tests results, *e.g.*, GMAT, GRE, MAT, LSAT, MCAT

✴ Financial requirements: completed financial affidavit by sponsor (promise of financial support), official bank statement and letter from the sponsor's financial institution (if required at the time of application); many institutions wait to gather this information until after an admissions decision has been made.

✴ Statement of purpose, resume, portfolio

✴ Letters of recommendation

APPLICATION FORMS

The application for admission is likely to be the only portion of an application that varies from institution to institution. To keep your form from discouraging applications to your institution, work to keep the document clear and concise. Require only the most pertinent information; balancing brevity with legitimate and necessary questions is the key to a well-constructed admission application. An institution may elect to create a separate application for international students or use one application for all students. Regardless of the format, the application should request the following basic information:

✴ Name. In some countries, the standard practice is to place the family name before the given name or use only the family name. The application should use the terms "family name" and "given name" to avoid confusion for the applicant and the data entry staff.

✴ Date of Birth. This identifier will help distinguish applicants with the exact same name. It is helpful to specify the order you prefer to receive these elements in, *e.g.*, DDMMYYYY.

✴ Gender. This is not always obvious from the name.

✴ Complete Address. Your database should allow for more address lines than are needed for domestic addresses.

✴ Desired Term of Study. Be specific with regard to restrictions, such as fall-only start terms.

✳ Desired Degree Level

✳ Desired Academic Program

✳ Complete Academic History. Maintaining information on the previously attended institutions of your applicants provides an excellent source of data for recruitment purposes and helps you better understand your applicant pool.

✳ Applicant's signature.

In addition to requesting this basic information, the admission application should also clearly explain the supporting documentation necessary to complete the application. These include letters of recommendation, required examination results, financial certification (if required for admission) and, most importantly, academic transcripts. With regard to transcripts, very clearly state your institution's policy regarding what constitutes an official transcript, mark sheet or examination result. You should also explain your policy regarding official English-language translations. Finally, explain your policy regarding incomplete applications. This will help alleviate frantic phone calls and emails to your office.

Depending on the format of your admission application, additional forms may help international applicants more easily and readily provide the necessary information. Consider including the following additional forms with your application packet:

✳ financial affidavit form, if this information is required before admission

✳ recommendation form(s)

✳ scholarship and financial assistance applications (not to be confused with the FAFSA used for applying for U.S. federal financial aid); these documents are only necessary if your institution awards financial aid to international students.

✳ graduate assistantship application

✳ information release form, to allow sponsoring agencies to monitor academic progress or allow for the work of family intermediaries

PROCESSING PROCEDURES

Ideally, processing international applications will not differ significantly from the processes and procedures already used in your office for processing domestic applications. Written policies and procedures pertaining to admissions requirements and quality standards will help maintain consistency. Apply consistent standards and practices as much as you can, but understand the need for exceptions and flexibility. While it is important to pay heed to recommendations and prevailing opinions that come from within our profession, each of us must look at the standards, policies and procedures that are mandated and work at our individual institutions.

CREATING A PROCESSING MANUAL

Develop a manual to ensure standardized processing, making sure to address:

✳ date stamping received materials

✳ fees for processing the application

✳ detailed procedures on data entry, including a format for names and addresses

✳ instructions on conducting name searches, discussion about name variations and DOB verification to facilitate matching documents to files

✳ file completion and preparation for academic evaluation

✳ timely correspondence, as it pertains to acknowledgement of application received, notification of missing documents, unmet requirements and admission decisions

✳ orientation, housing, registration information

In a section on processing international applications, add the following:

✳ discussion on official documentation as it pertains to transcripts, translations, bank statements and bank letters

✳ entry of test scores, such as TOEFL, ACT, SAT, GRE, GMAT, etc.; minimum acceptable scores

✳ the importance of the I-20 in the admissions process; laying out the steps required for the issuing of the I-20 from your institution

Once the international application is received, it should be processed according to the same policies and procedures applied to domestic applications. The most significant challenge for staff members in processing applications is determining the completeness of an international application. Academic documents from abroad can look very different than domestic credentials. In order to prevent bottlenecks in the processing stage, identify members of the admissions staff to assist in determining the completeness of the application in terms of academic credentials.

EVALUATING INTERNATIONAL ACADEMIC CREDENTIALS

Once complete, the application is ready to be evaluated. The evaluation of international academic credentials to determine U.S. academic equivalency is probably the most daunting aspect of processing international applications. Most people believe that one must possess vast knowledge about foreign educational systems and years worth of experience evaluating international credentials. While it takes some time and experience with different documents and educational systems to become expert, an admissions counselor who approaches the task with openness and armed with resources can become a competent credential evaluator in a surprisingly short time. The key is to recognize what you do not know and, when in doubt, stop and check with your resources and more experienced colleagues.

An important consideration for the international admission office is how best to perform the credential evaluation process. Depending on the volume of international applications and the number of staff in the office, one of the following models may work for your particular office:

✳ *The International Expert.* One staff member handles the evaluation of all international applications. This model generally works best for an office with a lower volume of international applications.

✳ *Country/Regional Specialists.* In this model, several staff members become country or region specialists. Applications are divided by country or region and the staff specialist for the country/region performs the evaluation. One of the drawbacks to this model is the lack of cross-training. If the Asia expert must leave the office for an extended period of time, who will perform those evaluations?

✳ *Alphabetical.* International evaluations are divided by the first initial of the applicant's last name with several staff members taking responsibility for a range of the alphabet. This model implies that all staff members involved in evaluation will learn all systems and regions.

✳ *Discipline.* This model works well in a graduate admissions setting. The caseload of evaluations is divided by discipline. For example, depending on the range of programs your office handles, sciences, social sciences, humanities and business can be four distinct disciplines. This model allows for cross-training and specialization at the same time. In addition, evaluators become more familiar with institutions and programs within foreign institutions.

Chapters 6, 7 and 8 of this publication offer extensive information on the various aspects of international academic credential evaluation.

Communicating With Your Applicants

Once an application has been received by your office, your institution has a responsibility to communicate with the applicant. Most student systems allow for the preparation of these communications in the form of boilerplate form letters or emails, in which most of the text is the same for all applicants.

Typically the first notification an applicant receives during the admissions process is an acknowledgment of the application. This can be a letter, a postcard alerting them to the receipt of their application or an email.

There are decisions to make when developing the text. Should it list materials received along with those still missing from the application? Many institutions still do this by hand, checking each application as it comes in and marking the missing pieces on a preprinted postcard. The most robust admissions databases can create personalized notifications for each applicant, including information on what documentation may be missing from a file. The institution should decide whether it is worth the extra effort (and possible mistakes and phone calls it will engender) to include information about which documents have been logged into the student system. Alternatively, the acknowledgement might merely list all the needed materials as a reminder to the applicant about the requirements.

In any case, the acknowledgement should confirm the department and degree applied for, as well as the desired term of entry so that the applicant can alert the office of any discrepancies. This information can, and probably should, print directly from your database. You will want the communications this letter may create, as it will help you correct any errors on the part of the applicant or those made in data entry.

Of course the most important communication an applicant will receive is the decision letter. Regardless of the decision, it is crucial that your staff proofread all communications with your applicants.

Denial letters are fairly standard in terms of processing, as no specific information beyond student name and address is needed. The text can simply state that the institution received a large number of high-quality applicants, and the student has not been admitted. If your institution chooses, you can include more specific information, such as program and degree, but this is generally considered unnecessary.

Acceptance letters require a bit more attention. These should confirm all the basic information about degree, field of study and term of entrance. The text should be warm and congratulatory, welcoming the successful applicant to continue his/her success at your institution. It should also include relevant information,

such as whether a deposit is required and the next steps necessary for enrollment.

For international students, you may discover a need for several types of admission letters. The type depends on the completion of financial requirements and your institution's requirements for proficiency in the English language, in addition to being academically admissible.

* COMPLETED REQUIREMENTS: send letter of admission and I-20 (notification of scholarship or graduate assistantship, if awarded)
* ENGLISH LANGUAGE TRAINING REQUIRED: send letter of conditional admission with language program I-20, if institution has a language training program (promise of admission once English language requirement has been met)
* FINANCIAL RESOURCES REQUIRED: send letter of admissibility that states the financial resources required before the I-20 can be sent (I-20 is sent separately after the financial resources are proven and acceptable)

Other forms that can accompany an acceptance letter include:

* intent to enroll form (when returned by students, will help plan for orientation and provide closer estimates of enrollment numbers)
* detailed orientation schedule
* clarification about requirements upon arrival, *e.g.*, testing, health insurance, health and vaccination records
* housing information and contract

International students may find the following information helpful:

* quick reference/cheat sheet in the I-20/visa/port of entry process
* arrival information request form (helps with airport pickup and initial settlement)

The last type of decision letter is a withdrawal letter. These are sent to applicants whose applications are being withdrawn, citing the reason for this action, such as the application was never completed, or the applicant requested his/her application be withdrawn. Some institutions choose not to send withdrawal letters, believing that the applicant, by his/her own actions, has decided not to pursue admission. If the applicant is not qualified for admission based on level of completed education, he or she should receive an individual communication about what might be missing in his/her educational background.

See Chapter 4—"Technology in International Admissions"—for more information on communication with applicants.

NEW STUDENT ORIENTATION

International students coming to the U.S. to study are simultaneously excited by the opportunities that lie ahead of them and nervous about the strange new world they are about to encounter. A good orientation program will help new students make an easier transition into their new academic community. Acclimation and an understanding of services provided will result in well-adjusted and successful students.

Consider the following logistics when creating a new student orientation program:

* determine the length of the orientation program (the length will be determined by the program agenda, two to five days is common)
* schedule orientation just prior to the beginning of classes (most students will schedule their arrival in the U.S. to coincide with the beginning of orientation and usually enter the U.S. no earlier then thirty days before classes begin)
* orientation should be coordinated with academic advising

* orientation must be coordinated with housing (available just prior to orientation to avoid temporary situations and then resettlement)

The following list is not all inclusive, but provides some topics that should be covered during orientation:

* academic structure and process
* styles of instruction
* class work and attendance expectations
* semester/quarter credit explanations
* grading structure
* degree requirements: major, minor, general education
* academic advising process
* registration process
* student services
* learning and writing centers
* tutoring
* health care
* housing and food services
* on-campus employment
* student involvement and campus organizations
* additional discussions and activities
* cultural norms
* social life
* spiritual life
* personal finances
* campus tour
* community tour: banks, shopping, services, entertainment, worship

Again, a good orientation program will help students adjust to a new environment: academic, cultural and community. Through these efforts we can better ensure success and, ultimately, program completion and graduation.

FOUR

Technology In International Admissions

ELIZABETH WHITE

Assistant Director
International Admissions
University at Buffalo, State University of New York

2010 AACRAO INTERNATIONAL GUIDE

Technology In International Admissions

As recently as the late 1990s, many international admissions officers at U.S. colleges and universities relied on traditional postal services in order to communicate with applicants. While email and the Internet had existed for years, they had become broadly available in the United States only in the early 1990s. By the latter part of that decade, the telecommunications infrastructure was improving abroad, but was not yet mature enough to allow for reliable communication, particularly in developing countries such as China and India, which, then and now, send large numbers of international students to the United States (Press, Foster, Wolcott, and McHenry 2003).

The now-common term "snail mail" accurately describes the slow pace of first-class mail delivery between most countries. Consider the cycle of a typical international student's application using regular mail: By the time an application is mailed and received, the institution acknowledges the application, and any missing documents are subsequently submitted to complete the application, eight weeks or more may go by. When mailing time for acceptance and enrollment packets is added, the three- to four-month turnaround time that was once the norm is understandable.

The way colleges communicate with prospective students—so crucial to the business of admissions—is just one example of the way the international admissions process has been changed by technology. Other technological trends of the last decade have also had an impact. The development of more sophisticated student information systems has given admissions offices better tools with which to admit applicants and then track those admitted students throughout their university careers. Online applications dump applicant information into these systems, reducing staff time devoted to data entry. These systems, in turn, feed data warehouses, which give easier access to information about applicants, allowing for better trend analysis.

In fact, today it is impossible to imagine doing business without email, the Web, and other forms of technology that have grown up in their wake. Technology is now an essential part of recruiting, admitting, and enrolling international students at American colleges and universities. In and of itself, however, technology is not a panacea. In order to use it most effectively, you must understand the needs of your campus and of your prospective students, as well as be aware of current technological trends.

Assessing Your Needs

Not every campus will have the resources, the staff, or the will to take advantage of every new technology; nor should they. As with any significant investment, enrollment managers must feel confident that the perceived benefit will be worth the investment. One of the most salient factors of technology is its rapid pace of change. The newest trend this year may be passé in a year's time; the most amazing new equipment will be obsolete in fewer than five years. Unless an institution is blessed with unlimited resources, it is not possible to embrace every new trend. Choices must be made. Several factors should be considered when making these choices.

BUDGET

One paradox of the technology available to admissions professionals is that it is both expensive and inexpensive. Certainly, the constant upgrades in hardware (computers, printers, scanners, copiers, etc.) require significant, ongoing investment. Software, however, can be relatively cheap and offer good bang for the buck (as with desktop publishing or Web design programs), or it can be enormously expensive (as with new student information system packages or enterprise resource planning systems [ERPs]). Offices that adopt a "do-it-yourself" approach, using the amateur talents of existing staff to create Web sites, maintain blogs, or create podcasts or video clips can have a fairly sophisticated marketing campaign without a huge investment. On the other hand, professional marketing companies that specialize in the higher education arena can take these homegrown efforts to new heights—for a cost. Developing a detailed enrollment plan in conjunction with your budget will help determine where money can most effectively be spent.

IT SUPPORT

The support of information technology staff is critical to the smooth functioning of any professional office. When considering which IT initiatives to embrace, consider the staff support that will be required. If you have IT staff members in your office, you may have more ability to influence their priorities. For example, if you want to establish a presence on various social networking sites, internal staff can probably do it; in fact, you do not even need to rely on IT staff for this kind of basic initiative. Some projects, however, will need to be addressed by institutional IT staff. If you need to revamp your Web site, for example, you may have to depend upon your campus Web master, which could dictate a longer timeline.

Whether you have in-house dedicated IT staff members, or rely on the institution's central IT professionals, remember that many technology projects require not only start-up time, but also maintenance. In the social networking example above, you need to remember that once your school's profile is up, someone will need to be dedicated to keeping it up-to-date.

SIZE OF APPLICANT POOL

Campuses with a small number of international students may find that it is not worthwhile to embrace every trend. If you are processing only one hundred international applications per year, you probably do not need the most sophisticated database software. You also could decide to put less emphasis on marketing efforts that rely on impersonal email blasts or e-flyers; a more personalized approach may be possible, and also more effective.

APPLICANT ACCESS

As web-based communication and email have become more prevalent, staff in international admissions had to become cognizant of the difference between Web access and speed in the U.S. versus the rest of the world. In recent years, the telecommunication infrastructure in many developing parts of the world has improved immensely. Many students today have access both to computers and high-speed Internet connections, particularly in the metropolitan areas of the countries that send the largest numbers of international students to the United States. This makes browsing Web sites with graphical content or applying online much easier than it was even five years ago. However, in rural regions of these countries, as well as in other parts of the world (such as Africa), students may not find it so easy. Even in some developed countries, connections will be slower than in the United States. And, in some cases, access may be controlled by the government, preventing your information from reaching its intended audience. Remember that the way a certain application performs on your state-of-the-art office computer (with high-speed Internet access) may not be experienced the same way by your applicants.

If your college's international applicant pool is made up largely of the typical prospective international student—city dwellers in India, China, and Korea—then issues of applicant access may be less important. However, schools with pockets of applicants from rural regions or other countries should research access issues for their specific feeder areas. Become knowledgeable about what your applicants are experiencing. If your campus recruits overseas, ask your recruiters to research this in-country. Certainly they will have some sense of access from using the Internet themselves while on the road. Since large Western hotel chains may have better Internet speed than that experienced by the average citizen at home, school, or in an Internet cafe, your recruiters should also talk to students, parents, counselors, and educational advisors about their ability to use the Internet and your school's Web site in particular. If your school does not recruit overseas, develop a survey (low on graphics) to be sent to your applicants by email. Or, ask current students about Internet access issues in their home countries. With more information about what your "customers" are experiencing, you will be able to make educated decisions about how to structure your Web site and your communication plan.

Communicating With Prospects and Applicants

One of the great advantages of electronic communication is its speed. Particularly for those who must interact with people all over the world, the way email and the Internet have sped up the delivery of the messages we must send to our students, and they in turn to us, is an amazing thing to behold. When developing a communication plan for your prospects and applicants, there are several facets to consider.

WEB SITES

One of the most important recruiting tools for any college or university today is its Web site. In years past, a prospective student's introduction to your campus was often the first printed piece he or she received in the mail. Now, students immediately go to the Web when they want to find out more information about your school. What will international students find when they visit your campus online? If your site has been designed only with typical U.S. Internet users in mind, including lots of graphics and multimedia applications (such as Flash), it is possible that you may be shutting

out a pool of prospective students who cannot download portions of your site. As already mentioned, if you have done your research and feel confident that most, if not all, of your visitors can view sophisticated graphical content, then you need not worry. But if you find that access is an issue for some of your prospective students, you may need to become an advocate for a simpler Web site design. Get to know your campus's Web master, and be sure that he or she is aware of the issues faced by your overseas visitors. Whether it means less use of Flash, simplifying the site's design (requiring fewer downloads), or, in extreme cases, having a special international student gateway with very few graphics, you may need to educate your IT staff about the needs of your international population.

For many campuses, blogs are now a component of the admissions Web site. A blog (short for "Web log") is a site listing the owner's "posts" or entries, usually in reverse chronological order, along with comments from readers. Its interactive nature is one of its advantages; blogs can be used to create online communities, where students can "meet" before they even arrive on campus. However, this feature can also be worrisome to admissions staff, whose goal, of course, is to portray a positive image of their institution. A true blog is free-flowing, with no moderator or censor. An institution can start a blog and post entries, but it cannot control the comments made by readers. If someone has a negative opinion to express, it will be there for the entire community to read. The good news is that some blogging software allows an owner to moderate the site, with the ability to delete comments and remove users. Before creating a blog, check the rules of the software carefully to be sure that it will meet your needs. Blogger (www.blogger.com) and WordPress (www.wordpress.com) are just two examples of free blogging software sites.

Social media have more recently become another tool in the admissions office's online arsenal. Many colleges and universities now have profiles on sites like Facebook and MySpace. These profiles may be formal, resembling an institutional Web site, or they may be set up by individual admissions staff members or student recruiters, with a more informal feel. (Some admissions professionals even find "friend" requests from applicants on their personal Facebook profiles; whether to accept these requests recently became a hot topic as an older demographic embraced Facebook for personal use [Anderson 2009]). Twitter is also gaining in popularity, as colleges establish accounts and ask their prospects or applicants to "follow" them. Either way, the point of having a presence on these sites is all about marketing: social networking is one more way to put your institution's name out there for the college-bound demographic. Furthermore, it is not just Americans who participate on these sites. In 2009, for example, Facebook's Press Room reported that 70 percent of its members lived outside the United States. It seems clear that prospective international students can be reached via social media.

EMAIL

Email has been a boon to international admissions offices, which now can communicate with individual applicants in a much more timely way than was previously possible. On the other hand, it has created more work. International students often prefer to communicate by email, since it is free and they can send messages at any time. Their anxiety about the application process, and differences in time zones, may cause them to send multiple repeat emails when they do not receive a timely response. Because of the high volume of emails received, most admissions offices now have staff dedicated to monitoring the office email account and responding to students' questions. To head off repeated messages, it is a good idea to have an automated reply explaining the typical length of time it takes for your office to respond to a student's message.

More beneficial has been the ease of sending mass mailings via email. Sending a message to hundreds, or even thousands, of people is fairly simple. Unfortunately, it may be too simple, as anyone who has been spammed (and who hasn't?) can confirm. Even legitimate email blasts from retailers, banks, college alumni offices, and many other businesses now clutter our inboxes. When using email, colleges and universities must proceed carefully, attempting to maintain a delicate balance between being informative and just plain annoying.

Some have argued that college admissions offices should completely stop sending mass emails (Bonfiglio 2007). There may be a place, however, for judicious use of mass emails with your applicant pool. If a student is truly interested in your institution, they will pay attention when they see the name of your school in the "subject" line (as long as it is not the fifth message they have received from your institution that week). If you reserve your messages for reminders about deadlines or other important information, students should pay attention, and it is still a good way to reach a group of people quickly and efficiently.

Sending attractive, graphical electronic flyers and newsletters does not require extensive knowledge of HTML. With software such as Front Page or Dreamweaver, a novice can easily create a basic Web site, copy the background coding into an email message, and blast it out to a group of applicants. E-flyers are basic, resembling the reminders you receive from your favorite retailer about an upcoming sale. E-newsletters are more complicated, containing what are essentially links to a series of Web sites. In both cases, there is a significant cost savings compared to printing and mailing a full-color postcard or newsletter. There is, of course, the start-up cost associated with purchasing the software and training staff, but that expenditure is minimal when you consider the savings over time.

The uses for these electronic forms of communication are practically endless. For prospects, you can send out targeted messages with dates of upcoming recruitment fairs in a given city or country. For applicants, you can send reminders about application, scholarship, or tuition deposit deadlines. For committed students, you can send information about orientation or housing check-in. Universities commonly use this medium to send marketing or branding messages about the institution, although it is here, particularly, where caution must be exercised; too many messages of this nature may cause your applicants to delete future messages.

One other caveat: put a standard statement at the bottom of your messages asking recipients to add your sending address to their list of contacts. This is important so that your messages do not end up in junk mail folders. In addition, as with any email subscription list, you should provide the ability for a recipient to unsubscribe from the mailing list.

REAL-TIME COMMUNICATION

In the past, if a student could not come to your office personally, the telephone was the best alternative way to communicate in real time. However, international long-distance rates per minute, especially during business hours, are prohibitively expensive. International admissions offices now have several other alternatives which are available for a much lower cost.

In Voice Over Internet Protocol (VoIP) two parties talk using an Internet connection rather than traditional phone lines. Both users must have computers with microphones and a high-speed Internet connection. Video calls are also possible if one or both users have Web cameras. There is free software available online (such as Skype—www.skype.com) that allows members to talk for free or at international rates that are a fraction of regular long-distance rates. Some of these sites only allow members to talk, meaning that the person you want to call may also need to sign up for the service. Also available are VoIP phone services, such as Vonage, where a monthly fee is paid, allowing you to call anyone, just like your regular phone service. Sound quality is generally good, although problems may occur, especially when calling overseas. Due to sound quality concerns and connection limits, it is not currently feasible for admissions offices to use VoIP exclusively instead of regular long-distance calls. However, it serves as a low-cost way to contact prospects or applicants when a more personal touch may be effective.

Instant messaging (IM) also allows for live communication via the Internet, but it is typed rather than spoken.

A number of free IM networks are available, including AOL Instant Messenger, Yahoo Messenger, and Google Talk. Meebo is a newer service that allows members of any IM network to talk to each other, also for free. These conversations can be between two individuals, or they can be among groups of people in chat rooms. Similarly, admissions staff can use IM to communicate with individual applicants, or groups of prospects or applicants. Many campuses now promote IM as one more way for students to contact the admissions office to ask questions or obtain information about the status of their application; a Meebo or other chat window is prominently displayed on their Web site, and a staff person is available to respond to anyone who wants to chat. Group chats can also be organized and publicized as a way for prospective students to learn more about the campus or to have specific questions answered. In group chats, a number of admissions advisors can answer questions simultaneously, to manage both time and the topics discussed.

Because of the issues involved in sending mass emails to applicants, some colleges are now using cell phone text messaging as another way to reach pools of prospective students. There are several obstacles that could prevent the widespread use of texting by admissions offices. First, cell phone numbers are not commonly collected on recruitment and admission forms at the current time. However, this may change in the near future as more and more students use cell phones as their primary phone. Second, there is often a charge for the recipient of a text message. Mass emails are annoying, but at least you do not pay for them. Student resistance to these charges may limit the usefulness of texting at the current time, but if free texting becomes more common, it may emerge as a feasible way to reach students (Fratt 2006).

Technology in the Admission Process

As has been discussed, technology has fundamentally changed the way we communicate with prospective students. However, not only has communication changed; the way we receive and process applications has as well.

APPLYING ONLINE

In the last edition of this publication (AACRAO 2001), online applications constituted a major technology issue. At that time, the web-based application forms that we now take for granted were fairly new on the scene. Today, applicants expect institutions to have an online application, and most campuses do, either through a form developed in-house using institutional resources, or via a contract with a vendor such as ApplyNow or CollegeNet. A homegrown online form is desirable, since the form will be customized to meet your needs, but it is expensive, both in terms of time and money. By participating in a vendor-developed application, a campus can have the application up and running quickly. Certainly, the cost of such a contract is not insignificant, but may be more easily justified since the costs are borne out over time rather than up front.

It is safe to assume that most students, even (or, perhaps, especially) those living overseas, now prefer to apply online. However, it is still a good idea to have a paper application available. If an applicant does not have his or her own computer and is using one in their school or an Internet café, they may not be able to finish a long application in the allotted time. This problem is compounded if the available Internet service has a low bandwidth. In this case, it could take minutes, not seconds, for each page of your application to load. A good "halfway" measure is to have a PDF version of your paper application available on your Web site. Even if Internet service is slow, at least the file must download only once. The student can then print the application, which also saves time spent waiting for the application form to arrive in the mail.

DATABASES

Perhaps the most important piece of technology used by an admissions office is its application database. Without an efficient means of gathering and storing information on applicants, it would be difficult to process applications in a timely way.

The database used by administrative offices on college campuses is broadly referred to as a student information system (SIS). The admissions office typically creates the initial student record for this system, either by manually entering data from a paper application or by uploading information submitted by the applicant on a web-based application form. These student records are then used by other administrative offices during that student's career at the institution. Typically, the admissions office uses the campus's SIS. However, since it can be difficult to find one software program that will meet the needs of many offices with divergent needs (especially on larger campuses), some offices purchase "shadow" databases to meet their unique needs. Ideally, these software applications will work in conjunction with the SIS, but technical issues sometimes prevent this, leaving the shadow database with no connection to the larger system.

The international admissions office, in particular, may find that the SIS used by the campus does not meet its needs. Student addresses can present a problem, since foreign addresses rarely fit the standard U.S. format common in American database software. In addition, since the advent of SEVIS, the information tracking now required of international student offices may not be possible within the current SIS.

The major developers of SIS software, however, have been releasing more and more sophisticated products in recent years. As campuses upgrade to newer versions, or move from in-house legacy systems to ERP software, they may find that fewer shadow systems will be necessary. The most important thing to note here is that the international office should have a place at the table as decisions are made about the software applications used on the campus. Because the international population's needs are unique, they could be overlooked without a strong advocate for a system that can serve the international office.

APPLICATION STATUS WEB SITE

Since so many applicants now have access to the Internet, some campuses have developed secure Web sites that provide application status information to applicants. In order for these sites to be efficient, a link must exist between the database information and the site; you will need the help of IT staff to build this. The advantage of having such a site is that, ideally, it should reduce the number of times that an applicant contacts your office by phone or email to check on the status of his or her application. Whether this is always borne out in reality can be debated. A critical issue here is timing; if a student sends a document to be added to his or her file, and it is not reflected on the site right away, he or she may contact your office anyway to confirm that the document was actually received. (This is especially true of the current "millennial" generation, many of whom expect instant communication, having grown up with technology.) At certain times of year, the admissions office may easily and quickly file and review new documents that are received. The nature of the admissions cycle, however, may make it difficult to match documents efficiently during the peak application period, when most applications are received. If your office is using such a site, make sure to provide applicants with information about the typical turnaround time for new information to be posted to the site.

DOCUMENT IMAGING

Paper is a seemingly inescapable feature of college admissions, especially for those working with international student applications. More and more campuses, however, are reducing their reliance on paper by implementing document imaging systems. Such systems allow scanned images of paper documents to be stored electronically, allowing an entire application to be accessed and reviewed on a computer. There are many benefits to an imaging system. Numerous application reviewers can view and comment on an applicant without waiting for a paper file to be handed to them. If the applicant contacts the admissions office with questions, front-line staff can answer them without tracking down a paper file. Since paper files do not need to be as readily accessible, more compact, locked filing cabinets can be used, saving physical space.

There are numerous vendors offering document imaging software and equipment. If a campus is implementing an ERP, this optional add-on can be integrated into the system. Or, the imaging system can be purchased and integrated with an existing legacy system. Either way, the institution's IT staff must dedicate significant time and money to ensure that the document imaging system integrates effectively with the admissions system.

The University of Texas at Austin has employed a document imaging system since the mid-1990s, when only a few American universities had implemented this new technology (Ellison 2009). The impetus for imaging came from the sheer volume of paper applications received by UT Austin—around 60,000 applications for a typical fall semester—and a lack of space to store them. The development of document imaging was undertaken carefully: five years were spent mapping workflow and business processes before the system was implemented. In the decade since UT Austin put their system into action, the technology has continued to develop. Until recently, standard flatbed scanners were used, but high-speed scanners have recently been purchased. New software also allows for less time spent sorting documents by color and size prior to scanning, as was necessary in the past.

With document imaging, a careful verification process is crucial to ensuring application and system integrity. For international documents, this begins with a careful review of the original paper document upon receipt. Since the look and feel of foreign documents play a significant role in ensuring their authenticity, this step must happen prior to scanning. Once trained staff verifies authenticity, the document is prepared for scanning. A document ID is assigned to match it to the correct student's application. Once scanned, the image must be checked for quality. While trained and permanent staff must verify the authenticity of international documents, most of the other steps in the verification process can be handled by clerical staff, or even student staff.

After application materials have been scanned and matched to a student's record, the paper file is stored for a specific time period before being shredded. This time period may be shorter than what is required under traditional FERPA guidelines, since the electronic file can serve as the official record. At the University of Texas at Austin, where paper documents are kept for one year after the last activity on the file, careful research ensured that the imaged documents met FERPA guidelines. Time is saved for staff in the registrar's office as well, since a paper file does not need to be transferred and audited upon a student's enrollment.

CREDENTIAL EVALUATION

We have already discussed the implications of increased speed of communication with applicants due to the Internet and email. Perhaps just as important for the international admissions officer is the ease of obtaining information about educational systems. Credential evaluators have a wide network of electronic resources at their fingertips and can cultivate relationships with experts in countries around the world much more easily. Table 4.1 lists of some key resources that can help someone new to the field get started.

The three references shown in Table 4.2 are well-respected foreign credential evaluation services. Each

TABLE 4.2: Evaluation Services

AACRAO International Education Services	www.aacrao.org/international/
World Education Services (WES)	www.wes.org/educators/index.asp
Educational Credential Evaluators (ECE)	www.ece.org

organization's Web site provides excellent—and free— resources for international admissions professionals.

SEVIS

In the aftermath of September 11, 2001, it was discovered that a few of the terrorists involved in the plot to attack the United States had entered the country on student visas, obtained on the basis of admission to American flight schools. This discovery led the federal government to put new emphasis on a plan, known as CIPRIS, in existence since the mid-1990s to track international students during their stay in the U.S. using an electronic system. In 2003 SEVIS (the Student Exchange and Visitor Information System) was launched, with the requirement that all schools hosting international students and scholars on F, M, and J visas must participate. This new technology application has brought significant change to the field of international education.

TABLE 4.1: Key Resources for Getting Started

Inter-L	An email discussion group for international educators. Introduces you to an immediate network of colleagues, many with years of experience and a willingness to answer questions.	http://groups.yahoo.com/group/inter-l
EducationUSA Advisors	Lets you tap into the global network of educational advising centers funded by the U.S. Department of State. The centers' advisors are excellent resources for questions about their educational systems.	http://educationusa.state.gov/centers/
World Higher Education Database	Provides basic information about educational systems in most countries.	www.unesco.org/iau/onlinedatabases/index.html
AACRAO EDGE	A fee-based subscription provides access to excellent summaries about many educational systems.	http://aacraoedge.aacrao.org/
NAFSA International Admissions Resources	By country, provides a good list of available publications and online resources.	www.nafsa.org— click on the following succession of links: ▸ Knowledge Community Networks and Resources ▸ Recruitment, Admissions, and Preparation ▸ Admissions and Credential Evaluation ▸ Document Library ▸ "Researching International Education Systems and Institutions" (download PDF)

SEVIS is a web-based system administered by U.S. Citizenship and Immigration Services (USCIS). If your campus issues Certificates of Visa Eligibility (Form I-20s) from the admissions office, the most pertinent change in the admissions process is the way colleges and universities issue I-20s to admitted students. Prior to SEVIS, campuses used basic software to create I-20s. Now, the campus must first create the student's SEVIS record by entering data into the secure SEVIS Web site. Only after the student's record is created can the I-20 be printed.

An institution can enter data into the SEVIS Web site in two ways. The first is by entering records one at a time using the Real-Time Interface (RTI). This method can prove efficient for campuses with small international student populations. The second method is to upload records in batch, using a software interface such as SunGard's fsaATLAS or Oracle's international student module in PeopleSoft. The batch method has obvious benefits for schools with large international student populations, although it is not seamless. Certain types of I-20s, such as those for students changing programs or degree levels at the same institution, or for students transferring from one U.S. institution to another, cannot be processed in batch. In addition, time must be spent troubleshooting after records move correctly from the software to SEVIS.

Even more fundamentally, SEVIS has changed the way campuses must monitor international students during their careers at American colleges. There are strict reporting requirements that schools must meet, or they risk losing their SEVIS certification and hence, their ability to enroll international students. Updates of information such as changes of address, funding, program, and degree level; failure to enroll; completion of program; and authorization of on-campus employment must be reported in SEVIS within thirty days of the event. As with the creation of I-20s, such updates can be entered using RTI or in batch; either way, international student advisors must now spend a significant portion of their time on SEVIS-related tasks. As a result, some campuses have created new full-time positions within the international student office devoted solely to SEVIS issues.

WIKIS

The site that introduced most people to wikis is Wikipedia, the online encyclopedia, now one of the most popular sites on the Web. On www.wiki.com, a wiki is defined as "a database of pages which visitors can edit live." Anyone who has ever tried to edit a document with a group of people via email can see the advantage of this model. Rather than reattaching a new version of a document to an email and then waiting for the next person's version to arrive, a wiki is more efficient, allowing for a more fluid, real-time editing process.

For admissions professionals, there may be several applications for wikis. If you have documents that need regular updating and must be viewed by a group of people (such as a training manual or admission letters), a wiki can help you move to a paperless, online editing process. A wiki can also be used for social networking, creating a community of students at any point in the admission process. There is free wiki software available on the Web; www.wiki.com is a good place to find an overview. Sites also exist that allow for creation of a Web page that can be edited by the public, wiki-style, or not, such as www.wetpaint.com.

DATA ANALYSIS

One of the critical aspects of a successful enrollment management plan is data. It is essential that you have the ability to pull good data from your admissions database and analyze it to spot trends and inform your decisions regarding recruitment, admissions standards, and follow-up communication.

Obviously, technology is integral to the process of extracting information from a database. The way you do this will be determined by the systems in place on your campus. Regardless of how you pull the data, you will likely need a separate software application for full analysis. Novices can learn to use Microsoft Excel with minimal training; basic charts and graphs are easy to prepare. In particular, Excel's pivot tables and charts allow for relatively easy manipulation of complex data. Some enrollment managers use SPSS or other more sophisticated statistical analysis software.

Conclusion

The dizzying pace of technological change can feel overwhelming. Once you become comfortable with a software program, an updated version is released. It seems that there is always a new gadget to learn to use. The reach of the Internet appears far from nearing its end. In the decade since the last publication of this guide, the number of technological applications available to international admissions professionals has exploded, making it likely that the decade ahead will bring more of the same. How can international admissions professionals keep up? It is critical to stay informed about trends in technology, but, even more importantly, we must understand how, and if, our prospective students are using the newest applications. Attend conferences and workshops, talk to your colleagues, and consult with high school and college-aged international students about the ways in which they use technology in their daily lives. Advocate for international students with your campus's IT staff, to be sure that the needs of this important population are not overlooked. Challenges lie ahead, but in meeting those challenges, new opportunities for success will emerge.

Ethical Practice:

The Core Value for International Educators

BRIDGET E. CANTY

Student Service Associate/Designated School Official
Office of International Student Services
Houston Community College

Ethical Practice: The Core Value for International Educators

Ethical practice defines who we are. At this time in our history, we are facing challenges that force us to re-evaluate and discover our core values. As international educators (IEs) our jobs force us to confront and maintain ethical standards on a daily basis. There are fundamental components to ethical practice in international education: 1) leadership, 2) communication, 3) competency, and 4) training.

Leadership by example is not a cliché, but an integral ingredient to the success of any institution. A strong leader is one who communicates the institution's mission, setting goals and guidelines that allow all members of the staff to work at their optimum level. He or she must have the courage to regularly challenge all policies and procedures to ensure that they are in place and are of the best interest for the institution and the students or clients. "For many organizations, the first step in managing ethics is to establish a code of conduct, or a document of some kind that articulates the organizational values, principles, and standards" (Kaptein, Huberts, Avelino, and Lasthuizen 2005, p. 301).

The main criteria, however, of an effective and positive leader, is a strong work ethic. In an international environment, what is considered ethical or unethical is contingent upon one's belief and cultural experience. Differing beliefs should not interfere when putting policies and expectations in place in the ethical work environment. While sensitivity and knowledge about the cultures and ethical beliefs of customers are essential, it is also crucial for the leader to set fair and comprehensive standards and guidelines to direct employees, particularly in the field of international education.

Rules regarding ethics establish order and provide a public statement of what should be expected of everyone who works for the school system (Wickersham, 2009, p. 20.)

A leader who portrays a strong work ethic through his or her actions is one that employees will respect, follow and look to as a role model. Subordinates feel a kinship and a sense of pride when they have a boss who demonstrates a strong work ethic. An ethical leader thinks, evaluates and assesses any given situation to ensure it is fair to all parties that will be affected before putting a policy in place. Employees may not agree with their bosses' decisions, but a comfortable level of trust exists when the employees know the boss will stand by their convictions and not yield to pressure whenever policies are questioned or disagreement arises.

The criteria for an ethical leader in international education are not much different than those of any other profession. However, because IEs often play the role of "ambassador"—a representative of the U.S. seeking to bridge the gap between internationals and those with whom they guide during their stay in the U.S.—IEs need to be knowledgeable in their area of expertise, as well as fair and honest in their decision-making when dealing with those transitioning into an often unknown environment. Hence, an essential component of an IE job consists of understanding the various cultural norms. The most important criterion for an international educator is to remain current on the profession's code of ethics.

International educators have always acknowledged the field's uniqueness of "constant change." For some, it is this constant change that attracts them to the field of international education. Conforming to new federal regulatory mandates with little prior notice or funding is part of the status-quo for foreign student advisors (FSA). As changes take place in educational systems abroad, international credential evaluators and recruiters (ICER) have to reflect and analyze the possible effect these changes may have on their admissions policies and requirements. Study abroad advisors (SAA) are challenged with staying abreast of any changes, whether political or educational that will affect their students' study during their educational experience abroad. Leaders in the IE field should be aware of the complexities of the responsibilities assumed by their employees and understand that, like many jobs, the need for continuous and effective communication to the students, institution, government entities and customers—both internal and external—is a fundamental necessity to maintaining an ethical standard.

Effective communication is a fundamental criterion for ethical practice, because of how and what we communicate. Furthermore it brands who we are, defines our knowledge of the subject matter, and provides an honest representation of the services provided. IEs often encounter a diverse audience, therefore it is essential that the message is clearly comprehended by all recipients. In addition to the traditional ways of communicating, *e.g.*, print materials, it is necessary to communicate effectively through the use of current technology, such as interactive Web sites, social networking, instant messaging and text messaging. These forms of communication are instantaneous (and rarely retractable), thus requiring a clear and concise message. Real-time communication forces us to be ever mindful of the need for ethics as our guide in all of our communication.

Communication is the ability to convey a complete thought or concept, have vision to inspire and excite, and enlighten the youthful, natural curiosity of our minds. Just as our daily actions reflect our "ethics," our method of communication is one tool by which these ethics are externally reflected and shared every day, in every moment of our conscious being. Dilenschneider

and Salak (2003) state the importance of how information is disseminated.

The ethical shift has done more than change the way we think. It has also placed new demands on communication professionals. They now need to create and maintain more reliable information-distribution systems, while also educating senior management to the new communication realities and keeping line employees and middle managers on the proper information track. The task is enormous, but headway has been made (p. 1).

We should always be conscious of not only *how* we communicate, but also *what* we communicate. Effective and ethical communicators must ensure that information is presented in an honest fashion, providing full disclosure, projecting the desired image which embodies the philosophy and mission of one's institution.

Ethical communication is a crucial proficiency of admissions officers and recruiters (AO/R), SAA and FSA professionals. Colleagues in all these areas must stay intimately attuned to the importance of effective, honest communication and how daily interactions between disciplines play into the projected image of the institution. One must bear in mind that many in the field of higher education wear multiple hats. For instance, many admissions officials are recruiters as well as foreign student advisors—all of whom may coordinate the study abroad programs, contribute to community initiatives and develop sponsorship programs. Because of such a complexity and overlapping of responsibilities, information must be constantly reviewed and updated by the administration leadership and, most importantly, refined almost daily for disbursement of knowledge to a wide target audience.

For instance, in the case of AO/Rs, their primary communication—which typically includes Web sites, brochures and all other tools used to communicate or promote institutions—should clearly define institutional requirements, deadlines, the tuition and fee costs, programs offered and expectations for applicants.

In many cases refinement of information must occur on a weekly or monthly basis to ethically ensure their audience the most current information. FSA and SAA officials are also tasked with clearly communicating the current services their institution provides to students, as well as providing a complete and thorough communication of federal regulations as they pertain to the individual students' visa status.

Moreover it is vital for IE professionals to communicate a persona of concern and empathy to their international students and scholars. Ethical communication requires professionals to be aware of their clients' local customs, so that the international visitors might more effectively receive the desired guidance and assistance. It is also paramount that international educators communicate not only with words but, during personal communication, also with their body language. SAA responsibilities are equally complex, as the advisor must communicate with students from the U.S. the challenges of the unknown, as well as inspire the students to take advantage of the experiences which combine education with external cultural events. Additionally the SAA officials need to be well versed in the transfer credit compatibility of the course work or research project of the student, as well as be able to effectively communicate information such as costs. Equally important is a clear and accurate delineation of all environmental factors that the student may experience.

SAAs should ensure that they ethically communicate an accurate assessment of the study abroad program opportunities, including 1) educational program details, 2) transferable academic credits, 3) which opportunities are considered an excursion, 4) what to expect at the foreign institution, 5) port of entry experiences, 6) cultural norms, 7) accommodation possibilities including home-stay or other student options and 8) the general attitudes toward students from the USA.

There is an interwoven relationship between an individual's core competence and ethical standards. The core competencies represent an interrelationship between a high level of skill and knowledge and the application of the duties. How well this symbiotic relationship works determines the effectiveness of the international educators.

Obviously international educators are required to have a high standard of competency in their respective fields. Norona (2004) states three key criteria needed for competent employees:

+ *The knowledge to do the job*
+ *The skills to put that knowledge into practice*
+ *The commitment to apply the knowledge and skills in the appropriate way* (p. 1)

Although being knowledgeable is crucial, knowledge without ethical standards is detrimental to one's institution and the field of international education as a whole. Take, for example, international recruiters, who constitute the first impression of a college or university to prospective international students. It is the recruiter's job to represent their institution in foreign countries. However, to do this effectively, the recruiters must honestly and transparently represent themselves and their school. They must be aware of both the visiting countries' educational system and their own institutions' requirements. They must also exhibit pride in their home college or university.

Recruiters' presentations, whether they are PowerPoint slides, brochures, Web sites or poster boards, should have an honest representation of the institutions' costs, programs offered, expected length of academic programs, special requirements, potential funds, location, local climate and a reasonable time span for the application process. An ethical presentation is a gain for all parties as it allows prospective applicants to clearly decide if the institution is a match in terms of fitting their goals, affordability and a suitable climate, as well as offering the ambiance that fits their individual needs. Although the above stated requirements may at first glance appear obvious, this is what most recruiters learn during their first three months of training. On the other hand, if being honest, knowledgeable and having pride in your institution were as simple as we would like to believe, employees and members of professional organizations, as well as big and small businesses, would not need to be taught ethical standards and principles.

As an example, many international university and college recruiters are set important goals. Given these high expectations and faced with rigorous competition, some may tend to accept "gray area" standards rather than clearly perceiving higher ethical standards as they should. In fact "gray area" tends to be the term often used to mask false statements and unethical decisions. For instance, replying to a student's question about one's institutional costs, by directing the student to the school's Web site, with the knowledge that it shows last years' costs which have since jumped markedly, would be unethical. When asked a question for which they do not have an answer, recruiters should be frank regarding their limited knowledge. Since the collapse of Enron in the late 1990s, our society has begun to demand ethical and honest behavior from those with whom we do business, report to or socialize. Our prospective students seek nothing less from their recruiters. I would wager that most would rather be informed of the truth than hear things that mislead or that will hinder them in the future.

A recruiter who holds to ethical standards successfully works hand-in-hand with the admissions officer. The work of one unquestionably affects the work of the other. The success of the recruiters' effort hinges on the ethical and effective work of the admissions officer once the applicants apply to the institution. A recruiter can increase the applicant quota by 50 percent. However, the work would be futile if the admissions office is unable for various reasons to provide expedient and quality service to the prospective applicants.

The relationship between the recruiters and admissions officers is akin to a track relay race; the team succeeds or fails together. The first runner can be in the lead, but once the baton is passed, how well the receiver of the baton does will determine the success of the team. This suggests that once the applicants are passed on to the admissions office, the effectiveness of the recruitment efforts begin. Even as technology becomes increasingly synonymous with good customer service, the number one marketing tool has not changed from twenty, thirty or even fifty years ago: word of mouth. Family and friends will discuss their personal experiences with an admissions office: how smoothly and quickly the process went, how knowledgeable and personable the staff was with them, and how fully their questions were answered as they went through the process. These experiences will dictate if 'word of mouth' is indeed a positive marketing tool for one's institution. Ethical behavior transcends international borders and cultures and will quickly spread through word of mouth in most countries outside of the United States.

The tools required for an admissions office that claims to uphold the highest level of ethical standards include up-to-date technology: at a minimum, an online application; a Web site that is easy to navigate; automated systems that streamline the process; electronic communication to prospective students and an electronic notification system for admissions officers that informs them of records ready for review. The staff should have the ability to analyze complex documents, utilize critical thinking, exhibit strong objective skills and practice intermediate computer knowledge. Most important is the skill to listen, understand and assess the information and needs that are being expressed.

The staff should be current on the latest educational changes around the world and assess foreign credentials accurately, ensuring that they are compatible with the institutions' policies and based on a comparison between u.s. and foreign educational systems. The very basics of an international admissions office centers on setting admissions standards for foreign credentials; what is decided will reflect the ethical practices of an institution. For instance, if an admissions office's fundamental practice is to require sixteen years of education as the minimum requirement for eligibility to enter graduate programs based on the premise that this is equivalent to what is required of students who have studied in the U.S. this would be justifiable. However, if this rule does not apply across the board, then guidelines should be put in place that explain and support why the rules differ from one country to another. Institutions have the right to set guidelines based on the needs of the institution and the potential for success of the students at the university or college.

However, guidelines should be subjectively written by someone with knowledge of foreign educational systems and the university's mission and academic programs. Adherence to strong ethical guidelines does not require universities and colleges to limit their possibilities, nor do these guidelines result in the restriction of opportunity for the international student to reach their goals in the United States. They do, however, compel us to implement practices that are justifiable and fair, thus resulting in success for both the institution and the student. These ethical guidelines also help eliminate confusion, adverse publicity and staff uncertainty resulting from inconsistent decisions and actions.

As mentioned previously, IEs grapple with explaining without bias why one educational system of fifteen years is acceptable when it differs from the standard sixteen-year benchmark of the U.S. educational system. To say one country's educational system is better than another would be irresponsible, unethical and expose students and their future to subjective interpretations. This is not to say that an institution cannot set different requirements from one country to another; quite the contrary. As long as the institutional policy can be logically explained, tangibly supported and proven to be in the best interest of the school and its prospective students, while also conforming to the guidelines set by the National Association of Foreign Student Advisors: Association of International Educators (NAFSA: AIE) and the American Association of Collegiate Registrars and Admissions Officers (AACRAO), differential country specific requirements may exist.

Another part of providing quality service coupled with ethical standards involves making the decision to admit or deny a student with expediency and accuracy,

allowing the student to determine his or her educational options. If the student is accepted, the approval packet should provide the applicant with as much information as possible that will prepare the student to transition from their home country to a new country.

Once the admissions office has passed the baton on to the foreign student advising office, the latter should at minimum provide, 1) an orientation about the institution and its policies; 2) registration and fee procedures; 3) the city and country; 4) visa and immigration regulations and 5) cultural adjustment. The institution should maintain trained and qualified foreign student advisors (FSAs) who exhibit a high standard of ethics. They must be prepared to attend to a large array of issues that international students may face upon first arriving at their new home. It is imperative that the FSA stay current on immigration regulations, despite their ever-changing nature. Without question, ethical best practices play a key role in the institutions' attempt to remain compliant with all current and newly adopted regulations.

The FSA should work closely with the institution's faculty and staff to assist with any problems or concerns that may arise between the student and others in the college or university community. The FSA serves at times as a mediator between the student and faculty, while also holding the responsibility of designated school official (DSO), representing the U.S. government's reporting and tracking mechanism for all international students. As a mediator, the FSA-DSO should ensure that the practices and policies of the institutions are in alignment with high ethical practices. At the same time the FSA must carefully balance the regulations with the human needs of the students, so that they do not suffer as a nonentity in the process. The role of the FSA-DSO is highly multifaceted in that they act as an advocate for the student; they are responsible for the institutions' compliance with the government and they work with faculty. In all ways, however, this tentative balancing act must be covered by the principles of ethical practice.

Sufficient competency in international education requires IE professionals to have strong ethical decision-making skills for complex interpersonal interactions and ever-changing situations. Clearly stated purposes and mission statements for international offices are essential for supporting one's decisions as based in strong ethical practices. For instance, FSAs oftentimes utilize the community volunteers to support programming activities for their international students and scholars. In fact, the J Exchange Visitor Program requires educational and cultural programming as a part of their compliance.

Volunteers, in general, have an intrinsic motivation for giving of their time, efforts and expertise. It is the ethical obligation of the FSA to appropriately manage the community volunteers' motivations, so that their actions support the mission and purpose of the office. The FSA must be aware of any attitudes, deeds or actions that do not fall in line with ethical behavior or support the core values of the office.

If, for example, the volunteer wishes to influence the students, either religiously or ideologically, the FSA should have written guidelines that instructs them as to the expectations and purpose of the program.

The purpose of the participation of community volunteers should be facilitating cross-cultural exchange and adjustment, as well as helping the international visitors to familiarize themselves with their new home.

As a constantly changing field demanding new thoughts and ideas, training is an essential component in international education. Training allows the educator to remain abreast of the changes and the knowledge needed to ensure that ethical practices and procedures are in place to address these changes. Training also allows for networking, obtaining the names of experts in the field to contact when problems or questions arise.

Employees may personally possess high ethical standards and principles, but without proper training and adequate knowledge of their duties, the professional setting may hinder these personal principles. Well-documented training manuals are essential to any new employee and should be designed at minimum in two different ways: 1) for someone new to the field with no

experience or knowledge and 2) for intermediate employees who have some working knowledge in the field but require additional knowledge that will bring them up-to-date. All instructional manuals should have a list of key players in the institution with names, positions, emails and extensions. Step-by-step instructions, along with snapshots of the various computer screens the employees will need to effectively perform their duties, are vital. Manuals, training procedures and business processes should be customized in accordance with individual areas of responsibility and presented simply so that a new employee can readily gain a semblance of knowledge of the processes. For an admissions officer, manuals should include instructional examples of previous agendas and brochures for those who prepare orientations; for FSAs, cases should include the institutional interpretation of federal regulations.

Training on the student records system should be scheduled in advance for all new employees and held prior to each new semester for current employees. The training and manuals should be geared toward the needs of the department. The training should be designed for presentation in intervals with a seasoned staff person equipped as an instructor. If possible, a virtual training should also be available that walks employees through the process. Planning for the frequency of new employee training that is appropriate for each department is an ethical business practice; for example, if an area has high turnover or hires seasonal employees, frequent training is necessary.

Conclusion

The field of international education is an exciting and fulfilling one for anyone interested in meeting people from other cultures and learning about the world from other perspectives. As universities and colleges embrace international students they must do so employing the highest professional ethics. This entails having a strong, ethical leader; effective communication throughout the organization; employees who are competent in their area of responsibility; and ongoing training. Technology has forced us to change almost every component of our life, the way we communicate with one another and our expectation of the services we receive. As international educators we are often the first introduction for many of our customers to the United States. This requires us to maintain the highest ethical standards in our work and personal life.

In the international arena, international educators struggle with issues of right and wrong. They are occasionally faced with the question of whether a correct decision is always the best decision. Is it possible that an ethical decision could, in the end, be damaging to all parties concerned? International educators are at their best when they constantly question and challenge their principles and ethical conduct. This ensures that the field grows and continues to represent high ethical standards.

SIX

International Credential
Evaluation and Methodology

ROBERT WATKINS

Assistant Director of Admissions
Graduate and International Admissions Center
University of Texas at Austin

International Credential Evaluation and Methodology

The evaluation of international academic credentials poses a distinct challenge to admissions officers at higher education institutions in the United States. The reasons are several but the most basic challenge comes from the fact that these credentials are different, especially if one's prior experience is solely with domestic U.S. credentials. With the knowledge of some key components, however, the process can be made somewhat less daunting. In this chapter we shall examine some of these components so that the new international credential evaluator finds it easier to make the transition from evaluating U.S. credentials to those from overseas.

Key Principles

The first key principle in evaluating overseas credentials is to refresh one's knowledge and understanding of the U.S. educational system in terms of years, benchmark academic credentials, the Carnegie unit and credit system, content of various U.S. higher education degrees, and the common A-F grading scale with its associated numerical values, to name but a few. But before we begin the analysis of these aspects of U.S. education, one very important decision must be discussed.

The field of international admissions and credential evaluation at higher education institutions (HEIs) has evolved tremendously in the past quarter century. A number of the pioneers in the field of international admissions and credential evaluation have now retired from their institutions, and newer and younger persons have stepped into these roles. While international student populations have rebounded significantly since the low point in 2002 immediately following September

11, 2001, institutions have begun to increasingly question the need for retaining on staff individuals with this very specific skill set. True, many high profile institutions with large international populations will continue to maintain a trained evaluation staff that is fully conversant with the principles of international credential evaluation and admission. But more and more institutions, including those which have historically had a section of the admissions office dedicated to evaluating international credentials, are finding it more cost effective to send the international applications and credentials from their applicant pool to some of the many private credential evaluation firms, both for-profit and non-profit. There are many reasons for this. Much of the expertise in evaluating these credentials that once resided in various (often larger public) institutions has now moved into the private sector or left the field through retirement. New young talent in the admissions offices certainly has no difficulty with stepping into the vacancies that have been created, but it is also clear to these younger administrators that specialization in international credential evaluation is not a path to rapid promotion within the administrative ranks.

Consequently, institutions that heretofore always processed their own international applications and credentials now seek to outsource this task to private entities rather than commit the necessary resources (which also include expensive non-personnel-related resources) to this task. Financial resources instead tend to go toward recruitment and other enrollment management strategies. Thus, the admissions office now must decide how to go about farming out these credentials to outside players.

Selecting a credentials evaluation service is difficult due to the wide range of options from which to choose.

However, if institutional needs are factored into the equation, choosing the right service or services can be a very logical process. First, quality is essential, making it logical to look toward those services that have a long history in the field. Private credential evaluation firms only date back to 1969 and even the most prestigious only back to around 1980. Naturally, longevity is no guarantee of quality so this must represent only one (perhaps minor) factor. Larger firms tend to see more diverse types of credentials and so this may be a component to consider. Some firms specialize in credentials from certain countries, or at least tend to evaluate certain geographic areas more than others. This may be useful to the office that tends to see more applications from one or two areas of the world than from multiple locations. If the office is familiar with some of the individuals who have been in the field for a long time, heard them present at conferences and/or read their books and articles on overseas educational systems, then name recognition may play a role in the selection process. Turnaround time is obviously important, as well as how much the service costs, since that cost will almost assuredly be borne by the applicant. Finally, credential service philosophy should match, as closely as possible, that of the end-user institution. In other words, if degree comparisons, credit conversion or other benchmark approaches utilized by the evaluation service do not reflect the same or similar philosophy of the selecting institution, then conflict over evaluation decisions is inevitable. Institutional policies regarding outside contracting must also play a significant role in the use of a single versus a multiple list of providers from which applicants may choose. Opinions vary as to the efficacy of choosing only one service versus several. Consistency would be most realized through the choice of a single service, although allowing applicants a choice may be preferred or even required by institutional (or even state) requirements.

Once the decision has been made to retain the international credential evaluation process in-house, the first key necessity is training the staff involved with the pro-

cess. The simplest way to begin the training is to refresh the evaluators on the U.S. educational system since this will be the final indices by which the overseas educational systems will be measured. Also, reaffirm (or, in the case of staff recruited from outside the institution, acquaint them with) the specific needs, strategies, policies and history of the admissions process of the institution itself. An historic commitment to the recruitment and retention of an international population is important for staff to know. It is crucial that evaluators know the nature of an associate's degree versus an Associate of Applied Sciences degree, or any terminal technical program versus the academic parallel. They should be aware of the singular needs of a given college or department compared to some other program needs. One should clarify the English proficiency policy of the office with regard to which instruments are accepted, the scores required and which countries need not present these credentials. The chapter in this book on International Transfer Credit explores in detail the concept of the Carnegie unit, which is based on seat time; as a result, there is no need to expand on that topic here. But familiarity with this concept is vital to understanding the award of transfer credit from overseas.

The major components of the U.S. educational system necessary for international credential evaluation that leads to a sound admissions decision are 1) understanding full time course loads in the USA and then the overseas educational system under review, 2) how to compare academic benchmarks using the U.S. system as a guide, 3) grading scale comparisons, with the U.S. 4.0 scale as the yardstick and 4) an appreciation of the decentralized nature of accreditation in this country and how that compares with the approach found in most other countries. First, we begin with the course work concept.

Under the Carnegie unit concept of class hours converting to semester hours, fifteen to eighteen hours maximum per semester or thirty to thirty-six hours per year is considered a full load. This is the base line by which another country's postsecondary attendance is measured. If the other country uses a credit system with numerical values in excess of that, then one must correspondingly reduce the credits. The rationale is simple: a full load THERE should be equal to a full load HERE. No overseas system should be granted MORE credit in transfer per year than the U.S. college student gains in normal attendance. Thus, evaluators need to keep the overseas educational experience within the parameters of the U.S. model and not grant more than thirty to thirty-six semester hours per year regardless of the number of credits awarded or class hours spent in the overseas educational institution. Their full-time load should equal our full-time load. This concept is closely linked with the second of our key components, benchmarking of credentials.

Basic Methodology

There are two basic methodological approaches to evaluating international credentials, particularly with respect to degree comparisons. The first method is year counting or, as I prefer to label it, the quantitative method. In this method, the evaluator compares the overseas system to the U.S. system by means of counting the years required for benchmark credentials (high school diploma, short-term postsecondary degrees, first full university degrees, advanced postgraduate degrees, terminal academic attainments). The final admissions decision, therefore, is based on a favorable or unfavorable variance resulting from the comparison. Three-year degrees from abroad, for example, that follow from a standard twelve-year primary/secondary experience fall short for purposes of graduate admissions in a comparison with the four-year bachelor's degree in the USA, which succeeds a similar twelve-year primary/secondary sequence.

The second method is that of comparing benchmark academic credential awards between the USA and the overseas country under evaluation. A first university degree, even if less than the U.S. four-year model, nevertheless is considered sufficient for graduate admissions at the U.S. school based on the fact that it is the first university degree in the subject AND allows entry into

higher advanced degrees at a university in that country, just as the U.S. bachelor's degree allows entry into a master's degree program. The high school diploma awarded in the Philippines, under this methodology, which comes after ten total years of primary/secondary education, would be fully comparable to the U.S. high school diploma because they both represent the same thing: completion of upper secondary school and entry into postsecondary programs in-country. This method is not tied to number of years of education within the programmatic experience but recognizes instead the conceptual notion that conclusion of upper secondary and entry into postsecondary education over there compares favorably to the same thing here, completion of the first degree there equates to completion of a first degree here, etc.

The problem, of course, is that in the latter method there are no particular set boundaries for each benchmark except those of the beholder. Would a ten-year Philippine high school diploma holder of sixteen years old be completely ready to enter the same university in the U.S. as his/her domestic counterpart after twelve years and age seventeen to eighteen? Is a two-year Pakistani general bachelor's degree sufficient for admission into a U.S. graduate program? These are but two of the equity questions that come to the fore in embracing the benchmarking method. Most institutions and private credential evaluation agencies tend to use a mixture of BOTH methods. When an eleven-year primary/secondary system in South America, for example, yields the qualification required for entry into university in that country, it is almost universally accepted by evaluators in the U.S. even though it is a year short of the U.S. model. Three-year first degrees awarded in other countries, on the other hand, are not as uniformly accepted. Most evaluators tend to START with the quantitative or year-counting method and then segue into the benchmarking mode when logic and the overseas system dictate. At this point, before turning to grading and accreditation, it is important to discuss placement practices and the history behind them.

There is no single entity in the United States, either state or federal, that issues placement recommendations or guidelines to be followed by those involved in international credential evaluation and admission of international students. Overseas, such organizations do exist, often at the central governmental level. But in the United States, the responsibility and authority rests with the individual actors. In the case of colleges and universities, institutional autonomy allows the school to make its own decisions regarding overseas credentials. Nevertheless, institutions generally want to act in concert with other like institutions and with commonly accepted standards and best practices. The problem is defining "commonly accepted." International credential evaluation is, as the AACRAO International Education Services (IES) office frequently reminds us, "an art, not a science." Consequently, what may be useful for, say, the University of Texas at Austin with regard to upper secondary credentials from Germany may not be the same for Austin Community College or even another component campus of the University of Texas System.

Fortunately, the void has been filled for fifty years by the National Council on the Evaluation of Foreign Educational Credentials, often referred to simply as The Council. During the period 1955–2006, representatives of the key organizations active in international student recruitment and admissions met to review forthcoming publications in international education and approve placement recommendations regarding the handling of the credentials discussed in the publication. These organizations have included over time AACRAO, NAFSA: Association of International Educators, the Institute of International Education (IIE), the College Board, Council of Graduate Schools (CGS), the American Association of Community Colleges (AACC) and the American Council on Education (ACE). The placement recommendations were then included in the book, usually at the end. These recommendations were advisory in nature since, again, no single source is authoritative in the U.S. with respect to placement practices. The recommendations

during that fifty-year span tended to be somewhat conservative and reflected generally the year-counting approach (though not invariably). As funding from the United States Government for these publications began to evaporate, the need for a Council, historically seen as tied to specific and individual publications, began to wane. Finally, in 2006, participating organizations within The Council agreed to disband that group.

The need for a replacement of The Council began to grow as AACRAO moved forward on two levels, first with their own series of publications that would be considered more useful with some sort of guidelines, and secondly with the birth of a research project known as AACRAO EDGE or the Electronic Database for Global Education, that contains over 230 country entries with listings of credentials, grading scales, resources, institutions, etc. Prior to the creation of EDGE and as The Council was moving toward dissolution, the AACRAO Board of Directors, with prodding from then Vice President for International Education Gloria Nathanson of UCLA, approved the concept of a replacement entity that ultimately became known as the International Education Standards Council (IESC). This group would analyze new AACRAO publications and provide placement guidance, as well as review each country entry in EDGE to fashion the placement advice included in that resource. Currently the IESC is comprised of Gloria Nathanson (UCLA), Robert Watkins (UT-Austin), and Johnny Johnson (formerly of Monterey Peninsula College, now retired). Future successors to this trio will be determined by the sitting Vice President of Group II: International within AACRAO.

The IESC, and The Council before that, tended to utilize the year-counting scenario, though frequent determinations based on benchmarking also appeared in publications. Also, though a greater understanding of technical and professional education (as opposed to, for example, vocational education) is evident in more recent years, the tendency is to make recommendations that reflect mainstream large school policies and needs. Deciding whether any credit should be forthcoming from a terminal technical program abroad will vary from institution to institution and should reflect the needs of the receiving institution. There is also a difference of opinion within the private evaluation community on year counting and benchmarking, largely due to the very different mission that these entities have versus the situation found at academic institutions, particularly large, selective admission schools. Whether a three-year holder from whatever country is suitable for graduate admission in the same or similar field as the first degree is a very different question than the question of whether or not that person holds a degree comparable to the U.S. bachelor's degree for professional licensure purposes.

Before leaving this intriguing topic, it is useful to note that one can fashion their own set of placement recommendations and guidelines even without the help of The Council or the IESC. Once the evaluator has had enough experience dealing with overseas credentials, becomes familiar with the literature available on that country's educational system and credentials, and has gained a feel for what others in the field do with that or similar credentials, creating one's own placement guidelines becomes a simple exercise provided three simple questions are asked and answered: what academic credential precedes the credential under review, what does this credential lead to in the education system of that country, and what is the nature of the credential itself (length, content, teaching location/venue, etc.)? Associated questions might include whether or not the credential leads to professional practice in-country, is the instructional venue comparable to that of the receiving institution, and what has been the success rate of the credential holder within U.S. higher education (if known)? All that one needs to render such determinations locally is experience and, above all, confidence!

Terminology and Standard Phraseology

In training new evaluators, it is very important to understand and appreciate nomenclature and standard phraseology used by practitioners in the field. Already

mentioned were the terms "year counting" and "benchmarking." It is also important to note that when comparing credentials from abroad with those in the United States, finding "equivalence" is not possible. Experts in the field long ago gave up use of the word 'equivalence' to denote a comparison between the overseas document and its closest U.S. cousin. The reason is glaringly simple: there is NO credential out there truly equivalent to the U.S. bachelor's degree (for example). Rather, the term used is "comparable." The first degree in Mexico, the *Licenciatura* level degree that comes after four years of university study (itself following a twelve-year primary/secondary system of education), is therefore found to be comparable to the U.S. bachelor's degree. This becomes particularly important when comparing overseas degrees to the U.S. counterpart in that same field or profession and for which there is a significantly different educational approach.

An example of this is found in the field of medicine. Medical education in the U.S. comes after a first undergraduate degree in some other field (usually, though not invariably, biological sciences). Abroad, medicine is very frequently a first degree following upper secondary education that leads to university admission, though very often longer than other first degrees in that country. The U.S. medical doctor degree flows from a prior undergraduate degree that includes pre-med courses. Abroad, that medical first degree has the pre-med component built in to the first two years or so of the degree itself. The U.S. degree of Doctor of Medicine is about eight years in length, counting the first degree (with internships and residency following), while the overseas medical degree totals perhaps six years after high school graduation. Is the overseas credential therefore comparable to the United States MD degree? Ostensibly one would answer in the negative due to two factors: length of overall education leading to the degree (six versus eight years), and the fact that the U.S. degree is a second and higher degree than the overseas counterpart.

The terminology used for this sort of comparison where they are seen as functionally comparable (in terms of the outcome for the graduates in the two countries), despite the structural difference in their educational length and levels, is not that the overseas version is "comparable to a Doctor of Medicine awarded in the United States," but instead the evaluator states that the overseas version of the medical degree "is the first professional degree in medicine" in that country. This denotes that this degree is the one obtained by medical doctors in that country to practice medicine or become licensed (if the country has a structured licensing process). Thus the statement of precise comparability is not being made due to the accentuated differences of the educational approach found in the two countries. The straight line comparison is still being drawn, however. It enables the admissions officer or credential evaluator to establish for the layman reading the evaluation the distinct similarity of each degree without getting into nomenclature differences such as Doctor of Medicine in the U.S. versus Bachelor of Medicine in China or Bachelor of Medicine, Bachelor of Surgery (MB BS) in Nigeria that might otherwise confuse or concern the end-reader. This phraseology has been quite useful as degrees in the health professions in the United States have altered significantly from bachelor's degrees to the current entry-level first degree in the profession that often is called Doctor (*e.g.*, of Physical Therapy or Pharmacy).

In addition to determining degree comparability, evaluators must also arrive at grade comparisons and credit conversion as they work through overseas documents. Here again the yardstick for measuring the other country's grading scheme is the U.S. model. Therefore, whatever the grading scheme used overseas, it must be compared to the U.S. 4-point scale of A–F with grade points 4, 3, 2, 1, and 0 respectively. If one has a tiered grading scheme with three levels of passing grades, then this can be seen to coincide nicely with the U.S. grades of A, B, and C. Beware of positing a grade of D to another country's grading scheme! A grade of D is a relatively (though certainly not exclusively) American grading phenomenon. It is the lowest grade allowable for passing the course, but will NOT result in graduation

with a degree should that grade level constitute the overall average of the student nearing potential graduation. Therefore, it should be seen as a condoned or conceded pass. This seldom exists outside the U.S., but may sometimes be found in countries such as France where 10/20 is the lowest passing grade, but grades of 8 and 9 (considered failing grades) are excused provided the overall annual average is 10 or higher. In Australia the universities simply label this grade forthrightly as "Conceded Pass (CP)." Conversely, in Mexico, the grade of 6/10 is a passing grade in some states and a failing grade in others. Where the grade is considered passing, it is part of the C range and *not* a D. It should also be noted that many overseas grading scales use a greater numerical range than the U.S. where only 70 percent and above are considered satisfactorily passing grades and the entire bottom end of the range unsatisfactory. Anglophone countries, however, approach grading in an entirely opposite fashion. The median grade range on a 100 point scale is 50, and it is the very top part of the range (80–100) which is rarely given. Always check the range of the scale on the document or in the resources you have accumulated to find out the lowest and the highest grades awarded, along with the lowest passing grade; then determine if the lowest grade is a satisfactory pass.

Credit conversion for the award of transfer credit can pose a challenge even greater than that associated with discerning grade equivalents! Until recently, few countries actually used a credit system. Countries using the Commonwealth style educational structure constructed their degrees according to subjects or courses with exams at the end. Those that did employ a credit system often used a startlingly high number of credits per year leading to the award of degrees. Australian universities and some newer British universities might have 120 credits per year as the full load for a student. Or one might find a number closer to the U.S. model as in Norway with forty credits (*vektall*) per year. These numbers do not pose a problem provided the evaluator remembers that the U.S. educational structure is the ultimate guide. Since the standard full load in U.S. colleges is thirty semester hours per year (fifteen per semester), then one simply compares the overseas annual number of credits constituting a full load to the U.S. figure of thirty. Thus, the 120 credits in Australia per year results in those credit totals being divided by four. As the Norwegian model is a bit more complex, it would be wise to build a comparison table grid where 40=30, 20=15, 10=7.5, etc. Evaluators should feel free to round up or down in order to keep the conversion logically within U.S. parameters of thirty per year or so.

This exercise became somewhat easier with the introduction of the Bologna Process when the European Credit Transfer System (ECTS) was adopted (from the Erasmus Mundi program begun in 1989). The full load per year of ECTS credits is sixty which means that the ECTS credit is half of a U.S. semester hour since that full load amount is twice the U.S. college norm. European educators point out that the ECTS credit is predicated on outcomes rather than simple "seat time" or contact hours. However, the Carnegie unit concept (upon which the U.S. degree and credit system is based) stipulates that for every hour of lecture, students are expected to spend two hours on outside preparation. This would certainly lead to an outcome of specific knowledge gained over time, yet these additional study or preparation hours are *not* included in the credit value of U.S. college courses; only the contact hours are calculated. Therefore, cutting the ECTS in half is consistent with the idea that a full-time study period (semester or year) abroad should yield the same amount of credit in the U.S. for that same time period; it is only a difference in numbers. And, because a year is a year, then 60=30 or 120=30 or 40=30, whatever the baseline number for the time period may be.

Another important aspect of international credential evaluation pertains to the documents required by the evaluator for analysis. Practitioners must require their applicants or clients to submit official documents for review. These should either be original documents issued by the institution (or, in the case of those countries that issue them, from a centralized authority such as the Ministry of Education) or copies that have been made of the originals and stamped by an appropriate certifying authority such as the registrar or some similar institutional administrator. A faculty member or even head of a department is insufficient since the ultimate issuing authority is administratively above these types of educational officials. A copy prepared by a notary public should never be relied upon since the individual simply copies the original certifying that the copy is a true duplication of the original. The original, however, has not been analyzed by the notary to determine authenticity, etc.

Similarly, translations can prove problematic since none of us are polylingual. However, one thing we CAN become is proficient in the indigenous educational terminology in each country such that we can recognize the foreign terms for various credential names, grades, numbers, etc. Jim Frey, the founder of Educational Credential Evaluators, Inc. and a long time practitioner (and many would say, pioneer!) in the field, calls this practice "learning to read transcriptese." The reason that one must be able to pick up a transcript in French or Slovenian and discern key phrases is that the alternative to not knowing sufficient indigenous educational terms is to remain at the mercy of the translator who is often *not* an educational expert. They render in English literal translations of the words they see in the foreign language, rather than use a term more familiar to us given the context within which it is being employed. This problem becomes particularly acute when trying to determine educational level. The Mexican student who completes *preparatoria* and earns the *Bachiller* en *Ciencias* has not earned a Bachelor of Science, as the translator might be tempted to write, but a diploma comparable to the high school diploma in the United States. And yet the term "bachiller" might be rendered "bachelor" by the translator who is simply translating the words literally. Thus, the international admissions officer or credential evaluator must have the original language document along with the English translation and be armed with the knowledge of enough indigenous educational terms to do a basic spot-check of the translation and reassure themselves of its essential accuracy.

Evaluations should never take place using a substitute for the proper academic documentation (transcript, marks sheet, or certificate of studies). In other words, an evaluation by a credentials service, while a very helpful supporting document, is not the actual document required. The evaluator should be able to see that the individual did in fact take these courses and earn these grades. Furthermore, evaluations should never take place using transcript re-creations. When an applicant presents a standard syllabus from their degree program at their institution telling you that they do not have the actual transcript, but can assure you they took the courses as listed in the syllabus and then earned the degree (which they do have to show you), the only proper answer is to express regret and indicate that no course-by-course review is possible unless an actual transcript is presented. A syllabus represents what SHOULD have happened, not what DID happen. Applicants who leave their country without transcripts unfortunately do not have official evidence that they took specific courses. They should be handled according to institutional policy toward those lacking the usual required documentation.

Resources

Finally, the evaluation of international credentials remains impossible without a solid foundation of resource material. Many volumes are still available from various sources on the educational systems of countries around the world. Some of these are quite old but still useful. Students are not always in the classical eighteen to twenty-two age range. Students older than average continue to attend two- and four-year schools, therefore the resource from the 1980s or 1990s can be just as valuable as one published last year. AACRAO and NAFSA both offer numerous publications that are invaluable in the international admissions process. The credential evaluation services are increasing their out-

put now that U.S. Government funding for publications has dried up and the associations themselves are increasingly finding publications an expensive proposition. The credentials services offer workshops, newsletters, and books, all designed to help practitioners evaluate international credentials. AACRAO continues to offer many of the Projects in International Education Research (PIER) volumes that have been published in the last decade or so. In addition, AACRAO's International Education Services holds two annual seminars on international credential evaluation, the Summer and Winter Institutes. The former is for beginning practitioners, while the latter is aimed at those with a bit more experience and specifically covers transfer credit practices from abroad.

The most invaluable tool to come to the forefront of international education research in the last fifteen years has been the Internet. Now, international evaluators have at their very fingertips institutional Web sites, monographs on overseas education, official government ministerial home pages, and a communication avenue to ask questions about an institution's programs or even its former students. Online databases also provide immense amounts of information on educational systems. A few are free, but most have a fee associated with their use. AACRAO offers one of the most comprehensive in the form of EDGE, the Electronic Database for Global Education, a subscription information database covering well over 200 country educational systems. Even in this day of declining institutional budgets, the fee for one year of a tool such as EDGE is less than what it would cost to purchase any three or four major international education resource books.

Once practitioners begin to feel comfortable with evaluating international credentials, they are ready to face some of the more imposing challenges in this field. These challenges are great and promise to become even more significant in the years ahead. The Bologna Process, which did not mandate but essentially produced a spate of new three-year European degrees, promises to continue to be a complicating factor in the U.S. graduate

TABLE 6.1: Resources for International Credential Evaluation

American Association of Collegiate Registrars and Admissions Officers (AACRAO)	www.aacrao.org
AACRAO EDGE	http://aacraoedge.aacrao.org
AACRAO Publications*	www.aacrao.org/publications/catalog.cfm
AACRAO International Education Services	www.aacrao.org/international/
International Association of Universities, World Higher Education Database:	www.iau-aiu.net
NAFSA: Association of International Educators	www.nafsa.org
NAFSA Admissions and Credential Evaluation Network	www.nafsa.org/groups/home.aspx?groupid=16
NAFSA Bologna Special Focus Network	www.nafsa.org/groups/home.aspx?groupid=15

* Includes non-international publications, so look for those with an international focus

admissions process. If one persists in the quantitative or year-counting approach in comparing overseas degrees, inevitable clashes with faculty and deans feeling the heat of financial pressures will result. This will be exacerbated by the equity issues that call for treating ALL three-year degrees consistently across national borders and the concomitant pressure to address the fairness issue with U.S. four-year degree holders competing for those same graduate admission slots and assistantship positions. There may be a need on the part of the graduate admissions professional to give serious thought to considering Bologna-compliant three-year degrees. Should that situation arise, the admissions officer is advised to look closely at the quality assurance mechanisms undergirding the European Higher Education Area (Bologna Process) as this may well set these three-year degrees apart from those found in other countries which may not possess as stringent and pervasive an approach to quality. Even then, the U.S. graduate admissions officer

should establish a firm set of guidelines under which those degrees would be considered, such as prior entrance qualification to the degree in question, type of institution awarding the degree, similarity to the graduate program desired, and agreement of the prospective faculty to which the degree holder is making application. While other challenges will surface, at present this seems to be the most direct current concern for U.S. graduate admissions professionals.

The evaluation of international credentials may indeed appear overly complex to the relative newcomer in the field. However, as long as the evaluator understands that there are resources at hand to help answer questions, that organizations and individuals exist who specialize in this sometimes arcane profession, that there is a common methodological approach to this process, and that much foundational groundwork has been laid over the years, he or she will not feel quite so overwhelmed!

Fighting Fraud

in the Admissions and

Registrar's Offices

2010 AACRAO INTERNATIONAL GUIDE

EDWARD DEVLIN

Credentials Evaluator
AACRAO International Education Services

ANN M. KOENIG

Southwest Regional Director
AACRAO International Education Services

Fighting Fraud in the
Admissions and Registrar's Offices

In the sphere of education, fraud does exist. Although we, as educators and education administrators, prefer to think that our sector is safe from fraud and misrepresentation, the reality is that fraud involving your institution has occurred, is about to occur or is in progress. Fraud in education can take many forms among students, instructors, administrators and other members of the institutional community. It can include cheating, plagiarism, academic and professional misconduct, misuse of the institution's name, misrepresentation of the institution and credential fraud. Recently AACRAO has published several resources on fraud as it relates to the admissions and enrollment management environment, including the *Guide to Bogus Institutions and Documents* (2006), *Accreditation Mills* (2007) and *Counterfeit Diplomas and Transcripts* (2008). Another highly recommended resource is *Degree Mills: the Billion-Dollar Industry That Has Sold over a Million Fake Diplomas* (2005) by Allen Ezell and John Bear. Several other web-based resources are included in the list at the end of this chapter.

This chapter identifies some of the common types of fraud encountered in the admissions and registrar's offices and presents suggestions for best practices in admissions and student record review processes. The goal is to help your institution become proactive about fraud and develop procedures and policies to minimize the incidence of fraud in your environment and protect the integrity of your institution.

Types of Document Fraud

The most common types of document-related fraud seen by the admissions and registrar's offices are incomplete or misleading applications for admissions; altered or fabricated academic documentation; intentionally misleading English translations; counterfeit transcripts and documents from real educational institutions; documentation from fictitious or bogus universities or colleges that sell "degrees" (so-called diploma or degree mills) and documents from bogus accreditation bodies that often operate in tandem with degree mills. Other offices on campus that require students, faculty or administration to present academic credentials, such as the human resources department or research and development units, might also encounter problems with document fraud, including misleading, incomplete or fraudulent résumés.

Misrepresentation of the Institution as Fraud

Every vendor that sells your institution's name on fake documents is misrepresenting your institution and degrading the value of its reputation. But misrepresentation extends beyond the sphere of fraudulent documents. Other examples include the unauthorized use of an institution's or organization's materials, products and services; false advertising that implies the involvement or endorsement of an institution; unscrupulous recruiting agents gaining unwarranted financial benefits from an institution's international student applications, and bogus entities such as degrees mills and accreditation mills including an institution's name in lists of its members, associates, etc. without the institution's knowledge or consent. Registrars and admissions officers are sometimes shocked to discover such cases of misrepresentation.

The Causes of Document Fraud and its Growth

The value of any product reflects the demand for that product. In an environment in which education or a degree is seen as a product, the market value of education increases as demand grows. When access to education is limited or removed, or when authentic academic documentation is not available, an opportunity for fraud is created.

We usually think of such things as natural disasters, war, political crises, economic disasters and social upheaval as conditions that can limit access to education or authentic educational documentation. We must keep abreast of current events so that we can give informed and careful consideration to applications from individuals who have been affected by such conditions. The list of countries and regions experiencing disruptive conditions changes with world events. As international professionals, we need to be familiar with resources that can confirm information about these types of conditions and give suggestions as to how to handle these cases.

However, we must also pay careful attention to other factors that create an opportunity for fraud. One common example is countries or regions with high rates of corruption or very complex bureaucratic systems that make it difficult for the average person to navigate. Other factors may relate to an individual student's academic history: for example, a student with outstanding education-related debt who cannot get official transcripts; an applicant who has completed coursework requirements but not other types of additional graduation requirements; an applicant to a graduate program who may have insufficient undergraduate coursework in a particular discipline or an insufficient grade average to be eligible for the program; an executive who has advanced professionally without commensurate formal education. All of these situations might lead an individual to resort to presenting fraudulent credentials.

The thread that connects all of these scenarios is the desire to gain access to education. Academic credentials have become a commodity in the world market. The proliferation of fraudulent documents has, of course, been fueled by the development of the Internet and e-commerce. Be it counterfeit transcripts from real institutions, "replacement" transcripts and diplomas from replica services or "novelty" degrees from degree mills "accredited" by bogus accreditors, it is the "commerce" in *e-commerce* that drives the growth of this industry. Degrees = dollars (or any other currency in the world). What "sells" in this milieu is the name recognition and reputation of your institution and every other school whose name or logo appears on fraudulent documentation, or that becomes a victim of this type of fraud.

High School Documents and Fraud

Fraud in education is not limited to the higher education sector. The answer to the frequently-asked question of whether fraud in higher education also applies to the high school level is, unfortunately, a resounding "yes." Although it appears that less fraud is connected with high school level documentation, when it comes to the benefits that one can gain from presenting fraudulent high school transcripts, "diplomas = dollars" remains the standard. Consider the case of any individual who has not actually completed secondary or high school in the United States or abroad, thus being shut out from many types of jobs or education/training programs. Or the person who has completed secondary school in a different country, but is constantly asked for a "high school diploma or GED" by people in the United States and is not aware of the existence of foreign credential evaluators. Or the high school athlete who possesses talent in his/her sport, but does not have the academic ability for college admission. Imagine the possible results of one of these scenarios when the individual discovers the possibility of buying a "high school diploma" or "GED" online. It may seem far-fetched or desperate to those of us who work at the level of higher education, but high school documentation has a "market value," too.

Why Due Diligence is Essential

There are many flags that might alert an international admissions officer to the possibility of fraudulent, altered or misleadingly-translated documents, including academic records, test results, letters of recommendation and financial documents. So why is due diligence essential? Why should an institution bother to request verification of suspicious documents? Why is it not enough to think that "the document is probably OK," or that *surely* the international applicant will not get a visa if the visa officer is suspicious about the document too? What is the harm in admitting a student with altered documents? The answers fall into three categories: ethical, legal and practical.

ETHICAL CONSIDERATIONS

The ethical imperative is simple enough. If a school admits students on the basis of suspicious or incomplete documentation, while denying admission to students who submit authentic documents, the institution is supporting and rewarding fraud. Good practice and simple fairness require that a school take care to ensure that its admission and transfer credit practices reward only real achievement for all applicants, international and domestic.

LEGAL CONSIDERATIONS

The legal issue is also straightforward. Institutions that receive state and/or federal funding, as well as those certified to accept international students, have entered into legal agreements with legal obligations. Not practicing due diligence is a clear violation of the public trust granted by state government support, as well as the partnership with the U.S. government that the institution has undertaken by applying for and receiving the right to admit international students.

PRACTICAL REASONS

The ramifications of ignoring due diligence are also rather clear-cut, although the interpretations may be more subtle and have long-lasting consequences for the reputation of an individual institution. On a macro level, if an institution admits international students based on suspicious or incomplete documents, the reputation of U.S. higher education suffers worldwide. The same warning applies more obviously to an individual institution. It is common practice in many countries to sell and buy bogus documents, from marksheets and transcripts to complete degree dossiers, including U.S. immigration forms. One single ill-gotten I-20 form from a U.S. institution that is not alert to document fraud can be reproduced and sold indefinitely. That institution's reputation is then tarnished. The reputation of an institution as an "easy mark" for questionable application documents is a hard one to repair. Once this reputation is public, excellent students will stay away. Weak ones will apply, fraudulently or not. Additionally, once word gets out about lax admissions standards, the number of fraudulent applications will skyrocket. The campus then has fraudsters in its midst and must deal with the consequences. Given the resource limitations these days, it is wiser to do a careful review during the admissions process than to have to manage problems created by fraudsters once they are on campus.

Good Practice is the Key

To safeguard the authenticity of our institutions, as well as to continue to attract quality international students who contribute to the vitality, diversity and quality of U.S. higher education, it is imperative that we follow principles of best practice in the admission of international students. This means that international admissions professionals should have the training and resources they need to make sound professional judgments about the documents that applicants submit, that they receive the encouragement and support of enrollment managers to research and seek verification of questionable documents and that they share the results of the verification process with their colleagues. There is too much at stake to disregard or fall short on our responsibilities in this area.

Document Review and Verification

Our best protection against fraud is a solid knowledge-base among our foreign credential analysts and a strong network of information-sharing about document fraud and verification successes. Best practice in international admissions and foreign academic record review calls for:

* training and continuing professional development for foreign transcript evaluators, so that they are knowledgeable and up-to-date about country educational systems, documentation practices and events that impact on international education;

* clear communication to applicants about the documentation required for admission;

* careful review and research of the documents that are submitted;

* requests for verification of suspicious documents;

* appropriate follow-up when verification is received from the issuing institution or educational authority; and

* the sharing of success stories in the verification process.

THE INTERNATIONAL EVALUATOR'S PROFILE

Too often the job of reviewing foreign transcripts is given to an inexperienced front-line person. Perhaps nobody in the office is familiar with documents from other countries. Sometimes a "fear factor" associated with documents in strange envelopes written in foreign languages exists. International credential analysts need to be experienced, engaged, detail-oriented individuals who are given the resources required to develop their expertise. They are the first line of protection in the battle against fraud.

TAKE A METHODICAL, CONSISTENT APPROACH TO DOCUMENT REVIEW

The following outline presents a step-by-step approach to best practice in assembling, reviewing, researching and seeking verification of documents. Following these practical guidelines will help safeguard your institution against fraud.

STEP 1: ASSEMBLE THE DOCUMENTATION IN THE APPLICATION FILE AND ASSESS ITS COMPLETENESS.

* Learn where to find accurate information on country educational systems, names of credentials awarded and the documentation practices in the countries from which you most often see applicants—how are documents issued, in what format, in what language, what is the procedure for students to obtain official documentation, etc.

* Establish guidelines for the documentation required for a complete application file, including English translations and the use of translations in the evaluation process. Evaluations should never be based on English translations alone. See below for more on the use of English translations.

* Develop a procedure for cases in which the required documentation is not available.

* Inform prospective applicants of documentation requirements and procedures as early in the process as possible. Be proactive and include this information on Web sites and all printed information.

* Inform prospective applicants of the method(s) for submitting application materials and timelines or deadlines in the process.

* Develop a procedure to follow when an applicant submits incomplete or unacceptable documentation. How and when is the applicant informed of this procedure?

* Are any of the above points negotiable? Under what circumstances?

* In applicant information, clearly define the consequences to the applicant if incomplete, untrue or falsified information or documentation is submitted.

* Communicate all of the requirements, procedures and timelines clearly. The keys to actually *receiving* complete application files that include all the necessary documentation are to *know what you need to receive* and then *communicate to applicants what is required* in a precise, clear manner. Using indigenous terminology for the foreign academic documentation is very helpful.

STEP 2: OBTAIN RELIABLE RESOURCES TO HELP YOU REVIEW THE DOCUMENTATION.

* Determine what you will need to research about the documents in the file, and assemble your research tools.

* Resources include publications and information on educational systems, maps, foreign language dictionaries, periodical articles, documents and information provided by previous applicants, etc. You can find information about the availability of such materials from professional associations like AACRAO, conference and workshop materials, online tools, etc. Do not forget that experienced colleagues are also an excellent resource.

* Update and expand your resource collection. As new resources become available, educational systems change, and technology expands, your research needs to change and grow.

STEP 3: USING YOUR RESOURCES, REVIEW AND ANALYZE THE DOCUMENTS RECEIVED.

* Arrange the documents in chronological order.

* Confirm the origin of every document. Is it an original, copy or duplicate? How did the documentation get to your institution and into the applicant/student's file? Is this pathway appropriate for the country involved and the type of document?

* Review the biographical data provided by the applicant and compare with the "story" told by the documents. Pay attention to detail (location, age, level of education, quality of performance, test results, military service, employment history, etc.).

* Locate and confirm key information on the documents, using your resources: name and type of document; biographical information about student; name, location, recognition status, type and level of the institution; level, type and length of program or courses shown on the documents; dates of attendance and graduation or completion dates.

* If there is a course or subject listing, do the courses correspond to the field of study in which the student was enrolled, and were courses completed? Compare assessment or grade results with information about the country/institution's grading scale. Does the document show credits, units or other relative weighting of courses? Are they appropriate for that country/institution?

* If the document is presented with an English translation, check the accuracy of the translation by comparing it to other documents from the same country or institution. See below for more on the use of English translations.

* Pay attention to the format of the document as well as the contents. Does the layout of the document match confirmed sample documents shown in resources or in your files, including size of paper, typeface fonts, placement of text, signatures, stamps/seals, date, photograph, etc.? Are the lines of text aligned correctly? Are borders consistent with those seen on verified sample documents? Does the document appear to be unaltered? Are there any noticeable changes to the document, such as erasures, handwritten alterations, deletions or covering of text? Is there any information missing from the document that should be there? Is there information on the document that should not be there? Are words spelled correctly in the native language?

STEP 4: HANDLING DISCREPANCIES, PROBLEMS, OMISSIONS, INCONSISTENCIES, ETC.

* Have "another set of eyes" review the document and your resource materials with you. Ask colleagues who are knowledgeable about the particular country, institution or field of study to review the document with you.

* If the problem cannot be resolved by checking resources and with input from colleagues, request verification of the documents.

A Step-by-Step Approach to Verification

The following steps are guiding principles for verifying questionable documents. To accompany these steps, we've included Sample Document Case 1, three real-life documents illustrating the complete verification process. An altered transcript from University of Tirana in Albania was received in our office, a verification letter was sent out and a negative response was given by the university (*see* Figures 7.1–7.3 on pages 75–77).

STEP 1: PREPARE A VERIFICATION REQUEST.

✳ Using reliable resources, identify the office to which the verification request should be sent, locate the appropriate contact information for this office or person and consider the most effective way to send the verification request (postal service, courier service, fax, email, telephone, etc.).

✳ Formulate the request for verification. It is helpful to develop a standard form or letter to request verification. Some suggestions:

◆ Determine whether the letter should be written in English or another language, or both, to get a response as soon as possible. If in a language other than English, prepare the request in English first and have it translated by a reliable translator, such as a faculty or staff member. Send the request both in English and the other language.

◆ Clearly state "Request for Verification" in the opening of the request letter.

◆ Introduce yourself, your institution and the reason you are requesting verification (student has applied for admission at your institution; student has requested transfer credit based on these documents; etc.).

◆ Include the student/applicant's name and date of birth or other identifying information for the institution. If the documents include a student identification number from that institution, include that in the letter.

◆ Be clear and specific about what information you need to receive from the verifier. For example, if the document is not authentic, what further information do you want to know?

◆ Include a copy of the documentation. If there are discrepancies in the document, highlight them.

◆ If your institution has applicants sign a form authorizing release of information from the individual's file(s) at previous institutions, include a copy of that as well. In many countries, student information is the property of the institution, not the student. But in cases in which student information is protected by privacy laws, such an authorization may be required.

◆ Specify a date by which you need a response, if you have a specific time frame, the format in which a response would be acceptable (for example, must be in writing) and the language in which you need to receive the response.

◆ Include your contact information for the response.

◆ Request confidentiality. This information is not to be shared with the student or anyone else.

◆ Thank the reader and offer to assist in the future or send informational material from your institution.

STEP 2: KEEP A RECORD OF VERIFICATION REQUESTS.

✳ Once you have sent the verification request, put a copy of it in the applicant's file.

✳ Also start a "Verification Requests" file for copies of request letters with attached copies of the questionable documents. Cross-reference the files so that you can easily retrieve the applicant's file when the response is received.

STEP 3: FOLLOW UP APPROPRIATELY WHEN A REPLY IS RECEIVED.

The receipt of a verification letter is one of the most thrilling experiences in the international admissions office. There are many countries from which it is difficult to get verification due to factors that we in the U.S. higher education community may take for granted—limited financial, human and technological resources; differences in record-keeping systems; corruption; or disruptions in civil life because of natural disasters or warfare. Despite the best intentions of our colleagues abroad, we cannot always count on their cooperation in

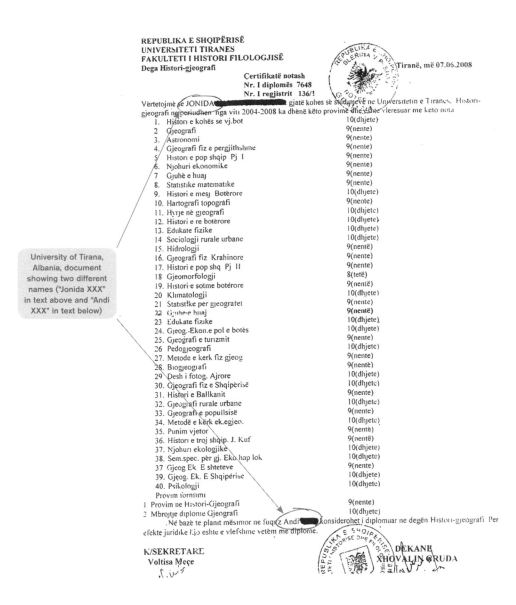

REPUBLIKA E SHQIPËRISË
UNIVERSITETI TIRANES
FAKULTETI I HISTORI FILOLOGJISË
Dega Histori-gjeografi

Çertifikatë notash
Nr. I diplomës 7648
Nr. I regjistrit 136/!

Tiranë, më 07.06.2008

Vërtetojmë se JONIDA _____ gjatë kohes së studimeve ne Universitetin e Tiranes. Histori-gjeografi në periudhen nga viti 2004-2008 ka dhënë këto provime dhe është vleresuar me keto nota

1.	Histori e kohës se vj.bot	10(dhjete)
2	Gjeografi	9(nente)
3.	Astronomi	9(nente)
4.	Gjeografi fiz e pergjithshme	9(nente)
5	Histori e pop shqip Pj I	9(nente)
6.	Njohuri ekonomike	9(nente)
7	Gjuhë e huaj	9(nente)
8.	Statistike matematike	9(nente)
9.	Histori e mesj Botèrore	10(dhjete)
10.	Hartografi topografi	9(nente)
11.	Hyrje në gjeografi	10(dhjete)
12.	Histori e re botèrore	10(dhjete)
13.	Edukate fizike	10(dhjete)
14	Sociologji rurale urbane	10(dhjete)
15.	Hidrologji	9(nentë)
16.	Gjeografi fiz Krahinore	9(nente)
17.	Histori e pop shq Pj II	9(nente)
18	Gjeomorfologji	8(tetë)
19.	Histori-e sotme botérore	9(nentë)
20	Klimatologji	10(dhjete)
21	Statistike per gjeografet	9(nente)
22	Gjuhe-e huaj	**9(nentë)**
23	Edukate fizike	10(dhjete)
24.	Gjeog. Ekon.e pol e botès	10(dhjete)
25.	Gjeografi e turizmit	9(nente)
26	Pedogjeografi	10(dhjete)
27.	Metode e kerk fiz gjeog	9(nente)
28.	Biogjeografi	9(nentë)
29	Desh i fotog. Ajrore	10(dhjete)
30.	Gjeografi fiz e Shqipërisë	10(dhjete)
31.	Histori e Ballkanit	9(nente)
32.	Gjeografi rurale urbane	10(dhjete)
33.	Gjeografi e popullsise	9(nente)
34.	Metodë e kërk ek.egjeo.	10(dhjete)
35.	Punim vjetor	9(nentë)
36.	Histori e troj shqip. J. Kuf	9(nentë)
37.	Njohuri ekologjike	10(dhjete)
38.	Sem.spec. për gj. Eko hap lok	10(dhjete)
37	Gjeog Ek E shteteve	9(nente)
39.	Gjeog. Ek. E Shqiperise	10(dhjete)
40.	Psikologji	10(dhjete)
	Provim formimi	
1	Provim ne Histori-Gjeografi	9(nente)
2	Mbrojtje diplome Gjeografi	10(dhjete)

.Né bazè te planit mësimor ne fuqi z Andi _____ konsiderohet i diplomuar ne degën Histori-gjeografi Per efekte juridike Ljo eshte e vlefshme vetëm me diplome.

K/SEKRETARE
Voltisa Meçe

DEKANE
XHOVALIN GRUDA

FIGURE 7.1

Case 1: Suspicious Document

University of Tirana, Albania, document showing two different names ("Jonida XXX" in text above and "Andi XXX" in text below)

a procedure that is part of the standard of professional practice in educational administration in the United States. Thus receiving a response to a verification request is the first step in the resolution of a tense and difficult situation involving the institution and the student.

✻ Assess the response:

◆ Does the information provided adequately answer the evaluator's concerns about the authenticity of the document? Is it conclusive?

◆ If the information provided is not conclusive, what further action needs to be taken? Will another round of correspondence be fruitful? To whom should it be addressed? What other avenues can be pursued if it seems that further contact with the verifying authority would not be productive?

◆ What if a verification fee is requested? Some educational authorities have begun assessing a fee for verification, particularly in areas where resources

FIGURE 7.2

Case 1: Verification Request Letter

University of Tirana, Office of the Rector
Deshmoret e Kombit
Tiranë, Albania

Re: Question about *Certifikatë notash* (please see enclosed copy)

       Name of student: Jonida xxx
       Diploma date: 07 June 2008
       Diploma number: 7648
       Registration number: 136/1

Dear Sir or Madam:

Greetings from xxxx University. Ms. Jonida xxx has applied for admission as a graduate student at our university. A copy of the diploma and the *certifikatë notash* that she sent to us are enclosed with this letter. Would you please review the enclosed documentation and answer our questions:

1.) At the bottom of the *certifikatë notash*, it states that "Andi xxx" graduated, not "Jonida xxx" Is this just a clerical error? Did the typist make a mistake?

2.) Is the rest of the *certifikatë notash* correct?

3.) Are Ms. Jovinda xxx's documents authentic? Did she really graduate with Diploma number 7648, registration number 136/1?

Thank you very much for your assistance. We would appreciate it if you would please return your reply to us as soon as possible, by post to [address] or by fax to [fax number].

Sincerely,

XXXX

are limited or a large number of verification requests are received. How does the evaluator handle such a situation?

✳ Take appropriate action. If the documents are verified as being fraudulent, follow-up should be immediate, according to established procedures and guidelines for the consequences to applicants who submit falsified documents. These policies should be defined and communicated to staff and applicants well before this stage of the admissions review process. See below for more on establishing policies and procedures.

Communicating with Applicants about Suspicious Documents and Verification

Strategies for communicating with students or applicants can range from saying nothing at all to the applicant; to informing the applicant that there are concerns about the documents and asking for explanations and/ or assistance in getting verification or "better" documents; to informing the applicant that verification has been requested and that nothing further will be done until verification has been received. Each case involving suspicious documentation needs to be reviewed on an individual basis and handled with sensitivity specific to the circumstances of the particular case. Working with

UNIVERSITY OF TIRANA
INTERNATIONAL RELATIONS DEPARTMENT
SHESHI "NËNË TEREZA" REKTORATI I UT, TIRANA, ALBANIA, TEL: +355 4 250166 / FAX:+3554 223981
E-mail:infokomunikimi@unitir.edu.al

Nr. 5 02/ Prot
/3

Tirana on, 8. 4. 2009

AACRAO
INTERNATIONAL EDUCATION SERVICE
SOUTHWEST REGIONAL OFFICE
15029 N THOMPSON PEAK, SUITE B 111 · PMB 606
SCOTTSDALE AZ 85260 USA

RE: CONFIRMATION OF THE DOCUMENTS

We would like to confirm that:

The Diploma No. 7648 and the Transcript of Marks submitted by Mrs.
Jonida I_____ **are not authentic.**

For further information, please do not hesitate to contact us at the above
address.

RECTOR
Dhori KULE

FIGURE 7.3

Case 1: Verification Response Letter

trusted resources, including experienced colleagues who have successfully navigated cases like these, helps admissions officers and evaluators to develop good professional judgment about how to handle cases involving suspicious documents.

Use of English Translations

In order to do an accurate assessment of applicants' previous education, evaluators should insist on receiving official documents in the original language in which they are issued. English translations may be needed, and evaluators need to establish guidelines on how English translations will be used in the evaluation process. Evaluation should always be based on the original credential in the language in which it is officially issued, never on an English translation alone.

Translations should be literal, complete, word-for-word representations of the language in the original documents, prepared in the same format as the original, by a person familiar with both languages. If the evaluator is not familiar with foreign languages, a professional English translation may be required. However, evaluators should keep in mind that the most important feature of a translation is *accuracy* in representing exactly what is written in the foreign language. The issue of *who* does the translation is secondary to the question of

FIGURE 7.4

Countries That Issue Official Academic Documents in English

- Afghanistan (transcripts in English)
- Australia
- Bahrain
- Bangladesh
- Bhutan
- Botswana
- Brunei Darussalam
- Cameroon (Anglophone)
- Canada (Anglophone)
- Caribbean Region (Anglophone): Antigua and Barbuda, Bahamas, Barbados, Belize, Bermuda, British Virgin Islands, Cayman Islands, Dominica, Grenada, Guyana, Jamaica, Montserrat, St. Kitts and Nevis, St. Lucia, St. Vincent and the Grenadines, Trinidad and Tobago, Turks and Caicos Islands
- Cyprus, Republic of (some institutions)
- Egypt
- Eritrea (transcripts in English)
- Ethiopia (transcripts in English)
- Gambia
- Ghana
- Gibraltar

- Hong Kong
- India
- Ireland
- Israel (some institutions)
- Japan
- Jordan
- Kenya
- Korea, South
- Kuwait
- Lebanon (U.S.-patterned institutions)
- Lesotho
- Liberia
- Macau
- Malawi
- Malaysia (U.S.-patterned institutions)
- Malta
- Mauritius
- Namibia
- Nepal
- New Zealand
- Nigeria
- Oman
- Pakistan
- Papua New Guinea
- Philippines

- Qatar
- Saudi Arabia
- Sierra Leone
- Singapore
- Somalia
- South Africa
- South Pacific Region (Anglophone): Cook Islands, Fiji, Kiribati, Marshall Islands, Nauru, Niue, Samoa, Solomon Islands, Tokelau, Tonga, Tuvalu, Vanuatu
- Sri Lanka
- Sudan
- Swaziland
- Taiwan
- Tanzania
- Thailand
- Tonga
- Uganda
- United Arab Emirates
- United Kingdom (England, Scotland, Wales, Northern Ireland)
- Western Samoa
- Zambia
- Zimbabwe

how accurate it is. In some cases, a student, friend of the applicant or faculty member may be able to provide an English translation that is as accurate as a translation done by a professional translator.

The accuracy of the translation should be confirmed by the use of reliable resources on the educational system of the country that show the names of institutions and credentials in the indigenous terminology. The evaluator should base the evaluation on the original document, using the English translation only as a tool.

If the translation appears to be inaccurate or misleading, then the applicant should be required to submit a different, accurate translation. There is no reason why an evaluator should hesitate to request an accurate English translation if one is needed. Likewise, evaluators should not jump to conclusions about the authenticity of the original document, or the applicant's intentions, if the English translation is not accurate. The translation is a tool to understanding the official document; any judgments about the authenticity of an official document should be based on the document itself, not on the English translation.

Official Documentation Issued in English

Some countries issue official documentation in English, even though English might not be the main or official language of the country (*see* Figure 7.4). In these cases, English translations should not be accepted. Only the official document issued by the institution in English should be considered official for use in the United States.

Counterfeit Transcripts and Diplomas

Counterfeit academic documents are produced and sold for the same reasons that counterfeit money exists. Education, or at least an educational credential, is "currency." A counterfeit document can be manufactured by an individual for his or her own use or produced for sale to others. In his book *Counterfeit Diplomas and Transcripts* (2008), fraud expert Allen Ezell presents information on at least three dozen online vendors that sell counterfeit transcripts from real educational institutions in the United States and around the world. The book also includes a list of at least eighty Web sites selling counterfeit Russian and Ukrainian educational credentials and describes the large-scale counterfeit document industry in the People's Republic of China. A table in the book shows a comparison of the characteristics of a genuine University of Florida transcript with the features of counterfeit University of Florida transcripts produced by three vendors of fake transcripts.

Vendors of counterfeit credentials may advertise the documents as "replacements," "replicas" or "novelty" items and issue disclaimers that they are not responsible for the consequences of attempts by customers to present the documents as "real." Some use the wording "fake transcript" and "fake diploma" throughout the text of their Web sites. Often the Web sites include samples of the documents available, testimonials about the quality and usefulness of the documents and "special offers." Some indicate which institutions' transcripts are *not* available; often they are schools who have taken some level of legal action against the supplier, such as a "cease and desist" warning.

How can you protect your institution's documents from becoming a victim of this type of fraud? A proactive posture is paramount: awareness of the problem is crucial, as well as vigilance in following a methodical approach to document review that includes a spectrum of verification procedures—from the use of standard resources to confirm information on transcripts, to written requests for authentication if necessary.

How does one determine the authenticity of a document from a real educational institution in an environment where potentially any institution's transcripts are for sale? Sometimes it is very difficult to tell whether a document is legitimate, especially when the fraudsters have stolen authentic templates or even bought them from unscrupulous employees of the issuing institution or authority. See Sample Document Case 2 comparing an original transcript from Cuttington University College, Liberia (Figure 7.5 on page 80) to a counterfeit (Figure 7.6 on page 81).

To clear up any suspicions about a document, a request for verification of the documentation should be addressed to the issuing institution. For guidance on seeking verification of documents from an institution outside of the United States, see the section on document review and verification above.

To request verification of documentation purportedly issued by a u.s. institution, contact the office of the registrar of the institution. The Family Educational Rights and Privacy Act (FERPA), a set of federal laws protecting the privacy of students in the u.s., includes a provision that student data called "directory information" can be disclosed to the public without specific authorization from the student/former student, unless the individual has requested that this information not be shared. This directory information includes data such as the dates of enrollment, level and mode of enrollment (undergraduate or graduate, full-time or part-time), major and degree, including date of degree, if awarded. For details on FERPA, see *U.S. Department of Education, Family Educational Rights and Privacy Act* (www.ed.gov/policy/gen/guid/fpco/ferpa/index. html), as well AACRAO's FERPA-related resources.

Degree Mills, Accreditation Mills and Bogus Foreign Credential Evaluation Services

A "diploma mill" or "degree mill" is an entity that produces and sells documents that appear to be academic credentials (diplomas, degrees, transcripts) from what appear to be universities or colleges, but in reality are academically worthless documents from fictitious "educational institutions" that represent inappropriately little academic work or none at all. These documents are meant to give the impression of academic achievement, but in actuality are purchased papers that have no academic value.

Awareness of diploma mill fraud is especially important for reviewers of international student records because many of these entities purport to be "foreign universities." Typically these entities claim to be a university in a country outside of the United States, while the operators themselves may be located in the u.s., located in another country or have different parts of the process located in different countries. For example, Bear and Ezell (2005) describe a well-known diploma mill

Key to Grades

A (4) - Very Good
B (3) - Good
C (2) - Fair
D (1) - Poor
F (0) - Failing
W-Withdrawal
Inc. Incomplete
Prior to 66 a three point system was in effect

From 1966 to 1978 a unit system was in effect as follows:

3.0 Excellent
2.0 Good
1.5 Fair
1.0 Acceptable
0.0 Poor
F- Failing

Effective in 1978 the Institution moved to a four-point system with the use of letter grades.

Transcripts of students enrolled prior to 1978 and still enrolled at time of the changeover reflect a combined average resulting from the use of a standard formula for conversion.

Transcripts of students enrolled prior to 1978 and still enrolled at the time of the changeover reflect a combined average resulting from the use of a standard formula for conversion.

PERMANENT RECORD – CUTTINGTON UNIVERSITY COLLEGE – SUACOCO – LIBERIA

ring called the "University Degree Program," an operation masterminded by a rabbi from New York, with telemarketing done in Bucharest, Romania, mail-forwarding services in Ireland, diplomas printed in Israel, and banking in Cyprus. The book lists three dozen known fictitious "university" names used by the University Degree Program. If one takes a comparative look at the documents from these "universities," one would see that they have the same format and essentially the same content, except for differences in the purchaser's name, the name and date of the "degree" and course titles on the transcript, depending on the field of "study." (*See* Sample Document Case 3, Figure 7.7 on page 82.)

There have been many spin-offs of this operation as former employees have started their own diploma mill businesses.

Accreditation mills represent a related area of fraud. Some diploma mills use claims of accreditation to sell their "degrees." It used to be more common for diploma mills to speak disparagingly of accreditation, stating in their descriptive materials that they did not need accreditation, did not agree with the philosophy of accreditors or otherwise were somehow exempt from or above the notion of accreditation. It appears that in the last decade or so, diploma mills have found that embracing the concept of accreditation can pay off. Some not

CUTTINGTON UNIVERSITY COLLEGE
POST OFFICE BOX 277
SUAKOKO, BONG COUNTY
LIBERIA, WEST AFRICA

ID# 2533
Armand O.
MAJOR: ACCOUNTING
DEGREE: Bsc. ON: 12/13/88

ADVISOR: Mason, Charles

ACTION DATE MO/DAY/YR	COURSE#	COURSE TITLE	GRADE	CREDITS	QUALITY PIONTS
01/15/85	1st SEMESTER FRESHMAN YR.				
	EDU. 100	FRESHMN ORIENTA.	B	0	0
	ACC. 110	MANAGERIAL ACCT.	B	4	12
	ENG. 101	FUND. OF COMPOS.	C	3	6
	FRE. 101	BEGIN FRENCH I	A	3	12
	MAT. 101	MATHEMATIC I	A	3	12
SEMESTER GPA: 3.23 CREDITS: 13					
CUMULATIVE GPA: 3.23 CREDITS: 13					
06/12/85	2nd SEMESTER FRESHMAN YR.				
	PHS. 101	PHYSICAL EDU.	B	3	9
	ENG. 102	FUND. OF COMPOS.	A	3	12
	HIS. 102	HIS. OF CIVILIZA.	B	3	9
	FRE. 102	DEG FRENCH II	B	3	9
	MAT. 102	MATHEMATICS II	A	3	12
SEMESTER GPA: 3.40 CREDITS: 15					
CUMULATIVE GPA: 3.32 CREDITS: 28					
11/12/85	VACATION SCHOOL FRESHMAN YR.				
	PED. 119	PHYSICAL SCIENCE	A	2	8
	ACC. 201	ACC PRINCIPLE I	A	3	12
	ECO. 203	ECO PRINCIPLE I	B	3	9
SEMESTER GPA: 3.62 CREDITS: 8					
CUMULATIVE GPA: 3.38 CREDITS: 36					
01/10/86	1st SEMESTER SOPHOMOR YR.				
	MGT. 202	MGMT. PRINCIP. I	B	3	9
	ACC. 202	ACCT PRINCIP. II	A	3	12
	ENG. 201	SOPHO ENGLISH I	A	3	12
	MTH. 203	CAL FPR CECISIO	C	4	8
	ECO. 204	ECO PRINCIP. II	B	3	9
SEMESTER GPA: 3.12 CREDITS: 16					
CUMULATIVE GPA: 3.12 CREDITS: 52					

FIGURE 7.6

Case 2 Counterfeit Transcript

only create their own bogus accreditors to try to add to the appearance of legitimacy of the "university," but also sell this bogus accreditation to other bogus entities. Instead of decrying accreditation, they have created ways to make it financially lucrative.

Some diploma mill operations are large fraud rings that also produce other types of fraudulent documents, such as driver's licenses, social security cards and other identification documents. Many offer associated "student services," including transcript verification, foreign credential evaluation and even alumnae associations. By calling a toll-free telephone number, the bogus documents can be verified, the accreditation of the "university" confirmed and an evaluation of the "foreign transcript" showing that the "degree" is equivalent to a U.S. degree received by the "graduate." These "services" are offered by the same people who set up the fraudulent diploma operation.

This was the case with the St. Regis University diploma mill operation. The masterminds and agents behind this organization, who operated in Washington State, Idaho and Arizona, created virtual "universities" and even "high schools" claiming to offer distance education from Liberia and recognition by the Liberian Ministry of Education. They created a bogus Liberian embassy Web site that showed that these "schools" were

THE REGENTS OF

Sherwood University

UPON THE NOMINATION OF THE COUNCIL OF THE UNDERGRADUATE DIVISION
HEREBY CONFER UPON

Alangir

HAVING DEMONSTRATED ABILITY BY GENERAL SCHOLARSHIP
CUM LAUDE - WITH DISTINCTION
THE DEGREE

Bachelor of Science
Physics

WITH ALL THE RIGHTS AND PRIVILEGES THERETO PERTAINING
GIVEN THIS TENTH DAY OF JUNE IN THE YEAR
TWO THOUSAND AND THREE

Carol Anderson
PRESIDENT OF THE REGENTS

John McCullogh
PRESIDENT OF THE UNIVERSITY

William Franklyn
DEAN OF THE UNDERGRADUATE DIVISION

Ronald R. Bowcort
CHANCELLOR

recognized and accredited by an equally-fictitious "National Board of Education." (*See* Sample Document Case 4, Figure 7.11 [on page 86], for an example of a St. Regis diploma and accreditation certificate.) This was accomplished by bribing a Liberian embassy official in Washington, D.C. In addition, they offered many "student services" and had a foreign credential evaluation service on board to give the "degrees" U.S. degree equivalencies. It was the tenacity of researchers such as Professor George Gollin of the University of Illinois and federal law enforcement agencies, combined with the hubris of the operators, that brought this outfit down.

How can the international transcript evaluator determine whether an institution is a real, recognized, legitimately-accredited educational institution that really teaches and awards recognized educational credentials?

Understanding the way in which diploma mills work allows for recognition of these entities. Diploma mills operate in many of the same ways that other fraud operations work—by imitating legitimate activity. Their goal is to look like a real university. Here are some things to watch out for:

✱ *Name:* The "institution" has a distinguished or traditional sounding name, or a name similar to a well-known or legitimate institution. (Is your institution's name being used? Check the Internet regularly to see how your school's name, or variations on it, appears.)

✱ *Location:* The "university" has a Web site but no physical address, or there is conflicting information about a physical location.

✱ *Foreign:* It gives the impression of being a "foreign" university, but may be operating from a completely different location. See comments above.

FIGURE 7.8

Case 3: Diploma Mill Transcript, Sample 1

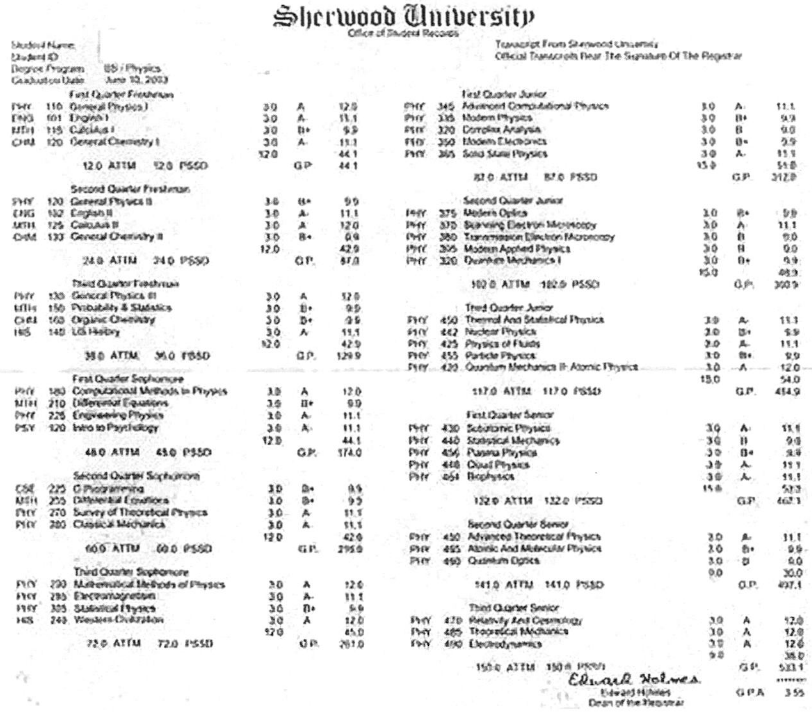

Sherwood University

Office of Student Records

Transcript From Sherwood University
Official Transcripts Bear The Signature Of The Registrar

Student Name:
Student ID
Degree Program: BS / Physics
Graduation Date: June 10, 2003

		First Quarter Freshman			
PHY	110	General Physics I	3.0	A	12.0
ENG	101	English I	3.0	A-	11.1
MTH	115	Calculus I	3.0	B+	9.9
CHM	120	General Chemistry I	3.0	A-	11.1
			12.0		44.1
		12.0 ATTM 12.0 PSSD		G.P.	44.1
		Second Quarter Freshman			
PHY	120	General Physics II	3.0	B+	9.9
ENG	102	English II	3.0	A-	11.1
MTH	125	Calculus II	3.0	A	12.0
CHM	130	General Chemistry II	3.0	B+	9.9
			12.0		42.9
		24.0 ATTM 24.0 PSSD		G.P.	87.0
		Third Quarter Freshman			
PHY	130	General Physics III	3.0	A	12.0
MTH	150	Probability & Statistics	3.0	B+	9.9
CHM	160	Organic Chemistry	3.0	B+	9.9
HIS	140	US History	3.0	A-	11.1
			12.0		42.9
		36.0 ATTM 36.0 PSSD		G.P.	129.9
		First Quarter Sophomore			
PHY	180	Computational Methods in Physics	3.0	A	12.0
MTH	210	Differential Equations	3.0	B+	9.9
PHY	225	Engineering Physics	3.0	A-	11.1
PSY	120	Intro to Psychology	3.0	A-	11.1
			12.0		44.1
		48.0 ATTM 48.0 PSSD		G.P.	174.0
		Second Quarter Sophomore			
CSE	225	C Programming	3.0	B+	9.9
MTH	255	Differential Equations	3.0	B+	9.9
PHY	270	Survey of Theoretical Physics	3.0	A-	11.1
PHY	280	Classical Mechanics	3.0	A-	11.1
			12.0		42.0
		60.0 ATTM 60.0 PSSD		G.P.	216.0
		Third Quarter Sophomore			
PHY	290	Mathematical Methods of Physics	3.0	A	12.0
PHY	295	Electromagnetism	3.0	A-	11.1
PHY	305	Statistical Physics	3.0	B+	9.9
HIS	240	Western Civilization	3.0	A	12.0
			12.0		45.0
		72.0 ATTM 72.0 PSSD		G.P.	261.0
		First Quarter Junior			
PHY	345	Advanced Computational Physics	3.0	A-	11.1
PHY	335	Modern Physics	3.0	B+	9.9
PHY	320	Complex Analysis	3.0	B	9.0
PHY	350	Modern Electronics	3.0	B+	9.9
PHY	365	Solid State Physics	3.0	A-	11.1
			15.0		51.0
		87.0 ATTM 87.0 PSSD		G.P.	312.0
		Second Quarter Junior			
PHY	375	Modern Optics	3.0	B+	9.9
PHY	370	Scanning Electron Microscopy	3.0	A-	11.1
PHY	380	Transmission Electron Microscopy	3.0	B	9.0
PHY	395	Modern Applied Physics	3.0	B	9.0
PHY	320	Quantum Mechanics I	3.0	B+	9.9
			15.0		48.9
		102.0 ATTM 102.0 PSSD		G.P.	360.9
		Third Quarter Junior			
PHY	450	Thermal And Statistical Physics	3.0	A-	11.1
PHY	442	Nuclear Physics	3.0	B+	9.9
PHY	425	Physics of Fluids	3.0	A-	11.1
PHY	455	Particle Physics	3.0	B+	9.9
PHY	420	Quantum Mechanics II: Atomic Physics	3.0	A	12.0
			15.0		54.0
		117.0 ATTM 117.0 PSSD		G.P.	414.9
		First Quarter Senior			
PHY	430	Subatomic Physics	3.0	A-	11.1
PHY	440	Statistical Mechanics	3.0	B	9.0
PHY	456	Plasma Physics	3.0	B+	9.9
PHY	448	Cloud Physics	3.0	A-	11.1
PHY	454	Biophysics	3.0	A-	11.1
			15.0		52.2
		132.0 ATTM 132.0 PSSD		G.P.	467.1
		Second Quarter Senior			
PHY	450	Advanced Theoretical Physics	3.0	A-	11.1
PHY	455	Atomic And Molecular Physics	3.0	B+	9.9
PHY	490	Quantum Optics	3.0	B	9.0
			9.0		30.0
		141.0 ATTM 141.0 PSSD		G.P.	497.1
		Third Quarter Senior			
PHY	470	Relativity And Cosmology	3.0	A	12.0
PHY	485	Theoretical Mechanics	3.0	A	12.0
PHY	490	Electrodynamics	3.0	A	12.0
			9.0		36.0
		150.0 ATTM 150.0 PSSD		G.P.	533.1
				G.P.A	3.55

Edward Holmes
Edward Holmes
Dean of the Registrar

- ✻ *Internet address:* It may use "edu," "ac" or "uk" in the URL, giving the impression of being a U.S. or British educational institution.
- ✻ *Contact:* No contact information is given on the Web site. The only way to contact the "university" is by e-mailing your contact information or providing it via the Web site.
- ✻ *Accreditation or recognition:* The Web site includes false, misleading or meaningless claims of accreditation, recognition, affiliation, membership or other types of status that are meant to give the impression of legitimacy, but really mean nothing in the legitimate higher education community.
- ✻ *Speedy degrees:* The amount of time required to get the "degree" is suspiciously fast. A large number of credits, or the whole "degree," might be given based on "life experience" only; "send us your résumé and receive a degree."
- ✻ *Costs:* The Web site shows a price list or lump sum prices for the various "degrees" and "transcripts." Different rates might be charged for including specific courses, grades, majors, etc. on the transcript. Payment may be acceptable by credit card or PayPal. There might be special deals or discounts for buying immediately.
- ✻ *Sample documents:* The Web site shows samples of diplomas and transcripts.
- ✻ *Network of diploma mills:* Several "university" Web sites may operate from the same computer or network. Researching IP addresses behind domain names, domain registry information and other "behind the scenes" computer information can yield valuable results in investigating a "university's" true identity.

FIGURE 7.9

Case 3: Diploma Mill Degree, Sample 2

THE REGENTS OF

Shepperton University

UPON THE NOMINATION OF THE COUNCIL OF THE GRADUATE DIVISION
HEREBY CONFER UPON

HAVING DEMONSTRATED ABILITY BY GENERAL SCHOLARSHIP
CUM LAUDE - WITH DISTINCTION
THE DEGREE

Master of Business Administration

WITH ALL THE RIGHTS AND PRIVILEGES THERETO PERTAINING
GIVEN THIS TENTH DAY OF JUNE IN THE YEAR
TWO THOUSAND AND THREE

PRESIDENT OF THE REGENTS

DEAN OF THE GRADUATE DIVISION

PRESIDENT OF THE UNIVERSITY

CHANCELLOR

* *Support services:* Diploma mills set up their own verification services available through a toll-free telephone number; the people answering the phone to verify are the same ones selling the degree. The entity might offer foreign credential evaluation and "Apostille" services if the institution purports to be foreign.

* *Advertising:* Print advertisements appear in well-respected publications, as well as in popular tabloids and comic books. Electronic media have made world-wide distribution easy and cheap and made it difficult to pin down just where such activity originates.

Using a methodical approach to document review, as outlined above, is essential to identifying whether the documents presented are from a real, legitimate and appropriately-recognized institution. Research using official and reliable resources is crucial. Mindful of the ways in which diploma mills operate, the evaluator first needs to identify what country the institution purports to be operating in, then determine the legal body in that country that supervises higher education. Is it a national ministry of education, a commission or council for higher education, or a provincial or state authority? Does this legal body publish a list of recognized institutions? Does the suspected diploma mill appear on the list of officially recognized institutions? Once the appropriate authority has been identified, the evaluator should contact that office to ask about the status of the institution in that jurisdiction.

Legal Issues in Degree Fraud

"Aren't diploma mills illegal?" is a commonly-asked question.

The response is, "It depends." Diploma mills exploit legal loopholes. Where laws are weak, vague, complex or not enforced, diploma mills thrive. Some diploma mill operations move around the United States and the world to avoid legal trouble and/or set up various parts

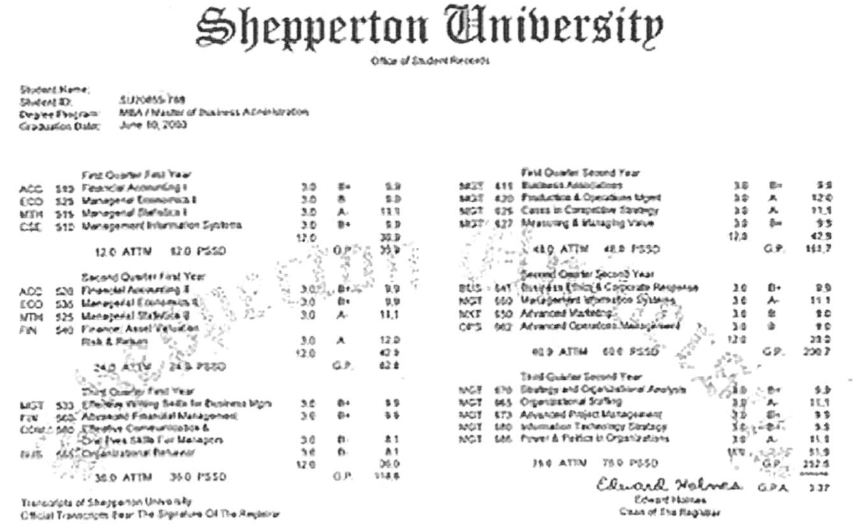

Shepperton University

Office of Student Records

Student Name:
Student ID: SU70855-788
Degree Program: MBA / Master of Business Administration
Graduation Date: June 10, 2003

First Quarter First Year

ACC	5[illegible]0	Financial Accounting I	3.0	B+	9.9
ECO	525	Managerial Economics I	3.0	B	9.0
MTH	515	Managerial Statistics I	3.0	A-	11.1
CSE	510	Management Information Systems	3.0	B+	9.9
			12.0		39.9
		12.0 ATTM 12.0 PSSD		G.P.	39.9

Second Quarter First Year

ACC	520	Financial Accounting II	3.0	B+	9.9
ECO	535	Managerial Economics II	3.0	B+	9.9
MTH	525	Managerial Statistics II	3.0	A-	11.1
FIN	540	Finance: Asset Valuation Risk & Return	3.0	A	12.0
			12.0		42.9
		24.0 ATTM 24.0 PSSD		G.P.	82.8

Third Quarter First Year

MGT	533	Effective Writing Skills for Business Mgrs	3.0	B+	9.9
FIN	560	Advanced Financial Management	3.0	B+	9.9
COMM	580	Effective Communication & Oral Pres Skills For Managers	3.0	B-	8.1
BUS	66[illegible]	Organizational Behavior	3.0	B-	8.1
			12.0		36.0
		36.0 ATTM 36.0 PSSD		G.P.	118.8

First Quarter Second Year

MGT	615	Business Associations	3.0	B+	9.9
MGT	620	Production & Operations Mgmt	3.0	A	12.0
MGT	625	Cases in Competitive Strategy	3.0	A-	11.1
MGT	627	Measuring & Managing Value	3.0	B+	9.9
			12.0		42.9
		48.0 ATTM 48.0 PSSD		G.P.	161.7

Second Quarter Second Year

BUS	641	Business Ethics & Corporate Response	3.0	B+	9.9
MGT	660	Management Information Systems	3.0	A-	11.1
MKT	650	Advanced Marketing	3.0	B	9.0
OPS	662	Advanced Operations Management	3.0	B	9.0
			12.0		39.0
		60.0 ATTM 60.0 PSSD		G.P.	200.7

Third Quarter Second Year

MGT	670	Strategy and Organizational Analysis	3.0	B+	9.9
MGT	665	Organizational Staffing	3.0	A-	11.1
MGT	673	Advanced Project Management	3.0	B+	9.9
MGT	680	Information Technology Strategy	3.0	B+	9.9
MGT	686	Power & Politics in Organizations	3.0	A-	11.1
			15.0		51.9
		75.0 ATTM 75.0 PSSD		G.P.	252.6
				G.P.A.	3.37

Transcripts of Shepperton University
Official Transcripts Bear The Signature Of The Registrar

Edward Holmes
Edward Holmes
Dean of The Registrar

FIGURE 7.10 Case 3: Diploma Mill Transcript, Sample 2

of their operations in different states/countries so as to make legal prosecution difficult.

In the United States, the establishment of educational institutions is regulated at the state level. Regulations vary from state to state. Some states have no laws, or lax or poorly-worded laws, while others have clear laws but little enforcement. The number of states that regulate the use of degrees is growing and now includes Alabama, Illinois, Michigan, New Jersey, Oregon, South Dakota, Texas, Virginia and Washington. Oregon in particular is a model of a state with clear laws, effective law enforcement and a commitment to public information on degree fraud. The Web site of the Oregon Office of Degree Authorization (www.osac.state.or.us/oda/) has a section for information on diploma mills, including maps of the U.S. showing states with good and poor track records in controlling diploma mill and degree fraud, a list of diploma mills and an employer's guide to college degrees.

On the federal level diploma mill operations have been prosecuted successfully on the basis of federal offenses such as aiding and abetting, conspiracy, false identification, mail fraud, fraud by wire, obstruction of justice, money laundering, criminal forfeiture, trademark violation and tax evasion.

In other countries education is regulated by law either at the national level or at a sub-national level. Governments oversee the establishment, funding, operation and administration of educational institutions. Public institutions established by law or private institutions that have the same legal standing as public institutions are "officially recognized" institutions. Government entities bestow the authorization to offer academic programs and awards.

Complex legal systems and cultures of corruption invite diploma mill fraud around the world. Some countries or regions are noted for problems with diploma mill activity. Many examples of diploma mills

FIGURE 7.11

St. Regis University

The Regents of the Board of Directors and the President & Chief Provost by virtue of their Authority have conferred upon

The Degree and Academician Status of

Bachelor of Science
in
Nursing

and granted all the privileges and rights accorded thereto.
Be It Known that knowledge and proficiency has been demonstrated by completing and satisfying all requirements of the Regents of the Board of Directors in token whereof the President & Chief Provost has authorized this status.
In witness whereof, this Diploma is granted by the Board of Directors, and presented on the Twenty Ninth day of August, Nineteen Hundred and Ninety Eight.

Dean of Studies   Chief Provost

operating from areas outside of the United States that have no higher education institutions or where higher education is not regulated exist, such as some Caribbean islands, some Pacific Islands and some cantons of Switzerland. Two well-known examples of diploma mills hail from internationally unrecognized "self-declared autonomous" entities within sovereign countries, the "Hutt River Province" in Australia and "The Principality of Seborga" in Italy. For identification and discussion of problem areas of the world, see the section on degree mills in the Boston College Center for International Higher Education's newsletter (www.bc.edu/bc_org/avp/soe/cihe/index.htm).

Considerations for Policies on Fraud

Be proactive. Proactive policies and clear, viable procedures can be effective tools in fighting fraud. If your institution does not have policies, or if existing policies are not effective, not extensive enough, not current

enough or not backed up by effective procedures, the following are some things to consider in establishing or adjusting policies on handling cases involving fraud.

* Define "fraud." Identify the types of fraud to which your institution is vulnerable and the various scenarios in which fraud can play a part. Examine cases of fraud that you have encountered or instances you have seen or heard about from others. What could/should have been done to prevent the problem? What was learned as a result?

* Identify the "market value" of your institution, particularly to international students. What is attractive about your institution? Why would fraudsters want to capitalize on your institution? What is the reputation of your institution? Is it prestigious or an easy target?

* Review the policies of your institution on student and faculty/administrator behavior (academic dishonesty, honor code, code of conduct, code of eth-

FIGURE 7.12

Case 4: Bogus Accreditation Certificate

ics). Are any of these relevant to the type of fraud your office might see?

✳ Identify the various offices or departments in your operating environment that should be involved in discussions about policies on handling fraud cases.

✳ Work with your institution's legal counsel to become informed about appropriate federal, state, county and city laws and ordinances for the cases you might encounter.

✳ A procedure or protocol to be followed in fraud cases should be clearly spelled out and communicated to all those who might deal with such cases. Who does what? What is the procedure, step-by-step? Should it be the same in every case? Is there an appeal process if the applicant disputes the findings? What is the procedure for that?

✳ In addition to policies and procedures, another effective tool in identifying and preventing fraud is a team to coordinate anti-fraud efforts across the campus or organization: keep an eye on the "big picture," continuously educate and inform, train others, proactively function as "watchdogs" and monitor the Internet for usage of the institution's name, assist with questions, prepare cases for review and judgment, track results, review and critique policy, etc.

✳ Publish your institution's policies and procedures, as well as the consequences for breaking the rules in clear, concise, unambiguous language and in easily-accessible locations (in application packets, in publications, on the Web, etc.).

✳ Incorporate a section in your application materials that must be signed by the applicant, attesting to truthfulness, completeness and accuracy of information provided; the understanding that institutions issuing the documents submitted may be contacted for authentication of the documents or further information relevant to the student's education there;

agreeing to abide by relevant policies, regulations, etc. and accepting consequences if rules are broken.

✳ Act quickly when a case of questionable documentation is uncovered. Address the situation immediately, to squelch the flames that can quickly escalate into a raging inferno. Be a confident and assertive first responder, with appropriate policies and procedures to support your work.

✳ Seek the advice of experienced, expert, neutral third parties if you need help, in accordance with the guidance of your legal counsel. Only use trusted, informed resources, keeping in mind that parties that produce or use fraudulent degrees and transcripts may also operate or use fraudulent verification, accreditation and foreign credential evaluation services, thus possibly having duped other otherwise reputable institutions and services into recognizing their "degrees."

✳ Keep a log or record of cases involving fraud. Cross-reference information and notes between various files so that data is easily retrievable. Note general information in generic files and information specific to a particular student or applicant in the individual's file. This recordkeeping is useful should the person ever apply again.

✳ Incorporate what you learn from each case into the institution's response to such cases. Each scenario presents a different set of circumstances, with new twists and perspectives. Review institutional policy regularly, adjusting it as appropriate.

RESOURCES ON FRAUD

AACRAO RESOURCES

Bear, J. *et al.* 2006. *Guide to Bogus Institutions and Documents.* Washington, D.C.: American Association of Collegiate Registrars and Admissions Officers.

Ezell, A. 2002. Degree diploma mills—past, present, and future. *College and University*, Winter.

———. 2005. Transcript fraud and handling fraudulent documents. *College and University*, Winter.

———. 2007. *Accreditation Mills.* Washington, D.C.: American Association of Collegiate Registrars and Admissions Officers.

———. 2008. *Counterfeit Diplomas and Transcripts.* Washington, D.C.: American Association of Collegiate Registrars and Admissions Officers.

OTHER RESOURCES

Bartlett, T. and S. Smallwood. 2004. Degrees of suspicion: Psst. Wanna buy a Ph.D.? *The Chronicle of Higher Education.* 50(42): A9. Retrieved May 14 from: <http://chronicle.com/article/psst-wanna-buy-a-phd-/24239>.

Bear, J. and A. Ezell. 2005. *Degree Mills: The Billion-Dollar Industry That Has Sold Over a Million Fake Diplomas.* New York: Prometheus Books.

Bear, M and T. Nixon. 2006. *Bears' Guide to Earning Degrees by Distance Learning.* Ten Speed Press. The Bears (John and his daughter Mariah) have written many guides to non-traditional education over the past thirty years and their books list many "fake," "substandard" and "dubious" institutions and their equally "fake," "substandard" and "dubious" accreditors. Older editions are sometimes available from used book vendors.

Carnevale, D. 2004. Don't judge a college by its internet address. *The Chronicle of Higher Education.* November 26. Retrieved May 14, 2010 from: <http://chronicle.com/free/v51/i14/14a02901.htm>.

Contreras, A. 2001. International diploma mills grow with the internet. *International Higher Education.* 24(Summer): 5–6. Retrieved May 14, 2010 from: <www.bc.edu/bc_org/avp/soe/cihe/newsletter/ihe_pdf/ihe24.pdf>.

———. 2002. How reliable is national approval of university degrees? *International Higher Education.* 29(Fall). Retrieved from Center for Higher Education, Boston College at <www.bc.edu/bc_org/avp/soe/cihe/newsletter/News29/text005.htm>.

———. 2003. A case study in foreign degree (dis)approval. *International Higher Education.* Summer. Retrieved from Center for Higher Education, Boston College <www.bc.edu/bc_org/avp/soe/cihe/newsletter/News32/text004.htm>.

Council for Higher Education Accreditation (CHEA). *Degree Mills and Accreditation Mills.* Retrieved May 14, 2010 from <www.chea.org/degreemills/default.htm>.

Gollin, G. 2003. *Unconventional University Diplomas from Online Vendors or Fraud, Corruption and Scandal: Buying a Ph.D. From a University that Doesn't Exist.* August. Overview of how diploma mills operate. Retrieved May 14, 2010 from University of Illinois Urbana-Champaign at <www.hep.uiuc.edu/home/g-gollin/diploma_mills.pdf>.

Hallak, J. and M. Poisson. 2007. *Corrupt Schools, Corrupt Universities: What Can Be Done?* Paris, France: UNESCO International Institute for Educational Planning. See especially Chapter 7, "Exams, credentials and accreditation." Retrieved from <http://unesdoc.unesco.org/images/0015/001502/150259e.pdf>.

Noah, H. and M. Eckstein. 2001. *Fraud and Education: The Worm in the Apple.* Lanham, MD: Rowman & Littlefield Publisher, Inc.

Oregon Student Assistance Commission, Office of Degree Authorization. 2010. *Diploma Mills.* Retrieved May 14, 2010 from <www.osac.state.or.us/oda/diploma_mill.html>.

Transparency International, The Global Coalition Against Corruption. *Corruption Perceptions Index 2009.* Retrieved from <www.trans parency.org/policy_research/surveys_indices/cpi/2009>.

U.S. Department of Education. 2010. *Diploma Mills and Accreditation.* Retrieved May 14, 2010 from <www.ed.gov/students/prep/college/ diplomamills/>.

———. 2010. *Family Educational Rights and Privacy Act.* Retrieved May 14, 2010 from www.ed.gov/policy/gen/guid/fpco/ferpa/ index.html.

U.S. Federal Trade Commission. 2005. *Avoid Fake Degree Burns by Researching Academic Credentials.* February. Retrieved from <www. ftc.gov/bcp/edu/pubs/business/resources/bus65.pdf>.

———. 2006. *Diploma Mills: Degree of Deception.* October. Retrieved May 14, 2010 from <www.ftc.gov/bcp/edu/pubs/consumer/alerts/ alt149.shtm>.

University of Illinois at Urbana-Champaign. 2010. *Information Resources Concerning Unaccredited Degree-Granting Institutions.* A compilation of various resources, including news items and public legal documents by Prof. George Gollin. Retrieved May 14, 2010 from <http://web.hep.uiuc.edu/home/g-gollin/pigeons/>.

EIGHT

The Art & Science of
International
Transfer Credit
Evaluation

MELANIE GOTTLIEB

Director of Admissions Operations and International Campus Liaison
Webster University

The Art & Science of International Transfer Credit Evaluation

In a global education marketplace with an increasing focus on student mobility, the development of competencies in the evaluation of foreign credit for transfer becomes an institutional responsibility and a marketplace necessity for international admissions professionals. Since there is no single authority in the United States for the recognition of foreign degrees and other qualifications, institutions and professionals are tasked with the responsibility of synthesizing research on more than 200 country education systems around the world.[1] Whether an institution decides to outsource the evaluation of foreign credentials to a service such as AACRAO International Education Services or take on the responsibility in-house, it is essential for international admissions professionals to have a solid grounding in the principles by which such decisions are made.

Foundations: Know the U.S. system

Before taking on the task of evaluating foreign credentials for admission or credit transfer, the professional should gain a thorough understanding of the U.S. system of education. One might have earned a postsecondary degree in the U.S. system, but may not be able to articulate clearly the nuanced definition of the *credit hour*: this discussion will focus on its key standard definition as a functional requirement for the transfer of credit at the tertiary level.

The definition of the credit hour provides the key to unlock the various formulas required to assess foreign transfer credit. As the quantifying unit of measure of a U.S postsecondary degree, the U.S. credit hour measures what is known as the *contact hour*. The contact hour is an indicator of teaching hours, and assumes that there is a fixed correlation between time in class and total student workload.

The International Affairs Office of the U.S. Department of Education (2010) provides clear functional definitions of the credit hour, categorized into lecture, laboratory and practice coursework:

✳ One lecture (taught) or seminar (discussion) credit hour represents one hour per week of scheduled class/seminar time and two hours of student preparation time. Most lecture and seminar courses are awarded three credit hours. Over an entire semester, this formula represents at least 45 hours of class time and 90 hours of student preparation.

✳ One laboratory credit hour represents one hour per week of lecture or discussion time plus one to two hours per week of scheduled supervised or independent laboratory work, and two hours of student preparation time. Most laboratory courses are awarded up to four credit hours. This calculation represents at least 45 hours of class time, between 45 and 90 hours of laboratory time, and 90 hours of student preparation per semester.

✳ One practice credit hour (supervised clinical rounds, visual or performing art studio, supervised student teaching, field work, etc.) represents three to four hours per week of supervised and/or independent practice. This in turn represents between 45 and 60 hours of work per semester. Blocks of three practice credit hours, which equate to a studio or practice course, represent between 135 and 180 total hours of academic work per semester.

---

[1] The AACRAO EDGE database currently provides 231 country profiles.

Most U.S. colleges and universities follow either a quarter-based or a semester-based calendar system. The *quarter system* divides the calendar year into four quarters, three of which constitute a complete academic year. Quarters are typically ten weeks long so that three quarters amount to 30 weeks of instruction. The *semester system* divides the calendar year into two semesters of 15 weeks each, plus optional summer sessions of varying lengths. The two semesters together constitute 30 weeks of instruction, so that three academic quarters equal two academic semesters. Thus, three quarter hours = two semester hours.

The average full-time student load in the U.S. system is 15 credit hours per semester (or quarter hours per quarter) or 30 credit hours (45 quarter hours) per year. In order to effectively evaluate transfer credit, one must make the additional assumption that that the basic academic content and student academic load is similar across universities and higher education systems. It is generally assumed that over a similar period of time, the notional hours of student learning must be similar, as clock hours and human capacity for learning have natural limits.

How to Decide What to Accept

When developing a policy for the acceptance of foreign credit, a best practice guideline would suggest the following four principles: consistency, clarity, flexibility, and the recognition of the diversity of educational systems around the globe. The National Association of Credential Evaluation Services (NACES 2010) is an association of private educational credential evaluation services committed to formulating and maintaining ethical standards in the field of non-U.S. education evaluation. Its Code of Good Practices outlines some concrete principles that are generally accepted amongst professional credential analysts:

✳ The methodology employed in credential evaluation is based on professionally accepted resources and reference material available to the field of credential evaluation;

✳ To ensure evaluation policies and procedures are periodically reviewed so they are accurate, appropriate, and based on information that takes into account the diversity of educational systems;

✳ To evaluate an academic credential after the recognition/accreditation status of the academic institution and/or program has been established;

✳ To employ in the evaluation process a range of criteria, including, but not limited to:
  ◆ Admission requirements
  ◆ Length of program
  ◆ Program type, structure, and intention
  ◆ Credential/qualification award requirements.

When faced with an unfamiliar credential, it is useful to assess it using a standard set of questions that will allow you to fit the credential into a framework that will illuminate a strategy for the transfer of credit. This exercise will assume that: 1) you have made the commitment to consult standard print and Web resources provided by organizations such as AACRAO, 2) you have already determined that the document is authentic, and 3) the institution has appropriate recognition that will allow you to consider transfer credit. Accepting these assumptions, a standard set of questions would look something like this:

✳ What do you know about the foreign institution/program?

✳ Where does it fit in the country's educational framework?

✳ What is the language of instruction?

✳ What is the level and type of the program? Is it vocational, professional or academic?

✳ What are the normal admission requirements for entrance to the program?

The above set of questions speaks directly to the transfer credit policy of your institution. The discussion as to what might be considered for transfer credit is essentially a discussion that should be a balance between the above overarching principles and the philosophy and institutional policies of the receiving institution. An effective transfer credit policy for foreign credit should be informed by the general transfer credit policies of the receiving institution. These policies are impacted by numerous factors including mission, institutional history, partnerships and market factors. A highly selective institution would normally have more conservative transfer policies than those of a more moderately selective or open enrollment institution. Consider the following:

* What are the general transfer guidelines at your institution? Are those guidelines conservative or liberal?
* Does the transfer policy differ by academic program or department?
* Does your institution award credit for professional or vocational coursework? Military training? Experiential learning? Physical education? Doctrine-based religious studies?
* Does your institution round credit in calculations, and, if so, to how many places?

These are all considerations when developing a strategy for transferring credit from foreign institutions. The basis of each decision should be a sound reflection of the policy for a U.S. institution of the same type and caliber, informing your international credential evaluation policy in a way that is both clear and consistent with overall institutional philosophy and mission.

Upper and Lower Division Credit

The concept of lower division and upper division credit seldom exists outside of the United States. The U.S. undergraduate degree is broad as opposed to deep (or major subject-intensive). European-style degree programs, for example, immerse the student in the major subject almost immediately, so an assumption that 'upper division' course work would only occur during the third and fourth years would be incorrect. Rather than a strict adherence to institutional upper and lower division guidelines, it is better to consider a logic that presumes subject progression, deeming the first course 'lower' due to its introductory nature but allows the second and third courses, regardless of semester or year taken to represent an 'upper division' course in that education system.

Advanced Standing

Secondary study in the U.S. and other countries does not generally warrant advanced placement; however, there are several advanced standing credit opportunities that exist in the U.S. system including The College Board Advanced Placement (AP), the International Baccalaureate (IB), and dual-credit agreements between colleges and high schools. In addition, there are some education systems that are longer in length, encompassing a level of study that is comparable to first-year general education requirements at a U.S. tertiary institution.

In the case of those countries with longer primary/secondary education than that of the U.S., advanced credit standing may be considered. A British "Advanced Level" (A-Level) General Certificate of Education (GCE), after 13 years of education, generally receives credit by institutions all over the United States. Germany, which formerly had a 13-year primary/secondary system, was often given credit for the culminating Abitur examination.

Some U.S. institutions have continued accepting advanced standing practices regardless of the reduction of the system to 12 years; others have discontinued them. As for whether your institution will choose to engage in these practices, consider whether your institution allows credit for dual-enrollment students and whether your IB and AP credit policies are conservative or liberal. These decisions are to be made by each institution based on the same institutional philosophical approach taken with U.S.-based advanced standing mechanisms, so long as credit for longer high school experiences does not extend beyond the freshman courses of the receiving institution.

English-Language Credit

Working with English from non-English-speaking countries (English as a medium of instruction does not mean it is an English-speaking country) is always a challenge for U.S. international credential analysts since the content and level is unlikely to be comparable to the first English or Rhetoric and Composition course offered in U.S. institutions. Know your school's policy on this issue, and err on the side of conservatism. Familiarize yourself with the description of these courses before considering them for transfer. Are the courses truly English Composition as taught on most U.S. campuses? Or are the courses more like English for Speakers of Other Languages (ESOL)? Some institutional policies might not allow for any transfer credit in the latter case; others might allow the coursework to meet a foreign language general education requirement.

Grades

The evaluation of student work (grades) is also a deciding factor in whether to accept coursework for transfer. There are a variety of resources with which to determine appropriate grade scales by country. Individual country-based publications will include grade scales. A more complete resource can be found on AACRAO EDGE, available by subscription, which includes comprehensive grade scale information at both the secondary and tertiary levels of education. World Education Services (WES) provides a free resource listing grade scales for tertiary education on their Web site, wes.org. You will note that a comparison of the offered scales will yield some inconsistencies that need to be reconciled by the credential analyst in accordance with institutional policy.

When adopting a grade conversion practice for your institution, it would be wise to keep several factors in mind.

First, grades can be norm-referenced to the cohort (grading on a curve), or fixed to the individual student performance. Until the recent developments in Europe that introduced the ECTS grade scheme, grades based on student performance were more common.

Second, grades are subjective and culturally located. Some cultures do not generally award the top grade in a scale, believing that to do so would imply impossible perfection; other systems award top grades more frequently. If grades must be converted from the native scale into a U.S. grading system, it should be recognized as a conversion of one subjective means of evaluation to another subjective means of evaluation. An institutional grade conversion policy must be flexible enough to take cultural context into consideration.

Third, consider the grade of 'D'. The definition of the 'D' grade in the U.S. system is a grade that is not satisfactory yet still passing. One must be very careful in determining what is or is not a U.S. grade of 'D'. Most U.S. institutions do not accept in transfer courses passed with a grade of 'D'. When considering a grade scale conversion, be certain that the grade identified from abroad as a 'D' is, in fact, the lowest passing grade in the class but insufficient for graduation if the student made that grade throughout their academic career. In other words, the grade truly needs to be some variation on a condoned pass to be truly labeled a U.S. equivalent grade of 'D'.

Developing a Methodology

The discussion of methodology will be limited to the transfer of postsecondary credentials into the U.S. system. Once the philosophical underpinnings have been applied, we are left with a second set of questions to identify the information required to make credit comparisons. The second set of questions, and the methodology that arises from them, are mathematical in nature.

* How is the work documented?
* What is the average workload (hours/units/subjects) in an academic year?
* What is the normal full-time duration of the program?
* How many hours/units/subjects are required to complete the program?
* Are the documented subjects theory, practice-based or both?

The first barrier to a successful approach is a psychological barrier for the professional who seeks to find the single correct answer to the transfer credit question. Without a single national authority providing concrete policy on the evaluation of foreign credentials, new professionals can find themselves lost in a sea of research that can often provide conflicting results. How does one find the "right" answer? In the words of Dr. James Frey (2003), Founder of Educational Credential Evaluators, Inc. and winner of the 2006 AACRAO Award for Excellence in International Education:

> *Experienced reasonable persons can reach differing conclusions concerning the nature of an educational programme and concerning the equivalence or lack thereof between two educational programmes* (pp. 36–37).

When the education systems of the world are studied, there are patterns that emerge from the above questions that allow one to develop an approach to the evaluation of transfer credit that will encompass most of the major world systems. The methodologies outlined below will allow one to approach the transfer of foreign credit in a clear and consistent manner while allowing for institutional character to influence decision.

There are four basic kinds of documentation of student work: Credit based systems, hours based systems, grade-based systems, and subject based. Following a description of these are recommended approaches to credit transfer for each of these four types of documentation. After understanding the philosophical side of transfer credit, what remains is simple mathematics. Table 8.1 shows basic credit hour equivalencies in the U.S. and can be used as a reference in conversion equations throughout the chapter. Table 8.2 (on page 100) is also a useful tool for a beginning credential analyst to help determine which methodology best fits the credential at hand.

TABLE 8.1: U.S. Credit Hour Equivalencies

Bachelor's Degree	120 Semester Credits (approx) or 180 Quarter Credits (4 years)
1 Year	30 Semester Hours (approx) or 45 Quarter Hours
1 Semester	15 Weeks
1 Quarter	10 Weeks
15 Lecture or Theory Hours + 30 Student Preparation Hours	1 Semester Hour
45 Lab Hours + 30 Student Preparation Hours	1 Semester Hour

Credit-Based Systems

Educational credentials that are credit-based measure and reflect student work in terms of units. We begin with credit-based systems, since this is the most similar to the education systems with which we are most familiar, that of the United States. Examples of credit-based systems can be found in Canada, Australia, throughout Europe, Japan, Thailand, and many others.

To convert a credit-based credential into semester hours useable for transfer:

1. Determine the number of units required to either complete the program, or if unavailable, in an average full-time year.
2. Determine the number of U.S. credits that would be completed in the same timeframe (reference Table 8.1).
3. Find a conversion factor:
   Equivalent U.S. credits in timeframe ÷ Total foreign credits in timeframe = Conversion factor
4. Multiply the foreign credits by the conversion factor to determine the U.S. credits.

See Figures 8.1a and 8.1b (on page 98) for an example of this conversion process.

Hours-Based Credentials

There are many countries, especially in Asia and Eastern Europe, that issue academic records reflecting hours of instruction rather than credits. A formula can be derived using the definitions of the U.S. semester credit

Credit system = ECTS (European Credit Transfer System) 1 year = 60 ECTS [a]

Length of study period = 1yr (approx 30 U.S. semester hours) [b]

Equivalent U.S. credits in timeframe (30) ÷ Total foreign credits in timeframe (60) = Conversion factor (0.5)

Multiply the credits shown by the conversion (0.5) factor to determine the number of credits to assign for each course.

a For a detailed description of the European Credit Transfer System, consult AACRAO EDGE at http://aacraoedge.aacrao.org.

b For our examples, we are assuming semester hours. If your institution operates on the quarter system, you would substitute the semester hour value (30) for the quarter hour value (45).

FIG 8.1B: Conversion Table

Course	ECTS	Conversion Factor	Semester Hours
Introduction to Business Administration	3	0.5	1.5
Private Business Law	4	0.5	2.0
Personnel Management, Leadership, Org Behavior	4	0.5	2.0
Principles of Economics I	4	0.5	2.0
Finance	4	0.5	2.0
Euro & Public Business Law	4	0.5	2.0
Principles of Economics II	4	0.5	2.0
Procurement, Logistics and Production	4	0.5	2.0
Marketing	4	0.5	2.0
Foreign Lang Business Communication I	4	0.5	2.0
Accounting & Management Control I	6	0.5	3.0
Statistics	4	0.5	2.0
			24.5

The following credits, semester and final examinations,
as well as practice and course work have been passed during the term of study.

Name of subject	Number of hours general	Number of hours class work	Final Grade
1. Azerbaijan Language	91.8	51	A
2. English I	91.8	51	A
3. English II	91.8	51	A
4. Survey of Calculus	91.8	51	C
5. Great Questions of Philosophy	61.2	34	B
6. Constitution of Azerbaijan Republic and Bases of Law	61.2	34	C
7. Human Communications	61.2	34	B
8. Great Questions of Philosophy	91.8	51	B
9. English III	91.8	51	A
10. English IV	91.8	51	B
11. Principles of Physics	61.2	34	C
12. Elementary Statistics	91.8	51	B
13. Multivariate Calculus	91.8	51	B
14. Survey of Azerbaijan History	91.8	51	B
15. Survey of Word History	91.8	51	B
16. Introductory Sociology	91.8	51	A
17. Principles of Accounting I	91.8	51	B
18. Principles of Accounting II	91.8	51	B
19. Principles of Microeconomics	91.8	51	B
20. Principles of Macroeconomics	91.8	51	B
21. Introduction to Computer Based Information Systems	91.8	51	A
22. The Environment of Business	91.8	51	C
23. Introduction to Business Statistics	91.8	51	B

Name of subject	Number of hours general	Number of hours class work	Final Grade
24. Generalized Modeling Techniques with Application	91.8	51	B
25. Corporation Finance	91.8	51	B
26. Management Concepts, Theory and Practice	91.8	51	B
27. Basic Marketing	91.8	51	C
28. Managerial Communication	91.8	51	C
29. Introduction to Organizational Behavior	91.8	51	C
30. Becoming A Leader	91.8	51	C
31. Introduction to Human Resource Management	91.8	51	C
32. Work Team Design	91.8	51	C
33. Entrepreneurship and New Venture Management	91.8	51	C
34. Enterpreneurship Field Study	91.8	51	B
35. Operations Management	91.8	51	C
36. Operations Planning and Control	91.8	51	C
37. Project Management Principles	91.8	51	C
38. Small Business Management	91.8	51	C
39. Numerical Analysis	91.8	51	B
40. English V	91.8	51	A
41. America's study	91.8	51	C
42. Strategic Management Policy	91.8	51	B
End of document			

FIG 8.2B: Conversion Table

Course	General Hours	Class Work	Conversion Factor	Semester Hours Precise	Semester Hours Rounded*
1. Azerbaijan Language	91.8	51	15	3.40	3
5. Great Questions of Philosophy	61.2	34	15	2.66	2

* If your institution prefers whole numbers, round to a whole number, as shown.

discussed above and the academic hours listed on the transcript.

To convert an hours-based credential into U.S. semester hours useable for transfer:

1. Determine the number of hours required to either complete the program, or if unavailable, in an average full-time year.
2. Determine the number of U.S. credits that would be completed in the same timeframe (reference Table 8.1, on page 97).
3. Find a conversion factor:

Maximum foreign hours in study period ÷ Equivalent U.S. hours in study period = Conversion factor

4. Multiply the foreign hours by the conversion factor to determine the U.S. credits.[2]

Figure 8.2a shows a translated transcript for a completed program, so we can determine the number of hours for the complete program if needed, but the document provides a better clue—a number of contact hours per course, designated as "class work." Often in this kind of document, the number of contact hours and the number of general work hours are combined.

[2] When dividing the hours by the conversion factor, pay special attention to lab or practice-based subjects, which will require a reduction by 2/3 before conversion.

TABLE 8.2: Credential Assessment Template

	Credit Based	Hours Based	Marks Based	Subject Based
	Units	*Hours*	*Numerical Grades*	*Number of Subjects*
Total in One Year				
Total in Program				
Length of Total Program				
U.S. Hours in One Year	30 or 45	30 or 45	30 or 45	30 or 45
U.S. Hours in Program	120 or 180	120 or 180	120 or 180	120 or 180
U.S. Length of Program	4	4	4	4

The document does not indicate the study period; since the document shows a completed program, our sources indicate that in this system (Azerbaijan), a Bachelor's degree is generally four years.[3] In situations of transfer credit, the document might only reflect coursework and hours with no timeframe. In such a case, an analyst would use the single course as the study period and translate each course accordingly. Since the coursework shown is consistent in terms of hours, this example shows one of each type of course listed. One can assume that the class work is equivalent to contact hours (*see* Figure 8.2b, on page 99).

Since a single course is the indicator of the study period, this example uses fifteen contact hours per credit to determine the conversion.

Marks-Based Credentials

Another type of academic documentation is what is known as grade-based credentials. In this form of credential, there is no specific and separate credit unit per subject taught. In this type of credential, the student's grade indicates the relative weight of the subject in the overall period of study. This type of documentation is often seen in France, India, Pakistan, and others.

To convert a marks-based credential into U.S. credits:

① Determine the maximum possible marks per subject and total marks in the study period.

② Determine the length of the study period and the U.S. credits that would be completed in that same time (reference Table 8.1, on page 97).

③ Find a conversion factor:
U.S. credits in study period ÷ Maximum marks in study period = Conversion factor

④ Divide the foreign hours by the conversion factor to determine the U.S. credits.

Figure 8.3 (on page 101) gives an example of a transcript from a marks-based system, showing conversions into U.S. semester hours.

Subject-Based Credentials

There are some credentials that provide only a list of subjects and the evaluation of those subjects, with no relative weight or other quantifiable unit to be used in conversion. Without any information on weight, credential analysts must assume that each subject carries an equal weight of one. You might find this kind of documentation from the United Kingdom, Australia, and Italy, to name a few. That said, documents of this type are becoming less common. For such documents:

① Determine the total number of subjects completed in the study period.

② Determine the length of the study period and the U.S. credits that would be completed in that same time (reference Table 8.1, on page 97).

---

[3] Consult EDGE country profile or other available reference sources to obtain general information about the system of education reflected in your document.

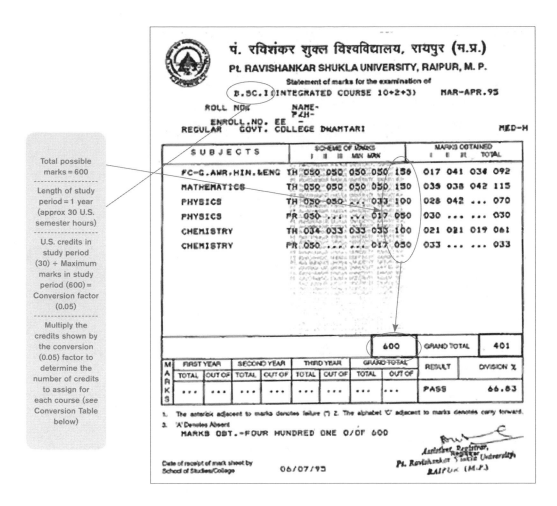

The sidebar annotations read:

Total possible marks = 600

Length of study period = 1 year (approx 30 U.S. semester hours)

U.S. credits in study period (30) ÷ Maximum marks in study period (600) = Conversion factor (0.05)

Multiply the credits shown by the conversion (0.05) factor to determine the number of credits to assign for each course (see Conversion Table below)

FIGURE 8.3B: Conversion Table

Subject	Max Marks	Conversion Factor	Semester Hours Assigned
FC-G. Awr, Hind, & Eng	150	0.05	7.5
Mathematics	150	0.05	7.5
Physics	100	0.05	5.0
Physics	50	0.05	2.5
Chemistry	100	0.05	5.0
Chemistry	50	0.05	2.5

Conversion of Marks-Based Credentials into Semester Hours

FIGURE 8.3A/B

FIGURE 8.4A/B

Conversion of Subject-Based Credentials into Semester Hours

OXFORD BROOKES UNIVERSITY		MODULAR PROGRAMME TRANSCRIPT	
NAME	TIMUR KAMALOV		
QUALIFICATION AWARDED	None		
DATE AWARDED			
REGISTERED SUBJECTS	Economics and International Relations		
ACCREDITATION	Not applicable		

YEAR 2009 - 2010

Module	Title	Grade	Mark
U23101	Democracy: the Individual and Society	B+	68
U23201	Introduction to International Relations	B+	62
U52002	Microeconomics 1	B+	63
U61500	Foundation A in French	C	46
U70910	Academic Writing for Business	B	56

**************************** end of this page ****************************

I hereby certify that this document is a true copy of the signed original seen by me on this day 20 01 2010, Winchester University

FIGURE 8.4B: Conversion Table

Subject	Relative Weight	Conversion Factor	Semester Hours
Democracy: The Individual and Society	1	3	3
Intro to International Relations	1	3	3
Microeconomics I	1	3	3
Foundation A in French	1	3	3
Academic Writing for Business	1	3	3

③ Find a conversion factor:

U.S. credits in the same study period ÷ Total subjects in study period = Number of credits per subject

Looking at the example in Figure 8.4a, a total of five subjects were completed in the study period.

Determining the study period can be tricky in this case—some institutions offer subjects in a year-long format; others offer them in a semester style format. We might need to consult the institution Web site or other documents in the student's file to determine the length of the study period. Based on other information in the file, it was determined in this case that the student studied at the institution for one semester, which translates to approximately fifteen semester hours.

We then divide the credit equivalent (fifteen) by the total number of subjects for the period (five), resulting in a conversion factor of three. Figure 8.4b applies this conversion factor to each subject.

Foreign Credential Evaluation: A Fluid Process Based on A Solid Foundation

It is important to note that some education systems might produce more than one type of documentation to reflect student work. In addition, the emergence of the European Credit Transfer System (ECTS) and other national and international projects aimed at increasing student mobility will ensure that credential analysts will need to stay current as systems adapt and change at uneven rates. We will continue to see varying credentials within a single education system for quite some time. A consistent application of the principles described in this chapter will help to hone the skills of a new credential analyst, building a base skill and confidence level that will allow them to approach more complex credentials.

In the end, it is a combination of research, accepted methodology, consistency of practice and institutional philosophy that allows the credential analyst to take the leap of faith required to come to a decision. The methodologies outlined above, in combination with a clear institutional philosophy, are designed to free the credential analyst from the need to find the absolute answer so they can develop an understanding of the continuum of correct answers that will serve both the student and the institution well.

NINE

The International Aspects of
Enrollment
Management

2010 AACRAO INTERNATIONAL GUIDE

CHRIS J. FOLEY | Director of Undergraduate Admissions
Indiana University–Purdue University Incianapolis

The International Aspects of Enrollment Management

Few concepts have been "hotter" in higher education in the past 40 years than "enrollment management." The efforts to define, refine and implement enrollment management throughout universities and colleges have led to massive reorganizations, new budgets and more research. Within the professions of higher education, we now have conferences devoted to the topic and a new classification of university administrator: the enrollment manager. Without a doubt, enrollment management is a critical element to today's higher education, and it must be understood by those who work within a university setting. This is ever more critical for international educators if they want to be successful within the modern university. This chapter will focus, not on the specifics of enrollment management—there are countless other resources for that—but instead on how international educators can learn the basic concepts of enrollment management. This chapter will also not provide comprehensive overviews of the parts of enrollment management (*e.g.*, admissions, recruitment, scholarships), but will concentrate on providing the guide by which to put the pieces of the puzzle together.

To begin, we must define enrollment management. For an academic definition, we will start with the one Hossler, Bean and Associates proposed in 1990: "Enrollment management is an organizational concept and systematic set of activities designed to enable educational institutions to exert more influence over their student enrollments. Organized by strategic planning and supported by institutional research, enrollment management activities concern student college choice, transition to college, student attrition and retention,

and student outcomes" (1990, p. 5). In short, enrollment management is a concept by which universities and colleges try to control the size and composition of its student body.

In a more applied sense, enrollment management can be traced back to the work of Frank Campenella and Jack Maguire at Boston College in the 70s. At the time, Maguire (1976) noted that "enrollment management is a process that brings together often disparate functions having to do with recruiting, funding, tracking, retaining, and replacing students as they move toward, within, and away from the university." Later, he would say, "enrollment management was developed to bring about a synergy among functions such as admissions, financial aid, and retention, which too often were viewed as independent and working at cross purposes" (Britz 1998).

Whether you prefer the academic definition of Hossler *et al* or the more practitioner-based version put forth by Maguire, it is clear that enrollment management focuses on determining how many students to enroll, what kinds of students to enroll and how to optimize student services. Research is needed on which to base decisions, as well as concern for the costs involved with recruiting, serving and retaining students. It is with the introduction of enrollment management that the concepts of "cost-benefit," "return on investment" and "sculpting" or "crafting" a student body have begun to gain traction in the conversations and debates among a university's administrators. Though enrollment management as a unit may reside in a single office on a campus, the terminology and concepts of enrollment management go far beyond those officially responsible for it.

FIGURE 9.1

Enrollment Funnel

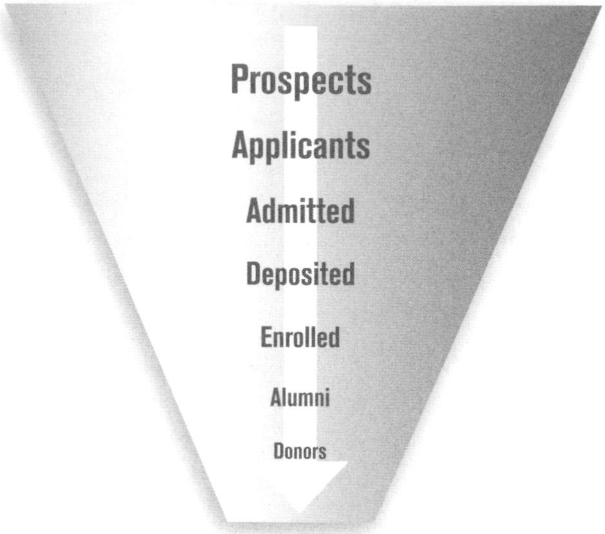

Prospects

Applicants

Admitted

Deposited

Enrolled

Alumni

Donors

FIGURE 9.2

Enrollment Life-Cycle*

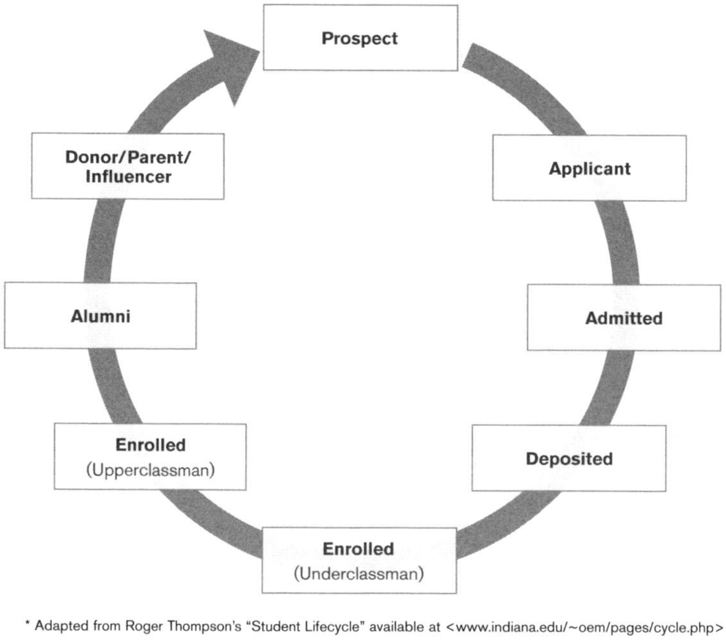

Prospect

Applicant

Donor/Parent/Influencer

Admitted

Alumni

Deposited

Enrolled (Upperclassman)

Enrolled (Underclassman)

* Adapted from Roger Thompson's "Student Lifecycle" available at <www.indiana.edu/~oem/pages/cycle.php>

There are two visual concepts that are common to enrollment managers. The first, the "enrollment funnel," focuses on the progression of students through their interactions with the university. Typically, the funnel begins with prospects (*i.e.*, those students who have shown or may show an interest in your particular institution). The funnel is wide at the top, indicating that it takes many more prospects to build your class. The bottom of the funnel may end with enrollees. However, some enrollment managers may extend the funnel to include graduates, active alumni and donors. (*See* Figure 9.1.)

Though the enrollment funnel is good at demonstrating the numerical differences between the separate stages of enrollment, it does not demonstrate the cyclical nature of university enrollments. The second concept, the "enrollment life-cycle," helps make this connection. (*See* Figure 9.2.)

Between these two figures, we see that enrollment management is based on the institution's relationship with students over time. Enrollment management acknowledges that this relationship changes and that not all students will progress to each next stage, but it also allows for an institution to better manage its enrollments and plan for the use of resources to accomplish its institutional enrollment goals.

The "Enrollment Portfolio"

In an interview with *The Greentree Gazette*, Art Kirk of St. Leo University[4] compared running a university to running a mutual fund. In his comparison, creating the right student "enrollment portfolio" is similar to developing an investment portfolio—an apt metaphor, in my opinion. Each year, institutions try to recruit and enroll not just the right number of students, but also the right "mix" of

----

[4] The interview is available at www.todayscampus.com/minute/load.aspx?art=1428.

students (for example, geographic origin, ethnicity, academic preparation, socio-economic status, etc.). As with investment portfolios, it is important to diversify your enrollment portfolio to minimize the impact of any single negative influence. If you put all of your eggs in one basket, you are open to significant trouble if that basket is dropped. Adding international students to your "enrollment portfolio" is another way to diversify your enrollment and insulate your institution from drops in enrollments from other segments.

For example, if Big Campus State University depends on a significant portion of its revenue from non-resident tuition (predominantly from New York, New Jersey and Chicago), and an economic crisis hits these particular cities (like the one which began in the latter half of 2008), Big Campus State University may look to ramping up its international recruitment as a way to replace these non-resident tuition dollars. Moreover, exchange rates can make your institution less expensive when the dollar is weak. So even though their countries may be having economic difficulties as well, a U.S. education may actually become cheaper due to fluctuating exchange rates.

An important note: the international portion of an enrollment portfolio is not a single segment, but a collection of smaller ones. You should also diversify within your international segment of the enrollment portfolio in order to minimize enrollment drops from one particular country. If a university relies on students from a single government scholarship program, for example, your segment may disintegrate overnight if the country's government discontinues the scholarship or shifts its scholarship dollars to another U.S. university. Or, in another example, if a university is overly concentrated on enrollments from a handful of countries, and the economies in these countries flounder, so could the international enrollments. This happened at the end of the twentieth century with Southeast and East Asia, and those schools that relied on students from South Korea, Malaysia and Indonesia were hit hard by the financial distress.

But just as with investment portfolios, over diversification can also impede success. Diluting your resources across too many international markets will dilute your results. It is important to know your institution's limitations and build an enrollment plan that is credible for your success. As a general rule, I recommend targeting 10 to 20 countries in two to four geographic regions of the world. Within these markets designate primary, secondary and tertiary markets (for example, Mumbai, Bangalore and Chennai may be primary markets and the rest of India may be a tertiary market). This allows you to prioritize how you will react to recruitment opportunities in each area. It also allows you to develop communities of students with common cultures on your campus.

Once you know the segments of your enrollment portfolio, you have to build pipelines. Pipelines cannot be built overnight, and it is important to be invested at the right time in a particular market to take advantage of a boom in interest from a particular country. Here, again, the investment portfolio metaphor is apt. Like investment positions, timing is critical. You have to invest over time (in the case of enrollments, these investments can take two to three years to develop) to build the right contacts, prospect pool, alumni, etc. to guarantee a good return. Moreover, if you see an opportunity develop (like a sudden shift in a country's interest in attending U.S. universities), those institutions who are already there will see the greatest benefit. Chances are, upon seeing the opportunity, it may already be too late.

Determining the right mix is important, and this must be done on an institution-by-institution case. You need to determine the resources you have to devote, your tolerance for risk and your enrollment goals, and you must have patience. All of these requirements are similar to those of developing an investment portfolio and, like investment portfolios, creating the right enrollment portfolio and establishing an international position in it can prove essential to weathering the changing winds of enrollment patterns.

The International Elements of Enrollment Management

To remain successful, international services and recruitment offices must understand the basics of enrollment management. Depending on the institution, enrollment management may focus on the recruitment and enrollment of students, or it may extend to retention programs, possibly even crossing into alumni and development. From an international perspective, enrollment management could include the programming and advising for international students, study abroad programs, institutional marketing, internship and co-op opportunities and alumni relations, in addition to the recruitment and initial enrollment of international students.

From a return on investment perspective, international recruitment is an expensive investment. International travel is expensive, the cost to evaluate international credentials is cumbersome and specialists to work with international students are also generally more costly than the typical "road warrior" of a domes-

International educators, then, must understand the enrollment management principles employed by their university or college (and, thankfully, not all of them revolve around revenue generation like the one above) to understand how best to engage administrators and develop support. Though the example above revolves around recruitment, it could just as easily revolved around on-campus services (international students require immigration advising and specialized programming), alumni (international alumni are more difficult to track) or academic services (international students are often more frequent users of academic support services [like writing centers]).

Note that the example above is highly quantitative. Enrollment managers often prefer to look at numbers and use "dashboards." Qualitative data, though helpful, is too cumbersome for most enrollment management decisions because it takes a long time to compile and analyze and may or may not be applicable to a general population. Instead, enrollment managers prefer easily-delivered (though often complex to design and develop) metrics that can be summarized in simple reports. These "dashboards" are the "vital signs" of the institution's enrollments and are used to quickly assess where there are problems and then quickly design and implement interventions.

TABLE 9.1: The Traditional Return-on-Investment Comparison of International Recruitment at a Public Institution

Student Type	Cost to Recruit 1 Student	Revenue from Tuition over 4 years		Return on Investment (Per Dollar Spent) for 1 Student
		Total	Per Year	
In-State Student	$200	$24,000	$6,000	$120
Out-of-State Student	$500	$60,000	$15,000	$120
International Student	$1,000	$60,000	$15,000	$60

tic admissions office. A simple example of this equation is the cost to recruit a student to a public institution.

In the example in Table 9.1 (which admittedly is very simplistic), the return for each dollar spent to recruit an international student is nearly half that for domestic students. If the discussion simply revolved around tuition generation and limited resources existed, the enrollment manager (or enrollment committee) would most likely place the university's resources in recruiting domestic students because he or she would have to spend more money to recruit fewer students if he recruited international students.

The challenge for international educators is to engage in these types of conversations, and be able to speak about their office's activities in the terms of enrollment management. This can be difficult for international educators who are accustomed to thinking in terms of international education as a "social good" that has positive consequences for the university (and even society) as a whole. However, in an enrollment management environment, simply saying something is worthwhile is not sufficient. There are many valuable engagements for a university; in a world of diminishing resources, a university must choose between many worthwhile activities. The challenge for international educators is understanding not only how to communicate the importance of international activities, but argue that they entail a better investment of university resources than other options on the table.

Market and Institutional Research

As noted earlier, decisions in an enrollment management context are typically data-driven. Anecdotes and information "from the field" can be helpful to understand the nuances of quantitative data, but any enrollment management decision will have quantitative data as its underlying foundation. However, perhaps the most remarkable difference between the data used in enrollment management and that of academic research, is that the enrollment manager rarely has complete data and analysis. A need to react quickly means that the enrollment manager must gather as much data beforehand as possible, establish regular reports to monitor key indicators, integrate new data as needed to determine what is happening in the enrollment landscape and take any necessary action to maximize the effect of programs to recruit, retain and graduate students.

In general, international enrollment managers have had a harder time getting data on their students. Often, they are excluded from discussions of key indicators and, worse still, from the systems that will be used to recruit, retain and graduate students. As a result, the first step for international enrollment managers is to not just access data, but start collecting it for future use.

There are two types of data to be reviewed: institutional data and market data. Institutional data will help you understand your current state of international enrollments and recruitment funnels, while market data will allow you to put the institutional data into context as well as identify potential markets.

INSTITUTIONAL DATA

Of course, planning must begin with an accurate review of your current situation, and a good effort at intro-

spection is the best place to start. International educators need to know not only how many international students are on campus, but more granular data points:

* Where do they come from?
* What are their retention rates (first to second semester, first to second year)?
* What are the graduation rates of international students?
* What is your yield on prospects to applicants? Admit rate? Admits to enrollees?
* What are your most popular majors?
* Do they require financial assistance?
* What are the graduation rates of students who study abroad? Do they come from specific majors?
* What portion of your graduate research assistants or graduate instructors are international students?
* Do your graduates return home?
* Do your graduates get jobs?
* Do your graduates donate to the institution?

Most importantly, how does this data compare to the similar data points for the general population of the university? If they compare positively, this can be a good reason to expand these elements of the institution's portfolio. If negatively, they may require resources to improve.

Unfortunately, many institutions neglect to build information systems that are sufficient to collect robust data sets for international students. Things as simple as sufficient space for international addresses in information systems or the ability to manage international naming conventions (for example, space limitations or students with single names) are often overlooked. However, for international students, information about visa status, schools of origin, and non-U.S. addresses can be just as critical to enrollment management as to domestic enrollment management.

MARKET DATA

From a recruitment perspective, knowing where to recruit is just as important as how to recruit international students. Though institutional data is most helpful, it is data about the students not currently at your institution that will help you place this data into context and determine the following:

* How mature are the markets you are currently strong in?
* Is there potential to grow these markets?
* Where are similar markets that you have yet to tap into?
* Who are your competitors in both established and new markets?

The first rule of thumb is to not ignore those international students already in the United States. For many colleges and universities, the U.S. is the largest feeder country of international students. These students are exchange students, dependents of staff working in businesses in the U.S., dependents of government staff, recent immigrants or students at boarding schools. Many times these students are overlooked by U.S. university recruitment programs because they are not "domestic" from a citizenship perspective as well as not "international" from an education background. But they are, in an international recruitment perspective, right in your backyard. And, for this population, market data is more easily accessible.

For students in other countries, the amount of market data available is not as robust as that for domestic recruitment. Still, there is information about international enrollments that will allow you to make some assessment of market potential. Here are a few sources:

* *Open Doors* is an annual survey of international student enrollments and study abroad published by the Institute of International Education (IIE). Though this report does not allow for granular analysis, it does allow you to determine a general idea of your market position. For example, if you see that there are 216 students from Kazakhstan studying in the U.S., and you have 22 of them, you understand that you have 10 percent of the market share of Kazakhstani students who are studying in the United States. Moreover, you can see that it would be

unlikely to recruit hundreds of students from Kazakhstan because that would represent a significant increase in these students, not only at your institution, but also in the United States.

* The *Atlas of Student Mobility*, also published by IIE, is a more thorough analysis of student flows to and from countries. Though not all countries are profiled in this resource, it does have a good representation. The data include not only numbers of students studying abroad, but their top destinations, as well as demographic data (like college-aged population and average income) that help enrollment managers understand the viability of expanding a market in a particular country.

* Testing services (like SAT or TOEFL) publish annual digests of their results. These digests include information on international students who took the examinations, and, in some cases, the testing service will provide greater access to this information for research (like the Enrollment Planning Service through the College Board). These latter tools allow you to see how many students took their tests and their grades, as well as family data. For a test like the SAT, you not only know how many good students are in a particular country, but how many of them are intending to study in the U.S. (since the SAT is an exam typically taken only by students hoping to study in the U.S.).

* Developing a data-sharing consortium with peer institutions can also be beneficial. Though perhaps more cumbersome than the other data sources (a quick web-search or book away), understanding what happens at similar institutions can be even more helpful because student flows will differ from institution to institution. Urban institutions, for example, will attract a different type of student than rural institutions.

Enrollment Modeling

Enrollment management involves understanding the future of your enrollments. Most often this leads to the development of a predictive model (usually based on a statistical analysis of historical trends) to estimate the size of the incoming class. In this case, the earlier you can predict the size and composition of the class, the greater lead time it gives the rest of the university to prepare for the incoming class. Other models might include retention rates or even models that would allow for interventions for students experiencing trouble. Because enrollment management incorporates return on investment (ROI), being able to predict the results of an initiative before it is conducted can assist in determining the initiative's worth. Accurate predictions of international enrollments not only impact the overall enrollment numbers, but also affect such disparate items as specific course enrollments (*e.g.*, English language training) and family student housing (for those students who bring their families with them to the United States.).

Enrollment modeling is both a science and an art. While statistical models can accurately predict the future in many cases, it can only do so reliably if the future behaves in a fashion similar to the past. Changes in the economy, admission standards, dismissal policy or a variety of other factors can throw an enrollment model, no matter how robust, for a loop. It is the art of enrollment managers, then, to compensate for what the model is not able to take into consideration.

From an international perspective, modeling can be especially difficult. The numbers are generally small; therefore it is complicated to do adequate analysis. In addition, the diversity of international students and their backgrounds (*e.g.*, different cultures, countries, educational backgrounds, economic shifts, country relationships) can cause significant shifts that undermine the value of past trends. For example, what enrollment manager could have predicted the Asian Economic Crisis of the late 90s or the decision by the Saudi government to fund large numbers of its students to come to the U.S. (as well as other countries)? It is difficult, then, to adequately include international enrollments (either new or continued) into a reliable model.

As a result, it is ever more important to incorporate your international team into conversations about future or continued enrollments. As a specialist in international education, you can add a perspective of what is going on "in the field" to help inform enrollment management decisions. With your experience and knowledge, you can adjust the models to reflect what is happening globally or at the specific country level. If presented appropriately, enrollment managers will appreciate the added input to help make their models more accurate and responsive to current international conditions—both on and off campus.

Admissions and Recruitment

International applications are usually handled by either a sub-unit of the admissions office or the international advising office. Though neither model is superior to the other, each does have particular strengths and weaknesses.

When housed with domestic admissions it is easier for the international admissions unit to stay on the same page with domestic admissions standards and recruitment. In addition, the unit can gain efficiencies in recruitment by piggy-backing with domestic initiatives, realize savings by bundling publications and tap into data entry pools and contracting with fulfillment houses that handle mass mailing tasks. However, because it becomes part of a larger admissions office, it is possible for the international admissions office to get sidelined or pushed aside. Since the bulk of most enrollments at U.S. colleges and universities are made up of domestic students, the international admissions professionals may have to fight to make sure their needs are met in this environment, and they can be seen as an irritant in recruitment initiatives (for example, always needing that extra address line in the database or determining for certain that the SAT may not be taken in some countries).

In the international services setting, the situation is almost the opposite. Here, the international admissions unit is valued because it is the source of the students they serve, and there is an understanding of "things international." However, here the international admissions group may not have the resources necessary to recruit and process applications from abroad (*e.g.*, travel budgets, adequate technology, etc.) or an office that values efficient processing of applications. In addition, staff may be pulled away to advise current students in busy times. Moreover, international admissions practices and policies may get out of sync with domestic admissions policies which can lead to equity issues.

Either model can be successful as long as there is sufficient support of the international admissions unit. Like many things in enrollment management systems, communication and coordination is the key. In some cases a hybrid model can be developed where parts of the admissions and recruitment responsibility are shared across departmental boundaries.

In most cases recruitment and admissions of international students are very similar to that of domestic students. In an increasingly globalized world, the expectations of prospective undergraduates are similar whether in New York or Seoul. The growing involvement of u.s. "helicopter" parents in the recruitment process is not new to international recruiters long used to recruiting parents as much as students. A focus on outcomes, rankings and speedy, personal responses are important to both international and domestic applicants. However, despite their similarities, international applications typically differ in three major ways that are important for enrollment managers to remember (or be reminded of): credentials evaluation, visa documentation, and language barriers.

CREDENTIALS EVALUATION

International students typically come from a different educational system. This means that somewhere in the admissions process, someone will need to interpret their international academic records so that they can be assessed using admission standards typically developed for students from u.s. high schools. This usually involves specialized skills, either held by in-house staff or obtained by contracting with a credentials evaluation agency. (For more information about which is better for your university, see Chapters 6 and 8.)

VISA DOCUMENTATION

Besides international credentials, international students also require visa documentation to gain entrance into the United States. Though not all international students will require international visa documentation, the majority will, and it is essential that universities maintain their ability to issue this documentation. This adds a crucial element to the international aspects of enrollment management because it involves an element of necessary compliance with federal policy. Like being a provider of financial assistance, universities assume a certain level of legal obligation to comply with federal immigration policies. This can come with investments in the training and staff necessary to remain in compliance with federal regulations, but it can also be a helpful trump card in debates over resources because remaining in compliance is not optional, it is a necessity.

Part of this process is, of course, the demonstration by students that they have adequate funding to support their studies in the United States. Collecting and reviewing this information can be cumbersome for the student as well as the office, and it is another element that universities must account for in their enrollment management plans. However, the benefit of receiving this information gives universities yet another indicator of a student's intentions to enroll. If a student submits this required information, enrollment is more likely, and, if they do not, odds are they will not be enrolling at all because they cannot enter the United States.

LANGUAGE BARRIERS

Though not applicable to all international students, language barriers can prove real issues in working with international students. Even those students whose native language is English are often unfamiliar with the vocabularies used in u.s. universities. Even familiar terms like "transcript," "high school," "college," "grade" or "credit" can be foreign to non-u.s. educated students, regardless of their native language. The concept of having to apply for college is commonly unfamiliar to non-u.s. students as well. Therefore, it is crucial for the international offices to continuously work within the enrollment management setting to ensure that student service units are linguistically "international friendly."

Scholarships and Financial Assistance

International students are typically not eligible for federal or state financial assistance, thus international students must privately fund much of their education. Because of this, scholarships can be important in recruiting and retaining international students. In addition to assisting students fund their education, scholarships are an important source of prestige for international students. U.S. parents generally appreciate being able to say that their student is going to university "on scholarship"—regardless of the size of the scholarship. This is often the case for international societies as well. A scholarship can "leverage" a student's decision to enroll at the university.

In many enrollment management systems, the role of scholarships is highly sophisticated. Because many scholarships essentially discount tuition, properly planning for them is critical to ensure that the institution maximizes its revenue while attracting the right types of students to the institution. Moreover, it is necessary to make sure the scholarship offer hits the right "price point," thus influencing the student enough to enroll. If the university offers too little financial assistance, the student may not enroll. However, if the university offers too much, then the university loses money that could be used for other things (including scholarships for other students). In the domestic context, these packaging strategies can be quite sophisticated. It is important, then, for international educators to be "at the table" during scholarship discussions.

The inclusion of international students in general scholarship schemes can differ by type of institution. It is more common for private institutions to package international students along with their domestic students. Public institutions, on the other hand, are less likely to do so because they may have fewer scholarships for non-resident students. Since international students are often lumped into the non-resident pool, they may not be eligible for scholarships at public institutions.

Criteria can be another common difficulty for scholarship awards to international students. For instance, if a scholarship requires a certain SAT or ACT score, but your institution does not require an SAT or ACT score for international students, then many will not be eligible. For this reason, it is important for international educators to be present in scholarship discussions to make sure that criteria do not inadvertently exclude international students or that alternative awarding criteria is available.

Study Abroad

Up to this point, we have been primarily focused on the elements of enrollment management that concern the degree-seeking student. In addition, we have also focused on the "import" side of the international equation—that is, the recruitment and serving of students coming to the U.S. from abroad. However, another element of this equation is the "export" of U.S. students to other countries. Study abroad incorporates both of these elements—the short-term, non-degree seeker from abroad and the U.S. student interested in studying in another country.

Study abroad is increasingly critical to enrollment management. As an education featuring an international component becomes ever more important, U.S. students are looking for universities that can offer a wide range of study abroad opportunities. While offering them is necessary, managing them requires resources. Advisors should possess familiarity with study abroad options, but it is still necessary to devote resources to developing and overseeing these programs. Destinations require continuous review to ensure the safety of students, and procedures need to be developed to handle emergencies and crises.

There is also a fiscal element to study abroad. Because U.S. colleges charge tuition to their students, they must plan for students to study at another institution and make fiscal arrangements that will not inappropriately compromise the university's budget. For example, in the traditional exchange program model, students typically exchange seats. The U.S. student continues to pay tuition to the U.S. institution, and the international student does the same at his or her institution. As long as these exchanges are 1:1, the U.S. university is generally fine. However, when not enough U.S. students participate in the exchange, U.S. institutions can find themselves giving away seats to the incoming exchange students. It is therefore important for institutions to carefully integrate exchange programs into their enrollment planning.

Immigration, Taxes, Health Insurance

There are very real legal obligations to enrolling international students. Failure to comply with federal regulations and laws can lead to an institution not being allowed to enroll international students. As with federal financial aid law or human subjects compliance, adherence to these laws and regulations is not optional, but mandatory. Though a university may debate how much to spend on international recruitment, they are not likely to endanger their ability to enroll any international students; thus making sure that your international student services is abiding by these regulations is imperative.

In addition to having to demonstrate that they have the funds to afford your institution, international students must also show proof that they have health insurance before they enter the country. In some cases, the health insurance from their home country may extend to their stay in the U.S., but in many cases it will not. As a result, international students need consideration during the negotiation of student health plans.

Thirdly, there is the issue of taxes. In many cases international students must file U.S. income tax forms, but these present complications due to tax treaties. Given that international students are often also graduate students on fellowships, assistantships or grants, deciding how to correctly file their taxes (or whether they have to do so at all) can seem a daunting task to international students. While the process may seem for-

eign to many U.S. citizens, for international students it is truly foreign!

Technology

Over the past twenty years, nothing has been more noticeable in the university environment than the integration of technology throughout the campus landscape. Thomas Friedman noted this impact of technology in his book, *The World Is Flat*. On the university campus, technology serves many purposes, whether it is email or instant messaging for recruitment, portals for enrolled students or text messaging for emergency notifications, technology is fast becoming the "go to" solution. Strong enrollment managers look to technological solutions to help them develop, implement and evaluate their plans. Moreover, they are looking to technology to reduce costs while providing better service.

International student offices are not unfamiliar with technology—especially since the roll-out of SEVIS after 9/11. However, there is a tendency to regard this sort of software as "niche," therefore it may not be as fully supported as other technologies. The risks of poor or flawed technology for international offices can be high. If an information system does not adequately track the visa status of students or if visa documents are not quickly and easily produced for prospective students, there can be severe repercussions—possibly even legal consequences for either the student or the university.

It is vital, then, for enrollment managers who are interested in adding an international segment to their "enrollment portfolio" to make sure that they are looking at solutions that will encompass the international student and that the expectation exists for technology to be integrated into the plans to improve the means of recruiting and retaining students.

For the most part students will demand technology. They will look for you on social networking sites, ask for your IM username and become annoyed if you do not have an online application. Moreover, they will expect the technology to function properly and, most importantly, to be *intuitive*. Students (especially prospective students) will walk away from a university whose technology is difficult to use. And if a student encounters difficulty, your help desk staff must be prepared to work with students who have communication difficulties and may even be out of the country.

Take Web sites, for instance. In my experience, U.S. universities have a great amount of information on their Web sites, but it is poorly organized and, even more disappointing, only accessible through a weak search engine. If your Web site is difficult to navigate, it gives the impression that your campus will be difficult to negotiate as well. The international student (or any student) is likely to walk away from it (and your institution).

A good enrollment manager, however, does not simply purchase technology for the sake of implementing technology. Technology can be expensive to purchase (direct costs) and implement (operational costs as well as opportunity costs), and those who look to be on the "cutting edge" often find that it is the "bleeding edge." It is also important to remember that technology does not always (and rarely does) equal savings in staff resources. In fact, technology typically allows you to do more than you were doing before, and that means that you will need additional staff to plan and execute this new functionality.

Therefore, though technology is increasingly essential to recruiting and serving students, it is important that a great deal of care and assessment be done to make sure that any new technology is a good investment—in other words, that the ROI is positive. Perhaps the best decision regarding a technological product is simply to walk away and consider it again at a different time.

Alumni

As we saw in the student life cycle, the relationship between the university and student does not end with graduation. Because of this, enrollment management should be closely linked with alumni associations and university foundations. The missions of each of these units co-mingle with those of enrollment managers,

and it is vital that they do the same for international alumni as well. Alumni can prove to be great contributors to recruitment (*e.g.*, by hosting receptions or contacting prospective students), retention (*e.g.*, by helping students see the value of a degree through co-ops or internships) and fundraising (*e.g.*, for scholarships). Not only that, but enrollment management activities (such as marketing) can also help support the missions of the alumni association and foundation by generating "buzz" about their alma mater. Education is investing in oneself, but the value of this investment can change over time—depending upon the reputation of the university. This reputation is built not only by the activities of faculty and athletics, but also by the students who apply and enroll to the institution. Just as growing interest from a prospective student is a good thing for an institution, so is it good for alumni because the "value" of the degree they already have grows as well. Therefore it is important for enrollment management offices to work closely with their alumni offices and their foundations for mutual benefit.

In Summation

Enrollment management is increasingly crucial to the enrollment success of universities and colleges. With an emphasis on resource management, data-driven decisions and long-term planning, enrollment management has become more than a simple office or division on college campuses; it is now a philosophy of developing synergies across units. International educators must adopt the language and methodologies of enrollment management to maximize their effectiveness in garnering support for the internationalization of their campuses. By being effective stewards of their resources, while also using elements of enrollment management to "plug into" conversations around the university, international educators can participate in, as well as lead enrollment conversations within U.S. colleges and universities.

TEN

International Undergraduate Admissions Checklist

MARILEE HONG | International Academic Specialist (Retired)
Office of Enrollment Services
San Diego State University

2010 AACRAO INTERNATIONAL GUIDE

International Undergraduate Admissions Checklist

This chapter will be devoted to the components of admitting international students (students entering with an F-1 visa), whether with international documents only, international and U.S. documents or U.S. documents only, and will focus on undergraduate admissions issues. As in any other area of international policymaking, this is an ever-changing arena dependent on current issues, budget, the political makeup of your campus and leadership.

The perspective for this chapter is based upon my 35 years of experience working in what is now Enrollment Services, which includes the admissions and evaluations/advising offices. This office handles the processing of international applications for both graduate and undergraduate programs, as well as the evaluation of international documents for incoming applicants and continuing students who study abroad internationally. The office also manages the entry of corresponding information in an automated degree-audit system.

As a public institution it is essential to adhere to legislative guidelines and policies. At the same time gray areas are handled differently within various sister institutions based on interpretation of policy. Whether your school is a public or private institution, has a staff of one or many or your office encompasses various offices on campus, invariably everyone deals with the same issues. Issues will certainly arise as you encounter the need to modify procedures from those followed for domestic students. The process continually evolves as new issues surface.

It is to be hoped that this chapter will provide awareness of the complexity of setting up the international student's admissions process, evaluation and notification. Other chapters in this publication will undoubtedly deal more in depth with some of these issues. The significant point is that you are not alone in facing these issues; hence it is a good idea to share your questions and concerns through networking with all types of schools, helping you to find what will work best for your institution. Perhaps a process will fail in the beginning making it necessary to reorganize or communicate with different areas on your campus. A single office is usually only a small part of a larger administrative whole. In addition, remember that, like anything else, mistakes represent learning experiences in the constant striving to improve our part of the whole.

Location—Enrollment Services versus International Student Center

❋ If a separate International Student Center exists, does that Center wish to assume responsibility for the admission and evaluation of international students? At what point will this Center's process merge with another office? From a budget standpoint, will this process be housed separately or in conjunction with another office such as Enrollment Services? In your institution, Enrollment Services may be the office that handles registration, recordkeeping of transcripts, notification of enrollment, evaluations, advising, prospective students, etc. What aspects will each office handle?

❋ What is the size of the population being served or processed?

International Application

❋ In the development of a separate application, determine paper vs. online, and obtain information from the appropriate entities on the data fields needed in this application. Is there a system ready to read online applications or staff to enter data from paper? Is a system with online access to and between different offices on the campus consistent with the purpose of the application process?

* If at a public institution, does your state have a system-wide online or paper application, or are you tailoring specifically for your campus only?

* Are you under legislative mandate to ask for specific information? Online information can also track statistics and maintain various reports you may be asked to provide for enrollment management purposes.

* Decide on the open period for the acceptance of applications, and, if a deadline is set, determine if it is firm or if appeals will be allowed. Is the staff provided with sufficient time to process and evaluate applications, as well as ask for supplemental information and documents and notify issuance of an I-20, etc.?

Initial Contact—The Person(s) Responsible for Disseminating Information to an International Student

* In the case of a prospective student, is your program set up to handle queries about the range of offerings and disseminate key information, including admissions requirements, filing periods and deadlines? Who notifies students when documents are needed to complete the applicant's file? Once admitted, who does the follow-up for enrollment verification, financial statements and intent to enroll? Is there a separate Web site for international students with information about an International Student Center and the services it provides? Is the Web site maintained and updated?

* Are there provisions for special populations (*e.g.*, athletes, undocumented, disabilities, etc.)?

Where are official transcripts received?

* Do all your incoming transcripts come to one office; if so, which office—your international center or

admissions? Are they then identified as an international document, scanned or routed (risking loss of documents)? Are transcripts mainstreamed so as to be treated the same as domestic transcripts?

Official versus Unofficial

* What is your campus's definition of an official or unofficial transcript? Can they be copied or hand carried in a sealed envelope? Is the policy on acceptance of tertiary documents different from that of secondary ones? Are copies accepted initially with the official version sent at a later date, and who is charged with tracking to make sure it is sent? Are there consequences for missing the deadline for documents to arrive, such as loss of registration for the next semester?

San Diego State University's (SDSU) Enrollment Services considers verification of originals against copies acceptable only in the case of secondary documents. For tertiary documents SDSU defines "official" as those sent directly from the issuing institution to SDSU. Failure to send these directly results in an incomplete file, which slows down the processing and consideration of the individual's entire application.

At SDSU this policy regarding official documents is largely consistent with that for receiving documents from domestic applicants. It should be noted, however, that an awareness of current international "crises" in some countries could affect this policy, and the normal procedure for receipt of transcripts could prove difficult. It is a good idea to track or keep copies of documents from those countries in order to know what has been received in the past.

* Is original language wording on the document part of the definition of an "official transcript?" Is it important to your institution who does the translation or how it is received?

International Student with U.S. Domestic Documents Only

* In the case of an international student who attends school only in the United States, is the application

processed and the admissions decision made as part of the domestic admissions process? If so, this may be more efficient if a computer program exists for domestic admissions that can easily incorporate the international contingent, provided this conforms to overall admissions policies.

The processing method for these unusual cases may well depend on whether an online application is used or applications must be dealt with separately by hand.

International Documents Only; International and U.S. Documents

❋ When evaluating or considering students with international documents only, what are the criteria for admission? Do these criteria align with that for domestic applicants? Are grade and credit calculations inclusive of all acceptable courses, while transfer credit reflects only those courses passed with an appropriate grade? For the benefit of major departments (especially those affected), is your office able to provide a familiar and transparent grade point average to those without international credential evaluation training?

❋ If you are considering both international and U.S. domestic documents, do you combine the cumulative grade point averages, keep the two separate or perhaps even avoid consideration of the international grade point average altogether?

Criteria for Admission Consideration— First-Time Freshmen, Lower Division and Upper Division Transfers

❋ For international students, an admissions decision must be made in a timely fashion. The time frame must allow for the evaluators to process and consider the application, render a decision and accommodate all required paperwork, including time for processing the I-20 and visa. A critical enrollment management question is whether or not the criteria reflect the school's targeted recruitment goals in terms of the desired international population for your cam-

pus. What are the budget constraints that affect this desired goal?

❋ Will the criteria be consistent for students with international work only, those with domestic work only, and those with a combination of both domestic and international study? How are the subjects on an international tertiary document reviewed? For a full evaluation do you require a course syllabus? What takes precedence in the admissions decision phase— examination results, class grades or both?

❋ Are you admitting students based solely on their grade point averages (using the country's and U.S. equivalent), or do other factors such as rank, essays, test scores, personal achievements etc. also play a role? What is the scope of the criteria for transfers from two-year schools and universities? Do criteria differ for those transfers coming from baccalaureate, technical-vocational or professional programs (*e.g.*, medical, law, nursing)?

TOEFL Requirement

❋ The Test of English as a Foreign Language (TOEFL) requirements and minimum results depend on your institution's policy. Two types of TOEFL tests are given: the iBT (Internet-based test) and the paper-based test (PBT). It is important to have a clear understanding of how tests are administered and what they measure in terms of preparedness for success at your university. Review test score policies periodically. Does faculty have an opportunity for input? In the case of a student with low test scores a need for additional English support may result. Does your institution have a connection with a language institute on campus? With this additional training, will the results of new testing be in time for admissions consideration? It is also imperative to meet with applicants undergoing additional ESL training frequently since many students tend to assume they will gain admittance either fully or conditionally once they reach a certain level of competency. This is particularly important when admissions requirements fluctuate or if other factors in the applicant's record may affect admission.

✱ How does your office determine which international applicants must take an English proficiency examination? Some institutions state their policy/definition in their catalog or Web site. Is this requirement different for transfer students with U.S. academic study? Will you consider "institutional" TOEFL results? An "institutional" TOEFL is given by a campus ESL program, therefore the tests may be recycled every so often and do not carry the same rigid security protocols of a national exam administered by the testing service. Working closely with the ESL Center will enable the admissions officer to have a fuller understanding of the English proficiency assessment process. The key is to make sure that the international student has the facility in the English language needed to compete evenly with domestic students in the same classroom.

✱ Regional visits and presentations by the Educational Testing Service (ETS) are very common. Take advantage of these free informational visits. They share current information as to how tests are administered, security issues, background, success studies, etc. If they have not contacted someone in your admissions office, be sure that you notify them.

✱ Be prepared to have an appeals process for waiver of assessment testing with knowledgeable individuals handling the review. What additional criteria would you consider? Do you take into account certain academic subjects studied in the U.S. in lieu of standardized testing?

✱ Will your campus accept results other than the TOEFL exam, such as the International English Language Testing System (IELTS), Pearson Test of English (PTE), the Michigan Test and perhaps others? Often in the case of state university systems a process exists whereby alternatives to TOEFL and other more well-known tests may be considered. Within an individual institution there may also be a system of due process for consideration and acceptance of additional English language tests; thus, it is a good idea to consult with the testing center and other entities such as faculty senate, graduate assembly, etc. to gain approval of alternative assessment measures.

✱ Once a desired exam score cut-off is determined, be sure to publicize this level on the appropriate page of the school Web site, as well as through communications with other colleges and their departments on campus.

Issuance of I-20

At what point will the documents be issued? Will this paperwork come only from the International Student Center or from the Admissions Office? Which office and which individual(s) will carry out the processing and provide the required information to the reporting authorities? Timing is important since the admitted student needs to apply for the F-1 visa at the U.S. Consulate in their home country.

The I-20 form cannot be issued from the Student Exchange Visitor Information System (SEVIS) until the student has been officially admitted to the institution. SEVIS is the database the Department of Homeland Security uses to track information about international students and scholars on the F-1, M-1 and J-1 visas while in the United States.

✱ Networking with other institutions, professional organizations and U.S. government contacts may help resolve issues that arise.

✱ The SEVIS process begins after admissions. Will the same office which issued the I-20 handle this process?

Financial Statement

✱ What kind of information do you require? What criteria are involved? What kind of supporting documentation (such as bank statements and sponsorship) must be supplied? Does a student have sufficient funds to cover his tuition and living expenses? What total amount is suggested for the financial guarantee? This amount should be broken down into costs for tuition and fees, living expenses, dependent expenses (if applicable) and other miscellaneous costs, such as health insurance. Determine when in the cycle of processing a student's file the financial guarantee form must be submitted and make this date available on the appropriate page of the school Web site. One of the most common questions international students ask is whether or not scholarships or grants are available. Information on this important question should appear on the Web site as well.

Evaluation of Documents for Admissions Consideration

The evaluation of international credentials is a specialized field that will require staff possessing independent judgment, research skills and attention to detail in evaluating documents from all over the world. Certainly one does not have to be multilingual, but often a number of years are needed to attain a confident familiarity with the intricate details of this somewhat arcane field. Even then many practitioners readily concede that new knowledge gained almost daily precludes one from ever knowing everything.

Working with international documents daily, attending professional conferences that specialize in workshop training or private workshops can be very helpful. Conference attendance increases your network of contacts with greater experience and knowledge of specific issues that may prove very helpful. The California system and the Texas public schools, to name two examples, have inter-l networks allowing the many campuses represented to keep in contact on similar issues.

Attending the professional conferences enables one to hear presentations from professionals in the field or specialists from a given country, learn about current and proposed publications, as well as attend forums that address mutual concerns and issues. You will find you are not alone in dealing with specific issues, and with this understanding the opportunity for networking begins.

* Champion an on-campus administrator that supports your efforts and interest in this field. Make them aware that a budget needs to be allocated for reference materials and programs, as well as professional development and support in this field. Often you are defending your decision against faculty, administrators and departments on your campus.

* Is a procedural manual written? If not, write one, including key information regarding procedures to process an international application at your institution!

Watch for Fraudulent/Altered Documents[5]

* This is always a concern when dealing with academic documents. How do you know if you are receiving a document that has been altered? Have you received enough documents from this country to realize when you need to ask for validation because the numbers do not seem to make sense or follow logical patterns; the paper upon which the document is generated does not feel right; or the type face is off. Always keep a file of questionable documents as well as copies of those that have been verified as genuine for points of comparison in the future. Familiarize yourself with what kinds of documents come from what country. This is critical because the first inkling that something is wrong with the document results from your sense that the record in front of you does not accord with those you have received previously.

* Does your institution have a policy when dealing with discrepancies? What kind of communication will you send the student when discrepancies occur? It is important to maintain professionalism while following a clear and well-established policy concerning altered documents.

Institutional Policy

* Whether in a private or public institution, institutional policy should cover how to handle decisions

---

[5] Refer to Chapter Seven for more details.

regarding the review of international academic records. One key decision concerns the extent to which international admissions follows that of domestic admissions requirements. Are they treated the same; if not, why not? There is no right answer, but crucially a need to fully understand and articulate the policy one way or the other. Senior administrators overseeing both domestic and international admissions processes must collaborate closely in order to establish policies, whether they differ or coincide. They must also work with those academic departments that have special admissions restrictions. Appeals of decisions, deadlines and exceptions to normal policy all need to have well- documented due process procedures.

✳ Public institutions must remain cognizant of legislative mandates that affect admissions policies. While institutional autonomy is paramount in the U.S. higher education arena, university system coordination often plays a role, and senior administrators need to be aware of this fact when fashioning admissions procedures for a distinct population, such as international students.

Utilizing Credential/Evaluation Services

✳ Do you have resources to evaluate international course work in-house? Which office will evaluate international documents?

✳ When considering the utilization of an outside international credential evaluation service, you will need to verify the accuracy of their work. Have you had previous communication with any of the services in your area? Have you seen discrepancies with their evaluation reports?

✳ If you require your students to use an evaluation service, you run into the question of who is responsible for the evaluation fee and the time frame for completion of the evaluation. The turnaround period negotiated with the service must take into account the time for departments to review transcripts and for them to arrive. The issue of offering only one service

for the sake of consistency versus more than one in order to allow for applicant choice must be addressed.

✳ If multiple services are allowed, familiarity with the different credential/evaluation services in the United States is needed so that understanding and comfort result from reviewing the methodology found in the report.

✳ After an evaluation/credential service has completed a report, the service will usually be glad to discuss any questions or concerns. You should select services that are responsive and forthcoming regarding their work.

✳ It is important to remember that they are reporting on the document, not providing a specific degree evaluation as you would for your own institution. Imperative to you is recognition of an institution, class level of the documents, type of program and units recommended. Not all institutions would utilize the information in the same way so be prepared to interpret the report in terms of your own institutional needs.

✳ The advantages of in-house evaluation staff versus private credential services needs to be carefully weighed. A transition to outsourcing of the evaluation process may well have a negative impact initially as the office deals with the payment issue, turnaround time, etc.

✳ Community colleges and private institutions lacking supporting staff to do the work will utilize private evaluation services so they can place their students in specific courses. These students, in turn, apply to senior institutions where the evaluation is done in-house or, if not, by a different evaluation service; this may lead to discrepancies in transfer credit between institutions. The receiving institution should make the possibility of differing transfer credit policies clear at the earliest moment in the transfer application process in order to avoid later confusion.

✳ Some institutions state their policy regarding the evaluation of international coursework in their catalog and publications. An example found in Thomas Edison State College's 2005–2006 catalog follows.

International Credit Evaluations

Course-by-course credit recommendations from the "XXXX" evaluation service will be reviewed by Thomas Edison Sate College based upon existing transfer and degree policies in place at the time of application. Students who are seeking information on international credit evaluations may contact XXXX at: Address, phone and Web site address of service

All fees associated with the foreign credit evaluation are the responsibility of the student.

The One-Person Office

* Your campus may have to rely on one person to handle the workload for international students. From prospective applicant, to acceptance, to orientation, to matriculation, international students have one point of contact. A backup is a good idea in the event you only have one person who can interpret international documents, check status and/or evaluate documents. This is critical to keeping processing from coming to a complete halt if your designated staff is out of the office.

* In such an environment, the paper flow must be organized carefully and visibly so that designated areas exist for prospective student applications, including a flow chart showing transcripts, evaluations and notification of admission in clearly marked containers allowing for efficient tracking.

* Ideally someone processes the paper documents, while another, more senior person deals with issues of compliance with federal regulations and reporting.

Mailings

* After identifying the types of mailings required, remove any unnecessary items, as well as duplicate material, especially those given out by other offices. It is necessary to have a communications area in which all publications are reviewed for grammar and text, as well as the message conveyed.

* Strive to move as much as possible toward a paperless process. Online applications, particularly for international prospects, are a good start. Cross-train support staff to enable them to participate as much as possible in the key aspects of the organizational process, even to the point of assisting in special projects, etc.

* It is important to have a system that enables the admissions office to ascertain applicant email addresses, likely including a Web portal through which all communications might be directed. While exceptions do exist, the vast majority of potential applicants anywhere in the world probably do have access, however tenuously, to a computer.

* Increasingly, schools all over the United States use online registration. It would be wise for the International Office to have a group of computers for registering in case international students do not initially have access to a personal computer.

* Another vital bit of material for new international students is the "Welcome" packet. This packet includes the I-20 form, information on paying the SEVIS fee, the acceptance letter, arrival and orientation information and housing information. This information should also be posted on your Web site (except for the I-20 and acceptance letter).

Budgeting for Resources

* Important items to have in the budget include international resources (books and reports on educational systems as well as immigration regulations), professional development (workshops, conferences, professional meetings), staffing, mailings and postage, dedicated email portal, official print notification pieces, publications for students and international recruiting efforts. An office also needs tech support to facilitate the creation of follow-up queries to track enrolled students and communication history, including information with respect to various holds on student files and/or compliance issues.

* While all of the above costs can quickly mount up, one helpful strategy is to work with various other offices/departments needing access to this same information.

Notification of Admission

✳ When notifying the student officially of their admission, brevity is important, however, some information is critical to the next steps in the evolving process a student travels from admitted to enrolled status. Key forthcoming dates, placement tests, documents needed to complete a student's file and brief information on registration are examples of the type of things to consider for this letter. If there is some special status the student holds initially (*e.g.*, provisional admission status), this must be addressed officially and as early as possible.

✳ Some form of student intent to attend should also be considered in order to better manage enrollment; this would need to be clearly emphasized in a notification letter.

✳ Reminders about important issues such as institutional requirements regarding health insurance, any additional requirements on financial statement verification and potential "holds" on records in return for outstanding documentation also need to be included.

Conditional Admissions from Language Schools on Your Campus

✳ Conditional admission to the institution as a whole for those enrolled in the ELS Center needs to be carefully and fully explained to the admitted student. The nature of the conditions that must be met and the time frame for their resolution are critical elements that need to be effectively communicated to students. While verbal and email communication is useful, this important concept requires official notification from the appropriate senior administrator. Conditional admission from an ELS Center may well be an effective recruitment tool, but clear and precise explanation of this status is crucial to avoiding future problems.

✳ Agreements with other language schools in the area, while potentially less confusing to the international applicant, nevertheless require careful language in all communications with the student.

✳ A close working relationship with an ELS entity that includes familiarity with their operations, testing schedule, U.S. college preparation skills and pedagogical approaches to teaching English ensure that transition for students from ELS enrollment to degree-seeking student is as easy and straightforward as possible. Build strong links to the language centers in order to facilitate this point of transition. This effort will require staff time, which may not be readily available, but will pay dividends in the future.

Preliminary Evaluation of Prospective Students

✳ This may seem like a luxury in an office where resources, particularly personnel, are limited. However, it has the potential to be a great recruiting tool; thus, it may be useful to set up a mechanism to advise prospective students with international documents on how their previous courses may be considered, particularly with regard to degree requirements at your institution.

✳ Identify the things it is important to know regarding prospective applicants and list them on the Web site. These documents may include a cover letter stating name, address, phone and email, along with educational goals and objectives. Require a copy of the original language documents, a translation and current educational courses in progress.

International Orientation

✳ What offices on campus are participating (*e.g.*, Financial, Cashiers, Testing, Enrollment, International and Health Services)? Orientation should be more than a welcome reception: it should be informative, but with a social component to ease the students' adjustment to campus. Make sure to include a section on the immigration roles and responsibilities they must follow while they are F-1, M-1 or J-1 students in the United States. Students also need to know about the services provided for them through the international student office and other offices on campus. Include representatives of the critical offices they will interact with most, such as financial services, student accounting, testing and credit by exam, registrar, health services, etc.

✳ The length of the orientation process depends on the number of students attending, but with so much important information to impart, one day is often too short. Moreover, consider dividing students by undergraduates and graduates, freshmen and transfer students or those new to the U.S. within the last six months and those in the U.S. for greater than six months. Be sure to include information on additional testing needed beyond that for admission, such as English composition and mathematics. Overviews of the online registration process and information on mandatory courses to fulfill graduation requirements are other critical components.

One hopes that this chapter has brought to the forefront the different issues that make up the overall undergraduate admissions cycle for an international student. Communication and collaboration are essential factors in making this whole process run as smoothly as possible, not only for the student applicant, but for staff, faculty and the entire campus. Advances in technology guarantee that the process will not remain stagnant and that the search for improvement is never ending.

For someone who began in international education more than 35 years ago, it is unimaginable that, for example, a system could be developed to automate the admissions process, evaluate and post credits in a degree-audit reporting system, enact online registration or build an orientation process for our international students. Technology has radically transformed the entire process for both the international student and the international education specialist. Imagine what the next 35 years holds for us and for our students!

ELEVEN

Graduate Admissions Issues

Assistant Director and Residency Official
Graduate and International Admissions Center
The University of Texas at Austin

DEANA WILLIAMS

Graduate Admissions Issues

Regarded by many as the foundation of our educational system, graduate education is critical to the economic, creative, and competitive future of the United States. The u.s. is the leading destination worldwide for international students, and those who have graduate degrees from the u.s. have historically made major contributions to our knowledge-based economy. To ensure that we continue to reap benefits from the influx of international graduate students, graduate admissions offices need to implement strategies to best demonstrate why the u.s. is and should continue to remain the leader in educating the world's academic elite.

This chapter will outline the basic issues that are primarily unique to graduate admissions offices: remaining the leader in recruiting globally, determining how to balance centralization versus decentralization in the operation of an international graduate admissions office, the pluses and minuses of outsourcing credential evaluation, the role that testing plays in graduate admissions, and finally the challenges and opportunities that the future holds in international graduate education.

The Global Talent Flow

It has long been a recognized fact that international graduate students contribute significantly to the successful enterprise of graduate education at u.s. colleges and universities. Aside from the cross-cultural sharing of knowledge, international graduate students who choose to study in the u.s. often find their studies are an ave-

nue to employment and that they have significant representation in all economics sectors of the u.s. market. We are operating in a global economic and academic marketplace where the competition for top-rate talent is increasingly stiffer and more important.

A review of international enrollment in u.s graduate programs over the past ten years reflects a fluctuating but steady increase in numbers (see Figure 11.1).

While more than half of the international graduate students enroll in degree programs in engineering, business and the sciences (see Table 11.1 below), enrollment in social sciences and humanities approaches one-third of the graduate international matriculation numbers. Overall, international students comprise more than 30

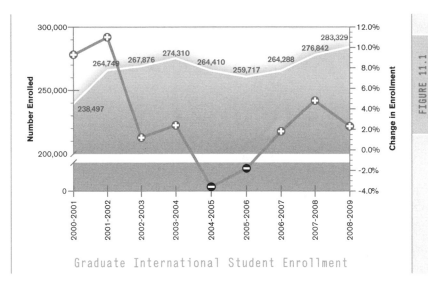

Graduate International Student Enrollment

FIGURE 11.1

percent of the master's degree seekers in u.s. institutions and almost half of the Ph.D. seekers.

India continues to top the list of sending countries with the combined total of graduate enrollment from

TABLE 11.1: Percentage of International Students Enrolled in Degree Programs 2008–09

Field of Study	% of Graduate Students in 2008/2009
Engineering	24.0
Business and Management	16.2
Physical and Life Sciences	13.1
Math and Computer Science	11.3
Social Sciences	9.0
Other Fields of Study	6.5
Health Professions	5.3
Fine and Applied Arts	4.3
Education	4.1
Humanities	3.9
Agriculture	2.1
Undeclared	0.2
Intensive English Language	0.0

SOURCE: IIE Open Doors 2009

TABLE 11.2: Graduate Student Top 20 Countries of Origin in 2008–09

Country	Number of Graduate Students 2008/2009
India	71,019
China	57,452
South Korea	25,463
Taiwan	15,332
Canada	13,185
Turkey	6,838
Japan	6,287
Thailand	4,709
Mexico	4,148
Germany	3,640
Brazil	3,019
Colombia	2,993
Saudi Arabia	2,903
Nepal	2,792
France	2,684
Iran	2,639
United Kingdom	2,468
Italy	2,336
Pakistan	2,216
Nigeria	2,153

SOURCE: IIE Open Doors

the top three countries of origin (India, China, and South Korea) comprising more than 50 percent of the total enrollment of international graduate students in the U.S. (*see* Table 11.2 and Figure 11.2).

Worldwide, the United States is still the leading destination for international graduate students. While institutions of higher education strive to recruit and retain the most attractive pool of international applicants, employers in the U.S. are likewise increasingly implementing global business strategies and, in the process, seeking out talent from amongst the U.S.-educated international graduate populations. More than half of the international Ph.D. recipients are still in the U.S. ten years after graduation. As documented in Richard Florida's book, *The Flight of the Creative Class,* regions of the country attracting graduate students to their programs have a better chance at retaining them for employment after graduation. Thus, the stakes are high for both educational and economic interests. Diverse cities that have a strong global job market and possess robust higher education institutions are natural destinations for graduate students. The relationship between the private and educational sectors in a city or region is critical for both groups who ultimately have the same agenda: enroll or employ the best and brightest.

When trying to craft strategies to attract elite applicants, one can turn to Richard Florida's concept of the three T's of economic growth: technology, talent, and tolerance, and apply them to higher education. Students are drawn to educational institutions that offer access to leading edge technology. They want to participate in an educational setting that incorporates and utilizes the latest emerging technologies in the curriculum, and they also want to reside in a city or region that has a strong high-tech knowledge-based economy. Where technology is emphasized, talent then follows. Florida uses the "global Austin" metaphor to show the effect of cities that transform and market themselves as progressive centers of industry, technology, and education and how such cities then attract a highly accomplished citizenry. Finally, technology and talent can both flourish in locations that cultivate an atmosphere of diversity and tolerance. Tolerance breeds innovation, which translates into economic and educational growth. It is in these regions that are centers of technology and talent and who offer a tolerant environment that high concentrations of foreign born residents reside.

Keeping this paradigm in mind, to be successful in retaining the best graduate students, consideration should be given to the following factors:

* *The use of cutting edge technology in your admissions processes.* Web pages, communication tools, and application materials are generally the first point of contact that institutions have with potential graduate applicants. Technological interactions that a potential applicant has with an institution lay the groundwork and signal the expectations that an applicant will have in terms of the emphasis an institution places on technology.

* *Market your program, institution, and city.* Create an institutional and departmental brand for your program that presents a global and progressive perspective. Fund campus visits and provide special recruitment programming for targeted applicants.

* *Provide competitive and creative funding.* Offer multiyear financial packages and other types of incentives to attract students. Think outside the box, including implementing collaborations with business and governmental entities to create programs and funding models that benefit all.

* *Expand overseas partnerships.* Develop dual-degree offerings, sponsored student initiatives, educational exchanges, and commercial opportunities for students.

(For a detailed review of the best practices and methodology of international recruiting, see Chapter 9.)

The race to find and procure the best academic talent for graduate programs is an ever-shifting game. The economic impact generated by international graduate students is significant, and thus the global competition for these students is constantly expanding. An institutional climate where education and research enterprises

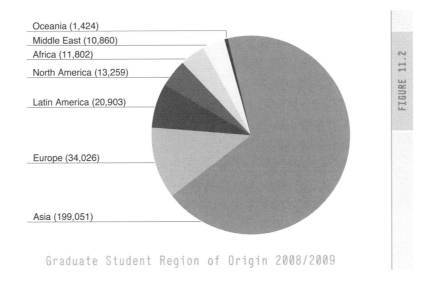

FIGURE 11.2

Oceania (1,424)
Middle East (10,860)
Africa (11,802)
North America (13,259)
Latin America (20,903)
Europe (34,026)
Asia (199,051)

Graduate Student Region of Origin 2008/2009

are complemented by an international and multicultural atmosphere will inherently be the primary factor that determines whether an institution is successful in attracting world-class applicants. Given the high interest shown by prospective international graduate students for U.S. graduate programs, it is critically important that graduate admissions offices have an organizational structure that allows for the rapid and efficient processing of these overseas applications.

Centralized vs. Decentralized Graduate Admissions

Management and processing of graduate admissions applications can vary widely across institutions, with the two primary models being centralized admissions and decentralized admissions. In a decentralized admissions process, although the graduate dean and perhaps a faculty assembly determine the admissions criteria for a college or university, the admissions process does not fall to a centralized admissions unit as it typically does for undergraduate admissions. The admissions process is left to the discretion of the individual departments with no basic oversight offered by a centralized processing/evaluation unit.

However, in a centralized graduate admissions process, generally one office will be responsible for receiving all application materials and distributing them to graduate departments, as well as evaluating the educational credentials to ensure that they meet an acceptable minimum standard for graduate admission. Centralized admissions can take on many different forms at different institutions. For example, many institutions may elect to have a single repository for incoming application documents, but not have oversight capability when making admissions decisions. Other models might employ a more overarching graduate admissions office, one directly involved in oversight of international student admissions, to ensure that institutional standards are upheld and that consistency is followed across disciplines.

DECENTRALIZED GRADUATE ADMISSIONS AND ITS CHALLENGES

At the graduate level, a decentralized admissions process can often lead to redundancy in the admissions process and inequity in the evaluation or review of international educational credentials. Without an office dedicated to ensuring consistency in the basic educational credentials required for admission to a graduate program, instances will often occur when one department admits an international applicant with a lesser credential than another graduate department on the same campus, sometimes within the same college. Consequently, decentralization can lead to unintended outcomes which allow for the admission of individuals who may not be qualified for graduate study.

In all graduate admissions models, it is important that departments maintain control of those issues most important to them, such as setting departmental deadlines and requirements for admission. However, holding on to processing of documents may not be necessary

to achieve the goal of admitting the most highly qualified graduate students. Without university-wide standard admissions requirements such as test scores, deadlines, and applications, an applicant can often find the decentralized admissions process confusing. A reading of various Web sites of universities around the country demonstrates the hodgepodge of procedural steps within an individual institutional that a potential applicant must navigate in order to simply apply for admission. Some institutions have deadlines and application fees which vary by department, and requirements are not standard across the various programs. Transcripts and test scores are often required by both the graduate department and another on-campus office, generally a graduate dean or official registrar office, which adds to the cost and the complexity of applying to a graduate program. A decentralized process may offer independence to graduate departments, but such redundancies will inevitably complicate the process for the applicant.

CENTRALIZED GRADUATE ADMISSIONS: THE PREFERRED MODEL FOR ADMISSIONS PROFESSIONALS

A centralized graduate admissions process is generally preferred by the professional administrative staff, but is often the model most feared by graduate faculty at institutions, who may have the perception that a centralized admissions office will be less efficient and add critical time to the processing of the application. Queries of graduate departments indicate that apprehension results from being asked to trust a centralized admissions office to collect and evaluate educational credentials, which creates the sense of losing control of the admissions process and selection of qualified candidates for a given program. Graduate programs often feel that they are giving up control of the process by allowing application materials to be collected and evaluated by a central admissions office that is often charged with processing applications for the entire institution, both graduate and undergraduate. In a centralized admissions model, it is key that the graduate processing units are given equal priority with undergraduate processing units and that the unit reassures the graduate department that selected staff members are dedicated to exclusively processing graduate admissions documents.

A centralized admissions process can also offer services that are generally not available in a decentralized process. Applicants benefit from the ease of sending all application materials to a centralized processing center which can then oversee the quality of the application process, guaranteeing consistency and safeguarding institutional integrity in the process. Providing services such as "customer" or applicant counseling, application status check, and implementing cutting-edge application tools such as document uploads and recommendation letter systems can all be made financially viable if managed within one centralized office. Thus, an efficient centralized admissions office will assist the graduate departments in a quick and easy review of application materials without transferring the cost or responsibility of maintaining and monitoring the various systems implemented in a dynamic admissions process.

Without a systematic admissions process, the collection of final transcripts and aspects of the oversight and auditing of an application can often fall between the cracks. A centralized office has the staff and the responsibility to make certain that final educational credentials are received and processed in an accurate and timely fashion. Also, a centralized admissions office can play a critical role in the maintenance of institutional policy related to admissions, can act as a front-line conduit for initiatives that will impact admissions processing (international updates, trends, and legislative mandates), and can maintain admissions statistics and reporting which are vital to maintaining quality graduate programs.

Key to the success of a centralized admissions process is a robust collaboration and cooperation with graduate department representatives. Building a relationship of trust and a confidence in the integrity and efficiency of the graduate admissions office operations is the cornerstone to developing the cooperation that must exist for operational success. The centralized admissions unit must view the graduate departments essentially as a "client" and be attuned to their needs and responsive to their requests. Providing technology and services to the department that enable the smooth operation of their admissions processes is critical in building the relationship between processing and departmental constituencies. Administering applicant customer service, which includes email, phone, and walk-in access to admissions processing representatives, assembling complete admissions files for departments, providing statistical applicant reports, and maintaining application systems and tools are areas of support that a successful centralized admissions office must provide.

Credentials Evaluation Outsourcing

One of the most pressing issues within the field of international graduate admissions is the issue of international credentials evaluation and degree comparability. How these decisions are determined can impact an institution's ability to recruit and enroll international graduate students. There is no "one size fits all," and each institution must make the decision on how to proceed with international credential evaluation and degree comparability determinations based on an assessment of the needs of the institution and its graduate departments.

CREDENTIALS EVALUATION

The issue of whether to retain a fully functioning and trained staff of international credentials evaluation experts is a hot button topic for international admissions office management staff, both at the graduate and undergraduate level. Over the past twenty years, a rise in the number of private credentials evaluation firms has allowed more and more colleges to outsource the evaluation of international credentials to experts outside of the university setting. With the increasing budgetary concerns placed on admissions offices, the thought of outsourcing this process and saving the institution the cost of training and retaining staff members by shifting the cost to the applicant is more appealing for many institutions. When weighing this decision, it is best to involve the major stakeholders at your institution, including graduate departments, the admissions office and the graduate dean, to determine the best course of action for your institution.

REASONS TO OUTSOURCE

✳ BUDGET: Outsourcing credentials evaluation will reduce the number of staff members needed to evaluate and process applications and thus would be a cost savings for an institution.

✳ ACCESS TO EXPERTS: Private credential evaluation agencies typically are staffed with highly trained experts in the field who have up-to-date information on the changes in worldwide educational systems. However, it is important that when choosing an outside agency, the institution takes steps to ensure that the agency is reputable with a knowledgeable evaluation staff experienced in higher education. Due to the lack of a regulated accreditation body for international credential evaluation firms, companies can operate without oversight or standards. Thus it is critical to do extensive background research on the agency prior to engaging in a contractual service agreement.

✳ REDIRECT OFFICE RESOURCES: Outsourcing will free up staff time and funds so that an admissions office can focus on other tasks such as application processing, customer service, technology, etc.

✳ REMOVE A DIFFICULT PROCESS: The evaluation of international credentials is a time-consuming venture which requires staff members trained to recognize and understand documents from around the world. By outsourcing this process, an institution would transfer a possibly cumbersome portion of the international admissions process to an outside agency who could then guarantee an efficient and expedient timeline for producing an evaluation.

✳ REDUCE RISK: When evaluating international credentials there is always risk involved. Fraudulent documents, unaccredited overseas institutions, incorrectly identifying and assessing the comparability of inter-

national credentials documents can ensnare even highly-trained evaluators on occasion. The time and money needed to adequately train staff members in the techniques required to understand and navigate international academic credentials can be challenging for institutions. This is especially true for institutions whose infrastructure is small and whose staff members must process applications, evaluate credentials, provide customer service, and advise on immigration matters. Significant time, cost, and effort are needed to keep staff up-to-date on the constant changes in educational systems and credentials. Developing a network of resources plus active involvement in local, regional, and national organizations is required to stay in-tune to the latest trends and changes.

REASONS NOT TO OUTSOURCE

✳ COST: Application fees are a major revenue source that many institutions depend upon to fund international admissions operations. By keeping the evaluation process in-house, an institution can use the application fee to fund the office and provide much-needed financial support in other office areas such as technology infrastructure. Also, an institution must be cognizant of the cost of outsourcing to the applicant to ensure that shifting the evaluation fee to the applicant will not require an unreasonable increase in the application fee.

✳ RETAIN INSTITUTIONAL EXPERTS: Keeping the process in-house will ensure that experts in the area of international educational systems and credential evaluation are represented on campus. Outsourcing the evaluation process often results in an institution having no internal staff member who understands the complexities of international credentials. Thus, leaving no "go to" person on campus when issues arise requiring such knowledge and expertise.

✳ KEEP THE PROCESS STREAMLINED AND EASY FOR THE APPLICANT: Outsourcing adds an additional layer of bureaucracy to the application process if the student is required to communicate directly with the third-party agency involved in the evaluation process. Keeping the process in-house generally provides more seamless application procedures for the applicant and for the institution which does not have to communicate with an outside agency or set up processes for receiving data from the agency and incorporating the evaluation information into a local database.

✳ QUALITY CONTROL: Electing to keep the evaluation process in-house guarantees that the institution has more autonomy with credential evaluation outcomes. Inevitably, credential evaluation companies will have different opinions on the U.S. comparability of international education credentials. An institution that does not outsource the evaluation process can be assured that the determinations are made in keeping with institutional policy and precedent and can also choose to examine and make changes to the policy on a case-by-case basis as needed.

Three-Year Degree Comparability and the Bologna Process

With the emergence of the Bologna Process—an agreement among forty-seven European countries to create a European Higher Education Area by the year 2010 (*see* Chapter 21 for more details)—the issue of three-year international first-level degrees and whether they provide adequate preparation for admission to U.S. graduate degree programs has become one of the more prominent issues in the field of international graduate admissions. The Bologna Process has as its basis a structure built upon a three-year first university-level degree. Upon full implementation of the Bologna Process, three-year first degrees will be the norm in many European countries.

In the rapidly evolving and competitive world of higher education, credentials evaluation methodology is paramount in guaranteeing academic mobility. How institutions view the three-year international degree is central to this discussion. International students comprise approximately 17 percent of the overall enrollment numbers in graduate degree programs in the U.S., with

enrollment in the science and engineering programs at 30 percent of the overall enrollment. In India, the single largest sending country for graduate study in the U.S., the three-year varieties of bachelor's degrees in the fields of arts, sciences, and commerce are prominent.

The central question to be answered by institutions is how they will view the three-year bachelor's degree holder for admission to graduate study. Currently there is no consensus among U.S. institutions on this issue. A thorough assessment of your institutional needs and policies is required to make this determination. Things to consider during this process would include:

✳ REVIEW OF THE INDIVIDUAL CREDENTIAL: What is the entrance requirement for admission to the three-year degree program? If the secondary curriculum is a thirteen-year program, this should be considered when assessing a three-year bachelor's degree. Most institutions do recommend graduate-level placement for a holder of a three-year bachelor's degree which was preceded by thirteen years of secondary study.

✳ REVIEW OF THE INSTITUTION OFFERING THE PROGRAM: Is the institution a "top tier" institution within the country? Some may choose to evaluate a three-year degree program based on the standing or ranking of the institution awarding the three-year degree. Others may elect to consider graduate-level placement for persons completing a three-year degree at a "top tier" institution only if the applicant was awarded the degree with high academic marks or grades.

✳ CONTENT OF THE DEGREE PROGRAM: Does the three-year degree represent adequate preparation for graduate study? An examination of content for most three-year bachelor's degrees would generally show that the missing element of the degree is the general education or elective component found in the standard U.S. four-year bachelor's degree. The typical three-year Bologna degree or three-year Indian degree would include more hours of study within the major field, and thus many institutions would deem it to be acceptable preparation for entry into a U.S. graduate program in the same field of study. Also, consideration of a "bridge" semester or year which would incorporate basic graduate preparatory coursework or general education study deemed missing from a three-year degree would be an option for institutions that are hesitant to grant direct admission into a graduate program.

✳ **FUNCTION OF THE CREDENTIAL IN THE HOME COUNTRY:** Is the three-year degree intended as preparation for graduate-level study in the home country, and if so, is direct entry into graduate study possible in the home country with the three-year degree? Institutions may choose to consider the recommended level of post-bachelor's degree study for graduate placement. If a particular three-year degree program represents primarily preparation for vocational or professional standing, an institution would potentially choose not to grant admission into a graduate degree program.

✳ **EQUITY:** Would there be an issue of fairness or legal concern if an international student was granted admission based on a three-year degree when a domestic applicant or an applicant from a country whose bachelor degree is more than three years in length is required to complete a bachelor's degree that is four or five years in duration? The issue of the quantitative versus the qualitative value of a three-year degree is one of debate within the field of comparative education. One must also consider the evolving nature of the U.S. bachelor's degree. Some institutions now offer bachelor's degrees that are less than four full years of full-time study. Also, many U.S. students enter degree programs with an accumulation of advanced placement credit based on a high school curriculum or on a testing mechanism (either institutional testing or testing done as part of a high school program), thus reducing the four-year degree program to less than four years of study.

✳ **NEED TO ENROLL THE BEST STUDENTS:** Is an institution reaching the enrollment and recruitment goals that reflect the best interest and needs of the institution? Often the need to matriculate larger numbers of highly qualified international students will influence the institution's three-year degree policy. The stakes are much higher in the international graduate recruitment arena than ever before and thus the competition for academic global talent often influences policy decisions. An institution can possibly increase their "odds" of enrolling the best and the brightest from overseas if they open the admissions option to a larger applicant pool by including three-year degree holders.

✳ **OUTCOMES:** Will a three-year degree holder be successful in a graduate program at the institution? Ultimately an institution may want to consider internal outcomes when assessing the viability of three-year degree holders. If three-year degree holders are routinely found to be as successful in all aspects of a degree program as their peers who hold degrees of four or five years in length, then a reasonable argument can be made that a policy allowing graduate admission to three-year degree holders would be supported. Higher education is, at the core of its structure, an outcome-based system. Thus, applying an outcome-based standard to persons who legitimately hold a first-level degree, be it three years in length or more, from an accredited institution within their home country, is a logical conclusion that some may choose to draw.

Testing

A significant factor in graduate admissions is the requirement that an applicant submit standardized test scores (GRE, GMAT, TOEFL, IELTS, etc.). Today's standardized tests are high in quality and reliability with the testing agencies going to great lengths to ensure equity in the design and security in the test delivery. The value of a standardized test requirement is its quantifiable measurement evaluating an applicant's proficiency in critical thinking, analytical writing, and verbal and quantitative reasoning skills, in relation to other applicants from varied educational backgrounds. It is important to understand that standardized tests are not perfect measures of ability, but, when used properly, they can provide graduate departments with useful information not found in any other standard educational evaluation instrument. Ultimately, with international student populations and the disparate nature of grading across educational systems, the standardized test is the only equally administered tool in the decision-making process.

While most accredited graduate programs elect to require standardized tests as an admissions requirement, in some cases institutions may choose to waive the requirement on an individual basis. Within an institution, an individual major or department (applied fine arts fields for example) may often find that while the TOEFL is a critical measure of success for incoming international students, the GRE is not of great value when assessing the performance potential of an international graduate applicant. Waiver procedures should be clearly outlined on both the institutional admissions' and the graduate department's Web pages. Departments that do elect to use standardized tests should thoroughly understand the scope of test measures and appropriately use the scores. Guidelines for test score use include using the score only in a holistic file review process, accepting only official score reports, consider-

ing test sections as independent measures instead of looking at the overall numeric value of the test as a whole (do not institute cutoff scores), avoiding making decisions based on insignificant score variances, and conducting institutional validity studies to correlate the scores with the success of your enrolled international graduate students.

Conclusion

Ultimately, it is the goal of all international graduate admissions professionals, regardless of the method they choose to implement procedures and policy, to facilitate and direct a process by which institutions can be successful in their efforts to enroll the most highly qualified and talented graduate students from around the globe. The graduate admissions office plays a critical role in supporting the objectives of the graduate departments and provides the tools needed to accomplish their enrollment goals. How successful we are at implementing an efficient and effective admissions process for international graduate applicants will depend upon our ability to collaborate with graduate departments, to target and communicate actively with the most gifted applicants worldwide, to make wise choices on complex international admissions issues, and to administer a technologically savvy product to the applicant and to the institutional clients that depend on our services.

12

Community College Issues

2010 AACRAO INTERNATIONAL GUIDE

CHRISTINE KERLIN

Vice President
University Center of North Puget Sound and Strategic Planning
Everett Community College

Community College Issues

ommunity colleges in the United States occupy a fairly unique position in the world of international student enrollment. As multi-function institutions, they offer high school completion, basic education, ESL, technical training, university transfer programs and sometimes bachelor's degree programs. Programs may span one week to several years. Most community college programs are open entry and generally have lower tuition rates than the baccalaureate sector. This is a combination of features that can prove very attractive to some international students, and for some it is their best way of entering higher education in the United States.

Before going much further, it is worthwhile to note that the two-year college sector embraces a wide variety of institutions—public, private, not-for profit, and for-profit—numbering about 1,685 out of a total of 4,300 colleges and universities in the U.S. (*The Chronicle of Higher Education* 2010). The two-year colleges may be comprehensive in mission, as described above, or they may focus exclusively on technical programs, or some other specialization. This chapter will refer primarily to comprehensive community colleges, though much of the commentary may apply to the more specialized technical colleges as well.

According to Open Doors, enrollment of international students in 2007–08 in all types of U.S. institutions was about 624,000, comprising 3.5 percent of all enrollments (IIE 2008a). Reports on two-year college enrollment of international students vary, but it appears to hover around 93,000 to 95,000 in recent years, compared to a total two-year college enrollment of about 6,500,000, or about 1.4 percent. The community col-leges with the largest international enrollments over the past several years are Houston Community College System (TX), Montgomery College (MD), Santa Monica College (CA), and De Anza College (CA), with their enrollments varying between 2,000–4,200 during that period (IIE 2008b). Relatively few community colleges, however, have international enrollments that reach that size; most enroll between 25–800, and some do not enroll international students at all.

In addition to enrolling international students on their U.S. campuses, some community colleges provide rich options in study abroad and special student and faculty exchanges. Some community colleges have taken deliberate steps toward infusing their curriculum with global perspectives. Howard Community College (MD), for example, selected by NAFSA: Association of International Educators for one of the 2005 Senator Paul Simon Awards for Campus Internationalization, offers extensive study abroad programs, and has exchange partnerships with other governments and agencies around the world (NAFSA 2005).

This chapter will describe selected aspects of the community college sector that relate to the field of international education. In particular, those features of the community college that are distinctive will be high-lighted.

A Competitive Environment

Attracting international students to a campus is a competitive process. The community colleges face a unique challenge insofar as their model of 2-year education may be either unknown to the international student, or poorly understood since few countries have such a model (Powers 2007).

Since student mobility and inter-institutional transfer is not typical in many countries, many international students, parents and funding agencies may not intuitively perceive the community college as a satisfactory option. This is further complicated by the desire of an international undergraduate to "settle" somewhere, something which may not be predictable given the student's need to transfer to a baccalaureate institution upon completion of lower division coursework at the community college. Also, since most community colleges do not provide residence halls, students seeking a college campus which can meet all of their school, social and living needs may prefer the residential environment found on most baccalaureate campuses. These challenges are not insurmountable, and indeed can be offset by opportunities not found on many university campuses, such as low tuition, small classes, short-term technical training, and, in some cases, lower admission requirements.

In addition, some community colleges may not market themselves very heavily, perhaps due to low interest in attracting international students, or perhaps due to not having the funds to support international recruitment. Furthermore, the baccalaureate and graduate schools have a much longer history in international education, more alumni, and, in many cases, better name recognition.

Thanks to some recent and strong efforts by the American Association of Community Colleges (*see* Appendix 1, on page 152), community college consortia such as the Community Colleges for International Development Inc., and some individual institutions, the visibility of community colleges as an option in the u.s. is becoming more positive.

International Student Recruitment

Community colleges interested in attracting international students can look to a number of their sister institutions in the u.s. for successful models. For example, Green River Community College (wa) utilizes the income from international tuition to directly fuel its outreach efforts as well as its programs, and assigns staff

persons to designated geographic areas for recruitment. Kirkwood Community College (ia) uses its consortial connections to build its visibility, and provides strong student services.

Community colleges interested in building their international student enrollment are wise to invest in solid planning. The foremost tasks of a recruitment plan are to identify the goals of the effort, as well as the resources available. These should include budget, staff resources, and the expressed support of the college leadership.

Second, it is advantageous to identify the desired mix of students in relation to current trends in international education. Over-reliance on a particular country or region can be risky, though a sharp focus often is the best use of limited resources. Also, some countries are more likely to yield students interested in a u.s. community college education than others. Certain technical programs may have varying attractiveness to students in different regions of the world.

Third, an analysis of college strengths and weaknesses, programs, and services should be completed. For example, strong and flexible technical programs may be conducive to marketing to governments and agencies looking for training contracts. Technical programs with internship partnerships with local businesses and industry can be appealing. Also, specific university articulation agreements can strengthen the appeal of the transfer program. Open entry esl programs can lend themselves to strong promotion as well.

As the desired geographic targets emerge, consideration needs to be given to the best method of reaching those students. Advertising, mailings to overseas advising agencies, the use of agents, personal recruitment travel abroad, participation in fairs and trade missions, and promotion of the college's Web site will vary in suitability. Social networks are another method of attracting student interest and contact.

Community colleges can employ some relatively low-cost strategies in attracting and retaining international students. The college's student-friendly Web site and portal, its ability to respond quickly to inquiries and applications, its development of relationships with reputable overseas agents, its partnerships with overseas institutions, its support of accessible housing options for students, its participation in consortial recruiting organizations, its utilization of alumni who have returned home, and its support of campus services for student advising and student activities can have a positive effect on enrollment. These efforts rely more on personal efforts than on an expensive international travel schedule, and are sometimes referred to as "armchair recruiting".

Stronger enrollment can result by employing not only those activities mentioned above, but also by traveling abroad and connecting with key organizations and individuals who themselves attract students interested in studying in the U.S. These types of relationships offer several outcomes: 1) individual students are referred to the community college, 2) groups seeking focused short-term training programs are connected to the community college, and 3) the college's visibility and reputation are significantly raised. Travel abroad also alerts the college to emerging trends and needs which can aid in shaping strategic recruitment activities.

An emerging trend in community college recruitment is the consortial approach. By pooling limited resources and by enhancing the presence of the community college in the higher education landscape, consortia can be a valuable tool for individual community colleges. For example, "Study Washington" is an association of colleges, universities, independent schools and education service providers in Washington State with a mission to promote the State of Washington as the best destination for international students who wish to study in the United States. Member schools represent all levels of education and are located in every part of the state.[6] Together they produce print material and advertising, as well as host booths, receptions and tours for overseas visitors. For the community college which may have few resources this can represent a significant opportunity to expand its reach.

Community colleges will also find it advantageous for themselves and their students to develop transfer agreements with partner universities in the U.S., a strategy that is discussed below.

Inquiry and Admission Processes

Inquiries for admission as an international student have become increasingly complex. Inquiries may arrive via letter, fax or email. They may come from a student already in the U.S., or from a local resident interested in a sponsorship. They may come via an overseas agent acting on behalf of the student. The inquiry might be generated from a Web site interaction or from a recruitment visit. The inquiry may be from a student who knows little about your college, or who is quite knowledgeable as a result of a sister-college partnership. For the community college that is eager to enroll international students, the timely and appropriate response to an inquiry can be critical in attracting and retaining the student's commitment.

Because more colleges are competing for international students, speed is of the essence in responding. College staff can make use of email, fax, the phone, and overnight mail. Colleges may have "chat" functions that allow both synchronous and asynchronous responses. The response should include the information and forms pertinent to the next steps in application and admission. If a college has been aggressive in placing material on the Web, the first inquiry might actually be a complete application packet. In fact, material on the Web often answers most students' initial questions and should be as comprehensive as possible, including forms and perhaps an online application.

Many community colleges offer the same open admission to international students as to their domestic students. Others may establish some moderate criteria, such as requiring high school completion, or a minimum grade point average. Some may require English languages scores that demonstrate a minimum level of proficiency; others may not. Admission criteria should be based on

---

[6] See <www.studywashington.org>.

an institution's own assessment of what background an international student should have to be successful.

Schools that provide a robust ESL program for international students may be able to accept students who arrive with varying levels of competency in English; schools without such programs, or programs that are not geared to lower levels of proficiency, should establish a method for evaluating English level prior to admission. There are a number of ways to do this, as described in other sections of this book. For example, the TOEFL test, or the International English Language Testing System (IELTS) yield scores or results that can be used in determining proficiency and placement. In some cases a community college can benefit from engaging in a referral partnership with a local English language school.

Though generally far less selective in admission than their baccalaureate counterparts, community colleges must meet with the same standards of application and admission in terms of complying with regulatory requirements for documentation and the ability to issue an I-20 and enter data into the SEVIS system, referred to in more detail in Chapter 13 of this book. Specifically, financial documentation that demonstrates the student's ability to meet all costs, either through their own resources or a sponsor of some type, should be required, as well as an application form that captures such data as birthdate, birthplace, address, former schools, etc. In the case of a student transferring from another U.S. school, a review of the student's status will make the admission and data entry process easier and more accurate.

There have been incidents where a student admitted to a community college may have been denied a visa in their home country because of a perceived bias against community college education or inadequacy in the prospective student's statements about their educational plan. While it is always difficult to accurately identify the reasons for a visa denial, the community college can make efforts to assure that the admission packet provides the student with information that has a positive effect on their visa application. The letter of admission should clearly state the admission status, preparation for attending the college, the arrival process and the pathway toward their goal. The packet should include information about the college itself, such as its accreditation, degrees, international population, public or private status, articulation agreements, ESL instruction, etc.

The timeliness of the application and admission process can be an issue for community colleges. Unlike many baccalaureate institutions, it may be perceived that community colleges are more accessible at any time. While flexible deadlines are certainly the prerogative of any admissions office, it is wise to assure that proper time is allowed for the review of all qualifications, credentials, financial standing, and visa application or status.

One final note regarding admission concerns the maintenance of student records. Community colleges, because of their open door process, and because their enrollment processes are usually continuous as so many students move in and out of enrollment, may need to create a separate records retention process for international records submitted at the time of admission. In fact, record retention for "F" and "M" visa students is specified in 8 C.F.R. 214. Good record-keeping will assure that the official transcripts from the home country, the original financial statements, etc., are available if needed during the student's attendance and after.

Credential Evaluation

Like colleagues in baccalaureate institutions, community college enrollment services personnel must make decisions about the process of credential evaluation. At the application stage, a process should be in place to assure that the applicant has the appropriate educational background, if one is required. At the admission or entry stage, credentials should be reviewed to determine if the student is eligible for transfer credit; this is a particularly critical issue for students who are monitoring the costs of their education and want their previous post-secondary education, if any, recognized.

The use of transfer credit from a non-U.S. institution goes beyond the purposes of the community college's own degree requirements, since it may affect the student's experience of gaining advanced standing at a university to which he or she might transfer. The inappropriate use of transfer credit from a non-U.S. institution might give the incorrect impression that the university to which the student transfers may accept the credit in the same manner.

The text above provides an argument for community college personnel to devote adequate resources to the admission and foreign credential evaluation process, and to develop a thoughtful approach with trained staff. Some community colleges decide not to devote extensive resources to foreign credential evaluation—the staff, the training, the library of resources, etc.—and utilize credential evaluation agencies. (In those cases, the student most often bears the expense of the credential evaluation.) Other colleges are able to support the continuous training of staff in understanding and evaluating foreign educational credentials. However, even the colleges that receive the reports from the credential evaluation agency must be in a position of interpreting them, and applying the credits suggested as college-level by the agency. The implication is that colleges must take responsibility for supporting basic training in credential evaluation, or take the risk of making poor decisions. This responsibility is particularly important when using credit from non-U.S. institutions toward an articulated degree or toward a degree that is linked to license requirements.

Student Services

As emphasized through this Guide, international student support systems are a vital ingredient in program and student success. In fact, student support services can be seen as an ethical responsibility of any institution that admits and enrolls international students. Too often, boosting international student enrollment is not accompanied by preparation for the impact on student services. Community colleges may experience challenges slightly different than those of their colleagues at baccalaureate institutions.

HOUSING

For those community colleges without on-campus or nearby residence halls, there is a large responsibility to work with carefully selected host families or with a homestay agency. In some cases arrangements may be made with local apartment owners. Options vary widely, but the central issue is enabling incoming students to arrange accommodation upon arrival, and to assure that the college supports safe and suitable options. This information should be provided in the early stages of student interest and in the admission packet.

STUDENT LIFE

Community colleges do not typically have the same student life environment as a residential baccalaureate institution. This can sometimes leave international students with a tenuous sense of community and fewer connections to other students. The story does not end there, though. Good planning can produce activities such as U.S. and international student buddy programs, conversation partners, international week events, club activities, outdoor recreation excursions, and international student participation in cross-cultural programs to name a few. Colleges may place this responsibility in a dedicated International Education office, or in a mainstream student services office.

ADVISING

The ability of international students to start at a community college, earn about two-years of college credit at a low tuition rate, and then transfer to a university, is a positive aspect for community college recruitment strategies. Careful attention should be given to how prospective students are advised of the opportunities, how their language proficiency may affect their plans, and how continuing students connect with possible destination institutions to meet their international admission criteria. The role that credential evaluation plays in that advising can be critical.

Advisory information should be contained in materials for prospective students. Specifically, many prospective students may base their decision for whether or not to attend a community college on how clearly the college communicates about the transferability of credit to baccalaureate institutions. New students should participate in a thorough advising session upon their arrival, and be assigned a method for continuous contact with an advisor. Perhaps more so than our domestic students, international students have a significant investment riding on their academic planning and transfer decision making.

Not all community college international students enroll with the intention of long term academic studies and/or transfer. Many enroll for the purpose of pursuing a one- or two-year technical program, or simply for a cultural experience in the U.S. that will also help them improve their fluency. Advising is very important to their success as well. For example, knowing that the student's goal may not necessarily be a specific degree may afford the student more flexibility in the selection of courses. Or, the special vocabulary of a technical program may present unique challenges to evaluating their readiness, or the rate at which they will progress. Schools that have a selective admission process for their technical programs need to make a clear statement of this at the outset.

Whether a community college centralizes advising with its international staff specialists, or whether international students are mainstreamed into the regular advising scheme, the college has a responsibility to offer the international students the advising resources he or she needs to make sense of a new system and new expectations. Such advising should also be provided in the context of strong cross-cultural knowledge and sensitivity. Staff development workshops that aid advisors and other support staff in learning about other cultural norms will forestall problems in misadvising or student dissatisfaction. Though community colleges often

enroll large numbers of persons from other countries who now reside in the U.S. in their basic education programs, international students generally do not have the same issues and needs and community college personnel need to anticipate their special perspectives.

While the foregoing emphasizes the critical need for educational advising, international student specialists are needed for what is commonly referred to as "immigration advising." This term covers the wide range of international student issues from accurate reporting through the SEVIS system, to approving part-time enrollment, to employment, and more. This topic is covered thoroughly in other chapters, but the implication for community colleges is that this requires special staff training and the ability for international students to have access to the staff persons who can help them maintain their non-immigrant status and comply with regulations.

Articulation Relationships

Many community colleges maintain transfer agreements with nearby or regional baccalaureate institutions, often identifying specific degrees and/or courses that transfer. These relationships and agreements are of inestimable value to the international exchange process. However, the existence of these agreements may not necessarily include some of the special situations relevant to international students. For example, baccalaureate institutions may apply different admission criteria to international students than domestic students, or the use of credit from non-U.S. institutions may be restricted. Community college leaders would be wise to understand the differences, if any, and convey these to their students.

In addition to articulation relationships that may already exist, it is possible to construct special agreements for the benefit of international students. For example, baccalaureate institutions that are interested in boosting their international enrollment may be willing to recruit in partnership, and/or to make special agreements, such as waiving TOEFL requirements if appropriate coursework is successfully completed at the community college. In some cases, universities will target scholarship programs at international students who transfer from a community college.

Articulation agreements with other overseas institutions are also valuable. Appendix 2 demonstrates an agreement between a U.S. community college and a Japanese college that offers benefits to both the students and the institutions.

Study Abroad and Exchange Relationships

A recent report produced by the Institute of International Education notes that less than 3 percent of those who study abroad are community college students, yet community colleges enroll about half of the undergraduate students in the United States. Added to this dismal picture is the observation that community colleges historically have enrolled the types of students who are largely underrepresented in study abroad programs (Raby 2008). If this trend continues, a significant population is marginalized in an increasingly globalized world.

This topic is almost too large to be included in a chapter on community college issues, but it is worthwhile to note that a number of community colleges are tackling the goal of enabling their students to learn through study and travel abroad; as mentioned earlier, Howard Community College (MD) has been commended for the opportunities it provides students. Aided by scholarship opportunities such as the Benjamin A. Gilman International Scholarship program, community colleges students may find affordable options. Community colleges themselves can form consortia that bring the costs down by organizing their own educational programs abroad.[7]

In general, community colleges are well-positioned to develop less traditional study abroad options. For example, technical programs can provide short term travel options such as South Seattle Community College's trip to English gardens coordinated by their Horticulture

program. With respect to the community college's emphasis on community development, Seattle Central Community College's Global Impact program takes students to developing countries for volunteer service.

Community college faculty can support international exchange by participating in Fulbright programs and other government supported programs. Doing so often plants the seeds for exchanges as another way to develop opportunities for students to experience other cultures.

Issues Related to Non-F-1 or Immigrant Students

The term "international student" can refer to many types of students, such as refugees or recent immigrants, not just those on a student visa. It is particularly important to clarify this on the community college campus, since students with a wide variety of immigrant and non-immigrant statuses may be enrolled. Program directors need to explain the differences between and among various programs for non-nationals, or non-English-speaking, or non-immigrants. Eligibility and appropriateness may vary for such programs. Given the diverse population within most community colleges, it is necessary to train staff in proper procedures in working with students of such different needs.

Non-visa students may present the community college with the challenge of foreign credential evaluation. As described in the section above, community colleges need to make clear decisions about their capacity to understand and evaluate credentials.

Enrollment Management Issues

Like baccalaureate institutions, community colleges may regard international student enrollment as an important factor in their enrollment management. The added tuition revenue is one advantage, and the enhancement to the campus climate is another. Sometimes, proximity to a local university results in enrollment pressure by dependents of the university's F-1 students, or by international students who need to improve their eligibility criteria to enter the university.

---

[7]   For an example, see the Web site of the Washington Community College Consortium for Study Abroad at <www.wcccsa.com>.

The risks and successes of identifying international student enrollment as a significant factor in enrollment management are several. Primarily, there is the ever-present possibility of fluctuations in international enrollment due to external causes, such as economic crises or a shift in government relations. Another challenge is defending international student enrollment when many perceive the community college as a locally-funded, locally focused institution.

Nonetheless, the opportunities that arise with international enrollment, the revenue benefits, and the springboard to building more international partnerships in an increasingly global education market make the effort worthwhile.

In conclusion, the community college environment engenders unique challenges in international enrollment. Thoughtful planning, trained staff, and strong partnerships can have a positive effect on the success of students and the viability of the international program.

Appendix 1: American Association of Community Colleges Policy Statement on International Education

The United States must remain a leader in the global community of the 21st century to maintain its educational and economic vitality. In light of the events of September 11, 2001, the citizenry must be prepared to engage in worldwide activities related to education, business, industry and social interaction. To ensure the survival and well-being of our communities, it is imperative that community colleges develop a globally and multiculturally competent citizenry. Community colleges are strategically positioned and experienced to respond to this educational and economic development imperative by educating and training individuals to function successfully in a multicultural and advanced technological environment that crosses all boundaries of education, communications, language and business. Meeting this challenge, community colleges provide:

* Internationalized curricula;
* Multicultural activities and programs;
* Language programs;
* Cultural and ethnic studies;
* Study abroad programs;
* Faculty and student exchange programs;
* Professional development;
* Technical assistance to other countries and their businesses/industries;
* Local, state, national and international forums;
* International student enrollment;
* Community education forums; and
* Other appropriate education and training programs to ensure a well-trained and technically literate workforce, functioning collaboratively with other countries of the world.

Community colleges are in a strong position to meet these international challenges with a widely dispersed national network committed to accessibility and service to the local community. AACC will actively advocate this international role for community colleges and will articulate this mission to the Congress and the administration, federal agencies and other appropriate national and international organizations.

Adopted April 1997 and Amended by the Board of Directors November 2001.

Appendix 2: International Exchange Agreement—ABC International University & Regional Community College

In order to promote international understanding and cooperation between the people of the United States of America and the people of Japan, as represented by Regional Community College (here-in-after called RCC) and ABC International University (here-in-after ABC International), the Presidents of these two institutions approve of the following agreement. The primary purpose of this agreement is to provide graduates of ABC International with the opportunity to complete an Associate of General Studies degree program at RCC.

STUDENT ACCEPTANCE AGREEMENT

A. RCC agrees:

✳ To accept students from ABC International, as recommended by ABC International, as sophomore standing students at RCC.

These students recommended by ABC International shall be accepted by RCC on the condition that they fulfill the criteria provided in Articles B1 and B2 of this agreement.

✳ To accept 60 credits earned by ABC International graduates and provide the graduates with a statement of courses needed to complete the Associate of General Studies degree. The typical courses required for completion are attached to this agreement as Appendix I.

✳ To issue the appropriate I-20 forms for ABC International graduates admitted to RCC by March 1 of each year.

✳ To enroll each ABC International student in a "bridge" intensive English language program in their first term, Spring Quarter. During that time students are expected to take an intensive ESL course and may be allowed to take one regular course, and to prepare for the regular courses in the Summer Quarter. Intensive English language classes are available to them after their first quarter, but are optional.

✳ To provide the same academic, residence and student services for ABC International graduates as are provided for all RCC students. This is contingent upon the payment of all applicable fees—including international student tuition, student fees, living expenses and host family program costs. Homestay arrangements will be facilitated through the same agency available to other international students, for the same fees; this will also support airport pick-up.

✳ To provide a transcript of each ABC International graduate to ABC International University within one month after the completion of each term, in accordance with a signed release by each ABC International graduate.

✳ To award the Associate of General Studies degree to ABC International graduates who successfully complete degree requirements.

✳ To advise ABC International University of the student's progress.

B. ABC International agrees:

To select participants for this program who have:

✳ Demonstrated general aptitude and proficiency for college level education. ABC International graduates must achieve the equivalent of a U.S.A. 2.00 Grade Point Average (GPA) on all previous college work;

✳ Demonstrated proficiency in the English language, in February of the year of enrollment, by scoring at least 440 on either the paper-based international or institutional TOEFL, or 123 on the computerized TOEFL.

✳ Satisfactory attitude towards study in a foreign culture.

ABC International will select its students from the results of a final examination to be held in February of each year. ABC International will notify RCC, no later than February 10, of the students selected for the program. For each student selected for the program, ABC International will forward to RCC the following application packet by January 1:

✳ International student application form and fee;

✳ Affidavit of financial support;

✳ Certificate of immunizations;

✳ Certificate of TOEFL score;

✳ ABC International transcript as of the date of submission, in English;

✳ Letter of recommendation from the ABC International University President.

Note: A final student transcript will be sent from ABC International University between April 1 and July 1. (Students must request the transcript.)

It is understood that individual ABC International graduates will bear the cost of all applicable fees including tuition, student fees and room and board fees at RCC.

ABC International will require its students to be covered by medical and hospitalization insurance that is satisfactory to RCC.

To consult with RCC to confirm the English language ability of ABC International graduates in late August or early September of each year before the commencement of the Fall term.

To tailor its curriculum at ABC International to assure that ABC International graduates can complete their associate degree at RCC in approximately one year.

Alternatives

Students who do not meet the minimum TOEFL score described above may still be considered for admission to RCC as long as they meet all other criteria. Students whose TOEFL score is below 440 may be required to enroll in ESL courses at RCC for a period longer than one quarter.

Students who wish to pursue a different Associate degree, such as a transfer or technical degree may also be considered for this program. However, RCC will make an individual degree plan with the student, and it may be necessary to spend longer than one year at RCC to complete all requirements.

EVALUATION OF THE PROGRAM

Ⓓ The term of this agreement shall be for five (5) years, commencing September 1, 2009, or as of the date of the last signature—whichever is later. This represents a continuation of an agreement begun in 1999. Both parties agree that continuing assessment is important.

Ⓔ If this evaluation provides information that leads either RCC or ABC International to conclude that it is not successful, twelve (12) months prior notice on the part of either party will be required for termination of the agreement.

Ⓕ Even if the agreement is terminated, both parties will continue to perform their obligation until all currently enrolled students have completed their education at RCC.

This agreement may be modified by mutual accord through an addendum signed by the Presidents or Vice Presidents of both RCC and ABC International. The provisions herein established fully represent the understanding of both parties. There are no additional interpretations, oral or written, that are not already incorporated within this agreement.

[SIGNATURE]	[DATE]
Vice President for Educational Services	Date
[SIGNATURE]	[DATE]
Vice Chair of the Board	Date

Appendix I

Students who attend RCC under the terms of this agreement will be pursuing an Associate of General Studies degree and will need to complete, at least, these courses at Regional Community College:

✳ English 98 or 101, or Speech 100 or 101.

✳ One 5-credit math course, numbered Math 17 or higher.

✳ One 5-credit Humanities course as listed on our AAS-Option II distribution list.

✳ One 5-credit Social Sciences course as listed on our AAS-Option II distribution list.

✳ One 5-credit Natural Sciences course as listed on our AAS-Option II distribution list.

✳ (The Humanities, Social Sciences and Natural Sciences courses must be selected from three different disciplines).

✳ At least five additional credits in college-level courses.

THIRTEEN

Student Visa and Immigration Issues

TERI ALBRECHT | Director of International Student and Scholar Services | The University of Texas at Austin

Student Visa and Immigration Issues

Navigating the student visa process can prove challenging for both the student and the school administrator. Multiple procedures involving the school, the immigration agencies and the U.S. consulate easily make the visa process seem overwhelming. However, with a basic understanding of the student immigration process, confusion can be lessened. This chapter will provide an overview of visa classifications most commonly used by students; define terms used during student immigration advising situations; describe the function of the agencies involved in student immigration processes; detail the ways in which advisors can successfully work with prospective students; explain the process by which students enter the United States; outline the responsibilities of the student and school upon the student's arrival at the home institution and provide resources for both school administrators and students.

Visa Classifications

There are many visa classifications that a student may hold while attending an institution of higher education. There are over twenty U.S. visa categories ranging from A1 to V3, and while students in many of these visa statuses can attend college on their respective visa, the majority of students attending programs and schools are in F-1 or J-1 visa status.

✳ F-1 VISA: The F-1 visa is the most common visa status for international students attending programs (*e.g.*, English as a Second Language programs) and schools (*e.g.*, institutions of higher education). Students who plan to receive an F-1 visa will receive an I-20 document from the school they are planning to attend.

The F-1 visa status is regulated by United States Immigration & Customs Enforcement (USICE).

✳ J-1 VISA: The J-1 visa is also used for international students attending institutions of higher education. A common use of this visa status, for many institutions, is to facilitate reciprocal exchange programs. Students who plan to receive a J-1 visa will receive a DS-2019 document from either the school they are planning to attend or from the program sponsor. The J-1 visa status is regulated by United States Department of State (USDOS).

✳ Other visas categories common at universities: While the F-1 and the J-1 visa are most common to university study, some students may present other visa documents and may not want to change their immigration status to F-1 or J-1. The majority of visa statuses will allow students to attend school incidental to their primary purpose in the United States (*e.g.*, an H1-B visa holder whose primary purpose is to work in the United States could simultaneously attend school and pursue a degree as long as the individual does not waiver from the primary purpose of working). However, there are two visa statuses, F-2 and B1/B2, which specifically restrict individuals from matriculating into a program or school.

Immigration regulations specifically restrict F-2 visa holders (the dependents of F-1 visa holders) from engaging in full-time study at the university level. The regulations also limit any part-time study unless it is considered to be "avocational or recreational in nature" [8 C.F.R. 214.2(f)(15)(ii)]. B1/B2 visa holders (travel for business and tourism) are also prevented from studying while on the B1/B2 visa. While immigration regulations restrict these visa categories from studying, schools should create their own policies regarding enrollment practices. For example, if a student in an unauthorized status chooses to study, the program/school may allow the student to do so with the student's understanding that he or she is violating his/her immigration status in doing so.

To learn more about U.S. visas, see the USDOS Web site: http://travel.state.gov/visa/questions/questions_4429.html.

Immigration Documents

Regardless of visa status, international students will have specific documents that prove their immigration status in the United States.

❋ PASSPORT: A passport is a "document issued by competent authority showing the bearer's origin, identity, and nationality, if any, which is valid for entry of the bearer into a foreign country" [INA § 101(a)(30)]. With the exception of Canadian citizens who enter the United States through a land or sea entry, every foreign national must have a passport to enter the United States. An individual's passport should be valid for the duration of time spent in the United States. Passport extensions can usually be processed by the foreign consulate located in the United States. In some cases, the passport must be sent outside the United States for processing.

❋ VISA: The visa, a stamp that is issued in the individual's passport, is issued by the U.S. consulate/embassy outside the United States. While most visas are issued in the person's home country, it is not always the case. Most foreign nationals are required to have visas to enter the United States. The exception to this is Canadians entering from the western hemisphere who are not required to have a visa if they are entering in a visa category other than A, G, E, K or V and tourist/business visitors who may enter the United States for a period of up to ninety days under the Visa Waiver Program. Countries eligible for the Visa Waiver Program are posted at the Department of

State Web site: http://travel.state.gov/visa/temp/types/types_1262.html#2.

Visa costs, duration of the visa and number of allowable entries into the United States are based on reciprocity. To better understand the reciprocity agreements, the Department of State Web site can be beneficial: http://travel.state.gov/visa/frvi/reciprocity/reciprocity_3272.html.

Although visas have an expiration date, the expiration date does not indicate how long the individual can remain in the United States. The visa is like an entry ticket, it must be valid for the person to enter the United States. Once the visa expires and the person departs the United States, it must be renewed at a U.S. consulate/embassy outside the United States in order for the individual to reenter the United States.

❋ I-94 ARRIVAL/DEPARTURE CARD: The I-94 card is issued and validated by United States Customs and Border Protection (USCBP) at the port of entry. The I-94 card is an important document because it provides proof of legal admission into the United States. The card also indicates the length of time for which the individual is valid to remain in the United States. For students in F-1 and J-1 status, I-94 cards are issued for "D/S," meaning Duration of Status. Duration of status means that a student can remain in the United States as long as he or she maintains valid student status and the I-20/DS-2019 is valid.

❋ SEVIS FEE RECEIPT: All F-1, J-1 and M-1 students must pay the SEVIS fee before applying for their respective visa. Students pay for the fee online and are sent a receipt showing proof of payment. The fee receipt should be kept as a part of the student's permanent immigration documentation.

❋ I-20/CERTIFICATE OF ELIGIBILITY FOR NON-IMMIGRANT (F-1) STUDENT STATUS: Students who enter the United States in F-1 status will be issued an I-20. Programs and schools must be approved by U.S. Immigration & Customs Enforcement (USICS) to issue I-20 documents.

✳ **DS-2019/CERTIFICATE OF ELIGIBILITY FOR NON-IMMIGRANT (J-1) STUDENT STATUS:** Students who enter the United States in J-1 status will be issued a DS-2019. Programs and schools must be approved by the U.S. Department of State to issue DS-2019 documents.

Understanding the Structure of Federal Agencies Involved with International Students

There are a number of federal agencies that are involved with the presence of international students in the United States. The main agency is the Department of Homeland Security, which under its auspices has three separate agencies that interact with international students.

✳ **U.S. IMMIGRATION AND CUSTOMS ENFORCEMENT (USICE)** administers the SEVIS system, the federal database used to issue immigration documents and track international students while in the United States. USICE is also involved in investigating possible anomalies with a student's SEVIS record, including situations where students are no longer enrolled in a program but are believed to still be present in the United States.

✳ **U.S. CUSTOMS AND BORDER PROTECTION (USCBP)** is the first agency with which students will come into contact. USCBP will inspect the student's documents upon entry to the United States and make a determination to admit the student into the country. Upon admission, the student's I-20/DS-2019 and I-94 card are processed to indicate a legal entry into the United States.

✳ **U.S. CITIZENSHIP AND IMMIGRATION SERVICES (USCIS)** is the designated agency that approves benefits for foreign nationals in the United States. International students will interact with USCIS to apply for certain types of work authorization, replace lost I-94 cards and other applications that facilitate their status in the United States.

The U.S. Department of State coordinates the U.S. consulates and embassies throughout the world and also administers the J-1 Exchange Visitor Category. Students who apply for a student visa to enter the United States must submit a visa application to, preferably, the U.S. consulate or embassy that is located nearest to their residence in their home country.

Preparing to Work with an International Student

KNOW THE STUDENT'S CURRENT IMMIGRATION STATUS

When working with prospective international students to determine what documents they need to enter the United States, there are some important questions that the student should be asked. These questions could be a part of an intake form or asked of the student directly before processing any documents.

Is the student entering from his or her home country? If so, then the student will not have a current immigration status in the United States and will need to be sent a Certificate of Eligibility (I-20 or DS-2019) to his/her residence abroad.

Is the student already in the United States in F-1 or J-1 status? If the student is already studying at another school in the United States in F-1 or J-1 status then a transfer of the student's SEVIS record will need to take place in order to issue an I-20 to the student.

Is the student already in the United States but in another visa category? If the student is in another visa status, it must first be determined if that visa status allows the student to enroll in courses. If the visa status does not allow enrollment or the student wishes to change to a student visa status, the student must submit either a Change of Status application to USCIS or travel outside the United States, apply for a visa at the U.S. consulate or embassy and enter on the student visa. In either case, an I-20/DS-2019 must be issued for the student to facilitate the change of visa status.

DOCUMENT ISSUANCE

The use of SEVIS, the Student and Exchange Visitor Information System, became mandatory in 2003 for any program or school wishing to bring international students to the United States in F-1, J-1 or M-1 status. SEVIS is an electronic database that facilitates the issuance of I-20 and DS-2019 documents and also serves as a mechanism to track students' progress while in their respective programs. Schools must be certified to use SEVIS through submission of the Form I-17 and a certification process. School officials must be designated within the SEVIS system to access and make updates to students' records. For F-1 programs, school officials are defined as Designated School Officials (DSO), and a Principal Designated School Official (PDSO) must also be designated within the system. The PDSO is responsible for insuring compliance with SEVIS and is also the primary contact person for the immigration agencies when contacting the school. When changes are made to school officials or when institutional information changes, the Form I-17 and I-17A must be resubmitted to update the information that was originally submitted through the initial Form I-17. For J-1 programs, school officials are defined as Alternate Responsible Officers (ARO), and a Responsible Officer (RO) must also be designated to serve as the primary contact.

SEVIS is slated to undergo a complete overhaul in 2010, and the changes to the SEVIS database will ultimately be paired with new regulations that affect international students. It is imperative, when working with international students, that regulations that affect international students be monitored at all times to ensure the best possible advising to students.

SEVIS can be used through either a Web interface or through batch processing. Many schools use the Web interface to create documents and report events. Examples of reportable events are confirmation that the student enrolls in the program of study each semester, a student's change of address, infractions against the student's visa status such as not enrolling in a full course of study or being dismissed from the academic program.

For more information on SEVIS and SEVIS reporting requirements, see the Student and Exchange Visitor Program (SEVP) Web site: www.ice.gov/sevis.

REQUIREMENTS TO ISSUE AN I-20 OR DS-2019

In order for an I-20 to be issued, two main requirements must be met: (1) the student has submitted an application and has been admitted to the school's program of study to enroll in a full course load and (2) sufficient proof of financial support has been submitted by the student to cover tuition and fees, living expenses, expenses of any dependents that will be brought to the United States and other specific expenses imposed or specified by the program or school. An I-20 can be issued for any program of study that is listed on the school's Form I-17 and has received USICE approval. Programs of study can range from an English as a Second Language (ESL) program, to a certificate program, to a degree program. The I-20 form requires the school official to indicate the level of English proficiency held by the student. While English proficiency is not required in all cases (for example, students admitted to an ESL program), students who are admitted to a degree program should either have a basic English proficiency as defined by the school's admission score requirements, or, if deficient, it must be stipulated on the I-20 that the student will receive English training upon arrival at the school. Consular officials may request that the student show proof of English proficiency or planned English instruction, thus students must be able to produce evidence of this.

In order for a DS-2019 to be issued, the school must have admitted the student to enroll in a full course load of study and substantiate that either (1) the majority of the student's funding does not come from personal or family funds or (2) the student is participating in an exchange program that has been formalized between the school and a foreign institution. Fewer students enter the United States as J-1 students, and programs/schools that are approved to issue J-1 documents must strictly adhere to the Department of State J-1 requirements.

FINANCIAL SUPPORT DOCUMENTATION

There is no written requirement as to what constitutes an acceptable financial support document. Schools have implemented their own policies as to what is acceptable for issuance of the I-20 or DS-2019. Certain considerations to make include:

✳ What is the minimum amount you will require for the specified academic term listed on the I-20/DS-2019?

  ◆ Working with the financial aid office on campus is often very helpful to determine both the cost of living amounts and tuition and fees estimates.

  ◆ Review the costs each year to reflect the rising cost of tuition and living expenses.

✳ Will you require original financial documents or will faxes, copies and scanned documents be acceptable?

✳ What types of financial support documents will you accept?

  ◆ Will you only accept documents written in English?

  ◆ Must the financial document be from an account which has readily available funds (this would exclude many pension/retirement funds or Certificates of Deposit that take years to mature)?

  ◆ Will you accept a tax return or a letter of employment verifying an individual's salary?

It is essential to answer the above questions in addition to other questions that will naturally arise when thinking about a policy regarding financial support documents. Deciding on and instituting a written policy will prove advantageous when dealing with the variety of documents and scenarios that will likely be submitted on the student's behalf.

CREATING AN I-20/DS-2019

Once the requirements for an I-20/DS-2019 have been met, the document can be issued through SEVIS. Within SEVIS specific data fields are required in order to process the document. The document can be generated immediately through the SEVIS Web site; once all required data fields are entered and the document request submitted, SEVIS will generate an I-20/DS-2019 in PDF format that can be printed immediately. The document will include the student's SEVIS ID number on the top right.

APPLYING FOR A VISA

To apply for a visa, the student must first pay the SEVIS fee. This can be done through the SEVIS fee Web site either in the United States or in a foreign country. Many consulates will not allow the booking of a visa appointment until the SEVIS fee is paid. Making an appointment at the U.S. consulate or embassy will vary by consulate and by country, thus students should be encouraged to consult the consulate/embassy's Web site. Waiting periods for an appointment also vary by location. The Department of State has a convenient Web site that estimates waiting periods at certain consulates and embassies: www.travel.state.gov/visa/temp/wait/tempvisitors_wait.php.

Depending on the country and location where the student will apply for the visa, certain documents will be required, at a minimum, the following: passport, Form I-20 or DS-2019, proof of SEVIS fee payment, visa application forms DS-156 and DS-158 (found on the Department of State Web site), a two-inch square photograph and visa issuance fees. Additionally, the following may be required: Form DS-157 (found on the Department of State Web site), transcripts and diplomas from previous study, scores from standardized tests, proof of financial support and proof of non-immigrant intent. The latter requirement, proof of non-immigrant intent, is probably the most ambiguous as there is no list of specific information for a consular officer to use in assessing whether a student meets this requirement. Students should be prepared to show proof of ties to their country through family members remaining in the country, substantiated bank accounts, ownership of land or other investments.

Visa difficulties that some students may encounter include background checks and security clearances.

While there is little that can be done to expedite these processes, it is often helpful for some students who undergo security clearances, especially graduate students, to have a letter from their academic department specifying the type of research in which they will be involved.

Entering the United States

An F, J and M-1 student can enter the United States up to 30 days prior to the program start date on their immigration document. During the flight to the United States (at the border for those that drive into the United States), the student will be issued an I-94 card. This card is essential for the student to have throughout his/her studies. It is also imperative that the student complete this card as accurately as possible and that his/her name on the I-94 card match exactly the name written in the passport.

With the launch of SEVIS II in 2010, the data on the I-94 card will become more critical. USICE has developed a handout detailing how to properly complete an I-94 card: www.ice.gov/doclib/sevis/pdf/migration_factsheet.pdf.

Upon entry into the United States, a CBP Officer will inspect the student's documents. The documents that should be readily available for inspection include the I-20/DS-2019, passport, visa, I-94 card, letter of admission to program and financial support documents. While these are the most common documents requested, the CBP officer may ask for any additional supporting documentation that proves the student's entry as a bona fide student and that he or she has non-immigrant intent in entering the United States.

If additional questions arise during the entry process, the student may be sent to secondary inspection. The secondary inspection area is an office within the airport (or in the port of entry station if entry is by land) where the student will be required to have a second interview with an immigration officer. It is common that students are substantially delayed and miss their next flight when secondary inspection is required.

Arriving at the Home Institution

Once the student arrives at the program for which the I-20/DS-2109 has been issued, several requirements must be fulfilled by both the student and the school.

Student's requirements:

* Report to the PDSO/DSO within 30 days from the program start date in order to have the SEVIS record activated.

* Provide a local U.S. address and report any change of address within 10 days.

* Register for a full course load of studies each semester.

School's requirements:

* Register the student in SEVIS and provide a current local address within 30 days of the program start date.

* Report any student not enrolled within 30 days of the program start date.

* Register the student in SEVIS each semester that the student is enrolled in the program of study.

* Comply with all SEVIS reporting requirements.

Schools have a critical responsibility to report to SEVIS. Failure to comply could result in the loss of school certification to issue I-20s and DS-2019s. It is imperative that school officials understand the importance of complying with SEVIS reporting requirements and knowing the deadlines in which to do so. Reporting requirements can be clearly found within the Code of Federal Regulations: 8 C.F.R. 214.2(f), *User Manual for School Users of the Student and Exchange Visitor Information System: Volume II Form I-20* located on the SEVP Web site and the *NAFSA Adviser's Manual*.

Advising Scenarios for Students Already Present in the United States

Once the student arrives at the program for which the I-20/DS-2109 has been issued, several advising scenarios could be encountered. The two most common are transfers and reinstatements.

An F-I or J-I student that transfers from one U.S. program/school to another must complete an immigration transfer of their SEVIS record to the new institution. This also applies to students that complete or graduate from one program and are admitted to a new program. Immigration transfers have very specific guidelines and deadlines that must be followed and a school official must ensure that both are being carefully followed. Failure to transfer the student to the new program could cause the student to lose his/her immigration status.

A number of scenarios can cause F-I/J-I students to lose their immigration status, also known as a violation of status. A student's immigration status should not be a determining factor as to whether or not the student is admissible to a program or school. An F-I or J-I student who is admitted to a program/school without a valid status should be counseled accordingly as to what the best route is to reinstate status. Some students who violate their status may be eligible to request a reinstatement to their valid status through a Form I-539 reinstatement application to USCIS. Other students may have to travel outside the United States and make a "new entry" to reinstate status. These decisions should not be made lightly as each has serious consequences if not successful. Advisors that are not comfortable with advising on these issues should consult other resources and colleagues in the field who can help.

Helpful Resources for Schools

Resources available to assist with the immigration advising process include professional practice information and trainings through conferences and workshops by organizations like AACRAO and NAFSA: Association of International Educators.

NAFSA: Association of International Educators (www.nafsa.org) specifically provides full-day workshops on F-I and J-I advising at both a beginner and advanced level. Additionally, the local, state and annual conferences often provide sessions that include government officials, best practices and technical sessions. NAFSA also publishes the *NAFSA Adviser's Manual*

which is notably the most comprehensive resource available for advising international students. Membership in NAFSA is not required to subscribe to the *NAFSA Adviser's Manual.*

The Student & Exchange Visitor Program (SEVP) (www.ice.gov/sevis/schools/index.htm), a program within the ICE agency, specifically focuses on SEVIS issues that affect schools and students. The SEVP Web site provides information, such as how to get certified as an F&M School; how to receive J-program designation; online DSO training course and training slides; SEVIS information, advising resources and user manuals and updates on the implementation and guidelines of SEVIS II.

Helpful Resources for Students

The most helpful resource for students is information that schools place on their Web sites to help prospective and admitted students prepare for their studies in the United States. Information should include the process by which students obtain admission to the program, the financial support documents required for the I-20/DS-2019, timeline for I-20/DS-2019 issuance, guidance on how to pay the SEVIS fee and check-in and orientation information.

There are also a number of online resources that are helpful for students:

* NAFSA's student Web site: www.nafsa.org/students.sec/international_students_2
* SEVP's Web site for students: www.ice.gov/sevis/students/index.htm
* Department of State's Student and Exchange Visitor's Web site: www.travel.state.gov/visa/temp/types/types_1270.html
* Education USA Web site: www.travel.state.gov/visa/temp/types/types_1270.html

Clearly, the student immigration process can be complex. However, the proper resources and training can minimize the complexities. This chapter has provided a very brief overview about student visas and their respective immigration processes. The best service an advisor can give to a student depends on adequate training and taking full advantage of available resources. Minimizing immigration complexities for students adds to the richness of their experience in the United States, which in turn promotes international education for the United States. It is in our best interest to guide our students with the most accurate information possible so they will, in turn, promote United States programs and schools to their colleagues, friends and family.

Orientation as a
Key Component
to International
Student Success

Executive Director
Office of International Students & Scholars
Rice University

ADRIA L. BAKER

2010 AACRAO INTERNATIONAL GUIDE

Orientation as a Key Component to
International Student Success

In U.S. colleges and universities, orientation is a time when new students are given instruction and programs are developed in an effort to integrate the students as quickly as possible into the school environment. The length of the program and the manner in which the programs are presented vary from institution to institution. However, students coming from another country to study should always be given a specialized instructional program before, preferably, or during the general university orientation days or week, in order to address immigration responsibilities and benefits, cultural differences, adjustment challenges, academic expectations in the U.S. and general logistics that may be unique to the U.S. and the host school.

International orientation programs should reflect the key objectives of the institution for their students and emphasize core values of the school's mission. Too often competing activities divert the orientation schedule, *i.e.*, filling the days reserved for the programs' primary purposes with events that avert focus from the principal objectives. Strategic goals and purposes for orientation need to be written, articulated to leaders and reviewed periodically to ensure priorities remain on track.

The process of orientation should begin well before the student arrives at the school. The continuum of orientation commences upon receiving admission documentation and preparation of immigration documents, such as the I-20 for F-1 students or the DS-2019 for J-1 Exchange Visitor students. An arrival packet should accompany the immigration documents, including a wealth of initial information such as logistics needed to apply for an entry visa or transfer to the new school if already in the U.S. as a student.

In this modern day of multiple avenues for communication online, creating connections with the school and among peers is quite accessible. The international student office should first evaluate who and what information across campus is being sent to orient the international student; this ensures that 1) the information is clear as to the parameters of the international students' admission and expectations upon arrival at the school; 2) the visa information, documentation and guidance for gaining entrance to the U.S. is comprehensible and 3) conflicting pieces of information are not being sent from academic or administrative departments, residential offices and student activities or clubs. Pre-arrival orientation represents an excellent time to offer training opportunities to begin preparing international students for some principal challenges—culturally, logistically and academically—they may face as soon as they arrive in the United States. Creative online programs, Web site recommendations and handouts are excellent resources for orientation preparation.

As a general rule, key social goals for orientation include creating opportunities for students to, 1) build their own network systems; 2) assist in developing a sense of "community" for international students and 3) ease the adjustment to a new country, culture, mores, education system and school as much as possible. Pre-arrival is a time to encourage connections between the new incoming international students and current students. Oftentimes, the initial challenging adjustment period may be minimized if the new incoming students are able to develop an early support system, even before arriving to the school, with those students already on campus.

Key components of the international student orientation program for students who have just arrived include,

1) welcome, 2) immediate survival, 3) adjustment, 4) pragmatics, 5) regulatory and legal responsibilities, 6) resources, 7) academic preparation and 8) introduction to the community at large. Productive survival orientation for newcomers requires creating an atmosphere where international students feel particularly welcomed in their new host institution. A formal opening welcome speech by a high level official, such as a provost or vice president, is encouraged and sets the appropriate tone of value that international students bring to the institution. Following, and in contrast, the program requires a short segment that will create a relaxed atmosphere and help put the students at ease. The NAFSA: Association of International Educators' Intercultural Activity Toolkit is an excellent resource for finding an appropriate ice-breaker that fits one's campus culture. International student volunteers, staff members of the international student office and community volunteers also play a key role in creating a friendly and open first impression at the orientation program. The process of building "community" among the international group, as well as within the overall school, is a necessary first step for helping newly-arrived international students adjust to their new school, home, city and country. Teaching students about campus culture, traditions and opportunities for involvement while still pursuing academic success helps international students to feel a part of their new school and should be an integral part of orientation.

For students coming from abroad, survival needs are immediate upon arrival. Offering in written materials the necessary resources for available housing options, where and how to buy food, transportation options and other pressing needs are critical. A checklist is helpful in directing the international students to the proper offices on campus they need to visit online or in person, as well as their locations. This will assist them in getting registered and settled into the academic environment more quickly. Instruction as to where students need to go off campus, including visits to the driver's license office and other governmental offices should be included in the orientation program.

Although degree-seeking (non-intensive English language) students will have met a minimum language proficiency requirement in order to be eligible to receive SEVIS Form I-20 [see 8 C.F.R. 214.2(f)] for international students' admission to F-I status, there tends to be a language adjustment period for most students. Non-native English speakers may have strong reading and writing English language ability, but may lack practice with their speaking and listening English skills. Often, international students coming from countries where English is the native language find the extensive use of idioms and slang commonly used in everyday English in the U.S. confusing. Orientation programs need to include resource information about the opportunities available for building language proficiencies.

Other immediate orientation needs include information on "how do I...?" Issues of immediate concern include, communicating with family and friends abroad to assure loved ones of their safe arrival, as well as information on how to set up a telephone system. The orientation program should include resources regarding the most practical and economical places to shop for groceries, toiletries, clothes, cars, cell phones, etc.

The adjustment period varies for each individual, but usually will begin the first day an international student arrives in the U.S. The orientation program during the first days provides the best opportunity to introduce and describe the concept and process of cultural adjustment because the students will be more at ease asking questions about their new country and culture once the subject has been presented formally. Although most will feel excited initially about their new venture, surroundings and school, it is crucial that the international student orientation includes information about acculturation challenges and stages, which can be illustrated with the W-curve of cultural adjustment (Gullahorn and Gullahorn 1963). Being introduced to this concept early on tends to be a source of help as students move through the acculturation cycle common to internationals. The W-curve model illustrates the pattern of stages, beginning with eagerness and enthusiasm for learning about the new culture, possessing a positive view of the newness of their adventure. This tends to follow a sharp downward fall in mood and attitude toward the host culture. Afterward, cultural adjustment begins and the students gravitate toward more favorable and accepting views and attitudes. This pattern often finds repetition upon re-entry to one's home country, and the W-curve, which patterns an upward and downward track of the moods and perspectives, is replayed in one's own culture. The end goal is to seek out and adapt to one's values the best aspects of both cultures, thus becoming successfully bicultural.

International student orientation programs should provide practical information regarding differences between cultures and awareness about the concepts of U.S. culture that international students tend to find challenging. The training should include examples of societal traditions and norms that may be confusing to new international students. Examples commonly used to encourage discussions on how perspectives in the U.S. may differ from cultural norms in other countries include, 1) the value placed on time and punctuality in the U.S., 2) personal space differences, 3) greetings versus sincere interest in how one is doing and 4) the individualistic/independent society versus the collectivistic/interdependent group culture (Triandis 1989).

In general, the international student orientation program in the initial days serves as a type of "buffer" before classes begin and the hard academic and social adjustment work begins for the students. This is the opportune time to not only train the students on issues unique to international students, but to also assist them in completing as many logistics required for settling in as possible. International students need to officially register with the international student office in order to present their immigration documents and consult an international advisor about any problems. Intensive information as to the students' immigration benefits, responsibilities and limitations of their visa statuses must be made clear during this orientation program.

Further, non-immigration legal issues in the U.S. and student judicial policies for the school are essential topics for the orientation. Examples include, respectively, the legal drinking age in the U.S. and academic integrity including plagiarism. Due to cultural differences, problems may arise if the students are not made aware of how laws and policies work in the U.S. and at their school. To illustrate, many students from abroad are accustomed to working in study groups. As a result, they must gain a clear understanding of the difference between studying in a group and producing one's own knowledge and work. In some situations, distinctions may be discreet, yet the need for cultural precision in this crucial concept is vital. Lack of clarity could cause a student to violate the school's academic honesty policy, resulting in potentially harsh consequences, including expulsion and deportation.

International student orientation must provide information on procedures and policies for registering and paying for classes, receiving proper academic advising and obtaining transfer credit. Other practical, but often confusing, needs that international students have comprise opening a bank account, gaining access to a computer account, buying a cell phone, setting up utilities, getting an identification card from the school, applying for a state identification or driver's license, social security and related regulatory needs, etc.

Students are overloaded with so much information in their first days in the U.S. that it is impossible for them to retain all of the information presented in the international and general orientations. Although it is essential to introduce the students to the many key concepts, it is equally important to provide them with the ability to resource the information for future referral. Written handouts, booklets and Web information serve as key reference sources when the need arises.

During orientation, international students should be introduced to what support services the international student office provides, as well as when and how this office can best help them. Clarifying the following questions would serve as a useful reference for the new international students: Is the international office accessible only for immigration questions and employment authorization, or can it offer other necessary support? Which regulatory, financial and personal issues can the international office provide useful information on for international students? What is the best way for a student to meet with an international advisor? What services are provided by other offices on campus? Who can provide the best information on academic support, campus activities, networking, recreation or health and wellness? If I have financial problems or need to travel home for an emergency, to whom would I speak? Who can assist me on issues relating to conflict resolution with my advisor, my roommate or a study group member?

As mentioned earlier, legal issues vary from country to country. Remembering specific information on legal responsibilities may be difficult to retain, however, it is essential that the students be introduced to resource information so that they can review it at a less stressful time than the first days in their new home. Reference information on alcohol policies and laws, driving legalities, key concepts in signing contracts, lawful online downloads and other legalities are essential for helping students avoid potential pitfalls. It is helpful for students to understand the role of the schools' attorneys in representing the institution, if a situation requires legal assistance. In most cases they may choose to seek private outside legal counsel.

For many international students, the specialization of services provided to students by different offices on a U.S. campus may prove very confusing. The resource information should include the "where do I find...?" key contact offices, locations on campus, telephone numbers and e-mails of vital support people and Web site referrals. Extended services include providing mentor-like programs, which goes well beyond the formal services provided by the school's international office staff. Volunteer programs are an excellent source of help to the students, as they can help new students from abroad more individually. People from the community, student volunteers and student clubs and associations

can provide assistance, including pick-up from the airport, shepherding students around campus to meet all of the responsibilities they need for registration and payment, providing a friendly welcome, answering questions that are unique to fellow students, introducing them to other students with the same field of study and meeting with them periodically during their first year as they adjust to their new environment. Friendship community programs are particularly helpful for the students and tend to enrich the students' educational experience, as they gain a better insight into U.S. culture, behavior and thinking. Although many community volunteers and students genuinely welcome the opportunity to serve in a mentoring capacity to new international students, it is always a good practice to provide some type of appreciation or recognition for their efforts and time. International student offices need to be keenly aware, however, that motivations volunteers bring to befriending international students could extend beyond simply an intercultural exchange and plain kindness. Therefore, it is recommended that volunteers be informed as to the schools' code of ethics and perhaps sign a volunteer code of ethics agreement.

Students come from many different educational systems around the world, so successful orientations include academic preparedness topics unique to the U.S. educational system. Suggested topics helpful for international students to learn about their new scholastic environment include, 1) course credits and how a grade point average (GPA) is calculated; 2) degree plans and prerequisites for taking classes; 3) the overall educational system in the U.S., including primary, secondary and the various avenues of postsecondary education; 4) mores in the classroom; 5) various types of testing which include take-home exams, open-book and traditional tests, quizzes, etc.; 6) effective communication with teachers; 7) participation in class; 8) homework expectations; 9) balancing extracurricular activities with academic responsibilities and 10) individual thoughts while working in study groups (Lipson 2008).

Students will also gain from an understanding of how U.S. styles of logic and learning may differ from those in from other countries. For example, students in the U.S. tend to actively dialogue and question as they learn, while in other countries students may listen to the professor with little or no interaction. In fact, often international students find it quite difficult to question a professor's viewpoint, as this might not be culturally acceptable in one's home country. However, in the U.S., challenging a viewpoint of the instructor with strong rationale based on critical thinking and creativity tends to be an encouraged and acceptable method of learning (Lipson 2008).

Thriving international orientation programs include some type of introduction to the community at large and beyond the borders of the campus or school. City tours using private or public transportation can help students to venture out more readily, thus enhancing their stay in their new home. Opportunities in the city, community celebrations and access to what the area offers are helpful in assisting international students adjust in their new academic and cultural endeavors.

Although there are varying program models schools will use for international orientations, the avenues chosen should best highlight the schools' greatest values, as well as balancing the need to meet the individual and unique needs of students from abroad. Archetypes of orientation programs include the following variations, 1) integrated approach into the school's general orientation; 2) pull-out or stand-alone programs; 3) partnering with general campus orientation programming; 4) specialized orientations for majors, professional programs or academic levels; 5) a "course" for introduction to a new learning environment or 6) hybrids of the various above-mentioned models. The school's culture, size, resources, type of information needing to be offered and core values will determine which model(s) will be used and for which topics. As a best practice, a variety of the

Additional Resources

► Berkeley International Office. *Cultural Adjustment*. Retrieved February 16, 2009 from University of California, Berkeley at http://internationaloffice.berkeley.edu/multiple_use/cultural_adjustment.php.

► Fosnocht, D. J. 2007. *Desk Edition of the NAFSA Advisor's Manual*. Washington D.C: NAFSA Publications.

► National Center on Secondary Education and Transition. *Continuum of "Individualistic" and "Collectivistic" Values*. Retrieved February 15, 2009 from National Center on Secondary Education and Transition at http://ncset.org/publications/essentialtools/diversity/partIII.asp.

► Peace Corps Worldwise Schools. *Culture Matters: The Peace Corps Cross-Cultural Workbook*. Retrieved February 15, 2009 from the Peace Corps at www.peacecorps.gov/wws/publications/culture/pdf/workbook.pdf.

FIGURE 14.1

approaches tends to meet the unique needs of the many types of learners and the vast amount of comprehensive information that needs to be presented to the students.

Orientation is a continuum. The traditional orientation program lasting only over the first days of arrival is no longer an acceptable standard, given the growing complexities of the immigration and other regulatory responsibilities of international students, as well as the many portals for communication available day and night, anywhere in the world. Orientation continues at a different level, however, during the first year of study and appropriate programming should be made available. The needs of a first-year student may include learning how to resolve problems appropriately in one's new culture, working effectively with one's academic advisor or supervisor, time management and study skills for success in the U.S. and dealing with cultural and relational differences in their academic and social life. To complete the orientation cycle, many international students give back to fellow new arrivals by going through a specialized volunteer training and becoming an assistant in subsequent years' orientation. Their own experiences are shared and the tradition of learning and helping others becomes a next step in learning. Further, the value of volunteerism and giving back to the community becomes instilled in the students.

Some best practice recommendations for successful international student orientation in U.S. institutions include the following:

✱ Study the institution's mission statement and make sure orientation strategies follow principal priorities.

✱ Choose models and strategies that can be adjusted as needed for one's unique campus culture, and that are feasible for the program planners.

✱ Focus on topics and issues that are not included in "regular" or mainstream orientation programs. View the agenda with a focus on presenting information that is specific to international students, as opposed to domestic students.

✱ Meet the student where they are. There is a natural progression in cultural adaptation and acculturation; successful programs adjust for these stages, whereby the end goal in the learning process is to help the international student gain as much independence as possible.

✱ Offer opportunities for students to "give back" as a systemized continuum to orientation programs.

✱ Get feedback from the participants, analyze it and use it for future improvements.

✱ Be sensitive of individual physical and emotional needs when planning the schedule. These would include potential homesickness, which students may need time to talk about; otherwise this kind of distraction could derail academic goals. Jet lag, new foods and weather affect the learning environment and ultimately the effectiveness of one's program. Language skills need time to develop through the practice of listening and speaking. Formal opportunities for language advancement help with future academic success.

✱ Seek to foster a sense of community in every aspect of the orientation planning. Key support networks will develop during this time, which can positively impact the students' educational tenure.

✱ Build in follow-up programming during the first year in order to ensure a feeling of continuity and appropriate institutional support.

In conclusion, international student orientation stands as a key component for adjustment to the new home, culture, school and education for students from abroad. The process should not be considered as an initial programmatic need, but a continuous learning process where the students come full circle, eventually contributing to the orientation of other newcomers.

FIFTEEN

Special International Student Populations:
Undocumented Students

2010 AACRAO INTERNATIONAL GUIDE

DEANA WILLIAMS

Assistant Director of Admissions
The University of Texas at Austin

TERI ALBRECHT

Director
International Student and Scholar Services
The University of Texas at Austin

Special International Student Populations: Undocumented Students

Access to institutions of higher education in the United States by undocumented students has long been debated but is far from resolved. While undocumented students in colleges and universities have traditionally gone unnoticed, it is estimated that 65,000 undocumented students graduate from high school annually and over 126,000 enroll in colleges and universities nationwide (Passel 2006). The total population of undocumented persons in the United States is estimated at almost twelve million persons. (*See* Figures 15.1–2 and Table 15.1.) Undocumented students in the "pipeline" for higher education continue to knock on the doors of colleges and universities across the United States, and, depending upon the state in which they live, they receive mixed messages about accessibility. Laws and regulations vary between the states in relation to access and tuition practices. Adding to the confusion, federal law regarding the issue is written in a way that makes states wary about extending admission and tuition benefits to this group of students.

Definition of an Undocumented Student

An undocumented individual is a foreign national who enters the United States either (1) illegally, by circumventing proper entry inspection by an immigration official at a designated port of entry; (2) illegally, by presenting fraudulent documents; or (3) legally, in a valid immigration status but remains in the United States past the expiration of the authorized stay. The majority of undocumented students living in the United States are residing here because their parents brought them into the country at a very young age. These children did not have a choice as to how they entered the country, and now the United States is the only country they know.

Brief History of Undocumented Students' Access to Education

Prior to 1975, the issue of access to education for the thousands of undocumented students in the U.S. had not been addressed in any legal venues or approached in any official capacity. In 1975, a Texas law denied access to public education to students who were not "legally admitted" into the United States. The law

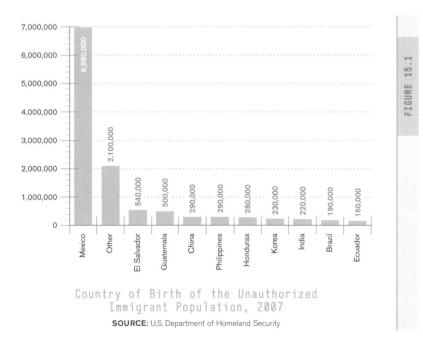

FIGURE 15.1

Country of Birth of the Unauthorized Immigrant Population, 2007

SOURCE: U.S. Department of Homeland Security

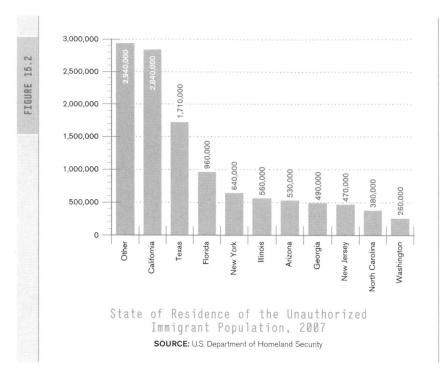

State of Residence of the Unauthorized
Immigrant Population, 2007

SOURCE: U.S. Department of Homeland Security

public services such as health care and education. The most notable among these attempts was the 1994 California ballot measure, Proposition 187, which was passed by voters but subsequently determined to be unconstitutional by a U.S. federal appeals court.

Prior to 2001, the laws and attempted legislative mandates were aimed at undocumented students enrolled at the elementary and secondary education levels. Then in 2001, the state of Texas passed legislation which would be the first to address the issue of undocumented students and their access to higher education benefits. The Texas law (House Bill 1403) guaranteed undocumented students access to in-state tuition and state-funded financial aid if they met certain criteria, including graduation from a Texas high school after three years of physical residence in the state. Soon thereafter, ten other states implemented similar laws allowing in-state tuition for undocumented students and state-funded financial aid in two of the ten states (*see* Table 15.2).

directed Texas public school districts to deny enrollment to undocumented students, which was then legally challenged as a violation of the Equal Protection Clause of the Fourteenth Amendment to the U.S. Constitution. The U.S. Supreme Court case, Plyler v. Doe (1982), overturned the Texas law, thus guaranteeing the right to free public education (K–12) to all children in the U.S. regardless of their immigration status.

During the 80s and 90s laws in many states attempted to restrict undocumented persons' access to social and

Numerous legal challenges to the various state laws have been offered but the most significant among them was Day V. Sebelius (Kansas 2005). Filed by The Federation for American Immigration Reform (FAIR), the case alleged that the Kansas law granting in-state tuition to undocumented students was in violation of Section 505 of the Illegal Immigration Reform and Immigrant Responsibility Act (IIRIRA). The wording in Section 505 of IIRIRA indicates that "Notwithstanding any other provision of law, an alien who is not lawfully present in the United States shall not be eligible on the basis of residence within a State (or a political subdivision) for any postsecondary education benefit unless a citizen or national of the United States is eligible for such benefit (in no less amount, duration and scope) without regard to whether the citizen or

TABLE 15.1: Unauthorized Immigrant
Population by Age (2007)

Age	n	%
All Ages	11,780,000	100
0 to 18 years	1,670,000	14
18 to 24 years	1,870,000	16
25 to 34 years	4,200,000	36
35 to 44 years	2,800,000	24
45 to 54 years	880,000	7
55 and over	350,000	3

* The total is not equal to the sum due to rounding.
Source: U.S. Department of Homeland Security

176

national is such as resident." The lawsuit was dismissed and subsequent appeal attempts were also found to be in favor of the state of Kansas. Similar challenges were made in California but were also rejected by the courts.

Most recently, a federal law known as the DREAM Act (Development, Relief, and Education of Alien Minors) has garnered support through introduction in the U.S. Congress 2009, as well as numerous efforts made by immigrant groups and their allies, but did not receive a vote. Provision of the DREAM Act would permit immigrants who have grown up in the U.S. to apply for temporary legal status and eventually become eligible for U.S. citizenship. It would also repeal Section 505 of IIRIRA which discourages states from providing higher education benefits to immigrants unless the same benefit is available to all U.S. citizens regardless of their state of residence. As of now, the DREAM Act remains stalled in Congress as the undocumented students, for whom its provisions are intended, continue to languish in legal limbo.

Challenges Faced by Students

Undocumented college students face many challenges as they navigate through their college years. Research conducted by Albrecht (2007) identified seven central challenges experienced by undocumented college students. These challenges include (1) coping with frustration and uncertainty; (2) struggling to succeed; (3) feeling the pressure of being a role model; (4) managing life as a "hidden" member of society; (5) missing out on opportunities; (6) perceptions of self as compared to other students; and (7) complications faced in utilizing campus services. Each of these challenges serves as an extra burden on their daily lives as college students.

✳ COPING WITH FRUSTRATION AND UNCER-
TAINTY: Feelings of frustration and uncertainty are often experienced by undocumented students due to the number of barriers they regularly encounter. These barriers include the uncertainty of national immigration policy, financial struggles, and an inability to plan for the future. Some of the more common

TABLE 15.2: State Laws Allowing In-State Tuition for Undocumented Students

State	Year of Passage	Legislation	Financial Aid
Texas	2001	HB 1403	YES
California	2001	AB 540	NO
Utah	2002	HB 144	NO
New York	2002	SB 7784	NO
Washington	2003	HB 1079	NO
Illinois	2003	HB 0060	NO
Oklahoma	2003	HB 1559	YES
Kansas	2004	HB 2145	NO
New Mexico	2005	SB 582	YES
Nebraska	2006	LB 239	NO
Wisconsin	2009	AB 75	NO

restrictions faced by undocumented students include the inability to legally drive since many are not eligible to apply for a driver's license, inability to fly for fear of exposure and oftentimes lack of official identification, and the inability to conduct normal daily business like opening a bank account or renting an apartment due to the lack of a social security number.

Students also face uncertainty regarding their undocumented status in the United States. At any given time, these students are at risk of deportation. Additionally, with state legislative bodies debating tuition benefits for undocumented students, students residing in states that provide in-state tuition are concerned that this benefit could be withdrawn at any time, leaving them unable to pay for college.

Undocumented students, due to their status, are not eligible to hold employment (even on campus) and thus, unlike many college students that support their studies through part-time jobs, must rely on family members' financial contribution and financial aid (in the few states where this is possible) to pay for college. One of the biggest challenges faced by undocumented students is the uncertainty of their post-graduation plans. Without work authorization, those students with academic credentials in hand are forced to retreat into the shadows for jobs. While some students do continue on to graduate studies to further advance their education, most are waiting and hoping for passage of the DREAM Act, which would provide them with the legal basis to hold employment.

✱ **STRUGGLING TO SUCCEED:** Many undocumented students find themselves caught in the middle, on the one hand feeling the need to prove to society that their college education is deserved and, on the other, facing the scrutiny of family members that do not always support or understand their college ambitions. The result of these pressures is that undocumented students report feeling the need to work harder than other students in order to persevere and succeed.

✱ **FEELING THE PRESSURE OF BEING A ROLE MODEL:** Serving as a role model for younger undocumented students preparing for higher education and for younger family members is another challenge faced by undocumented students. Students feel a high level of responsibility to encourage those younger than themselves to attend college. This self-assigned role adds to their pressure to proving themselves as successful college students.

✱ **MANAGING LIFE AS A "HIDDEN" MEMBER OF SOCIETY:** Many undocumented students protect their undocumented identity from others—school administrators, friends, and even significant others—for fear of being exposed. Because the risk of exposure could result in deportation from the United States, undocumented students experience fewer opportunities as a result of living in the shadows of society.

✱ **MISSING OUT ON OPPORTUNITIES:** Undocumented students tend to have fewer options for collegiate opportunities than their peers. For example, undocumented students cannot hold paid internships as many students do during the summer break. Complicating the issue, undocumented students studying in the healthcare and teaching professions often find that they cannot hold unpaid internships because they are unable to complete a background

check (due to their lack of a social security number). These students also miss out on study abroad opportunities because leaving the United States deprives them of their legal basis to reenter the country. As it relates to student organization activities, undocumented students find themselves less able to take advantage of group experiences such as business fairs, site visits, and distant conferences as these are often seen as a chance of exposure.

✱ **PERCEPTIONS OF SELF AS COMPARED TO OTHER STUDENTS:** Undocumented students also find themselves as members of other demographic groups. They are a subset of their ethnic/nationality group—many are first-generation college students—and college administrators may view them (or even classify them) as international students. Although undocumented students may be a subset of these other groups, they feel that they have significantly different needs than the majority of the group, often reporting that they have to work harder while having fewer opportunities. Even though most undocumented students do not relate to the experiences of international students, some students tend to "hide" within the population as it interacts with school administrators and their campus peers.

✱ **COMPLICATIONS FACED IN UTILIZING CAMPUS SERVICES:** Campus services such as career services, financial aid, and academic advising are all essential services for college students. For undocumented students, accessing these services can be viewed as a risky endeavor for fear of disclosing personal information. Because of their ineligibility to work and the potential of having to disclose their undocumented status, career advising is often underutilized by undocumented students. For students who attend schools that provide financial aid, the financial aid office can act as a facilitating office. However, students are not always comfortable disclosing their status making it difficult for the students' advisors to provide information useful in their specific situation. The same can be said for academic advising situations. Other services that undocumented students tend to underutilize include the counseling center and university police services—both helpful services on campus to the majority of the campus population but seen by undocumented students as services that could expose their status.

Challenges Faced by Institutions

Institutions also face many challenges as they assist students in navigating an admissions process and institutional policies not designed for persons without legal status. Making adjustments in procedures and systems to accommodate the undocumented student is paramount in securing their successful matriculation into higher education and ensuring that their retention rate remains at an acceptable level.

✳ DISSEMINATION OF INFORMATION: The issue of getting admissions information out to the many undocumented students in high schools across the country often presents a challenge. Institutional Web sites, applications, printed materials, and other admission documents are formatted with either the domestic applicant or the traditional international student in mind. Undocumented students do not easily fit into either category, thus understanding the procedure necessary for applying to institutions of higher education is challenging, not only for the student, but often for the institution. Institutions should have well-informed recruitment personnel and counselors; develop Web pages that are clear and contain concise instructions on the application process and benefits afforded to undocumented students; maintain close contact with high school counselors, including providing materials for them to reference during their counseling sessions; and distribute printed materials or brochures informing undocumented students of the benefits afforded them under the law. Remember that these students need special assistance, and having key contacts at your institution who can answer their questions is imperative to ensuring a smooth transition from high school to college or university enrollment.

✳ APPLICATION PROCESS: A problem encountered by many undocumented students when applying for admission to institutions of higher education is the dilemma of how to apply, as a domestic applicant since they are residing in the U.S. or as an international applicant since they do not have legal status. Without clear guidance, the application may restrict their access or their willingness to apply for admission. Most undocumented students lack parental support during the application process, primarily due to the concern of exposure felt by their parents, the language barriers they must overcome, or simply because their parents lack postsecondary education experience and thus do not understand the process. Providing bilingual application instructions (most commonly in Spanish) and bilingual advising for the parents can prove invaluable to assisting the families of undocumented students through the application and admission process.

✳ FINANCIAL AID: Because they lack access to traditional forms of financial aid and because their families can offer little in the way of financial assistance, one of the biggest obstacles that undocumented students face in achieving success in higher education is the inability to pay for their education. Federal financial aid is not available for undocumented students, and few states have laws explicitly allowing for state-funded financial assistance. A family's lack of financial documentation creates problems in the processing of financial aid packages for those institutions who do offer state-funded financial aid. Undocumented students cannot complete the FAFSA; thus states and institutions who do offer financial aid to undocumented students often must create their own financial aid application forms and process those forms outside the standard aid determination systems. Also, these students are often underfunded. In the modern financial aid age, most schools use federal guaranteed loans to cover the shortfall between the student's costs and the amount of grants they can afford to provide the student. As no undocumented student can receive these funds, this severely limits the student in total funding. Also, if an undocumented student can obtain a scholarship, the student and the institution have difficulty paying the student these funds in compliance with relevant federal tax laws since he or she has no social security number. Most rules and regulations allowing the student to access state funds mirror federal funding requirements. Many of these processes are easy if the student is a U.S. citizen or permanent resident, but are considerably more challenging when the student is not.

✳ IDENTIFICATION: Most undocumented students lack sufficient identification to enable them to accomplish all of the tasks in the standard admissions and enrollment procedures of a college or university. The absence of documents such as a valid passport, driver's license, and social security card inhibit their ability to conduct regular business that domestic students often take for granted. They cannot verify their identity for purposes of obtaining items and services such as opening a bank account, renting an apartment, obtaining a phone or utilities, or conducting educationally related travel. Even within institutions, identification requirements for items like official university ID cards can cause problems.

✳ FULFILLING DEGREE REQUIREMENTS: When trying to fulfill degree requirements, the lack of proper identification often leads to dead ends for departments and students. For example, an undocumented student who is in an education degree program and must complete student teaching to fulfill his or her degree requirements will face a barrier when they have no social security number for a required background check. Also, undocumented students whose educational pursuits require air travel will not be able to fly without proper documentation. Likewise, a student who must sit for an educational test or a licensing exam may lack proper identification required by the testing or licensing agency. These are but a few of the restrictions that undocumented students encounter and that institutions must consider when implementing policy.

✳ PROVIDING INSTITUTIONAL SUPPORT: Undocumented students are, because of their lack of status and also because of fear of exposure, an anonymous group within institutions. Trying to provide the special support services, both academic and non-academic, that they need is a difficult task that requires balancing their fear of exposure with the institutions' ability to provide individual support. Many undocumented students actively seek immigration advice from an institution in the hope of finding an avenue for gaining legal status in the United States. Having a network of outside referral agencies that can assist students with immigration matters is a way that institutions can provide assistance without going beyond the scope of institutional responsibility. Being sure that academic and career advising centers are sensitive to the special needs, and also aware of the barriers that undocumented students face, is necessary if an institution wants to provide assistance that is of value to undocumented students. Ultimately it is good to remember that all students, whether they possess U.S. citizenship or not, have the right to be treated in a respectful and courteous manner when being served by admissions counselors or by persons in any other university office. They can all use guidance and assistance, and, depending on their situation, it may be possible to help a student realize his or her goals.

✳ MANAGING STATE VERSUS FEDERAL LAWS AND MANDATES: Institutions are tasked with implementing state and federal laws which are not always complementary in their requirements. Deferring to the guidance of institutional legal counsel is always advised when dealing with matters such as immigration status that seriously impact a student's life. Balancing the privacy and protection of a student in relation to the institution's legal requirements should be undertaken with the utmost care and consideration.

Conclusion

The challenge for colleges and universities is to learn more about this population of students in order to provide services to them in a safe environment. The over-arching issue, however, is determining how to promote services to undocumented students without exposing or even advertising their presence on campus. The first step is to better understand the needs of this group of students. At any given time, an undocumented student could be seeking services or advice. Campus administrators should respect the difficult situation in which these students find themselves and be acquainted with resources that will help them succeed in their college journey.

SIXTEEN

Special International Student Populations: Students with Disabilities

DARCY E. MCGILLICUDDY

Coordinator
Sponsored Student Programs, International Office
The University of Texas at Austin

Special International Student Populations: Students with Disabilities

When serving international students with disabilities, there are a number of factors to consider. Statistics reveal that the number of students with disabilities actually traveling to the United States for study is low. Unfortunately, a common perception exists among international students with disabilities that the challenges of adjusting to a new culture may prove insurmountable. While the demands for the student may be great, there are some key things for university staff members to consider that could be of great help to the student.

Every student with a disability is an individual with a distinct background and circumstance. Every student faces different challenges and presents specific needs. Every disability is unique and requires careful thought in regards to appropriate accommodations. In the United States, an ethical and legal obligation for institutions of higher education exists to provide equal opportunities for any student with a disability. It is extremely important to treat each situation as distinctive and avoid making assumptions.

Much can be done to ease a student's transition even before a student boards the airplane! The following section, while far from exhaustive, offers a few options to consider prior to a student's arrival.

Different Types of Disabilities

First, it is important to understand the nature of the specific disability. The needs of a visually impaired student will be very different from those of a student with a hearing or mobility impairment. Additionally, dis-abilities of every kind range in their severity. For example, a student with a developmental impairment (*e.g.*, cerebral palsy, autism, or epilepsy) may be mildly to severely affected by his/her particular disability. The severity can make a tremendous difference in the types of support services needed.

It is important to learn as much as possible about a specific disability so that you can understand your student's situation. This may be particularly important when working with a student with a learning disability (*e.g.*, hyperactivity, hypoactivity, memory disorders), often referred to as an "invisible disability" because it is sometimes not obvious. The university disability services office may be able to provide useful information and expertise.

Cultural Implications

Secondly, if possible, it is helpful to learn more about the student's culture and family situation. Some questions to consider:

* How does the student's culture view disabilities, in general?
* How does the culture view the student's particular disability?
* Does the student require assistance from his/her family? Or are there other people in the community that may provide assistance? If so, to what level might they assist?
* Does the student need assistance with daily tasks, academic activities, or mobility?
* Will a family member or friend be accompanying the student for the initial period or duration of his/her study?

In the United States, there is a great emphasis on students with disabilities functioning as independently as possible; however, this is not the case in every culture. In some cultures, students with disabilities receive a great amount of personal assistance from family and friends. Therefore, it can be very jarring—in addition to the typical culture shock that every new international student encounters—for a student with a disability to adapt to the American view of independence. Leaving a familiar support structure can cause some students to feel further isolated and alone. By addressing some of the questions above before the student arrives, you can help to ensure a smoother transition.

Access to Technology

In today's U.S. university setting, access to and use of technology is an absolute must. Again, because the types of disabilities that exist vary, access to technology may or may not be an issue for your student.

Most students that study abroad come from high schools or universities that prepare them for the university's technological expectations. It is possible that the student has advanced skills and actually relies on technology to live his/her daily life. While technology can be very helpful in the management of some disabilities, it should not be assumed that all students have had access to such technology. For example, it is generally expected that a visually impaired student has access to a computer with assistive software and can use such technology from the first day of class. However, this is not always the case. If a visually impaired student comes from a country with less developed technology in this area, he or she may have succeeded in school using a Braille machine. The level of note taking sometimes needed in a U.S. university classroom would make the use of a Braille machine much more challenging. It is important to know your student's background and the demands your student will face in his/her typical university class. If it appears that there may be a challenge, you should speak with your disabilities office about potential solutions prior to the student's arrival. Often

times it is merely a matter of alerting professors in advance and working with the student individually until he or she feels comfortable in the new classroom environment.

Living Accommodations

Another factor to consider before the student arrives is living accommodations, both short term and long term. If your office is at all involved in arranging travel for students, make sure to notify the airlines of any necessary special accommodations. Ideally, it would be best for the student to have long-term housing available on the day of arrival. Your student may want to do all the research on his/her own, but may also either require or appreciate your assistance. It is always respectful to ask before assuming anything.

Consider creating a list of questions to ask housing providers. Here are a few examples, though this list is not exhaustive and may not apply to some disabilities:

* Does the room and property meet ADA (Americans with Disabilities Act) standards?
* Is it a single story building? If not, does it have an elevator?
* How wide are the doorways and hallways?
* Does each room have a personal bathroom?
* Is there any assistance available for persons with disabilities?

In addition, it may be important to consider whether or not the student needs on-campus or off-campus housing. For some students, dorm life may be very distracting and stressful. For other students, living far from campus may constitute an obstacle. Your student will be able to inform you of his/her needs are and can be your guide for potential questions.

KNOW YOUR CAMPUS RESOURCES

One of the most important things you can do to prepare for your student's arrival involves knowing your campus resources. Here are some helpful questions to consider when seeking out campus resources:

* What services are already available on your campus for students with disabilities?

* Does your campus have a specific disabilities services office? If not, where on your campus are these resources provided? Consider visiting the office and becoming acquainted with the staff if you have not already.

* If your student needs mobility training, does your disability services office offer this training, or will your student need to hire another professional?

* What accommodations can be made for students with learning disabilities?

* How do classrooms accommodate students with hearing disabilities?

* What accommodations are made for students in wheelchairs, especially in older buildings, which may not be equipped with elevators?

* What is available free of charge through campus services; for what services are the students expected to pay?

* How does your campus transportation work? What are the accommodations for students with special needs?

* Are there any student organizations geared towards students with disabilities?

* Are there student volunteers available for assisting students with disabilities?

* In addition to on campus, what resources are available in the community, and how can your student access these resources? Because international students may not qualify for some services, it may be helpful to check in advance.

Conclusion

If some of this information is new to you, you can expect that many of your fellow staff members may not have faced these issues either! If your office will be assisting the student in the first few weeks of arrival or at any time during his/her study, it may be helpful to arrange training for your staff in advance, possibly with your disabilities services office or a professional organization. Perhaps you can find another student or community member with a disability to come and speak with your staff. For example, if you know that a new visually impaired student will need mobility training, you can receive training on how to appropriately assist the student. Such preparation can really help your staff to feel more comfortable and, as a result, be able to provide appropriate assistance to your students.

There are countless issues that can arise during the period of adjustment. Perhaps the most important thing is to be prepared for anything! If you and your staff remain flexible and ready to serve your student, you are sure to share some incredible experiences and learn invaluable lessons along the way.

187

17

SEVENTEEN

Special International Student Populations: College Athletes

Assistant Director of Admissions
Graduate and International Admissions Center
The University of Texas at Austin

ROBERT WATKINS

Special International Student Populations:
College Athletes

Admissions officers face many challenges as they sift through the large volume of applications received for an upcoming semester. None are more challenging than those from students desiring to come to the institution to participate in college athletics. Although applications from domestic students interested in athletics are already more complex due to outside rules governing their handling, applications from international students can prove even more difficult. The National Collegiate Athletic Association (NCAA) creates much of the complexity surrounding athletic admission, but also provides the resources and support needed by its member institutions to chart a course through these difficult waters. In the case of the international athlete, the NCAA and its Eligibility Center provide invaluable assistance in dealing with this most demanding of admissions issues.

On the one hand, the NCAA adds to the complexity of athletic admissions through its voluminous rule book laying out a prodigious number of bylaws and subsections. Admissions officers not familiar with this massive tome operate at high risk when they admit athletes. This is even more pronounced in the case of the international athlete. The NCAA offers a free (to member institutions) *Guide to International Academic Standards for Athletics Eligibility* that is invaluable to those charged with analyzing international athlete applications. The *Guide* is written with the non-expert in mind, whether coach, admissions professional, or athletics compliance officer. But even with this extremely useful information, the final decision often involves the interpretive abilities of the reader.

The *Guide* is published annually by the NCAA and the content flows from one of the many committees of the NCAA. The International Student Records Committee (ISRC), in existence in this form only since 2002, is a standing committee of the NCAA (one of over a hundred committees in that organization). The consultants group that served as the predecessor to the ISRC, however, dates back to the middle 1970s. At that time the NCAA perceived a gap in the expertise of that organization with respect to overseas educational systems and credential evaluation. Consequently, a consultants group was formed under the leadership of Dr. Cliff Sjogren, then director of admissions at the University of Michigan and an acknowledged expert in international admissions, to examine domestic admissions requirements for athletes and propose academic equivalents to these requirements for those countries around the world that made up the then small percentage of foreign athletes participating in NCAA sports. By the time Dr. Sjogren and the original band of consultants he collected retired and the group transitioned to an actual standing committee, the international proportion of the NCAA student athlete population had grown exponentially.

While the percentage of international athletes involved in NCAA sports remains only five percent of all those processed in the Eligibility Center (in the four years culminating in 2009), the complexity of the credentials presented for review belies their smaller numbers. Many countries rely on national examinations as conclusions to the upper secondary educational experience, and thus, the vast majority of the countries sending prospective student athletes (PSAs) do not utilize a system of units as is the case in the United States.

Furthermore, many countries include an element of streaming or tracking at the upper secondary level that tends to run counter to the U.S. concept of a well-rounded breadth of core course units. Thus, the successful graduate of a European country, or one with a European model of education, admitted to the most prestigious higher education institutions in the world may not appear to be academically qualified to participate in NCAA sports because of what is perceived as a missing element of core course work; however, this is solely because such a course is not a part of the specialized curriculum followed. These and other similar issues constantly crop up when evaluating international athlete applications during the admissions process. Fortunately, the *Guide to International Academic Standards for Athletics Eligibility* exists to help one grapple with those complex questions arising from international athlete admissions.

The *Guide* provides country entries that lay out the necessary credentials for meeting NCAA initial freshman eligibility standards. Transfer student athletes, as well as those PSAs applying to Division III or to NAIA (National Association of Intercollegiate Athletics) schools, have a different set of admissions criteria. The *Guide* contains a series of country entries in which the high school credentials for that country that have been determined to represent both high school graduation and the equivalent of sixteen academic core units spread out over the four main subject areas of English, mathematics, physical or lab science, and social science. The experts in international credential evaluation and international admissions that currently make up the International Student Records Committee have systematically gone through the various country credentials recorded in the *Guide* to make certain that these represent the equivalent to both high school graduation and attainment of the appropriate number of core units required for the PSAs in the United States.

The international credentials listed appear in the form of categories with Category 1 defined as those credentials that meet BOTH graduation AND the necessary core units. The courses found on these credentials with grades then constitute the grade point average that is in turn matched to the SAT or ACT score achieved by the PSA. In a number of cases no credentials are Category 1 because the credential obtained does not assure the full range of core courses during the education leading up to its award. For example, Commonwealth countries allow for individual choice of the subjects taken leading to university admission since the university-bound student has a clear academic goal in mind, and degrees in Commonwealth universities (and many European countries as well) are highly concentrated in the chosen field with very little elective or outside (the major) study. Thus, if one chooses languages or literature, there is no requirement to take math and science at the upper secondary level. The *Guide* places those sorts of credentials in Category 2. Category 2 documents are those that clearly represent graduation from high school but do not necessarily assure the appropriate core distribution. Thus evaluators (and NCAA staff) must comb through the actual year-to-year course work to ascertain if the appropriate spread of core course content has been met in a Category 2 document.

Those documents that do not represent graduation from high school in that country but would be useful in supplying core course work are placed in Category 3. Alone they are insufficient for graduation and core courses, but they do represent part of the high school experience that could well yield some core courses and are therefore included in the evaluation. Category 4 lists those credentials that are found at the postsecondary level, the possession of which places the PSA in a transfer category with all the attendant rules governing that status.

The *Guide* is constantly being updated based on new information received from conference attendance by NCAA staff or committee members, information supplied by NCAA member institutions as a routine part of the registration process with the NCAA Eligibility Center (which replaced the former Clearinghouse in Fall 2007), or information that comes in from ministries of education abroad announcing changes in the secondary education system of that country. A change in the secondary grading scale for a given country would be an important piece of new information affecting the determination of eligibility for PSAs from that country. Whenever a country changes its educational system, the Eligibility Center and the International Student Records Committee move to incorporate that new information in the *Guide* as quickly as possible. Even if the old credentials in the *Guide* are replaced, the *Guide* continues to list the older (now defunct) information in subsequent editions of the *Guide* for five full years after the change (as the older credential may still be seen for a few years after the change).

While the listing of credentials and grading scales that meet the initial eligibility requirements for various countries sounds straightforward, in fact, many complex questions inevitably arise during the course of the evaluation. For example, did the PSA delay graduation beyond the normal for his/her cohort in that country's educational system? Is the technical or agricultural stream resulting in the document listed as either Category 1 or Category 2 sufficient for status as a full qualifier? What is full-time enrollment status at a post-secondary institution abroad? These are the sorts of questions that the Eligibility Center, the International Student Records Committee, and NCAA staff grapple with on almost a daily basis. In the area of international athlete evaluation, it is best not to assume! NCAA staff answer these and many other questions constantly so that institutions have a better understanding of the international credentials they receive and do not have to operate in the dark! The admission of athletes is a complicated process governed by numerous rules and regulations. International athletes pose an even more complicated variation on that process, but help is no farther away than the telephone or the computer. When in doubt, ask!

EIGHTEEN

Financial Aid and Regulatory Considerations

SANDRA BLOEM-CURTIS · Senior Associate Director, International Compliance, Systems Management, and Administration, Office of International Students & Scholars, Rice University

ADRIA L. BAKER · Executive Director, Office of International Students & Scholars, Rice University

2010 AACRAO INTERNATIONAL GUIDE

Financial Aid and Regulatory Considerations

Financing study in the U.S. for international students can be very expensive. It is common for international students to request information about what kind of financial aid and assistance the school can provide, if admitted. In reference to international students, the term "financial aid" has a more restrictive meaning than aid for domestic (U.S.) students. In general, financial aid in the U.S. connotes financial support coming from U.S. federal government funding. However, for students on nonimmigrant visas and for the purpose of this chapter, the term will encompass various funding sources, yet exclude any U.S. government funds.

Sources of Funding for International Students

Most often, financial support for international students will come from personal funds: a family or a friend's backing, a personal bank account or savings, or a scholarship by a private source from one's home country. This is by far the primary funding source for all international students (Open Doors 2008). In addition, often a student's host institution provides resources by means of a fellowship/institutional grant, teaching or research assistantship or scholarship. While many schools do provide scholarships for international students, it is more common for institutional financial support to be offered to graduate students than to undergraduates.

Scholarships tend to be specific in nature and usually include a merit component, therefore it is helpful to provide instructions on how international students can apply for or research the possibility of getting a scholarship. The application process may be confusing; as a result, clear instructions on how to apply, including supporting documentation, grades and other specialized eligibility requirements need to be made available. Each institution has unique processes for applying for scholarships, some with a centralized resource office and others with a decentralized approach, whereby students need to inquire through various academic and administrative departments.

Another funding option for international students is the students' home country government. These students are often referred to as "sponsored students" because of the unique nature of funding, as well as the special circumstances, obligations, benefits and limitations that tend to be attached to the government-sponsored student experience. For instance, the funding source could be a limitation that directly affects the visa category required. Most sponsored students study in the U.S. on a J-1 Exchange Visitor (EV) program visa, as opposed to the common F-1 student visa. The EV program is sponsored and administered by the U.S. Department of State (DOS) and jointly supervised by the U.S. Department of Homeland Security (DHS). An example of a well-known EV sponsorship is the Fulbright scholarship.

The J-1 visa allows for tighter control over the students' options, especially after graduation. One restriction a J-1 student might encounter is the obligation to return to the home country soon after graduation or before being eligible to apply for a change of visa status to a more permanent working visa, such as the H-1B specialty working visa or U.S. permanent residency [INA Section 212(e)]. Since the purpose of the Exchange Visitor (EV) program is an educational and cultural exchange, the "exchange" is enforced under the home residency requirement. This law ensures, through a mandate for the student to return to his or her country for a minimum of two years, that the sponsoring government's financial investment in the education and training of the student by the government will be reciprocated by the student's sharing of the skills acquired in his or her U.S. education and cultural experience.

Very often students' educations are financed by using multiple sources of funding in order to cover the high tuition, fees, insurance and other living expenses, *e.g.*, a student receiving a university assistantship in combination with personal family funds. Further, it is also common for funding sources to change during the students' educational tenure. While this is an acceptable practice, it is imperative that the students amend their SEVIS (Student and Exchange Visitor Information System) Form I-20 (for F-I students) or SEVIS Form DS-2019 (for J-I students) with any updates to ensure it is always up-to-date and accurate.

In addition, and upon request, the school may provide incentives for prospective students that can ease the initial financial burden, such as a waiver of application fees, paying or reimbursing the SEVIS fee, reimbursing the visa application, providing moving expense bonuses or special help with insurance costs.

While most international students secure funding for their education from 1) personal/family funds, 2) host institution fellowships/scholarships, 3) their home government, 4) a private sponsor, 5) their employer or 6) from their home university (Open Doors 2008), other potential sources of income may be available. Programs and loan resource information provided by the Institute of International Education (IIE), as well as scholarships and grants from non-profit organizations, are some of the alternative sources that may be available to assist in providing financial aid to international students (*U.S. Journal of Academics* 2009).

In some cases, education loans may be a good option to international students seeking financial aid. Although U.S. loans are typically quite restrictive, international students may qualify for assistance. These loans typically require a U.S. citizen or U.S. permanent resident to

co-sign as a guarantor on the loan, and interest rates can be quite high (EducationUSA 2009). Lending institutions may also require that students already be enrolled or officially admitted to the institution before applying for a loan and a copy of the I-20 or DS-2019 as proof. In these cases, students may need to initially provide a personal source of funding for the first academic year to secure their immigration documents and later apply for the loan to cover the remaining costs of their educational programs.

The IIE provides various programs and resources to aid international students. One excellent resource is the database that IIE maintains with information on scholarships, fellowships and grants for study in the U.S.; the database, available online, is searchable by region, area of study and program name. IIE also administers programs that promote international education, such as the Fulbright program, which provides funds for students, scholars and professionals to pursue graduate study, advanced research and teaching opportunities.

Additional financial aid resources can be found based on specific areas of study, exceptional talents in the performing arts or sports or programs focused on solving world issues. EducationUSA, a network of advising centers supported by the Bureau of Educational and Cultural Affairs at the U.S. Department of State, is an excellent resource for international students. They provide not only information about studying in the U.S., but also information on how to access those opportunities, including financial aid. Their Web site (http://EducationUSA.state.gov) provides links to funding resources including loans, scholarships, fellowships and grants. The *U.S. Journal of Academics* also maintains a list of additional resources regarding loans, grants, scholarships and non-profit organizations that provide funding to international students (*U.S. Journal of Academics* 2009).

Proof of Financial Aid and Sponsorship

Specific and adequate documentation to cover the estimated costs from each school must be provided as a part of the regular admissions process [8 C.F.R. 214.3(k)]. Required estimated expenses from the hosting school are mandatory fields on Form I-20, the Certificate of Eligibility issued to the prospective students to study in their institution. Requisite information includes tuition, fees, insurance, living expenses, books and supplies; but is uniquely determined by each individual school. Even within an individual school, different departments' tuition and fees may vary due to unique needs between programs.

Schools hosting international students are responsible for maintaining a clear and consistent procedure each semester when determining the required costs. A best practice is to seek funding estimates from the institution's budget office. Consistency in determining I-20 costs not only affects the hosting school's compliance records, but will shape financial decisions of the invited international students who must prove they can cover the estimated costs for the first academic year, as indicated on the I-20.

Proof of financial backing is not only required in order to provide immigration documents for admission, but it is also required by the U.S. government when an enrolled international student applies for an immigration benefit, such as a visa entry stamp, a change of visa classification, a request for an extension of status to continue with an educational program or a request to transfer to a new program, educational level or school.

When applying for an entry visa stamp at a U.S. consulate or embassy abroad, a student is required to present specific documentation, including a Form I-20 or DS-2019 issued by the sponsoring institution, a Form DS-156 for the visa application, receipts for payment of the visa fee and the I-901 SEVIS fee, a passport valid for at least six months into the future and two 2x2 inch photographs. The student must also be prepared to provide transcripts from previous institutions and scores from standardized tests used for admission to a U.S. institution (SAT, GRE, TOEFL, GMAT, etc.), as well as proof of financial support. The proof of financial support may be in the form of original bank statements,

sponsor letters of support, a letter of award from an institution providing a scholarship or fellowship indicating the specific amount of award, loan approval, etc. Because the immigration documents issued by the sponsoring institution will indicate the estimated costs for one academic year, the visa-issuing officer will also require evidence of support in at least that amount. Although the institution issuing the immigration documents already required the proof of support in order to issue the documents, the U.S. consulate or embassy serves as a secondary check point to ensure that the international student has sufficient funding to support him or herself while pursuing his/her studies [22 CFR 41.61(b)(1)(ii)]. As a matter of best practice, the financial documents should be original and dated within the last six months.

If a student is already in the U.S. and needs to change to a student visa classification, he or she may do so by applying for a change of status with the U.S. Citizenship and Immigration Services (USCIS). The student will be required to submit the following to the appropriate USCIS office: 1) completed form I-539 "Application for Extend/Change Nonimmigrant Status," 2) processing fee as indicated on Form I-539, 3) original Form I-20 or DS-2019 issued by institution, 4) receipt for I-901 SEVIS fee payment, 5) photocopies of passport biographical and visa pages, 6) original I-94 card and 7) proof of financial support. The documentation for financial support must show that the student or sponsor has the ability to cover the costs as indicated on the estimated expenses of the student's immigration documents. The documentation must be original documents from the bank, lending institution, private financial sponsor or educational institution in the case of scholarships, fellowships or assistantships. A change of status request may take between four to six months for processing, and, depending on the student's prior visa status, he or she may or may not be able to begin the educational program before receiving the change of status approval.

The documentation needed for proof of financial support does not change when a student is applying for an extension of his/her current status or when applying for a transfer to a new program or school. In the case of an extension of status to complete his/her program, the student will need to show proof of support for the additional time needed to complete the program. In the case of a transfer, a student would need to show the minimum amount required for one academic term.

Ensuring that the international student obtains original documents for proof of financial support will not only assist the student when he or she must apply for a benefit from the U.S. government, but will ensure that the sponsoring institution has the required documentation on file for compliance purposes.

Establishing Institutional Policy on Financial Aid

Financial support and information on financial aid for international students requires proper, consistent and updated documentation and record-keeping to ensure compliance requirements are met. Guidelines and policies should be posted in a manner that is easily accessible to all parties, including the departments who admit and host the students, the admissions offices, recruiters, prospective international students, the DHS and the DOS. Schools who host international students are always subject to audits, in order to maintain their F student and J Exchange Visitor programs. Regulations governing nonimmigrant international students also mandate that international students may not receive public assistance funding, which includes local, state or federal funds, in order to maintain their legal immigration status and/or apply for a new U.S. visa [INA 212(a)(4)]. The school's Principal Designated School Official (PDSO) for the F student program and the Responsible Officer (RO) for the J Exchange Visitor program must conduct periodic reviews to update and inform the government of changes in the school's financial estimates. For instance, any change in amounts for tuition, fees or other required costs will need immediate updates on Form I-17 for the F program and Form DS-3036 for the J program. Official updates are made online through the school's SEVIS

record and may require DHS and DOS approval. As mentioned previously, documentation used by the school's Designated School Official (DSO) for creation of the I-20 must be duplicated for use at the U.S. Consulate when the student is applying for a visa. Official student immigration records must be maintained by the school with the original and current financial verification documents for the school's audit purposes, as well. Once a student applies for a student visa and arrives in the U.S., he or she must immediately update any changes in financial sponsorship in their SEVIS I-20 record.

Policies for establishing adequate financial estimates and sufficient financial backing must be coupled with policies on what constitutes the official or acceptable documents that students must show to provide evidence that they can adequately cover all required expenses for a minimum of the first academic year. Documents must include an attestation of the sponsor(s) to meet the amount indicated, the sponsor's relationship to the international student and an official verification of funds available, *i.e.*, an official bank statement or letter. But *what* documents are considered acceptable may vary from institution to institution. Would a faxed or a scanned and e-mailed copy of a financial backing statement or bank letter be considered official? What documents sufficiently represent attestation that the financial sponsor is able to adequately support the student? Can a nonimmigrant visa holder serve as a financial sponsor for the F-1 student? If so, for which visa categories? For how many months is the sponsor's signed attestation for financial backing valid? For how long should the sponsor's bank account have been active and at what level of funding? Is a salary letter of the financial sponsor a valid document for support? For how long into the future should a student who is self-funded show proof of being able to finance his or her education? How much is appropriate for the school to add for each dependent? These are some of the questions that need to be reviewed and policies that need to be established by each institution in order to ensure consistency for all student records.

Employment Authorization and Legal Immigration Status

Since incoming students only need to show adequate financial proof for one academic year, financial sponsorships may change during the students' course of stay in the United States. As mentioned previously, changes must be officially updated in SEVIS immediately. However, in the event that the sponsor is unable to continue to provide the same level of support or any support at all, the student may be able to work on campus for up to twenty hours during the academic year and full-time during vacations and breaks to relieve some of the financial burden. Another solution may be for the student to apply for unforeseen severe economic hardship employment, which is adjudicated through DHS as well. While this option provides some needed assistance, its challenges include delay of the application decision by immigration for up to three months when financial need is usually urgent, a costly application fee, a high bar for the proof of change in the financial sponsorship and the inability of the student to apply before attending at least twelve months at their academic institution. In the end the application may or may not get approved [8 C.F.R. 214.2.(f)(9)(ii)–(iii)].

Students should be informed upon arrival about working possibilities and the reality of job availability for international students at one's institution. If regular on-campus jobs are readily available, information on the institution's Web site would be helpful. However, students must be warned that to indicate financial dependency on an on-campus job on the I-20 is usually not acceptable, with the exception of a teaching or research assistantship. That said, students may begin on-campus employment upon arrival to campus and after the semester begins. Off-campus employment opportunities such as practical training options and employment due to extreme hardship hold a prerequisite of a year of maintaining F-1 status, with rare exceptions, before eligibility for this work authorization.

Although international students may find themselves in situations whereby they need additional financial help, working without proper employment authorization should never be an option, as this would violate their legal immigration status. Moreover, rectifying one's legal immigration status, if violated, is risky and may prove to be financially costly, as well. Further, unauthorized employment is illegal and could result in a student being deported back to his/her home country.

Best Practices for Financial Aid

It is imperative for institutions to set institutional policies and guidelines to ensure consistency and compliance, which is key to maintaining certification to sponsor F Student and J Exchange Visitor programs from the DHS and DOS. Further, it is important to secure the support from central administration and establish institutional policies that apply across all admitting departments. Strong policies create an avenue for success by providing fairness, equality and ensuring that admitted students are prepared to meet their academic, financial and legal responsibilities. Once these policies and guidelines are developed, it becomes much easier to communicate the requirements to admitting departments and prospective students. Periodic training sessions for admitting departments may prove a helpful and useful tool in communicating requirements, updates and the reasons behind the policies and guidelines. Because immigration regulations and practices are in a constant state of flux, it is important to stay abreast of changes to ensure adherence to compliance requirements.

RESOURCES ON FUNDING

Another best practice recommendation is to build a central resource on funding for international students. A centralized information source minimizes the need for dedicated staff time to address this issue, while empowering students and prospective students to begin researching options on their own. Having a dedicated Web page that is easily accessible is vital, as it may be continuously updated as new information and resources become available. By linking to trusted external resources, such as those previously mentioned in this chapter, students may access other databases that provide up-to-date resources and opportunities.

SUPPLEMENTAL FINANCIAL SOLUTIONS

Studying in the U.S. does require a significant financial commitment, but there are creative ways for students to minimize the financial burden and reduce their educational costs. However, one caveat is that not all aid can be used as financial support documentation. Options that may provide supplemental solutions for relieving financial stress include on-campus employment, living with a friend or relative, working as a resident associate

regarding the evidence students must make available for financial backing to obtain their immigration documents from the sponsoring institution or their immigration status from the U.S. government.

On-Campus Employment

On-campus employment is an excellent option to assist students in relieving some financial stress. Students in F-1 status or J-1 status are eligible to work on-campus part-time (up to twenty hours per week); jobs may include working at the cafeteria, campus bookstore, academic department, library, recreation center, etc. F-1 and J-1 students may also be eligible to secure authorization to work off-campus in certain cases after they have completed their first academic year of study. Students should always confirm their eligibility for employment with their international student advisors and secure the necessary work authorization in each case.

Alternative Living Arrangements

Alternate living arrangements may provide another source of financial relief. International students may have the option of living with a friend or relative off-campus, thus providing a substantial savings with regard to monthly living expenses. Although this option may not qualify as evidence of financial aid to reduce the standard "living expenses" amount indicated on the immigration documents, it can be a source of savings for the student. Becoming a resident advisor in a campus dormitory often provides free accommodation and other financial benefits, allowing an international student the opportunity to get involved on campus and to reduce financial strain. Working in a cafeteria or on-campus restaurants may provide a salary and benefits such as free meals.

FIGURE 18.1

Additional Resources

- American Association of University Women. 2009. *Fellowships, Grants and Awards for U.S. and International Women Scholars.* www.aauw.org/learn/fellows_directory/index.cfm.

- NAFSA: Association of International Educators

- Financial Aid Basics for Advising Undergraduate International Students. www.nafsa.org/uploadedFiles/NAFSA_Home/ Resource_Library_Assets/ISTA/financial_aid_basics_4.pdf.

- Financial Aid Resource for International Education. www.nafsa.org/knowledge_ community_network.sec/education_abroad_1/education_abroad_2/ practice_resources_12/getting_started/nafsa_financial_aid_resource/.

- International Student Organization: Scholarships & Grants for International Students. www.isoa.org/list_scholarships.aspx.

- *Student and exchange visitor program.* U.S. Immigration and Customs Enforcement. www.ice.gov/sevis/.

- The World Bank Scholarships and Fellowships Program. http://web.worldbank.org

- U.S. Department of Homeland Security. 2007. *User manual for school users of the student and exchange visitor information system version 5.7: Volume II form I-20.* June 22. Retrieved February 4, 2009, from www.ice.gov/doclib/sevis/pdf/School_UM_Vol2.pdf.

- U.S. Department of State. Bureau of Consular Affairs. http://travel.state.gov/.

in an on-campus dorm or using health insurance from one's home government or parents. Although these options may provide sufficient funds to cover incidentals such as books, supplies, clothing, food and personal expenses, these alternatives do not provide reprieve

Alternative Health Insurance Options

Although the cost of health insurance in the U.S. is quite high, some students may have access to health insurance plans from their home government that will cover them while they study abroad, while others may still be eligible for coverage as dependents under their parents' health insurance plan. Both options may result in less costly alternatives to securing one's own health insurance, while still maintaining the legally required health insurance for immigration status, in the case of J-1 Exchange Visitor students (22 C.F.R. 62.14). Although immigration law does not require health insurance for the F-1 student, it is highly recommended that all international students secure sufficient health insurance. Having the less costly alternatives indicated above may be the necessary encouragement a student needs to ensure coverage. It is imperative, though, that international students make sure their coverage is adequate, because the financial consequences could be devastating in the event of insufficient coverage during a medical emergency.

Financing educational goals can get quite expensive, but the key to meeting those financial obligations is discovering creative ways to access the funds required while adhering to immigration regulation requirements.

In closing, most international students will find financial aid a crucial challenge while studying in the United States. The solution to meeting their financial needs will most likely be found through several avenues, including personal funding, support options from the hosting school, employment opportunities and unique ways of budgeting and saving on costs. Financial responsibility is not only required of the student studying from abroad, but concise record-keeping and consistent policies are necessary for the host institutions of international students, in order to maintain compliance with the laws that govern financial aid and related regulatory issues.

NINETEEN

English Proficiency Tests and University Admissions

2010 AACRAO INTERNATIONAL GUIDE

PATRICK COLABUCCI | Senior Academic Director
American Language Institute, College of Extended Studies
San Diego State University

VAN HILLIER | Teacher Training Program Coordinator
San Diego State University

English Proficiency Tests and University Admissions

English proficiency testing is a large and growing global enterprise. Millions of people, from elementary to university to graduate students, take English proficiency tests every year. Many countries have an English proficiency test as part of their high school exit exams. Many universities have English proficiency tests as part of the admissions and/or placement process. For aspiring students, the results of these tests play a critical role in determining their academic and professional futures. For schools, these tests help ensure the maintenance of standards while attempting to further the realization of a truly internationalized student body.

Standardized tests used by university admissions departments include the SAT, LSAT, GMAT, GRE, MCAT and others. As the number of applications from international candidates continues to grow, the importance of understanding the meaning of English proficiency tests increases. These tests measure competency at a particular point in time. Admissions departments use these scores to determine if a candidate has an adequate level of English to not only function, but succeed at the university level.

High stakes testing is common to most educational systems and disciplines. Testing English as a foreign language for academic purposes is no different. There are thousands of universities, colleges, professional schools, professional organizations, militaries, governments and immigration authorities that make use of the English as a Foreign Language (EFL) test.

The International English Language Testing System (IELTS) and the Test of English as a Foreign Language (TOEFL) are the two most widely used and recognized.

A new test, the Pearson Test of English (PTE), related to the Common European Framework (CEF), was developed in collaboration with and endorsed by the Graduate Management Admission Council (GMAC). It was launched in October 2009.

All these tests attempt to measure the ability of nonnative English speakers to use and understand English in academic settings. And, as universities around the world continue to open their doors to nonnative English speakers, the market for English competency tests grows. There may soon be nearly two billion new speakers of English, making the majority of English speakers in the world nonnative speakers. The information here is intended as a resource for admissions and registration officials.

For test takers, scores on English proficiency tests are of great importance. They represent a necessary component of the admissions decision for colleges, universities and other organizations. Like any other requisite, *e.g.*, a grade point average or SAT score, without it, doors close and opportunities become out of reach.

The TOEFL

The Educational Testing Services (ETS) was founded in 1947 when the American Council on Education, the Carnegie Foundation for the Advancement of Teaching and the College Entrance Examination Board contributed their testing programs, a portion of their assets and key employees to form ETS under the leadership of Henry Chauncey. The TOEFL was a paper-based test until 1997 when it became available as a computer-based test (CBT); by 2006 it was widely available as an internet-based test (iBT). The TOEFL is now available most pervasively as the iBT. While the paper-based and

TABLE 19.1: ETS Scoring Scale

Reading Skills	22–30 High	15–21 Intermediate	0–14 Low	
Listening Skills	22–30 High	14–21 Intermediate	0–13 Low	
Speaking—Familiar Topics	3.5–4.0 Good	2.5–3.0 Fair	1.5–2.0 Limited	0–1.0 Weak
Speaking—Campus Situations	3.5–4.0 Good	2.5–3.0 Fair	1.5–2.0 Limited	0–1.0 Weak
Speaking—Academic Content	3.5–4.0 Good	2.5–3.0 Fair	1.5–2.0 Limited	0–1.0 Weak
Writing Based on Listening and Reading	4.0–5.0 Good	2.5–3.5 Fair	1.0–2.0 Limited	
Writing Based on Knowledge and Experience	4.0–5.0 Good	2.5–3.5 Fair	1.0–2.0 Limited	

institutional versions of TOEFL are still available in certain areas and for certain situations, the iBT accounts for 95 percent of TOEFL tests administered.

For admissions purposes, ETS provides a general scale regarding what scores indicate. (See Table 19.1.)

Test scores are sent weekly to most institutions electronically through the ETS SCORELINK service or via mail on a CD-ROM. A few institutions continue to receive hard copies of scores from ETS.

ETS guarantees security before, during and after each test administration; numerous measures exist to ensure the integrity of the scores. One important measure is verifying the identity of the test taker: photo identification requirements are strictly enforced.

Currently there are several published reports on how a TOEFL or an IELTS score correlates to academic success. One study measured academic success by grade point average and/or the number of graduate credits received. In this study the TOEFL correlated more strongly to the number of graduate credits earned than to GPA. Studies suggest that in English speaking universities test scores do not necessarily predict academic success, thus indicating that more work on the testing side is needed to improve accuracy.

Comparing scores from the various available tests also presents a problem. Currently sufficient data does not exist to correlate scores of a TOEFL to those of other English tests. Nevertheless, the following from the Vancouver English Center may help serve as a guideline (http://secure.vec.bc.ca/toefl-equivalency-table.cfm). (See Table 19.2.)

ETS completes test scoring within fifteen business days of each test date. Score reports on all three versions of the TOEFL include a total score as well as sub scores measuring individual language skills. In both the PBT and CBT, the total score is an average of the three scaled sub scores, multiplied by 10. The iBT total score is an aggregate of the four sub scores. Scores are calculated on the four skills tested as shown in Table 19.3.

Sub scores, or scores on individual skills, are sometimes singled out by departments or institutions. For example, nonnative English speakers applying for nursing positions in the United States may need an overall score on the iBT of eighty-five, as well as a minimum speaking score (the sub score) of twenty-eight. At many U.S. universities, a single overall score may be required for undergraduate admissions, while a graduate department may require a specific minimum sub score.

The TOEFL tests four skill areas: Reading, Listening, Speaking and Writing. In the Reading section, there will be three to five passages of approximately 700 words with twelve to fourteen questions per passage. Questions in this section involve scanning for information, identifying accurate summaries and making inferences.

The Listening section consists of four to six lectures (six questions per lecture), each three to five minutes long and containing between 500 and 800 words. Two or three will be campus-based conversations about three minutes long with between twelve and twenty-five exchanges and five questions per conversation.

The TOEFL and IELTS diverge substantially in their assessment of speaking skills. In the TOEFL there are six speaking tasks, including two independent speaking tasks on familiar topics. In this section the test takers are asked to draw upon their own ideas, opinions and experiences. Four speaking tasks are integrated tasks where test takers respond to a reading or listening prompt. A Read-Listen-Speak task requires the test taker to read an academic text on a given topic, listen to a lecture on the same topic and finally speak in response to questions. On a Listen-Speak task, the test taker listens to part of a conversation or lecture and is asked to briefly summarize the information from the listening material and sometimes express an opinion about it. The spoken sections are recorded and later assessed and scored.

The Writing section comprises an integrated writing task in which test takers read a short text (230 to 300 words with three minute reading time) on an academic topic. They then listen to a speaker discuss the same topic from a different perspective. This latter portion is 230 to 300 words with two minutes of listening time. Finally a thirty minute independent task requires test takers to write an essay that states, explains and supports their opinion on an issue.

In 2007, there were just under a million registrations for the TOEFL test. Currently, there are approximately 4,268 test sites in 143 countries. Internal and external item writers are employed from a variety of countries, and all items go through an extensive review and sampling process as test items in actual tests. All TOEFL iBT test questions are reviewed by at least four trained and qualified TOEFL test developers, an ETS editor and a fairness reviewer. Also, as needed, a subject matter expert who can comment on the accuracy and the currency of the content reviews items.

TABLE 19.2: TOEFL Equivalency Table

TOEIC	TOEFL Paper	TOEFL CBT	TOEFL IBT	IELTS
0–250	0–310	0–30	0–8	0–1
	310–343	33–60	9–18	1–1.5
255–400	347–393	63–90	19–29	2–2.5
	397–433	93–120	30–40	3–3.5
405–600	437–473	123–150	41–52	4
	477–510	153–180	53–64	4.5–5
605–780	513–547	183–210	65–78	5.5–6
	550–587	213–240	79–95	6.5–7
785–990	590–677	243–300	96–120	7.5–9
Top Score				
990	**677**	**300**	**120**	**9**

TABLE 19.3: TOEFL Scaled Subscores

	Paper-Based	Computer-Based	Internet-Based
Total	310–677	0–300	0–120
Listening	31–68	0–30	0–30
Reading	31–67	0–30	0–30
Structure/Writing	31–68 [Str.]	0–30 [Str./Wr.]	0–30 [Writing]
Speaking			0–30

Test takers may take the TOEFL a maximum of once every seven days, although taking the test within such a short interval is unlikely to result in a higher score.

The IELTS

In the 1960s, the British Council used the English Proficiency Test Battery (EPTB), a traditional, largely multiple choice test series. The English Language Testing System (ELTS) replaced the EPTB in 1980. In 1987, the British Council and Cambridge University ESOL conducted a validation study under the academic direction of Charles Alderson of Lancaster University. Shortly thereafter, the International Development Program of Australian Universities and Colleges (IDP) joined the British Council and the University of Cambridge Language Examination Syndicate (UCLES) to form an international partnership. The International English Language Testing System (IELTS) was born.

Further modifications to the test were implemented in 1995 to improve security and administration, and an Academic Reading Module and Academic Writing Module were added. A revised IELTS Speaking Test was introduced in July 2001. New assessment criteria for the Writing Test were operational from January 2005.

IELTS has experienced a huge growth since it began in 1989: from 43,000 test takers in 1995 to over one million in 2008. Currently, there are over 500 test centers in more than 130 countries. Many test centers in China can test more than 1,000 candidates at a time. Tests scores are available thirteen days after the test.

IELTS is offered as a computer-based test in a select number of centers across the world. IELTS believes that the demand for computer-based testing will grow, but as of now, the preference for a pen-and-paper-based test amongst candidates globally continues.

The writers of the testing materials comprise EFL and ESL professionals with broad experience. Currently teams of writers work in the U.S., UK, Australia and New Zealand. Test writers receive intensive training and attend editing and training sessions as tests move through the production process. Item writers work from detailed specifications for each test.

Over 6,000 institutions globally accept IELTS scores as proof of students' English language skills. This includes almost all institutions in the UK, Australia, New Zealand and Canada. As of October 2008, over 2,000 universities, colleges and organizations in the U.S. recognized IELTS scores. An up-to-date list of U.S. institutions accepting IELTS is available at www.ielts. org/pdf/USA_Recognition_List.pdf.

Results can be sent to receiving institutions either by post or electronically. In addition, receiving institutions can register for the free IELTS test results verification service (TRF verification service), which enables institutions to authenticate IELTS test results in a secure, quick way online.

Like any high stakes test, IELTS is committed to protecting the integrity and validity of its test. Every aspect of the test is subject to internal quality controls and cut-ting edge security practices. All IELTS test takers must present a form of photo identification, usually their passport, a copy of which is required with the application. The identification of IELTS candidates is checked upon registration and also during every section of the test.

IELTS administrators receive regular training from Canadian border services in fraudulent identification and impostor detection. For example, staffs are well trained in face recognition and other document verification techniques.

The IELTS test covers all four skills. The Reading section contains three passages, each of about 900 words and totaling no more than 2800 in total, with eleven to fourteen questions per passage. The Reading section takes thirty minutes and includes a total of forty questions. This section has some multiple choice questions, as well as more productive questions, which may require the test taker to write between one and two words.

The thirty minute Listening section contains three scripts, which can have one speaker or two. Each is approximately three to five minutes long. Again, the number of questions is 40, split amongst the three scripts. The latter two are academic-oriented. It includes some multiple choice questions, as well as more productive questions, which may require the test taker to write between one and two words.

The IELTS speaking test consists of an interview between a test taker and an IELTS examiner lasting between eleven and fourteen minutes and usually recorded with, a digital voice recorder. The examiner asks the test taker questions ranging from the basic or mundane (*e.g.*, are you a student or do you work?) to topics of greater depth (*e.g.*, the changes in technology impacting education). Test takers are assessed on pronunciation, vocabulary, grammatical accuracy and fluency/coherence.

There are two writing tasks on the IELTS: a graph, chart or process illustration description of 150 words and a response to a topic requiring the candidate to provide an argument of 250 words. The writer is allowed sixty minutes total.

Each subsection of the IELTS is scored on a scale of one to nine. The numbers are referred to as bands: a test taker can score a band three in writing or a band five in speaking. Test takers receive an overall score based on their total in the subsections divided by four, the number of subsections. This number is then rounded to the nearest half band.

Speaking is scored on lexical range, fluency/coherence, pronunciation and grammatical accuracy. Each is scored on a scale from one to nine (except for pronunciation, which is scored two, four, six or eight) and the scores are averaged. Writing is scored on task achievement, coherence/cohesion, lexical range/resource and grammatical accuracy. Again, each area is scored from one to nine, and the total is divided by four to get the band.

For the Reading and Writing sections, the number of correct answers (out of 40 questions) is converted into a band.

A test taker's results, therefore, will consist of five scores, one for each skill area and the overall score. IELTS results are available 13 days after the test. Over one million (as of 2008) take the test annually in over 120 countries making it the largest international English language test of its kind.

The Pearson PTE Academic (PTE)

The PTE was launched in October 2009 in 22 countries, which, in total, account for 71 percent of the students taking English language proficiency tests. It is entirely computer-based. To date, the PTE has been piloted with more than 10,000 test takers, including both native and nonnative English speakers. The test takers represented native speakers of more than 100 different mother tongues, 38 cities and 21 different countries. The results have been analyzed and the test has been refined. All scoring of the PTE is automated to ensure impartiality.

The PTE is delivered via Pearson's Vue, a secure network of computer-based testing centers. Candidates have the option to choose and reserve where and when they take the test from a list of test centers and the times the PTE Academic are available at those centers.

The PTE is approximately two and a half to three hours long, similar to the IELTS and TOEFL. It consists of a total of 70 questions drawn from a library of different types of items. Test takers write essays of between 200 and 300 words and summaries of 50 to 70 words.

The PTE aims to provide test takers with their results within five business days. After receiving the scores, test takers can choose to send them to up to seven institutions. Universities and institutions are able to access and download test scores through a secure Web site. Universities and institutions also have the ability to listen to test takers' speaking segments. The Pearson PTE uses sub-skill scores in speaking, reading, listening and writing, which are further broken down into the "enabling" factors of communication. These comprise fluency, grammar, pronunciation, spelling, vocabulary, written discourse and textual skills and are similar to how the IELTS assessment of Writing and Speaking are profile scored using lexical range, communicative competency, grammatical accuracy and other factors.

The questions on the PTE are integrated and thus designed to measure more than one sub skill at a time. They are intended to accurately reflect the academic environment. For example, test takers who are fluent writers of English, but cannot understand spoken English well, would likely have difficulty competing in a lecture course. Also, a test taker able to converse easily, but who struggles with academic writing, may have difficulty in a course that is assessed heavily on written papers or projects. The PTE aims to manifest these scenarios.

Security for the PTE is rigorous and high tech. Each test taker is advised at the time of registration exactly what documentation he or she will need to bring in order to gain admittance to the test. They may need a fingerprint file, an electronic signature and/or an official photo identification, like a passport. The PTE is committed to the highest level of test integrity. The PTE tests are randomized, so no two test takers will have the same version of the test at any given test center.

The PTE scores tests based on the Common European Framework Descriptors. A concordance can be generated to correlate scores from different proficiency tests. Published minimum admission requirements for the iBT are typically 73 to 89 and for IELTS, 6.1 to 6.8. According to the PTE, these ranges correspond with scores from 50 to 54 and 60 to 64 on the new PTE Academic.

The PTE has specific scores for the four "Communicative Skills"—Listening, Reading, Speaking and Writing, as well as scores for the "Enabling Skills"— Grammar, Oral Fluency, Pronunciation, Spelling, Vocabulary and Written Discourse.

Based on a score range, PTE test takers fall into one of three categories: B1 (43–59), B2 (59–76) and C1 (76–85). B1 indicates an insufficient ability to participate in academic study, B2 indicates a language level sufficient to participate independently in academic education and C1 indicates an ability to be very comfortable with all postgraduate activities including teaching.

Public versions of previously used TOEFL and IELTS tests are readily available. Unfortunately a sample of the Pearson Test of English could not be offered for the purposes of this chapter.

So, all in all, EFL testing is used by a broad range of organizations for a wide range of purposes with admission to college or university representing just one of these purposes. University admissions professionals should bear in mind that these are typically high stakes tests, and decisions based on these test results may dramatically impact test takers' lives. Testing organizations need to ensure that great care and dedication to quality are observed in creating tests, analyzing test results and crafting accurate descriptors of what the results mean.

TWENTY

The Evolving Field of
Education
Abroad

2010 AACRAO INTERNATIONAL GUIDE

SARAH MARTIN

Graduate Programs Coordinator
Duke Global Health Institute

The Evolving Field of Education Abroad

S tudy abroad is now a well-established concept in higher education, in the minds of students and on the radar for college administrators. The breadth of credit-bearing opportunities available is making it increasingly possible for students from a wide range of institutions—from community colleges and liberal arts colleges to research universities—to find programs suitable to their field of study, as well as their schedule. Education abroad is professionalizing at a rapid rate, with more and more resources and training materials available for those responsible for study abroad, and elevating the level of discussion about program quality, health and safety, and transfer of credit.

By The Numbers

There has been a steady increase in the number of students studying abroad for academic credit over the past decades. The Institute of International Education's (IIE) *Open Doors Report on International Educational Exchange* series collects data and publishes statistics on international exchange. They began collecting data on the "internationally mobile student population in the United States" in 1948, and continue to survey international officers at U.S. institutions annually. The data on study abroad is updated every two years, and offers both big-picture information about the field—destinations, fields of study, duration, etc.—and detailed data about individual institutions sending students abroad.

According to the 2008 edition of *Open Doors*, using data from the 2006–2007 academic year, 241,791 students from U.S. institutions studied abroad for credit. This number represents an increase of well over 200

percent from just a decade earlier. While some statistics have stayed relatively the same, such as participation by gender—65 percent of study abroad participants are women—many are shifting. Europe is still the favored region of study, with Latin America solidly in second place, but Asia and Africa have seen steady increases over the past ten years, now comprising nearly 15 percent of students going abroad. The duration of experience is also trending towards shorter programs, with 60 percent of students studying abroad for less than one semester, up from 50 percent ten years ago. The top majors for study abroad continue to be social sciences, business, and humanities, which combined account for over 50 percent of students; however participation from science and engineering majors is slowly increasing.

Promoting Education Abroad

In 2004, the U.S. Congress, at the urging of the late Senator Paul Simon, formed the Abraham Lincoln Commission on Study Abroad, a body of educators and legislators exploring ways to increase the number of U.S. students studying abroad, and they came out with a report in 2005. The report and subsequent lobbying efforts, led by international education and higher education organizations and institutions (including AACRAO), have resulted in the Senator Paul Simon Study Abroad Foundation Act, which was approved by the U.S. House of Representatives in June 2009 as part of the Foreign Relations Authorization Act for FY 2010 and 2011.[8] The Simon Act, if passed by the Senate, would build on the Lincoln Commission report, allocating resources to establish a foundation that would

....
[8] See <www.nafsa.org/publicpolicy/default.aspx?id=16130>.

work to increase participation in quality study abroad programs, with an eye towards increasing participation of diverse students, and increasing opportunities in diverse locations such as developing countries. Resources would be allocated towards student grants and for grants to institutions and organizations (domestic and for use with international partners) to build capacity for study abroad at home in the U.S. and at host sites abroad.

Many efforts are being made to increase study abroad participation of historically underrepresented populations, including students of color, first generation and non-traditional college students, students enrolled in community colleges, and students majoring in the sciences, technology, engineering and mathematics (commonly called the STEM majors). In addition to localized curriculum integration initiatives, specialized program development and marketing, and larger-scale organizations offering advising and financial resources to underrepresented groups, there is active discussion at the policy level. IIE (2010), which publishes *Open Doors* reports, published an excellent series of Study Abroad White Papers that take an in-depth look at access, participation, and capacity building issues in select aspects of study abroad.

A Synopsis

This chapter focuses only on credit-bearing opportunities abroad. The term "study abroad" is used interchangeably with the term "education abroad." These are both common terms in the field of international education, with some preferring education abroad as a term more inclusive of the variety of learning opportunities available to students. You will find sections covering the basics of study abroad programs, guidelines for developing study abroad policy and procedure, ideas for study abroad outreach and programming, and a discussion on legal issues and considerations. While this chapter covers many important topics, it is by no means comprehensive and should be complemented with further reading, research, discussion, and innovation on your

home campus and with peer institutions. Many of the other chapters in this publication will inform education abroad activities and programs and should be read with your study abroad operations in mind. A short list of resources, including full books on topics that receive only brief mention herein, is included at the end to supplement those resources available through AACRAO.

The Nuts and Bolts of Education Abroad

As the field of education abroad grows, so does the range of program types and models available to students. Students can spend a week on a faculty-led program abroad or a year enrolled in a foreign university. They can pursue an intensive language study program with other international students, sit in a classroom abroad with students from other North American universities, and participate in hands-on learning in a non-traditional classroom setting like a research station or at a non-profit community development organization. More and more, international education is incorporated into degree programs and individual courses, and students at many universities expect to have an experience abroad as part of their undergraduate education.

Your own university's context and student body impacts the programs that you offer, and it is helpful to understand the different terminology used to describe education abroad program models. You can offer a range of programs that meet the needs of students wanting both shorter and longer programs, but must design them without compromising on quality of programs or courses offered for credit. You can also use a variety of approaches to develop and expand education abroad opportunities through creative partnerships with other institutions and organizations. In the NAFSA: Association for International Educators' *Guide to Education Abroad for Advisors and Administrators, Third Edition* (2005), sections of several chapters are dedicated to defining and discussing program "types" and educational "models," though there are many hybrids among these lists. The types and models described in the following paragraphs, adapted from the NAFSA guide, will give you a solid lexicon with which to approach your faculty, peer institutions, and outside organizations as you develop an education abroad portfolio for your institution.

PROGRAM TYPES

The term "program type" refers to the administrative category of a program. Each type infers a level of institutional ownership and responsibility, both for management of the program and advising of students. Most institutions develop a portfolio of options including several types of programs.

Reciprocal or Direct Exchange Programs

Historically, exchange programs are probably the most common type of study abroad program. The term direct or reciprocal exchange refers to agreements made between individual institutions, or consortia of institutions, to exchange students and often faculty, usually on a one-to-one basis, with minimum additional costs above the standard tuition and fees of the home university. Programs are often products of successful research collaborations between specific departments, relationships between administrators, network affiliations (*i.e.*, religiously-affiliated colleges and universities) and also outreach from organizations or ministries that represent foreign universities in North America.

Exchange programs often afford students an opportunity to become quite integrated into regular university life abroad, but also rely on student independence and initiative more than other types. They tend to be longer in duration, lasting a semester or year, since students are taking courses at the host university with local students. Exchange programs also require a lot of administrative oversight by the home campus, with responsibilities ranging from negotiating and maintaining agreements, to orienting and arranging housing for incoming students, to assessing incoming transcripts for appropriate credit transfer. The administrative burden can be relatively high in proportion to the number of students and faculty involved, but the benefits of

these programs done well are many, including a relatively low cost to students, direct communication with overseas peers and partners, and easy recruitment of international students to the home campus. Challenges include maintaining the exchange balance if interest is uneven, higher responsibility for developing resource materials and advising students (both outgoing and incoming), and accommodating for differences in curricular and administrative structures and academic schedules in universities abroad.

For new international education administrators, it is important to survey departments and programs to get a sense of how many of them already have arrangements with institutions abroad. Informal agreements may need to be reviewed and updated at an institutional level, in collaboration with the departments themselves, the university registrar and/or curriculum oversight committees, university legal counsel, and other upper level administrators.

Faculty-Led and Home-School Programs

In addition to creating relationships with institutions abroad to facilitate direct and reciprocal exchange, institutions frequently decide to create their own programs abroad. These can be occasional or one-off programs, led by a faculty member for 1–8 weeks, or they can be grounded, long-term centers abroad, hosting students and faculty for courses throughout the year. Such models offer an institution more control of the academic curriculum, the schedule, and student support services, but they also require a more robust administrative structure and management plan to develop, run, and maintain.

Faculty-led programs can take many forms, including a variety of lengths of time, models of host-culture interaction, and ranges of attachment to a specific course or department. Generally speaking, the term "faculty-led program" refers to a faculty member (or faculty members) leading a tour and/or teaching a course to a finite group of students abroad. While some are for a full term abroad, most fall into the categories of "summer" or "short-term" programs lasting eight weeks or less. While teaching in or leading these programs may be viewed as a faculty "perk," the logistical circumstances of the programs sometimes have the unintended effect of limiting student interaction with the host culture and their peers abroad, which is somewhat in conflict with the overarching goals for education abroad. Depending on the institutional structure and the level of faculty and department involvement and support, there may be significant or very little involvement on the part of the study abroad office or staff in organizing logistics, preparing the curriculum, publicizing the program, or selecting and preparing the student participants. At a minimum, it is important to be aware of these opportunities and advise departments and faculty on risk management and best practices for short-term programs, and to make sure that the programs meet your institutional curricular standards. You may be substantially involved in developing and managing these programs, including financial arrangements, recruiting and training faculty to lead programs, working with departments and faculty to assess how this type of program fits faculty development and tenure protocols, marketing and recruiting students, and arranging logistics for the program.

"Home-school programs" abroad may take the form of a permanent "center" abroad, or semi-regular offerings of longer-term faculty-led or coordinated programs abroad. Institutions with centers abroad often utilize a consortium model, to share administrative responsibilities and costs, as well as to ensure program sustainability through a broader base of potential participants and faculty instructors. Home-school programs may be taught by faculty from your home campus, faculty from other consortia schools, if relevant, or international faculty contracted to teach to students from your campus or consortium. Like faculty-led programs, they allow a school to have greater control over the curriculum, calendar, and academic and student support services. They also represent a more substantial investment in a location, given the need to invest in on-site staff, classrooms,

and housing options for students. Consideration must be given to local laws, including labor and taxation issues, and pedagogical issues like exposure to the host culture. Creating centers abroad and/or forming or joining a consortium for education abroad programs should be explored by the highest levels of university administration, and student and faculty interest in the location(s) should be well documented, given the investment in time and resources required.

There are many variations on both faculty-led and home-school programs. A survey of your peer institutions will likely result in many examples and ideas, each reflecting the academic culture and context of the school. While there is a tremendous amount of institutional responsibility required in developing and maintaining home-school and faculty-led programs abroad, most institutions take great pride in these programs as a reflection of their achievements in internationalization.

Programs not developed and offered by the home institution, or consortium of schools of which the home-school is a member, fall generally into two administrative categories for the home campus—affiliated and unaffiliated programs. Within those categories, there are differences between the type of institution or organization responsible for the program. Some accredited, degree-granting institutions (foreign or domestic) may open their classrooms or programs to students from other schools, or act as facilitators to enroll students in yet another institution. Other programs may be developed and managed by provider organizations, frequently called "third-party providers." Provider organizations may facilitate enrollment in a degree-granting institution and offer additional student programming and support, or they may operate independent academic programs, contracting with faculty abroad and frequently working with an advisory board or degree-granting school of record. Occasionally, students may also seek credit from private language schools. A more thorough discussion of accreditation and credit transfer can be found in the discussion on Establishing Policy and Procedures for Study Abroad, and both topics are covered more extensively elsewhere in this guide, though not specific to study abroad.

Affiliated Programs

The term "affiliated programs" is generally used to refer to education abroad programs or universities with which an institution has some sort of formalized agreement that is not direct or reciprocal exchange-based. There are many terms used by institutions to describe these programs, including "co-sponsored" or "approved" programs. The program may be hosted by another university (foreign or domestic), a provider organization, or some other type of exchange agency, and it exists independently of the home institution. A formal agreement may cover any range of items, but frequently would detail credit transfer, the transfer of financial aid, tuition and fee requirements, mutual expectations in terms of student recruitment, selection, support, and communication, and other topics relevant to study abroad programs.

Developing "affiliations" can greatly increase the range of international opportunities available to students, producing a lower administrative burden on an education abroad office than developing and managing institutional programs. A formal agreement might also ease other administrative processes related to study abroad. Maintaining a list of affiliations, however, requires substantial discussion about why some institutions might not be invited into such an arrangement. It is important to develop criteria for affiliations that reflect university goals for education abroad, including standards of academic rigor, allowable credit or financial aid transfer, program models and locations, as well as expectations for student development, safety, and support. Potential "affiliated" programs should be discussed with faculty and university administrators, and contracts should be developed or reviewed by university legal counsel.

Unaffiliated Programs

Unaffiliated programs are those programs with which an institution has no formal agreement, or which are contracted on a by-student basis. Like affiliated programs, the programs may be hosted by another university (foreign or domestic), a provider organization, or some other type of exchange agency existing independently of the home institution. The field of education abroad is growing and opportunities are evolving, making it hard to evaluate every program or institution proactively. Therefore, it is fairly common for any non-home-school program to be considered unaffiliated, leaving room for students and study abroad offices to determine appropriate opportunities on a case-by-case basis. While the administrative burden of unaffiliated programs is lower than home-school programs, they often present challenges around knowing program details, quality control, credit transfer, and use of financial aid. It is important to set clear policies for acceptable study abroad opportunities, credit transfer, financial aid, and timing of the experience, among other things, and it is critical that institutions involve decision-makers at every level of the university.

PROGRAM MODELS

The *NAFSA Guide to Education Abroad, Third Edition* (2005, pp. 345–371) outlines four education abroad program models. These are broad categories, with much variation, especially within the "independent study model."

Study Center Model

The term "study center" is generally used to describe programs that offer courses only for program participants, sometimes taught in English, and where students travel or live together during the duration of the program. These are also sometimes referred to as "island programs." Many short-term faculty-led programs are considered island programs, as are some university centers abroad. Island programs are considered somewhat easy to control, since the learning environment is determined by the sponsoring institution, though the administrative burden is high, since the program must account for nearly all academic and personal needs of the students during the program. This model limits cultural immersion opportunities, unless intentionally built into the program and carefully crafted to avoid seeming touristy.

Integrated Enrollment Programs

The term "integrated enrollment programs" refers to programs in which a student is integrated into the courses and campus culture of a foreign university. The type of program most often representing this model is the direct or reciprocal exchange, though there are a number of provider organizations that facilitate student enrollment in foreign universities, coordinating recruitment and placement, and sometimes providing additional support for the study abroad students at a local or country level. The provider organizations also offer support in the areas of financial aid and credit transfer. The integrated enrollment model affords students the opportunity to experience alternative education systems, through taking classes with their international peers and living in university housing. The administrative burden on the home school varies.

Hybrid Programs

"Hybrid programs" are those in which there is some combination of coursework and activities developed solely for program students, with some opportunity to enroll in classes alongside host university students. Housing may be with host families or in university housing, but it might also be in private dormitories managed by the study abroad program or organization. An example of a hybrid program might be an institution or provider organization that offers intensive language courses for students, and perhaps some country or region-specific history or cultural studies courses taught by contract faculty, but has arrangements with local universities allowing students to take one or two courses, too.

Independent Study Programs

The "independent study" category is described by the NAFSA guide as "the lump category for research-based field work, unpaid internships, service learning, volunteer projects, and individual language immersion."

However, several distinct models can be teased out from this category, and it can make more sense to title it "alternative program models" or "experiential program."

Internships, field-based programs, and service learning are often built using experiential education theory and design, with the idea that linking didactic coursework to hands-on practice is more productive and long-lasting for some learners. This type of program is especially valuable in an international context where one can combine academic learning with intercultural learning. International internship programs often combine a part-time internship with a classroom component used to discuss both key curricular concepts and to process the cultural dynamics of a workplace. Field-based programs are frequently, though not exclusively, designed around areas of study such as anthropology, sociology, and ecology. These programs may focus on topics like international development or social change, and students may spend much of their time learning from prominent community organizers, social activists, or government officials, bringing students together to discuss the variety of perspectives on the issue within one country or region while living with home-stay families to augment language acquisition and to add yet another voice.

Other field-based models might expose students not to an international culture, but to a culture of scientific research, with students living at environmental research stations and engaging in daily data collection or analysis. Service-learning programs combine coursework with community service, engaging students daily with host country peers and communities, connecting students to a place on a more personal level.

With alternative models and independent study programs, like many hybrid programs, the administrative burden for a home school is varied. Many programs may be run through institutions or provider organizations that offer student support structures and formal curriculum information, making credit approval and student advising more straightforward. However, institutions should also develop clear policies about what elements are required for a student to receive credit and where appropriate, the policies should be consistent with similar domestic programs and opportunities.

All international programs should be regularly reviewed for academic rigor, and student efficacy and safety. More detailed information about program evaluation and assessment is included later in this chapter.

PROGRAM LENGTH

The duration of an education abroad experience is a significant consideration as institutions develop programs. As participation has grown from 143,590 students in 1999–2000 to 241,791 students abroad in 2006–2007, the growth in study abroad programs has been primarily in short-term programs. Institutions and organizations have expanded their offerings of faculty-led, summer, and other short-term programs, giving students an opportunity to have an international experience without taking a full semester or year away from the home campus.

Short-term programs, classified by the IIE *Open Doors Report* as those programs lasting eight weeks or less, have opened up the possibility of study abroad for many students who—because of perception or circumstance—could not spend a semester or year abroad. While some areas of student learning and development might be compromised through a short-term experience, like foreign language learning or the opportunity to sit in a classroom for a full semester or year with international peers and faculty, program design has a significant impact on intercultural learning. Programs, both long and short, can be designed to maximize opportunities to interact with international counterparts, to engage personally with topics they are studying, and to step outside of the student's comfort zone. Simply traveling overseas does not merit academic credit or the title of education or study abroad. Students must be challenged to learn about their host country and counterparts both inside and outside of the formal educational component of the program. This can happen successfully in two weeks, or can be unsuccessful despite 16 weeks abroad, depending on the program design, student initiative, and preparation.

Other misconceptions about program length contributing to the growth of short-term programs include program cost and ability to earn relevant credits towards a degree. Both of these can be countered with a little research and good advising, and should not be perceived as true barriers to a longer experience abroad. Air travel, for example, is often the most expensive item for short-term study abroad programs, yet usually does not rise significantly for longer programs. Financial aid, which may be available for a semester or yearlong program, is not as frequently available for summer or short-term programs, therefore raising the direct costs to the student. Finally, given the vast number of education abroad programs, shifts in the academic calendars of many foreign institutions, and growing diversity of courses offered, students are increasingly likely to find a program with coursework acceptable for transfer at the home institution, if not a targeted program developed by the home institution itself.

In conclusion, each institution will have some assortment of program types, models, and lengths, largely determined by the institution's academic focus, student body profile, and administrative capacity. To quote the author of the previous version of this chapter (2001), "Study abroad programming, in order to be most effective and enriching (both to the student and to the institution), must be as carefully designed and planned as any other academic program in the institution." The next section of this chapter will explore development of policy and procedure for study abroad on your campus.

Establishing Policy and Procedures for Education Abroad

Academic bulletins and catalogs typically represent the academic offerings and policies of an institution. Student (and faculty) handbooks and honor codes accompany bulletins and catalogs through the establishment of further academic and behavioral expectations. Study abroad officials should develop similar materials, complementing the home university's guidelines and detailing policies and expectations that may come uniquely with participation in programs abroad. Host institutions will also have a unique set of guidelines, and it is important to make students aware of the need to adhere to both home and host institution expectations. You have likely already worked with academic and administrative departments on your campus to develop procedures. If not, you should work with others on campus to begin to address this gap, even if only pulling together relevant policies and procedures already adopted and in use. Either way, you will be most successful if you develop policies collaboratively and in the spirit of your institutional culture, and then implement and share information about policies and procedures with students, other offices and departments, and faculty in a consistent and transparent manner.

This section, which is not comprehensive, offers general guidance on establishing policies and procedures at your institution, referencing areas that you may wish to consider as you further refine the education abroad environment on your campus. For more detail about evaluating international transcripts, understanding foreign higher education systems, and developing guidelines about transferring credits taken overseas, please review the more extensive chapters in this publication, as no detail will be provided here.

WHO CAN STUDY ABROAD AND WHEN?

Among the first questions that institutions must address are "who can study abroad?" and "when?" Decisions about appropriate class year or standing, GPA achievement, behavioral record, etc., must be considered carefully alongside the institutional goals of promoting education abroad programs. Some of these decisions will overlap with existing policies regarding student work undertaken elsewhere, but others are quite subjective and unique to study abroad.

Discussion of the "ideal" term or year for study abroad can also lead into discussions of study abroad and enrollment management. Predicting (and/or engineering) study abroad participation by term has great importance to those trying to fill dorm rooms and class-

room seats each year. Successfully increasing study abroad participation can affect many other systems on campus (and is affected by many other systems on campus). Sharing early projections, detecting and reporting on trends, and working with other departments or offices to find the balance appropriate for an institution is an important responsibility for a study abroad official, especially as program participation flourishes. Additionally, developing creative study abroad programs for special constituencies of students (*e.g.*, first semester freshman) may allow for new enrollment management models much to the benefit of the institution for both recruitment and space allocation.

A final consideration is the study abroad application itself. How will students register their intentions and suitability for study abroad? What deadlines make sense for the types of programs offered? Will students apply directly to host programs or institutions, or will they apply internally to the study abroad office first? What criteria will be used to admit or approve students for programs abroad? What offices will be notified of a student's intent to study abroad, and who will notify them? Who needs to approve participation in study abroad outside of the international education office? If students apply to faculty-led or another home-school program abroad, what information is critical to include on an application and what information needs to be gathered in follow-up forms or requests? How (or) will the study abroad office gain access to information that students are not necessarily willing to disclose? If students are applying to outside programs, how much student information will be shared? Are there systems or technologies that will provide for more efficient study abroad operations, including the application data, risk management information, and/or information sharing?

AWARDING OF CREDIT FOR STUDY ABROAD AND APPROVAL OF PROGRAMS AND PARTNERS

The awarding of credit is perhaps the most important consideration as you develop programs or partner with other institutions to send your students abroad. If you are awarding credit for programs that will be used in any way towards a student's graduation requirements, you want to ensure that it is deserving of inclusion in their academic record and that you are awarding the correct amount of credit for work completed abroad. To establish policies and procedures around credit transfer, it is imperative that you work collaboratively with the admissions and/or registrar's office. Policies relating to in-residence credit are important for students planning a study abroad experience towards the end of their degree program, and general policies on minimum grade expectations or policies relating to taking pass/fail courses abroad will affect all students abroad.

Administrators can guide you on your home institution's credit transfer standards and processes, re-admission procedures, if needed, and help you understand host institution and/or international course-credit correlations, and together you can develop guidelines for education abroad. You will also work with the registrar's office to evaluate transcripts and award credit for study abroad programs, and in many cases, responsibility for these activities falls fully on that office. In addition to colleagues in the registrar's office, you should develop a network or advisory group of academic deans, department chairs, and faculty who, depending on your institutional structure, will help you to approve programs, evaluate and/or develop courses, and figure out how to most effectively integrate study abroad into the curriculum.

Courses developed by your own faculty and offered through your institution should be held to the same academic standards as any other courses on your campus. In many circumstances, the format and contact hours may vary from a course taught on the home campus, but elements of academic rigor and evaluation should be consistent. Likewise, courses that you approve as your own or accept towards credit—transfer or otherwise—should be evaluated for appropriate rigor, acceptable faculty credentials, and proper institutional accreditation. Standards will fluctuate by home institution, and the responsibility falls on each to decide what is acceptable for their students, but generally, standards

for accepting credits from international institutions should be transparent and consistent with the institution's policy for accepting domestic transfer credit in order to avoid awkward situations.

Many universities find it extremely helpful to have a process for pre-approving credit to be taken abroad, which serves many purposes. Through pre-approval of credit, students enter into a contract of sorts with their home university, removing much uncertainty about how courses will be applied upon return to the home campus. There is a natural opportunity to review expectations and policies before departure, and home institutions can also feel some level of comfort in extending financial aid to the study abroad experience. Of course, in some cases, course schedules or availability may not be known ahead of the student's arrival abroad, which necessitates some flexibility on the part of both the student and home institution. Other considerations with posting study abroad credit on a home-school transcript or academic record include whether or not to post full information (class titles, grades before translation, program location) and whether or not to include study abroad grades (especially if undertaken in a program not developed by the home institution) in the GPA calculation.

"School of record" is an important topic that arises with many international education organizations or program providers. Many (but certainly not all) program providers are not fully accredited institutions of higher education, often bridging relationships between U.S. institutions and those abroad. To facilitate easier transfer of credit between the accredited host institution (or program components taught in unaccredited organizations), provider organizations might provide transcripts through a "school of record." The school of record may convert course-hour calculations or provide grades already translated into the U.S. grading system, for ease of credit transfer. Though the burden is ultimately on the school of record to stand behind the credit being offered on their transcripts, schools (and students) receiving this credit must also be vigilant that it is legitimate and in line with the standards of your institution. As with any transcript, domestic or otherwise, that students submit for inclusion on their academic record, administrators must examine transcripts with a critical eye and develop policies that are clearly and consistently enforced. It is appropriate to question the level of oversight and ownership that a school of record assumes for study abroad transcripts issued under their name. In 2010, AACRAO and the Forum on Education Abroad formed a working group to examine School of Record issues and to work on a set of guidelines and best practices.

Institutions should also make clear their criteria for approving education abroad partners, whether formally, as in the case of affiliated programs, or on a case-by-case basis, as with unaffiliated programs. It is not necessary to have an approved list of program providers or partner institutions abroad, but there are compelling reasons to do so. On the one hand, not having a list of approved international programs allows students and faculty to choose or recommend programs that fit very individual criteria or academic needs. On the other hand, with an approved list, administrators and faculty can become very familiar with select programs deemed to fit a set of criteria for a given institution. Clear, consistently-applied and justified reasons will go a long way in explaining to faculty, students, parents, and the providers themselves why certain programs are approved and others not. If there are discrepancies as to how credits are transferred back to the home institution (*e.g.*, as transfer or home-school credit), study abroad administrators should also provide clear reasoning for such decisions or procedures.

As with specific courses and academic programs on the home campus, programs abroad should be evaluated on a regular basis for academic relevance, rigor, and quality. Working with faculty and administrators on campus, maintaining a strong relationship with program partners and host institutions, and gathering feedback from student-participants, is important in the evaluation of programs abroad. Of course, education abroad programs have additional criteria on which they should be evaluated, discussed later in this section, but institutions have a responsibility to themselves and their students to closely monitor the quality of educational experiences made available.

Institutions should prepare responses for students who study abroad outside the parameters of the institution and come later asking for that work to be considered for transfer credit. As with all other issues, a transparent, defensible, and consistently-implemented policy is important to have as such questions or cases arise.

FINANCIAL AID AND PAYMENT OF PROGRAM EXPENSES

Just as transfer of credit issues necessitate collaboration with academic departments and offices on a campus, transfer of financial aid requires collaboration with the campus financial aid office. The decision to transfer financial aid, however, may not be as clear cut as the decision to accept credit (or not) from host institutions. The financial aid administrators at your institution will be able to explain the different types of aid (federal, state, institutional, and private), and how each is administered or understood in regards to programs abroad. Study abroad administrators also have a role in working with financial aid administrators (and higher level university administrators) to develop and advocate for models of financial aid that reflect institutional goals for international education. At institutions with established study abroad programs, it is important to weigh the benefits and drawbacks of liberal financial aid transfer and, as with credit transfer, to implement policies that are consistent and transparent. Institutions may also wish to implement policies reflecting their attachment or ownership of certain program types, giving preference to exchange programs over those offered through program providers, or to affiliated programs over those unaffiliated. Program administrators need to work closely with financial aid officials to find the right balance of policies that support and encourage participation in education abroad among all students, regardless of economic background, while working realistically within the overall budget of the institution.

Decisions about payment amounts, deadlines, refund policies, etc. will be a part of establishing new faculty-led or home-school programs abroad, and many institutions also have procedures for payment when outside programs are involved. The study abroad administrator, with other administrators on campus, should discuss and create policy for issues such as:

* A study abroad fee (sometimes used to offset administrative support or fund scholarships, etc.);
* Payment routing for outside programs (direct-pay or billed through the home school, or combination);
* Balancing (or not) of participants in direct or reciprocal exchanges;
* Items (tuition, housing, and/or fees) included in exchanges;
* The application of financial aid (federal, state, and institutional); and
* Processes for disbursement of financial aid.

The concept of collecting home-school tuition from students, in exchange for more liberal financial aid policies ("home-school fees"), is often a method of equalizing opportunity for students with lesser means and creating a somewhat more predictable financial model for institutional financial administrators. In some cases, actual program expenses may be less than home-school tuition, though in others, they may be more. The idea, sustainable primarily at private institutions, is somewhat controversial, and institutions wishing to adopt this model should carefully plan the implementation process, as well as develop materials to explain the model to students and parents.

AFFILIATION AGREEMENTS AND OTHER CONTRACTS

As the topics of credit transfer and financial aid applicability highlight, the benefits of clear agreements between the home school and host organization are often immeasurable. Legal counsel offices will frequently have templates or strict guidelines about what needs to be included in institutional affiliations, and study abroad officials should involve their legal counsel in reviewing any type of agreement committing to a relationship between two parties. If no such agreements have been developed at your university before, a quick request to peer institutions will likely produce several examples, and professional organizations and institutions further afield will also generally share this type of information (check NAFSA education abroad resource guides, for example). Additional care should be taken around any contracts developed or signed with organizations or businesses providing services overseas, such as transportation or housing for short-term, faculty-led programs.

FACULTY POLICIES AND RISK MANAGEMENT

Basic policies must be developed to address and encourage faculty participation in and leadership of education abroad programs. Specifically, policies around faculty payment and contribution to tenure and/or teaching requirements are fairly common needs. In addition to leading programs or teaching in programs abroad, faculty involvement can also be critical in evaluating study abroad programs, developing relationships with host institutions, and advising students.

The basics of risk management are covered later in this chapter; however, an important component of risk management, primarily for education abroad programs run by the home institution, is faculty and staff training. In addition to covering the basics of program development and management (budgeting and reporting, human resources (HR)-related salary or teaching release issues, logistics, etc.), faculty should understand the different role that they might find themselves in during the course of a program abroad. Of course, the level and types of preparation will vary with different program models, sizes, and available support staff, but short-term, faculty-led programs may require the most intense faculty preparation. Study abroad officials should develop guidelines and training materials for faculty, collaborating with student affairs professionals and HR administrators. Whenever possible, space for faculty peer-to-peer discussions should also be developed.

Risk management extends far beyond faculty-led programs or home-school programs or campuses abroad. Education abroad administrators are well served to develop and disseminate policies and procedures addressing risk management and student safety, planning for scenarios on the home campus and abroad. There are many resources and professional development opportunities in this area, and study abroad professionals new and old should attend workshops and share resources with relevant colleagues on their campuses, involving a wide variety of administrators and faculty representatives in drafting and supporting such initiatives.

PROGRAM EVALUATION

Briefly mentioned in the section on credit approval and transfer, evaluating programs is a necessary component of running a sound study abroad operation and can be combined with assessing learning outcomes. Programs run through your institution and those on any type of approved or affiliated list should be evaluated regularly and thoroughly, including areas such as academic rigor and learning outcomes, student satisfaction, student health and safety, and program operations. Receiving input from a variety of sources, including faculty, students, program providers or host institutions, and even your peer institutions, will assist you in developing a fuller picture of the program, regardless of whether you have seen it "in action" or not.

Perhaps reflecting a general movement towards better assessment of learning outcomes on college campuses, or simply because the field has grown significantly and rapidly, assessment and evaluation of study abroad programs has also taken center-stage for many international education organizations. The membership of the Forum on Education Abroad (2008) compiled, refined, and released a handbook titled *Standards of Good Practice for Education Abroad* that should be read by study abroad administrators and other faculty and administrators preparing to undertake a review of study abroad offerings at your institution (and in preparation

for launching new programs). The *Standards* document combines the Forum's standards of good practice with a detailed list of queries into each. Though certainly not to be viewed as a one-size-fits-all document, the *Standards* were developed to encourage reflection and discussion on important questions for education abroad, and were created with input and participation from institutions and administrators around the world, filling a variety of roles in the field.

Other assessment guidelines and models are utilized within the field of education abroad, and many institutions may prefer conducting program assessment and evaluation using criteria agreed upon by existing institutional bodies. Site visits to international programs are often a part of program evaluation and assessment, but should not be the sole method of evaluation. Discussing plans and researching methods used by peer institutions, as well as professional organizations, is recommended, and creating a transparent and consistent approach is imperative.

As you may have ascertained, establishing policies and procedures for education abroad programs is a multi-faceted and collaborative process, requiring input from many different constituents on your campus and abroad. While it is an evolving process, there is much to be learned from those with already established programs, and in most cases, you will find colleagues willing to share information and experiences on that topic, and the topic to follow—advising, programming, and student preparedness.

Advising, Programming, and Student Preparedness

Institutional culture and philosophy will impact your level of involvement and approach to study abroad programming and preparedness activities. This section discusses student advising, building awareness on campus and marketing of programs, ideas for student programming, and involving parents in the study abroad process.

ADVISING STRUCTURES AND CONSIDERATIONS

There are many different ways that education abroad advising can be structured, depending on the size of the institution, study abroad participation, and scope of the office and its programs abroad. Other factors in how advising might be structured include faculty involvement, delineation of advising duties between offices, and institutional philosophy. Regardless of where your official reporting line leads, the study abroad office will deal with substantial academic and administrative issues, and staffing and advising structures should be designed with this in mind.

Smaller study abroad offices tend to take a more generalist approach to advising students on programs and opportunities, working in tandem with other academic and administrative offices on campus to advise students on credit transfer and financial aid issues, and with academic departments to develop faculty-led programs. Medium-sized offices often have the ability to develop regional or programmatic (summer or short-term programs, exchanges, by academic department, etc.) expertise among staff members, though they may wish to take a generalist approach towards advising, even while taking a more focused approach and assigning program management responsibilities. Large offices, or those offices on campuses serving larger student populations, may decide to define specific advising and program management roles, often with the necessary hierarchy that comes with a larger staff. Specialization and delineation of duties may be the best option towards managing large study abroad programs and associated activities without losing efficiency or the ability to take a more individual approach towards working with students and program contacts, but communication between staff members will take new importance, since many issues will apply across-the-board.

As mentioned earlier in the chapter, to increase both your expertise and a sense of campus-wide involvement, you may wish to develop an advisory committee—academic, administrative, or both—to evaluate programs, services, and new opportunities on a routine basis. For small offices, this can be crucial. Regardless of whether or not you formally rely on other on-campus offices to advise and track student academics undertaken abroad, it is important to develop a solid working relationship with offices such as the registrar, financial aid, risk management, and student counseling and/or health office, since each will hold specialized knowledge that applies to students studying abroad. Likewise, developing faculty allies within each department or school will allow you to work more in partnership with departments to develop and provide opportunities aligned with their curricula and the academic goals of your institution.

General Student Advising Areas:
* Program selection and application preparation
* Academics—institutional policies, credit transfer, educational model, academic expectations, enrollment process, etc.
* Student development/counseling abilities to match students with program models and types appropriate to their skill level and goals
* Health and safety—vaccinations, local context (political, health, cultural, etc.), personal and travel safety, etc.
* Housing and transportation (both international and domestic)
* Cultural adjustment and cross-cultural communication
* Finances and financial aid
* Communicating with friends and family in the home country

Structural Considerations:
* How many staff members are in my office? Are we faculty, staff, or a combination?
* What types of study abroad programs and opportunities are we managing? At what level—academic, administrative, both?
* How many students are we serving (or would we like to serve) each semester or year?
* What is our relationship with other support offices on campus?

✻ What is our relationship with the faculty and upper administration?

✻ Are we responsible for training faculty to lead programs abroad?

✻ Are we responsible for international financial accounts?

✻ What is the reporting line of our office (through Student Affairs, Academic Affairs)?

✻ Is my office driving new program development or approvals?

✻ Will our office advise for post-graduate opportunities, too (fellowships, etc.)?

✻ Are we working with strong off-campus partners, in so doing providing additional support to our faculty, students, and parents?

✻ What is our institutional philosophy about student support? Is this consistently applied among other student support (academic and administrative) offices?

✻ How can the office best support students before, during, and after the study abroad experience?

As has been stated in other sections of this chapter, it is important to remember that you do not have to re-create the wheel. Reach out to study abroad offices at your peer institutions or further afield to find out what iterations of advising structures they've tried, how they've worked to build relationships with departments and administrative offices, what types of programming they support, etc. There is a wealth of information out there, along with many experienced professionals willing to share with newcomers to the field.

BUILDING AWARENESS

In addition to managing study abroad activity at your institution, you will also be tasked with building awareness of international study opportunities on your campus. Part of this will be educating the campus and its constituents on your services—another part will be managing the presentation of opportunities offered by those coming from outside of your campus.

Your outreach efforts should be informed by your ultimate goals for education abroad on your campus—do you wish to grow participation, to pursue curriculum integration with specific schools or departments, to improve the reputation or rigor of opportunities, to build recognition of all-around student development through study abroad, or all of the above? Outreach goals need to be balanced with your staff and student resources, and relationships with faculty and other campus offices come into play when thinking about maximizing your reach. You can (and should!) also actively involve a diverse group of students, especially study abroad alumni, in your outreach efforts. If you would like to see more science majors study abroad at your institution, for example, make sure to feature a statement from a science major somewhere in your marketing materials. The same applies to other groups of students less commonly represented in study abroad participation statistics. It is helpful to design your outreach efforts to address students at different stages of exploration. For example, a freshman may be best served by general information sessions, a sophomore by a study abroad fair, and a junior by location- or program-specific meetings. Likewise, for faculty-led programs or programs targeting a niche of students, it is wise to work through non-traditional channels to reach the appropriate constituency of students.

Representatives from other institutions and provider organizations may wish to visit your campus, either at your invitation or on their own initiative. These visits can be quite productive, and will contribute to raising the profile of study abroad if planned well, but if the message is not consistent with your outreach efforts or school philosophy, a visit can also be damaging. It is wise to communicate your institution's policies and practices to outside visitors in advance and during your meetings with them, or their meetings with faculty or students, and you should follow up to learn about their visit if it extended to activities outside of what you had planned. Strong relationships with other institutions and provider organizations—especially those with programs utilized by your students—ultimately reduce the administrative burden for your office, since you will have more thorough knowledge of the programs and staff.

It is important to consider your desired "message" in all of your outreach activities. If you want students and faculty to take opportunities seriously, or if you want to present study abroad as an activity integral to both academic and personal development for students, it is best to highlight academic enrichment, student development, and future returns over and above the "fun" aspects of the experience. In every instance, you should consider your target audience(s) and your institutional context. In addition to reaching students, at some institutions it will be equally important to gain faculty buy-in to grow a study abroad program, while at others it will be important to educate parents on the benefits of study abroad. Looking at your institution's student demographics, successful strategies of other offices, and popular academic departments, as well as listening to students, faculty and others to learn perceived and real barriers, will help you in crafting a communications plan appropriate to your own context.

STUDENT PROGRAMMING

Study abroad experiences can be anchored into a student's academic experience, even if short-term. Study abroad offices should coordinate with faculty, administrators, and off-campus partners to develop programming for students appropriate to their experience. This section will briefly cover three areas—pre-departure orientation, communication during the program, and re-entry programs.

Pre-departure programming and preparation will vary greatly depending on the size of your institution, the types and models of programs you are using, and the number of students you are sending abroad. Some institutions have for-credit courses or mandatory day-long meetings; others may only have a 1-hour optional meeting supplemented by handouts—there is a huge range in the middle. If you are managing faculty-led or home-school programs, you will need to be more thorough in your orientations, especially if there will not be supplemental meetings abroad. If you are sending students abroad with or to another institution, it will be helpful for you to find out what information your students will receive upon arrival.

At a minimum, pre-departure meetings and information should cover logistical issues and expectations of students—these exist for every program type and model, regardless of the length of the program. You will want to reinforce topics you may have discussed during advising sessions, to ensure that students have a common understanding on issues such as:

* Institutional policies for earning credit for academic work.
* Financial aid details and policies.
* How to contact you/your institution, and who to communicate with in an emergency.
* Behavioral expectations and penalties.
* Health and safety resources available on campus and abroad.
* Resources—academic and personal—available to them while abroad.
* Explanation of any paperwork needed.
* Travel resources and requirements (visas, immunizations, etc.).
* Cultural adjustment issues and cross-cultural learning strategies.
* If semester- or year-long programs, information on housing and registration upon return.

More detailed pre-departure orientation sessions can go into additional topics or site-specific information such as:

* Academic expectations in the host-country setting.
* Language learning strategies.
* Global citizenship concepts.
* Self-reflection, exploration of individual's culture, motivation and goals for study abroad, etc.
* Overall expectations and/or fears.
* Anti-Americanism or racism abroad.

✻ By country/program explanation of schedule, students' expectations of daily life or adjustment, extracurricular opportunities, etc.
✻ Break-out sessions for groups, such as women, students of color, heritage-seeking students, and LGTB students.
✻ By-country discussion of history, culture, and current context.
✻ By-country discussion of specific logistical details (travel, health, safety, academics, etc.)
✻ Setting the stage for returning to campus post-experience.

As much as possible, try to include other presenters in your sessions, including other faculty or administrators on campus (*i.e.*, the registrar, housing, financial aid, counseling, public safety, etc.), to supply multiple voices to reinforce policies. If you are working with outside organizations, it can also be helpful to invite them to do a pre-departure session with students attending their programs. Involving study abroad alumni in sessions is an excellent way to give students an opportunity to ask questions about the program or site, but you should prepare the students well. Students trust what they hear from their peers, and you should ask students to emphasize issues relevant to your sessions and message (*i.e.*, study abroad as an academic pursuit, an opportunity to learn about other cultures and/or global perspectives, adherence to university policy, etc.).

The length and structure of the program, as well as your institutional context, will influence how you stay in touch with students while they are abroad. If they are on a faculty-led, short-term program, you may not need to communicate with the group unless there is an emergency. If they are abroad for a semester or year, you may need to send them information about course registration and housing for the coming term, or you may wish to send them updates from campus once or twice. Communications can be informational and proactive, but at times, they may also be critical. Developing a communications plan for reaching students abroad is an important aspect of risk management planning in this day and age. Knowing how to reach students, the institutions hosting them, and parents or guardians (when in line with your institutional policy) should be built into all program planning and approval.

Many schools are utilizing technology to create a continuous community for students regardless of their location in the world. Blogs, Facebook sites, Twitter posts, and other technology make it increasingly easy to stay connected. There are different perspectives on the ability to communicate easily with "home" while abroad, with some feeling that it is better for students to disconnect and participate fully in their study abroad experience. Others feel that the connection can lead to increased ability for schools to encourage student reflection on the experience, deepening its impact academically and personally. Keeping a blog, for example, is essentially keeping a journal chronicling experiences. As a study abroad administrator, you can use postings to demonstrate the impact of the experience to faculty and staff at your institution, or to allow students to share and communicate (in a more public sphere than email) with each other while abroad.

One caution—with others on your campus, decide how to approach topics or issues that come up in any sort of social network or blog site that you might develop. Posts can be educational, but they can also be alarming or harmful to their hosts or your institution, since students are often writing before they have processed an experience. Develop guidelines for public posts, and encourage students to reach out to you (or someone) directly if a post, including photographs, may be personally or politically sensitive. If your institution reserves the right to discipline students for actions off-campus and during the study abroad experience (which is advisable), remind students of this fact, and be prepared to respond appropriately if something comes up.

Re-entry programming is another important part of the study abroad experience. Like pre-departure programs, you can involve a variety of representatives from your campus (career services, counseling, academic departments) and plan programs ranging from a very minimal, optional meeting, to multi-faceted events over weeks or months. You may have a hard time reaching students when they return to campus, since they will be busy trying to integrate back into campus life, and they may not immediately realize the impact that their experiences abroad have had on them.

The *NAFSA Guide to Education Abroad for Advisors and Administrators, Third Edition* (2005, p. 305) offers four solid reasons to provide re-entry programming to students:

* To assist students in their readjustment to the home culture and to college or university life after studying abroad.
* To help students learn to reflect on and articulate what they learned from their educational experience.
* To facilitate opportunities for students to incorporate their international experiences into their lives at home, both academically and personally.
* To help students identify ways they may use and market their international experience in the future.

Ideas for programming might include study abroad alumni mixers, sessions on integrating a study abroad into a résumé or job interview, a writing workshop to develop essays or articles about their experiences, small group debrief sessions with study abroad and counseling center staff, open panels on research done abroad, or the organization of a study abroad photo contest or exhibit. Re-entry programming will also help you to identify those students best able to represent your office in pre-departure meetings or meetings with faculty and administrators as you build support for your office. Study abroad alumni will also be your most powerful marketing resource and tool, since they are likely to be enthusiastic about sharing their experience with others.

PARENTAL INVOLVEMENT

Parental involvement in higher education has fully arrived with the current generation of traditional col-lege-aged students. Numerous articles on the "Millennial Generation" and "helicopter parents" give a nice overview of traits and behaviors generally associated with these terms. Parents can both assist and challenge you in your role as an education abroad professional, and you are likely to talk to them before and during a student's study abroad experience.

Institutional demographics, policies, and philosophy will inform your involvement with parents as much as anything else, but at a minimum, you might wish to develop a parallel resource to prepare them for their child's study abroad experience. In the planning stages, you will want to share with them general information developed for students as mentioned in the "General Advising Areas" section above, with emphasis on logistical and practical information. At institutions where you are trying to increase participation among traditionally under-represented populations, it will be especially important to develop resources to demonstrate the value of study abroad to parents, who may be reluctant to allow their child to pursue this opportunity. Reaching parents early and highlighting success stories, in admissions and orientation events, and in the first years of college, is important, as they usually have a lot of influence—both mental and financial—over a student's decision to study abroad.

While students are abroad, you want to make sure parents understand some of the cultural adjustment issues students might face, and the need to balance the phone calls home. Also clearly communicate emergency contact information to them, so that they will feel comfortable with their ability to reach you if they feel it is necessary. Discuss privacy issues with your institution's legal counsel, so as not to violate students' rights. If you are sending students abroad using a provider organization, it is advisable to ask them what their approach is to working with parents. Involve the organization in the re-entry experience, too, if possible, offering information about common cultural re-adjustment issues, or possible questions they can ask their students upon return.

Regardless of your approach to working with parents, they are an important constituency. If you have the capacity to do so, you may wish to involve parents of study abroad alumni in outreach efforts before, during, and after the experience.

Legal Issues, Risk Management, and Education Abroad

As our society grows ever more litigious, professionals in the field of education abroad are increasingly aware of the potential legal issues inherent in advising for and managing study abroad programs. Recent legal issues involving study abroad programs have included everything from safety and institutional liability issues abroad to relationships between institutions and third party program providers to complaints over finances or the award of credit. It is important for a good study abroad program administrator or advisor to be aware of areas of risk and legal vulnerability, to develop contingency plans for what-if scenarios, and to seek and utilize advice from university counsel and risk managers regarding important issues, contracts, and the management of risks. Education abroad professionals can counter worry with the development of knowledge, a focus on preparation, and proactive, transparent communication with their institutional colleagues, faculty, students, and in many cases, parents. This section will examine several areas of legal issues in education abroad, focusing on areas of planning and preparation, operations, documentation, and questions that should be asked of risk managers and legal counsel at your own institution. All preparation can be considered risk management.

In the previous edition of this chapter (2001), the author gave a basic introduction to legal terms applicable to U.S. higher education law (and therefore U.S.-sponsored or accredited education abroad programs) which have been kept here, classifying the broad areas of law relevant to those advising for and administering study abroad programs. In general, most of the issues that are covered in this section could be grouped into two categories if pursued in the courts—contract law and tort law. Contract law deals with contracts and agreements, and tort law deals with wrongdoing outside of contractual matters, such as accusations of negligence. The author also introduced several federal laws that are applicable, most notably ADA, FERPA, and the Clery Act. I will include information about these under the relevant headings. In the nine years since that chapter was released, several issues have arisen that have led professional organizations in the field of study abroad to formalize and/or more widely promote standards of best practice and codes of ethics to guide institutions and individuals, which will be referenced here and which are cited in the "resources" section at the conclusion of the chapter. The information provided here is by no means comprehensive, but should be a good starting place as you establish a study abroad program at your institution. Forming a relationship with your institution's legal counsel and risk management personnel is critical, and similar topics are discussed with increasing frequency at their professional meetings, too.

STUDENT HEALTH, SAFETY, AND PREPARATION

Regardless of legal considerations, health and safety is likely one of your key concerns as a study abroad professional. It is also one of the hardest things to control. Since the world and the students scattered around it are unpredictable, the best course of action is to advise students well, make smart policy decisions, and plan for unexpected situations. Some of this has been discussed earlier in the chapter, and in the context of reducing liability, it is important enough to reiterate in this section. Discuss these items with your university counsel and risk managers, and agree on a standard for your institution. You may also choose to draft contracts or release forms with participants. These lists of recommendations are starting points for discussion, and are not comprehensive.

Student Safety

✳ It is critical that you inform students of potential risks of study abroad, in general and specific to the location they choose (political climate, risk of natural disaster, living conditions, local transportation), and give them access to resources that will allow them to make their own informed decision about participation.

* If you utilize provider organizations or send students to host institutions, you should review the materials that are given to students throughout the admissions, advising, and orientation process.

* Choose vendors and service providers carefully when planning your own programs abroad, asking for certifications, licenses, insurance documentation, and references.

* You should develop multi-layered contingency plans, include communications and student/group mobility, and make sure that every student knows who to contact in an emergency.

* Do not shy away from placing reasonable restrictions on students in the name of safety.

Student Health

* If you are administering your own programs or sites, develop a process through which a student's pre-existing health conditions are professionally evaluated given the context of the host site.

* Make sure that the student, the program director, and in many cases the student's home physician, share a common understanding of resources available in a host country to accommodate the student's illness, as routine treatment or in the case of an emergency. Involve parents as appropriate.

* Require that students have appropriate health insurance that offers coverage and support in the host country—a policy that explicitly covers medical evacuation and repatriation of remains.

* For faculty-led programs, also ensure that the faculty member or program leader has appropriate insurance coverage, and that the faculty member discusses contingency plans and emergency contact information (u.s.-based and within the host country) with a designated participant or co-leader.

Expectations for Student Behavior and Country/Culture-Specific Orientations

* Establish a code of conduct for students abroad that fits with your institutional philosophy, and make it widely known and available to students.

* Discuss the power of information-sharing technology (*e.g.*, Facebook, blogs) and make recommendations for appropriate or respectful use.

* Emphasize to students that they are subject to the laws of their host country and the policies or code of conduct of their host institution.

* Encourage students to reflect on how certain acceptable (and unacceptable) behaviors in the United States might be received by citizens of their host country.

* Provide students with ample resources or opportunities to learn about the host culture, including cultural norms around alcohol use, sexual activity and orientation, gender expectations, etc.

* Involve host institutions in preparing pre-departure resources (or familiarize yourself with resources they provide directly to students).

* Discuss academic differences related to academic honesty or plagiarism policies, if known and relevant, to prepare students for their new academic environment.

Faculty Preparation

* Share all relevant information and resources given to students with faculty members leading student groups abroad (if they have not been involved in the development of the materials).

* Make faculty members or program leaders aware of any relevant or potential health concerns (including mental health) and relevant medical information regarding the participants.

* Discuss the student code of conduct and develop guidelines and a process for documenting warnings, sanctions, or dismissal with faculty before the program begins.

* Develop a complementary faculty code of conduct and set of expectations.

✳ Document and review contingency plans with faculty or program leadership, and identify U.S.-based and in-country emergency contacts and protocols.

CONTINGENCY AND CRISIS MANAGEMENT PLANNING

Though inherent in all of the above mentioned suggestions, developing strong contingency and crisis management plans will serve you well in the (hopefully) rare instances they must be invoked. Crisis management plans such as a designated on-call system, phone tree, and contracting of outside assistance can be developed in a general sense, but many areas of contingency planning must be developed with specific programs in mind. Work with colleagues on your campus to develop plans for inconvenient but non-threatening situations such as a cancelled flight or transportation strike, and also for the most extreme situations like an earthquake, missing student, or violent political uprising.

✳ Do students have contact information for local contacts and home-school officials?

✳ Are students (and faculty) registered with the U.S. Embassy of the host country?

✳ Are there back-up methods of transportation? Are students traveling as a group?

✳ How will you contact students, faculty, and their parents or guardians?

✳ Will you be able to fulfill the credit expectations elsewhere if the program is interrupted and will you issue tuition refunds if not?

✳ Who will you call to help assess whether or not a program should begin as planned, or continue if the program is already underway, if a situation happens before students leave home?

Work with faculty and program staff to build bridges between the programs abroad and home campus student health, mental health, or crisis counseling services. In the circumstance of a student rape, violent attack, or mental collapse, having these connections ready to spring to action is critical, and your office may wish to develop these connections for students on outside pro-

grams as well. Extensive resources and training opportunities exist to learn more about planning, and study abroad administrators should make it a priority to take advantage of the experiences of peer institutions and colleagues on their own campus to develop a model that protects the students, faculty, and institution, and share the key concepts with all participants, so that they will know what to do if a situation occurs.

MARKETING AND PROGRAM ADVISING

Program marketing and advising also bears risk and should be approached thoughtfully. Descriptions and representations of the program should be reviewed for accuracy, adherence to established academic standards or goals, and for connection to the institution's philosophy. Program components, coursework, costs, and provisions should be easily available to prospective students and families, and advising sessions should assist a student in understanding available options rather than limiting options based on subjective reasons.

Some institutions choose to create a list of approved programs, restricting students to selected opportunities, and those decisions should be transparent to students and other program providers alike. There are many benefits to having a controlled list of study abroad options, or to promoting home-school experiences over outside providers (approved or not), and as long as criteria are clear and made based on objective factors, it should also be reasonably defensible if challenged. Institutions leaving program identification to students should be prepared to evaluate each program as proposed, especially if credit will be pre-approved and financial aid transferred. Both models (two of many models) are completely appropriate depending on the individual institutional culture and philosophy, not to mention policy.

Recently there has been a bit of negative publicity on relationships between institutions and third party provider organizations, and financial arrangements, board memberships, and/or perks provided to administrators in exchange for program approval. The field of education abroad has reacted by further developing a professional code of ethics; organizations and institutions have become more transparent in articulating mutual goals, contributions, and opportunities created by these relationships; and individual institutions have responded by releasing clear criteria on why certain programs make the list while others do not. While the negative connotations were not welcome, the outcomes have been quite positive.

Disclosing potential risks, preparing students and faculty for adverse situations, working to develop thorough knowledge of sites and programs, planning ahead, documenting advising conversations and policy information, and disseminating information honestly and ethically will go far in reducing institutional liability. If you are responsible for training a staff, it is important to impart this sense of responsibility on them and give them the necessary education and tools to do their job well. As officers of your institution, it is important to do your best to protect the institution from the risk of liability or lawsuits. As professionals, you should also discuss your potential individual liability with institutional legal counsel and determine what amount of protection, if any, they will provide should you be named in a lawsuit.

PROGRAM COMPLIANCE, CONTRACTS, AND FINANCES

Another area of great importance for study abroad administrators running their own programs and working with outside providers is program compliance, contracts, and finances. As discussed in the "policy and procedures" section of this chapter, it is important to develop policies and contracts around working with vendors or service providers overseas, both to protect your students and your institution. As stated in the earlier version of this chapter, contracts should be carefully drafted showing who is responsible for every aspect of the service, and program administrators should try to include a clause in the contract stating that the agency providing the service will reimburse or indemnify the U.S. college should it be sued as a result of said service. Likewise, you should develop similar contracts with any

international education organizations or program providers hosting your students overseas, especially if you have a more formal relationship or affiliation with the organization. There are, of course, areas of mutual responsibility, especially advising and preparing students. You should advise students and faculty on how to attain the appropriate visas or work permissions for the host country (using outside resources when appropriate or unclear), make sure that programs you are planning can operate legally, and provide additional protections (liability insurance, appropriate financial arrangements, etc.) for your program faculty and staff. Any outside programs recommended or approved by your institution should be held to the same standards and should be able to provide reasonable proof of compliance if asked.

Study abroad professionals should not have to bear the full burden of drawing up contracts, figuring out the details of international money transfer, or investigating complex compliance issues. Instead, drawing on the resources and expertise of your institutional legal counsel, human resources office, financial controllers, and risk managers offers more protection. While you may be responsible for much of the documentation or work, it is important to have the input of people for whom these issues are commonplace.

Federal Laws and Education Abroad

There are four important federal laws to understand as a study abroad administrator, dealing with safety, access, health, and student information. Though many more laws may touch the operations of a study abroad office, these are the most commonly discussed within the context of education abroad.

AMERICANS WITH DISABILITIES ACT (ADA)

Under the Americans with Disabilities Act, students with disabilities are entitled to receive reasonable accommodations to ensure access to study abroad opportunities. Though still open to much interpretation and complicated by disparities in standards of accessibility overseas, study abroad advisors should

FIGURE 20.1

Additional Resources

This chapter aimed to prepare study abroad administrators at a basic level and to inspire conversation and collaboration about study abroad programs on a much broader level. Myriad resources exist to answer questions, build knowledge, and develop professionally, both through the extensive publications of AACRAO and through other organizations. Select links to useful or cited resources are provided here.

- AACRAO Publications Web site: www. aacrao.org/publications/new.cfm
- The Forum on Education Abroad's Standards of Good Practice for Education Abroad. www. forumea.org/documents/ForumE AStandardsGoodPrctMarch2008.pdf
- www.forumea.org/standards-standards.cfm

Professional Codes of Ethics
- AACRAO: www.aacrao. org/about/ethics.cfm
- NAFSA: www.nafsa.org/_/File/_/ ethical_principles_2009.pdf

NAFSA Publications
- www.nafsa.org/interactive/core/ orders/category.aspx?catid=2
- Abroad by Design: Key Strategies, edited by Cori Filson

- Guide to Successful Short-Term Programs Abroad (2nd edition), edited by Sarah E. Spencer and Kathy Tuma
- Crisis Management in a Cross-Cultural Setting, edited by Patricia A. Burak and William W. Hoffa

Web-Based Resources
- U.S. State Department Travel Resources—http://travel.state.gov
- What's Up With Culture?: On-Line Cultural Training Resource for Study Abroad– www2.pacific.edu/sis/culture/
- IIE and IIE Open Doors—www.iie. org, http://iie.org/en/Research-and-Publications/Publications-and-Reports
- Mobility International USA—www.miusa.org
- Mobility International USA, National Clearinghouse on Disability and Exchange—www.miusa.org/ncde

Information on federal laws mentioned above:
- Americans with Disabilities Act—www2.ed.gov/about/offices/ list/ocr/docs/hq9805.html
- The Crime Awareness and Campus Security Act (Clery Act)—http://ed.gov/ admins/lead/safety/campus.html
- Family Educational Rights and Privacy Act (FERPA)—www2.ed.gov/policy/ gen/guid/fpco/ferpa/index.html
- Guidance on the Application of FERPA and HIPAA (Health Insurance Portability and Accountability Act) for Student Health Records—www2. ed.gov/policy/gen/guid/fpco/ doc/ferpa-hipaa-guidance.pdf

---

make every attempt to design inclusive programs or to identify opportunities that will be able to accommodate students with disabilities. In many cases, the study abroad advisor, the student, the campus ADA advisor (if available) and faculty or host institutions can work together to identify required accommodations, site or program limitations, and where adjustments can be made. Mobility International USA is a leading international organization promoting equality for people with disabilities, and their National Clearinghouse on Disability and Exchange offers resources and encouragement to students with disabilities considering study abroad, as well as guidance for administrators in the U.S. and abroad in helping students achieve their goals.

CRIME AWARENESS AND CAMPUS SECURITY ACT (CLERY ACT)

The Clery Act and its relationship to overseas programs or campuses is receiving ever-increasing attention. If you operate a standing program abroad, you may be obligated to report any crime statistics through your home university, which must also be disclosed to the larger university community. It is important to discuss the provisions of this Act related to educational activities abroad with your institution's legal counsel, since there are a variety of factors that go into reporting. Criteria established in the Clery Act handbook published by the Department of Education (2005) regarding if and what statistics must be reported include:

* Participation in federal financial aid programs.
* Categorization of property ownership or rental relationship.
* Relationship of the site to your student body.
* Whether or not crimes occurred at the location while your students were present.

International branch campuses of U.S. institutions may be obligated to report statistics separately from the home institution.

FAMILY EDUCATIONAL RIGHTS AND PRIVACY ACT (FERPA)

FERPA covers the student's right to privacy and protects academic records, as well as those relating to a student's disciplinary record, combining both under the term "educational records." At age 18, or when the student begins attending an institution of higher education regardless of age, the decision to share these records transfers to the student and away from the parent; therefore study abroad administrators must be very careful to understand where the line between "public record" and "private information" falls. Most campuses will have someone who is an expert on interpreting FERPA, and it is important to develop training materials for staff, as well as a policy statement to share with frustrated parents.

FERPA is more straightforward when it comes to liaising between two academic institutions or parties during the planning of student participation in programs abroad. FERPA allows for the exchange of education records between officials with legitimate educational interest, in connection with providing financial aid to a student, and when appropriate in cases of health and safety emergencies, among others. These exchanges are commonplace between the home institution and program partners, so students should be told in advance that such exchange will take place to avoid any misunderstanding. As an institution or office, you may also decide that you wish to have students sign a release allowing you to speak with a parent or guardian about their participation in (before, during, or after) a study abroad program. Institutional culture will likely dictate your approach to this topic.

HEALTH INSURANCE PORTABILITY AND ACCOUNTABILITY ACT (HIPAA)

HIPAA regulations are somewhat complex and institution type may influence what is considered protected. In many cases, treatment records of students at post-secondary institutions (in a Student Health Clinic, for example) may be included as protected "educational records" under FERPA. Due to the complexity of the regulations, it is important to bring in the counsel of someone very familiar with the law. Additionally, it is highly recommended that you ask the student to sign a waiver allowing a designated study abroad administrator to have access to information that may be relevant in an international setting. Many program administrators will also partner with student health or mental health offices, so that counseling or appointments can take a more focused direction to prepare specific students for any potential issues that may arise when abroad, based on their specific issues, and to offer program leaders valuable training information.

This section aimed to introduce you to many of the complexities of operating programs abroad and was intended to spur discussions around risk management, staff training, student preparation, and the larger context in which we work. As the field grows, so will the legal issues that arise, and it is important for study abroad to maintain awareness and vigilance, as well as on- and off-campus networks for help if questions or problems develop.

TWENTY-ONE

Transforming European Higher Education:
The Bologna Process

ROBERT WATKINS | Assistant Director of Admissions
Graduate and International Admissions Center
The University of Texas at Austin

2010 AACRAO INTERNATIONAL GUIDE

Transforming European Higher Education: The Bologna Process

For international educators 2010 did more than usher in a new decade, it represented the target date for full implementation of the European Higher Education Area (EHEA) commonly referred to as the Bologna Process. In this year, all participating countries in the process (a total of forty-seven as of 2010 with the addition of Kazakhstan) were to have fully transformed their country's higher education system to conform to the agreed upon models adopted at that first ministerial meeting in Bologna, Italy in June 1999. Certainly immense progress has been made, but the EHEA is far from fully implemented. Of course, the definition of full implementation is just part of the problem facing this concert of European nations. In this chapter we shall review the key points of the plan, how things are progressing (or not), and the effect outside of Europe of the changes implemented. Some attempt to discern the future of the process and its ripple effect outside Europe will be made as well.

After arriving at a political decision to accept the different European upper secondary leaving certificates for purposes of university admission throughout Europe in the mid-1980s, European educators finally embraced the need for reforming higher education at the 1999 meeting in Bologna. There, twenty-nine ministers of education from different countries agreed to create the EHEA which would radically transform higher education among the participating countries by

* creating a new degree structure;
* adopting a credit accumulation system as a basis for these new degrees;

* formulating a transparent reporting scheme that would reveal how these degrees were attained; and
* weaving together a quality assurance structure at multiple levels that would undergird the new degree structure.

Furthermore, the ministers agreed to meet every two years to assess progress among participating countries toward the goal of full implementation of the four key components by 2010. These meetings were held biannually in Prague (2001), Berlin (2003), Bergen (2005), London (2007), and Leuven (2009). For each meeting a lengthy report was prepared entitled Trends (I-V) that laid out in detail the decisions made and progress achieved. Between ministerial meetings a working group called the Bologna Follow-Up Group (BFUG) met to hammer out details of progress achieved, coordinate future progress, and transform the stated goals emanating from the meeting communiqués into concrete action.

Over the course of the decade since the first meeting in 1999, several major achievements took place. First, the group of signatory countries grew from the original twenty-nine to the current forty-seven. Secondly, what was originally envisioned as a two-cycle new degree structure (first degree/second degree or undergraduate degree/graduate degree) became a three-cycle track with the introduction of a third, terminal academic degree generally referred to as a doctoral degree at the Bergen meeting in 2003. Thirdly, signatory countries began formulating national qualification frameworks and national quality assurance bodies (though in many of the countries these already existed in some form or other). Finally, the systematic issuance of diploma supplements across the area, the addition of a new degree structure in all faculties within higher education institutions, and the recording of European Credit Transfer and Accumulation System (ECTS) credits alongside the courses taken for the degrees began to appear on documents consistently.

True, problems persist. Not all traditional degrees have been eliminated or fully replaced by the new degree structure in signatory countries. Despite the universal agreement of the need for the diploma supplement and the apparent consensus on content to be included, these documents vary, sometimes widely, not only across national boundaries, but even within the same country from institution to institution. The final structure of the third level, the doctoral degree, remains unclear as the deadline for full implementation nears. Nevertheless, the process continues to move forward and now seems inevitable. Though a political decision in which academics and administrators were not truly consulted prior to agreement on radical, sweeping changes to higher education, the process continues to move inexorably toward fruition, even if full implementation in 2010 now appears to have been an ambitious goal.

In fact, the official Bologna Process Web site since the 2009 Leuven Ministerial Meeting has begun to proclaim "The Bologna Process 2020-The European Higher Education Area in the new decade." In 2010, at a celebratory meeting in Budapest and Vienna in March, the ministers of the signatory countries requested that they be given reports on mobility and the social dimension, the development of transparency mechanisms, and efforts to construct a network for obtaining better information on and promotion of the Bologna Process outside the EHEA from the BFUG. The BFUG does the actual monitoring of the Process between ministerial meetings, and their reports are to be presented in 2012 at a meeting in Bucharest, Romania. The E4 group [European Association for Quality Assurance (ENQA), European Universities Association (EUA), European Association of Institutions in Higher Education (EURASHE), and European Students Union (ESU)] were asked to continue in their

efforts to oversee the development and refinement of the quality assurance mechanisms undergirding that dimension of the EHEA. External evaluation was a key component in this request by the ministers of the E4 Group. Finally, the ministers agreed to hold future meetings in 2015, 2018, and 2020 charting the continued evolution of the Process in the current decade.

Questions Remain

While the Bologna Process is undoubtedly irreversible, questions continue to arise among the students, educators, and even those outside the academic sector within the signatory countries. While no specific length for the first degree was mandated (other than that it be *at least* three years in length), the three-year first-level degrees chosen by most of the countries elicit uncertainty within the employment sector. In countries where the traditional first degree was long, as, for example, in Germany, the corporate world has become increasingly uneasy as it has begun to hire university graduates with the new degree. Will these graduates be as prepared to enter the business community as were their earlier degree-holding predecessors? Do those with professional degrees such as engineering have sufficient training to perform as well as those with longer pre-Bologna engineering degrees? In some countries higher education engineering institutions have opted, for the present, to keep aloof from the Bologna-compliant degree structure. France is a prime example of this sort of adherence to the old ways of providing engineering education. For the time being, the system of *grande écoles* with their 2+3 structure (two years of classes *preparatoire* plus three years of engineering leading to the *diploma d'Ingenieur*) have chosen to retain their educational structure separate from that found in the universities which offer the L-M-D sequence (*Licence-Master-Doctorat* or 3+2+3). In Germany, while the individual states which control education remain unalterably committed to the Bologna-compliant degree sequence, some voices are heard calling for an amendment to the sequence to embrace a four-year first degree. With the transition away from the thirteen-year primary/secondary system among all the states in Germany (in place by 2004 and beyond), questions arise as to whether or not a three-year bachelor holder is as qualified for employment as was the case with the thirteen-year system or would be if the graduate possessed a four-year degree.

Another concern focuses on mobility, the ostensible reason for this major alteration of the European higher education landscape. Is the movement from one university to another prior to a degree being awarded, or even after a first Bologna-compliant degree is earned, as seamless as the planners of the EHEA hoped when they met in Bologna, Italy in 1999? If one has a three-year first degree and then applies for a second higher degree in a Bologna signatory country where the first degree is four years, is that graduate able to be accepted for the higher degree without qualms by the receiving institution? If so, how does that institution justify to its indigenous applicants with a degree of 240 ECTS credits the admission of a non-native applicant with a degree containing only 180 ECTS? If the applicant is required to take additional pre-master's studies to "top up," what has happened to the concept of mobility? Mobility implies a relatively seamless transition meaning direct entry. Furthermore, if one has a four-year first Bologna-compliant degree (as is the case in Spain or Russia), does the applicant admitted to second-level studies at a university in a country where the first degree is three years receive advanced credit for that additional year?

Even if the degrees in two countries are the same length and credit requirement, does the graduate face questions or problems when it is discovered that the Bologna-compliant degree holder from country X, applying for a university second-level degree in country Y, possesses a degree from a very different type of institution? Is a Bologna-compliant degree from a *Fachhochschule* (university of applied science) fully acceptable to another country's university master's program? Is the degree from a *Berufsakademie* (university of cooperative education) fully accepted by the university master's

degree program in France or Italy? All have degrees containing 180 ECTS credits, but at some institutions, not all ECTS credits making up the bachelor's degree are awarded for academic course work. Anecdotal evidence gleaned from conversations with various German educators seems to indicate that graduates from some non-university institutions may, in fact, be required to do extra course work, perhaps as much as one year, before being admitted into a university second-level program (master's). Similar problems exist in other countries as with the case of the Romanian sub-*injiner* with a three-year first degree who does not obtain professional licensure or certification to practice engineering in Romania or other Bologna signatory countries. Some institutions within countries currently opting for the three-year first degree, such as Germany, are giving thought to moving toward a four-year first-degree model.

The precise nature of the third-level terminal degree commonly called doctor continues to be something of an open question. Incorporated formally into the Bologna Process in only 2003, traditionally the European doctorate has been largely the completion of a work containing original research under the supervision and guidance of a single professor and seldom including classroom instruction as part of the program. Since the addition of the third level to the Bologna Process, concrete steps are being taken in numerous signatory countries to create true graduate research centers for these degrees as well as add taught courses to the program of study. Of course this necessitates a closer scrutiny by educators of the doctoral admission process and the procedures for assessing the thesis produced by the doctoral candidates. Whether the addition of more classes (or classes where none previously existed) results in some sort of specific credit total for the award of the degree as is the case with new first- and second-level degrees remains to be seen.

Not all questions center on the new degrees. One problem that has continued to plague the members of the EHEA is that of consistency of documentation with respect to the diploma supplement. While the European

Universities Association (EUA) and the Bologna Promoters and Experts (individuals identified as the most knowledgeable about the requirements of the process within each country and each higher education institution) have labored prodigiously to move each country toward full implementation, disturbing inconsistencies remain. An attempt in the Netherlands to check for uniformity of diploma supplement format among higher education institutions in that country revealed that no clear adherence to the standard format outlined by the EUA and the BFUG was apparent among the institutions answering a survey. Significant format differences existed among these institutions necessitating a reminder from the Bologna Experts and Promoters in the Netherlands to adhere to the commonly accepted framework available from the experts. More disturbing was the fact that as recently as 2009 a questionnaire published in the Trends 2010 Report for the meeting in Vienna/Budapest that year revealed that 66 percent of the institutions in signatory countries automatically awarded the diploma supplement, with an additional 14 percent doing so upon student request. Thus, 20 percent of institutions in the signatory countries did not even issue a diploma supplement which is one of the four key components of the entire process! However, this is an improvement over the percentages cited in the Trends V Report issued at the London Meeting in 2007. In that Report, 48 percent of the institutions issued the diploma supplement automatically with 11 percent doing so upon request, while 41 percent did not award them at all.

One final area that has shown mixed results within the EHEA has been the evolution of the quality assurance mechanisms undergirding the new degrees in the Bologna Process. Charged by the ministers to effect progress in the quality assurance realm, the E4 Group responded at the 2005 meeting in Bergen with the European Standards and Guidelines (ESG) for quality assurance. In addition, the E4 Group established the European Quality Assurance Register (EQAR) which would assess and register national quality assurance bodies within the EHEA. The signatory countries were then implored to construct national qualifications frameworks (NQFs) that would "map out" the educational award structure of that country encompassing the three levels of new Bologna-compliant degrees. This would include generic descriptors predicated on learning outcomes, along with credit ranges for the new degrees. This was recently broadened to incorporate "lifelong learning" into the frameworks covering education in that country from "cradle to grave." In 2009 at the Leuven meeting, a deadline date of 2012 was set for the implementation of all NQFs among the signatory countries. Trends 2010 reports that only six countries have so far fully implemented their national qualifications frameworks. Some twenty-one more are in the process of implementing them.

In addition, the frameworks are supported by separate ongoing projects aimed at building descriptions and definitions of specific degrees and degree levels. The Dublin Descriptors came out of the Joint Quality Initiative Meeting in Dublin in 2004 which offered generic descriptive learning outcomes associated with various Bologna degree levels. Signatory countries were encouraged to use the Dublin Descriptors as a point of departure for further refinement of learning outcomes to be associated with the various levels ultimately enumerated on the completed individual national qualifications frameworks. In addition to the Dublin Descriptors, the Tuning Project began in Europe a year after Bologna and in response to the desire to create common ground for field-specific harmonization of degree content. A parallel process began three years later in Latin America. The Tuning Project has made substantial progress in mapping curricular commonalities in various academic disciplines and continues independent of, but closely related to, the Bologna Process. However, even with all of the progress made at the micro level, much remains to be done at the macro level in terms of national implementation by signatory countries.

Effect Beyond Europe

After more than ten years of higher education transformation, the effects of the Bologna Process have become more pronounced outside of the European Higher Education Area (EHEA). First of all, non-European countries with educational systems patterned on that of a former colonial mother country are mixed in their assumption of the need to adopt the Bologna reforms. Latin American countries, beyond the Tuning Project previously mentioned, do not particularly see the need to alter their indigenous degree or credit structure to conform to that of Spain or Portugal. Francophone Africa, on the other hand, has wholeheartedly embraced the French L-M-D (*Licence-Master-Doctorat*) degree cycle. Though not part of the EHEA, these countries deem it only natural to change the degree structure to conform to the French model just as the prior structure mirrored (for the most part) the traditional French university degrees. Whether this trend will extend to full adoption of all aspects of Bologna (*e.g.*, ECTS credits, quality assurance mechanisms including national qualification frameworks, etc.) remains to be seen.

In the United States the Bologna Process is now becoming widely known, if not fully understood, in higher education circles. Major higher education associations and entities routinely include sessions on the Bologna Process at their national and regional conferences. The two largest, AACRAO and NAFSA: Association of International Educators, generally schedule multiple sessions on various aspects of the process, usually with European presenters giving the latest information on the state of the implementation process. Articles in the various newsletters and journals of these associations on Bologna abound, and surveys by both the Institute of International Education (IIE) and the Council of Graduate Schools (CGS) are avidly read to attempt to discern the trend toward acceptance of Bologna-compliant three-year degrees into U.S. graduate programs.

Historically, graduate deans and other senior officers at graduate programs paid scant attention to policies regarding overseas degrees in general and European degrees in particular. What little notice was paid at this level generally consisted of taking stock of the high volume of applicants from India, China, Taiwan, and Korea. Among the Bologna signatory countries only Turkey factors in the top ten or so sending countries to U.S. graduate schools and that country retained its traditional four- year first degree. But as the number of signatory countries grew, as European educators involved in international exchange began to increasingly urge acceptance of Bologna-compliant three year degrees, and as difficult financial circumstances beset many U.S. graduate programs, greater attention and concern focused on admission policies from individuals at the more senior levels than had heretofore been the case. No longer were international admissions officers and credential evaluators routinely setting and enforcing graduate admissions policies regarding overseas degrees in quiet and almost unseen fashion. Suddenly, interest percolated down from the highest levels with respect to what had always been a rather arcane and complex art: the evaluation of overseas academic credentials and their comparison to U.S. higher education degrees.

This relatively small field of experts traditionally compared overseas degrees to U.S. degrees based on a quantitative approach that essentially counted the number of years of the full-time degree program from abroad (and often the years of primary/secondary education that preceded it) and established a comparison point. The principle reason for a quantitative approach to comparability largely centers on the fact that the American bachelor's and the European or European-style degrees are so dissimilar. The European degree explores a chosen subject in much more depth than is the case with the bachelor's degree in the United States. The U.S. bachelor's degree emphasizes breadth as opposed to depth to the point of keeping the chosen major at only one-fourth to a third of the overall degree program. General and distributive education requirements make up the rest of the degree, something simply not done in a European first degree. Given the wide difference in content, U.S. international credential evaluation experts defaulted to simply counting the years of the overseas degree program and comparing that to the U.S. bachelor's—accepting those that were four years and rejecting those that were not. To be fair, a more holistic view is generally employed by those more steeped in overseas educational systems so that a three-year degree preceded by more than the U.S. model of twelve years primary/secondary education is given full acceptance. Under this approach, however, the three-year degree emanating from a system that embraces a twelve-year primary/secondary sequence like that found in the United States does not gain acceptance.

As economic woes increasingly began to plague higher education institutions in the United States, senior university officials started to re-appraise the standard year-counting approach to graduate admission. International students pay more tuition at public institutions where fees are differentiated based on state residency. Furthermore, in the STEM fields (science, technology, engineering, and mathematics) graduate departments tended to experience a higher percentage of non-U.S. students, either because the U.S. students successfully entered employment after a bachelor's degree or because interest in non-STEM fields rose among that group of graduates. Deans of graduate admissions quickly learned from their faculty that European three-year first-degree holders were well prepared for graduate-level study in the United States because they had been immersed in those three years in the chosen field. Furthermore, standardized test scores tended to be equally as high, or perhaps even higher, among the European degree holders compared to the U.S. graduate applicants. For the senior university official attempting to maintain sufficient numbers in a graduate school, the efficacy of admitting students to their programs who had demonstrated a strong command of the subject matter *and* high test scores, that is, Bologna-compliant three year degree holders, became an easy choice to make.

Increasing exposure to information regarding the Bologna Process, rising acceptability among more and more U.S. graduate schools, and financial demands to maintain or increase enrollment all contributed to an evolution in approach to the Bologna degrees in the United States. However, critical questions with no simple answers continue to arise among the U.S. graduate admissions and international evaluation community. Access and equity remain the overarching principles of college admissions in the United States and admission only for the elite continues to be anathema. Why should three-year degrees from Europe be acceptable, but those from India not so favored? Why must the U.S. student planning a graduate school experience spend four years in undergraduate school while Europeans (or other non-U.S. degree holders) only attend for three years? Both are competing for places in U.S. graduate schools, in the usual popular fields, and coveting the same graduate fellowships and teaching assistantships. Is an institution favoring one group over another by requiring a four-year bachelor's for one group and a three-year degree/diploma for another? There is a major assumption within academia in the United States that merit is the overriding factor. In a society that all too often is prey to litigious tendencies, university administrators acknowledge, however quietly, that fairness may need to be defined or re-defined with respect to graduate admission.

Less controversial, perhaps, is the concept that admission to graduate study in the United States and what may, or may not, be comparable to a U.S. bachelor's degree are indeed two entirely different questions. That a three-year Bologna-compliant degree holder may be perfectly prepared for admission to a graduate program closely allied to the subject previously pursued is quite a different supposition than whether or not that same degree is comparable to a U.S. bachelor's degree. Thus, the U.S. international graduate admissions officer would be inclined toward a decision on admission that would be at odds with a U.S. international credential evaluator's final determination of degree comparability. And yet the two worlds do intersect when the credential evaluator is asked to make a determination on degree comparability for a school that depends on that evaluator's decisions on comparability.

Alongside the degree comparison question is the issue with converting ECTS credits to U.S. semester credit hours. The ECTS model posits a full load per year of sixty ECTS credits, thirty per semester. This amount is double the normal load for the full-time U.S. undergraduate who traditionally takes fifteen semester hours per semester, thirty per year in order to complete the four-year bachelor's in eight semesters. Smaller loads and changes of major without the corresponding use of the additional summer sessions delays graduation beyond that time frame. A maximum load is considered to be eighteen hours per semester which would yield thirty-six for the year. More than that amount usually requires special permission which may or may not be granted. Students with fewer than twelve semester hours per term face the risk of loss of scholarship, loss of visa status for internationals, and generally also calls for special permission of a senior administrative officer in that college subdivision. Thus, the standard Carnegie unit load on a semester calendar is around thirty hours or half the ECTS load. Not surprisingly, U.S. admissions officers and credential evaluators have adopted a conversion ratio for ECTS of 2:1 or 1 ECTS credit=1/2 of a U.S. semester hour. This was further codified by the now defunct National Council on the Evaluation of Foreign Educational Credentials, which for fifty years supplied placement recommendations in publications of overseas educational systems used by credential evaluators across the United States. In 2005, they came out with an official pronouncement suggesting a conversion ratio for ECTS to U.S. semester credits of 2:1.

The European response pointed out that ECTS were predicated on learning outcomes rather than simple "seat time." The ECTS credit reflects contact hours, tutorials, laboratory sessions, discussion sections, and outside preparation, all of which contribute to produce a "learning outcome." Therefore, a more reasonable conversion ratio of, say, 0.67 rather than 0.50 would be in order, the Europeans suggested. U.S. educators, how-ever, pointed out that the Carnegie unit, though predicated on contact hours, also carried with it a supposition that the student learner would spend two hours of outside preparation for every one hour of time spent in class. This was not an unreasonable assumption for a society that was in the main relatively wealthy, with the vast majority of students in possession of a computer or ready access to one through their university. Also, significant library holdings at most U.S. universities allows students to spend research and study time on their own rather than using class time for these sorts of tasks. Since U.S. students therefore received only three semester hours for their forty-five contact hour class and not the nine hours that would encompass the outside preparation time assumed as part of the Carnegie unit structure, the learning outcome argument for ceding more U.S. credit in the conversion of ECTS credits failed to gain a large number of adherents, though a significant minority have embraced the higher ratio. There is no particular requirement to adopt a 0.67 ratio in converting ECTS credits simply to derive a magic number such as 120 out of a three-year Bologna-compliant degree of 180 ECTS credits. If one is convinced that a graduate with such a degree *can* succeed in a given graduate program, the obvious answer is to simply admit them rather than attempt to stretch ECTS credits out in conversion in order to arrive at a total that is traditionally representative of a U.S. four-year degree (p. 120).

Institutional policy regarding the conversion of ECTS credits also represents a challenge with respect to other key campus officials beyond the international admissions office. Education Abroad offices which oversee exchange programs and study abroad transactions with European universities must explain to faculty and others at the institution how those ECTS credits earned in education abroad programs should be handled back at the home institution. The best model for such administrative oversight would be a close working relationship between the international admissions office and the education abroad office so that both treat the ECTS credits brought back to the home campus in a consistent fashion. A ratio like the previously mentioned 2:1 should also be tempered with a certain amount of "evaluator flexibility," exercised already by most admissions officers with respect to the conversion of quarter credits from U.S. colleges. A literal halving of the ECTS will frequently result in fractions of credit, which must be made whole for degree plan applicability. Rounding up from, say, 4.5 to 6 in the case of two courses taken abroad that convert from 9 ECTS to 4.5 semester credits hours would be a reasonable approach in such a case.

The topic of credit value leads to the fascinating discussion of injecting learning outcomes into the credit structure or at least using this pedagogical principle to aid in the perpetual search for quality assurance in higher education in the United States. The current accreditation model in the United States largely centers on issues of student-to-teacher ratio, financial stability, volumes in the library, percentage of Ph.D.s or advanced degrees on faculty, graduation rates, etc. Furthermore, much of accreditation is self-study and thus voluntary in nature. Site visits are made and re-accreditation procedures exist, but none of it truly focuses on the element of what a graduate should know when they are awarded the bachelor's degree in a given field. Certainly no question arises in the process of accreditation regarding curricular content except in the broadest sense when talking about the accreditation of schools by regional academic accrediting associations. Only in the discipline-specific professional accreditation associations do we find a close scrutiny of courses included in a degree, but these are aimed at program accreditation, not institutional accreditation. A school may be accredited by the regional accrediting body, while its engineering degrees are not necessarily accredited by the Accrediting Board of Engineering and Technology (ABET). This impacts the graduate only at the point of the job search and then usually only insofar as the local state licensing board is concerned.

This topic is becoming increasingly important as educators in higher education and governing entities grapple with time to degree issues, the soaring cost of higher education, higher education institutional accountability, and national versus regional accreditation. Accreditation exists in the United States but it is uneven; the six regional academic associations are inconsistent in their requirements for accreditation. All of it, of course, is built on the foundation of the Carnegie unit which dates to 1908. Degrees are built on units (whether quarter or semester), and those units are predicated on seat time as opposed to something more intangible: learning outcomes. And yet the Bologna Process contains a feature—quality assurance—which attempts to reconfigure quality in higher education. As previously mentioned, quality assurance within the EHEA is composed of several features including national qualifications frameworks which map education from the early beginnings to the highest degree offered. Simultaneously, various projects such as Tuning and the Dublin Descriptors attempt to harmonize degree structure through an agreed upon set of learning outcomes specific to the disciplines.

This degree content harmonization process has now come to the United States. From Europe and Latin America, the idea of having faculty draw concrete outcomes derived from the discipline-specific curriculum of a given degree, has now spread to the United States with the Lumina Foundation project, Tuning USA, which includes three states in the Midwest. Indiana, Utah, and Minnesota are participating in the project, which began in the first part of 2009 to bring faculty together to analyze learning outcomes for degrees in their respective disciplines with the goal of finding commonalities. If successful, this template may serve to enable faculty at schools in other states across the country to create a conceptual outline of what the degree(s) ought to contain. Whether this concept could ultimately weave itself into the fabric of accreditation (as the EHEA hopes to do) remains to be seen. Ideas that hint of centralized control or that might appear to threaten freedom of creativity among academia in U.S. higher education generally do not advance. However, the idea of injecting learning outcomes into the quality assurance aspect of U.S. higher education promises to generate excitement and discussion for some time to come.

The Future of Bologna Outside Europe

As previously indicated, the Bologna Process, for all of its shortcomings and uneven implementation, is clearly here to stay. Europe will not turn back from this radical experiment in harmonization of higher education; and the ripple effect will continue to widen around the world. Non-European former colonies in the developing world will continue to grapple with implementing some form of Bologna whether in part (degrees and ECTS only) or in all respects, even though these countries are not now, nor will they ever be Bologna Declaration signatories. Other countries will continue to express interest in the process simply for the sake of an intriguing aspect of the process or because of an assumption of higher quality by enacting reforms based on the Bologna model. Australia has a great concern with mobility and access for its degree-holders within graduate schools around the world, particularly North America. This interest particularly focuses on the Australian Ordinary three-year bachelor's degree, not generally embraced by North American institutions of higher education. Given the increasing acceptance of Bologna three-year first degrees, Australian educators naturally seek similar treatment for their similar length degree. India has a similar concern and closely monitors U.S. graduate school acceptance of Bologna-compliant three-year degrees. The first degree in India generally is three years in duration and very much modeled on the European concept of depth rather than the U.S. emphasis on breadth.

In the United States the effect of Bologna will continue to center on the three-year degree issue with quality assurance a secondary concern. As interest and fuller understanding of the Bologna Process grows, discussion and debate heightens around aspects of the U.S. higher education system. Degree length has now become a frequent topic of conversation among educa-

tors and governmental authorities as both groups seek to find answers to the problem of the rising cost of higher education and the ensuing debt levels resulting from those costs. Talk of embracing a three-year bachelor's degree in the United States is increasing, although for the moment none of it turns to the radical notion of changing the actual internal curricular structure of the degree itself. All comments so far appear to address only the alteration of the time taken to obtain the degree by speeding up the process of finishing the four-year degree either through college credit earned while still in high school or year-round schooling. None have so far suggested that some piece of the forty course 120-hour degree should be eliminated.

The analysis of current graduate admissions policies regarding overseas degrees, particularly those from Europe, will also continue to dominate discussion in graduate admissions offices. Key questions will continue to revolve around the efficacy of accepting a three-year degree from abroad while requiring the U.S. graduate to secure the four-year degree in this country. A major challenge for graduate deans and admissions officers will remain how to fashion a policy that treats European three-year degrees and non-European three-year degrees fairly and consistently. This challenge will necessitate closer scrutiny and understanding of overseas educational systems and the degrees that exist within those systems. All three-year degrees are not equal, and admission should never be based solely on duration in any case. Degrees and diplomas of similar length that emanate from very different types of post-secondary institutions represent outcomes that are comparable only in their length, and not necessarily in their purpose or scope.

It might be useful to review the suggestions found in the AACRAO online database EDGE (Electronic Database for Global Education) with regard to the three-year Bologna-compliant degree. In the Bologna Process profile in EDGE, the Overview concludes by suggesting that graduate admissions officers contemplating the acceptance of Bologna-compliant degrees take the following factors into account (advice that would also work well with other, non-Bologna, three-year degrees):

* Degree must be in the same or similar field of study.

* Bologna compliant degrees must lead to unrestricted admission to the next educational level.

* Awarding institution should be comparable in nature to the receiving institution, for example, a university degree versus a degree from a non-university higher education institution.

* A national quality assurance mechanism must be in place in order for a three-year degree to receive consideration for possible placement in graduate-level programs in the United States.

* A close comparison of the curriculum of the overseas degree and the content of the U.S. degree reveals significant compatibility according to the views of the faculty in the receiving graduate department.

* The Bologna-compliant degree holder is deemed prepared to undertake graduate-level study as would a student enrolled in comparable courses at an institution in the United States.

These suggestions also assume that graduate admissions officers have provided extensive information on the Bologna Process to the graduate faculty of the various departments and programs so that informed decisions can be made with regard to these degrees and that faculty willingness to even consider three-year degrees has been ascertained. Some departments may not wish to admit three-year degrees at all, due, among other reasons, to the content-heavy prior degree needed to be admitted at the graduate level. Naturally, admission decisions do not hinge entirely on prior degrees, but also on test scores, grades, nature and quality of undergraduate institution attended, and individual fit for the program based on personal statements, letters of recommendation, and personal achievements.

U.S. admissions officers and credential evaluators need to continually monitor the Bologna Process through associational conference attendance, pertinent Web sites, and constant consultation with colleagues around the country. Over the past decade the Bologna Process, confined to Europe in terms of implementation, has demonstrated that it has far wider ramifications than the geography and population affected would seem to suggest!

TWENTY-TWO

Professional Development

PEGGY BELL HENDRICKSON

Director
Transcript Research

Professional Development

The field of international education offers many opportunities for professional development. Indeed, professional development is an important component of all education but international education in particular. In general, the term refers to the acquisition of information and skills in order to further a career and is often seen as optional, as only for those who want to move up the corporate ladder or be seen as a team player. Within the realm of international education, however, professional development takes on even more relevance; the very nature of international education makes it impossible to learn all aspects fully. With hundreds of diverse educational systems that are constantly evolving—as burgeoning governments seek to make their mark on history, new alliances create new institutions and the global market creates exchanges never before imagined—professional development becomes a critical component.

There are many reasons to expand, or cultivate, professional development, as you will see throughout the next several pages. This chapter will also cover several specific ways to further professional development to fit numerous budgets, support systems and time constraints. An often overlooked aspect of professional development is that of personal development, and so attention will be paid to this topic as well. This chapter also discusses a variety of training options available to international educators, focusing specifically on the international admissions arena. Technology has become an important aspect of professional development that is continually evolving and growing in popularity. This chapter closes with a brief discussion of other aspects of professional development including funding, obtaining support, personal benefits and future steps.

Reasons for Professional Development

Professional skills in the field of international education can and should be developed for a variety of reasons, among these, fraud detection, networking, service leadership, following best practices, asset building and personal fulfillment.

DETECTING FRAUD

International educators realize that fraud is rampant in the field as discussed in Chapter 7 of this book. Falsified documents, diploma mills and bogus credentials are among the many important reasons for developing these professional skills. Falsified documents can refer to several things, from changed grades on a student's record to a completely new name on an otherwise legitimate document. Professional skills can teach the new international educator about certain measures commonly taken to reduce the risk of fraud. For example, many institutions request that African secondary exam results be sent directly from the exams council; accept only original, sealed transcripts with university stamps from places like China; or require attestations from specific bodies such as the registrar for institutions in India. In extreme cases, one may even send suspect transcripts out for verification, though the rate of return is not always reliable.

The term "diploma mill" refers to the billion dollar industry of selling fake transcripts and/or degrees from schools that do not exist. Bogus credentials are generally good (or at least passable) forgeries of legitimate schools, while diploma mills exist only on paper or in cyberspace. A number of books and Web sites exist to help with the detection of diploma mills, including John Bear and Allen Ezell's book *Degree Mills: The Billion-Dollar Industry That Has Sold More Than a Million Fake Degrees* and the Oregon Office of Degree Authorization Web site. Scandals get reported each year involving public figures, government officials and even homeland security authorities who have presented bogus credentials or diploma mill degrees.

By increasing professional development, the international educator can learn more about fraud detection, more easily identify diploma mills, become familiar with best practices for regions with high fraud activity, keep abreast of trends regarding official documents and become more confident in identifying potentially altered credentials. Building a network of colleagues will also help make fraud detection simpler.

NETWORKING

Networking has many connotations. In the traditional business sense, it can be seen as schmoozing or making connections to further a career, but the field of international education has a more practical need. Networking is one of the best ways to learn the intricacies of international admissions. A network of professionals allows for the sharing of limited resources when institutional budgets are tight, as they always are in an educational setting. It enables a forum for brainstorming and the opportunity to bounce ideas off others with similar experiences or greater expertise. Networking creates bonds of friendship and respect that can increase personal satisfaction. It provides opportunities for collaboration on conference sessions and publications. It can also be used in the more traditional sense to enhance career opportunities.

Networking also presents new international educators with the chance to find a mentor or, at the very least, to begin creating a list of experts to turn to in times of need. This is especially straightforward at the local, state or regional level, where networking opportunities abound in smaller groups with the same faces

and increase chances for communication. If local organizations exist, the minimal cost and time away from the office can pay for themselves threefold. In fact, local networking is especially critical for making contacts, getting training and setting institutional policies. The latter is especially important in international education since no school wants to gain a reputation for being inconsistent or more lax than its neighbors.

At medium and large forums or conferences, there are different strategies for networking. One such plan involves perusing the conference program beforehand since they are often sent out or posted online in the days and weeks leading up to a conference. Identify a person or group of individuals who are presenting on a topic that interests you or meets a need you currently have and send them an email introducing yourself or asking a question you hope they might address. Then follow up with them at the conference; newcomers will often be introduced to other established contacts after making that first connection. Introduce yourself to people with similar questions in the audience or even to the ones who give the answers. Occasions to volunteer abound in the education industry. Go to newcomer sessions and every event with free food—international educators love to chat and eat!

SERVICE LEADERSHIP OPPORTUNITIES

Professional development can also lead to service leadership opportunities. Many professional development activities, from serving on committees to presenting a conference session to holding office, are volunteer work. The organizations discussed later in this chapter provide countless chances to gain leadership skills that translate to all facets of a person's life and career even beyond the field of international education.

Like networking, leadership service can be done at local, state, regional, national or international levels. One of the easiest ways for a beginner to make her or himself known is to volunteer for a leadership position. Even if the role ultimately goes to someone else, the newcomer has shown a willingness to give back to the community, to make international education a priority and to take on some of the behind-the-scenes work. In addition, technology is enabling national leaders all across the globe to take a hand in mentoring from afar. As such, networking can be done at all levels.

FOLLOWING BEST PRACTICES

Another critical facet of professional development centers on the best practices in the industry. The field of international education is more art than science; there are no rules as much as guidelines. Previously, an inter-associational board, the National Council on the Evaluation of Foreign Educational Credentials provided non-binding guidelines for placement recommendations. With the dissolution of the Council in 2006, the advent of major changes to educational systems throughout Europe in the last decade and the growing trend of multi-country educational institutions, the work of international admissions offices and credentials evaluators has become increasingly complex and exciting. Professional development gives international educators the chance to communicate more regularly with one another to discuss and create best practices in the changing climate.

Best practices can refer to a variety of different aspects of international education. In the realm of credentials evaluation, they relate to the secondary, undergraduate and graduate equivalencies. They cover the broad spectrum of acceptable English language proficiency measures as well as determining what constitutes an official academic credential. For those offices that handle immigration concerns, finances and government documents also play a role. Whatever your institutional policies, whether they are publicly announced on your application or Web site, or whether they conform to neighboring schools or evaluation agencies, they should be consistently applied. Having a good working knowledge of the best practices can also help increase your own value to your organization.

BECOMING AN ASSET TO YOUR INSTITUTION

A less acknowledged aspect of professional development is that of becoming a greater asset to your institution or field. By subscribing to the other reasons to more fully develop your professional skills—fraud detection, building a network, engaging in service leadership and following best practices—you will have more training, knowledge and confidence in your daily job. This, in turn, enables you to help students and staff faster, more easily and more consistently. You will more effortlessly make the shift from inexperienced novice to skilled knowledge worker and to experienced mentor.

PERSONAL GAIN

The final reason discussed here to engage in professional development relates to personal gain. While it generally is not a strong motivator initially, personal growth and fulfillment often becomes a driving force behind those who actively contribute to the field. The acts of volunteering behind the scenes, serving on committees, submitting work for publication, presenting at conferences, mentoring newcomers, responding to mailing list queries and sharing training materials all go a long way towards making up for the low pay and long hours that often accompany jobs in the education sector. The friendships forged through professional development activities can make these events less daunting and more accessible. The skills learned make the efforts very worthwhile. Finally, the chance to help influence the state of the world through international education is awe inspiring.

Professional Development Providers

With so much incentive to develop professional skills in the field, it stands to reason that there should be many options for furthering these skills. At the highest level, national organizations exist to bring together large numbers of people and ideas, but many communities also run local, state or regional associations that may or may not be branches of national organizations. The field also allows for the expansion of international connections, communication and even training through EducationUSA advisors, Fulbright, AMIDEAST and other international communities. Many institutions also offer chances for professional development through their campus human resources programming. Individual educators can and should develop their own resource library.

A key element of professional development is volunteer work. Volunteer to be a table or room moderator at a session. Work the registration booth. Offer to make copies, pass out handouts or collect surveys. Make yourself known to the local arrangements committee or any other committee that emphasizes the skills you currently have. These volunteer opportunities are available at all levels—local, regional, state and national. This chapter will briefly cover some varied sources of professional development.

NATIONAL ORGANIZATIONS

The most obvious and straightforward way to receive professional development is through national organizations such as the American Association of Collegiate Registrars and Admissions Officers (AACRAO), NAFSA: Association of International Educators, the European Association for International Education (EAIE), the National Association of Graduate Admissions Professionals (NAGAP) and the Canadian Bureau for International Education (CBIE), to name a few that work directly with international admissions offices. These organizations are comprised of registrars, admissions officers, immigration specialists, recruiters, enrollment managers, education abroad advisors, private evaluators and others who are heavily invested in international education. All of them organize annual conferences, host electronic mailing lists, offer training programs and publish journals or magazines. We will briefly examine the organizations listed here, but know that this is not an exhaustive list.

AACRAO is the current leader in North America for the publication of international credentials evaluation materials including the revolutionary AACRAO Electronic Database for Global Education (EDGE).

Founded in 1910, AACRAO is one of the largest higher education organizations in the country. Its annual conferences typically offer 40 to 50 sessions on international admissions related topics. Though a member organization, it also provides numerous services such as training, consulting, foreign credentials evaluations, etc. to non-members. Its Web site even hosts an entire section on professional development with opportunities such as serving on committees, author projects, electronic mailing lists and members-only online guides.

NAFSA: the Association of International Educators is the largest organization in North America focusing exclusively on the many facets of international education. Founded in 1948 as the National Association of Foreign Student Advisers, NAFSA has always offered professional development directed at meeting the unique needs of international students. Since the organization concentrates on international education, its services run the gamut from credentials evaluation and recruitment to immigration and programming, while also addressing education abroad and ESL instruction. As a result, it is naturally less able to concentrate on one specific arena though it has increasingly highlighted immigration concerns. However, it provides 30 to 40 conference sessions under its Recruitment, Admissions, and Preparation (RAP) knowledge community. NAFSA also publishes the wRAP-Up newsletter, which includes credentials evaluation, as part of its Admissions and Credential Evaluation (ACE) Network.

The EAIE, focused on European higher education, stimulates professional development through conferences, training courses, seminars and other methods. Like its North American counterparts, EAIE provides wonderful opportunities for networking, publishing, volunteering and furthering professional development via conferences and committees.

NAGAP concerns itself entirely with North American graduate education. However, since nearly half of the approximately 500,000 international students working towards degrees in the United States are graduate students, NAGAP obviously has a vested interest in international education.

Finally, CBIE also conducts annual conferences, professional development training and online workshops. In addition, CBIE advocates for internationalization, co-establishes multinational universities, manages sponsored program scholarships and conducts research on international students.

Other national or international organizations also offer conferences, publications or other opportunities for professional development in the broad range of international education studies. The list includes the Association of International Education Administrators (AIEA), the Council on International Educational Exchange (CIEE), the International Education and Research Network (iEARN), the Institute of International Education (IIE), NASPA: Student Affairs Administrators in Higher Education and the Center for International Higher Education (CIHE), among others.

One of the best aspects of international education is that, unlike traditional business sectors, information is communal and power is shared. Best practices take the place of corporate secrets. Committees work together to make things happen rather than to further an individual's goals. National organizations rely on their members to keep them abreast of current trends and to discuss alternative ways of handling them.

LOCAL, STATE AND REGIONAL ORGANIZATIONS

While these national organizations offer great options for professional development, many institutions or individuals simply cannot spare the cost in travel, association dues, conference fees, meals, per diems, hotels and other travel-related expenses, not to mention lost work hours and time away from family and other responsibilities. Local, state and regional organizations can fill the needs of the time- and budget-conscious quite well. These close-to-home organizations may or may not be affiliated with the national organizations listed above, but they share a common goal of increasing international education and offering related profes-

sional development. In addition, members can increase their options by attending multiple conferences, or institutions can send multiple colleagues to different meetings. For example, in Texas, three major metropolitan areas host their own organizational meetings based loosely on existing national organizations and offer professional development and training to international educators in Houston, San Antonio and Dallas/Ft. Worth. In addition, AACRAO and NAFSA both have active state and regional affiliates that meet annually, providing yet further options to accommodate the needs of varied offices. Those with limited budgets should not neglect the international connection.

GLOBAL ORGANIZATIONS

Many organizations exist around the globe whose primary or secondary purpose is to assist international educators in understanding their educational system, credentials and learning objectives to help facilitate the transfer of students from one country to another. With more than 450 advising centers around the world, EducationUSA promotes U.S. higher education in other countries. Advisors in those countries can be excellent sources of information on institutional recognition, transferability of courses to local institutions and even transcript verification or authentication. The Fulbright Foreign Student Program offers many of the same services, and some of the offices house both organizations. These offices provide testing services, virtual recruiting, scholarship information and other assistance.

Like EducationUSA and Fulbright, AMIDEAST promotes American education from within other countries. Unlike its counterparts, AMIDEAST operates solely out of the Middle East with offices in twelve countries. In addition to providing the recognition, transfer and verification services of other organizations, AMIDEAST also offers training, publications and an email mailing list geared towards international educators. In addition to looking abroad for professional development opportunities, those international educators working at universities or colleges can look closer to home at their own human resource departments.

CAMPUS PROGRAMS

Often institutional human resources departments will offer campus programming designed to enhance professional development. These programs are intended to stimulate employee skills, increase employee satisfaction, enhance office work, augment promotion tracks and boost retention. For those who are unable to travel or have limited budgets, the on-campus option makes a tremendous difference in developing the skills relevant for a multitude of employment opportunities. Examples of professional development include business etiquette, employee motivation, résumé building, mentoring and coaching, customer service skills and change management, to name a few. These skills, augmented by developing a research library, can ensure that even those without any budget for training still have the ability to increase their professional development.

Building a Research Library

Building a resource library is a critical task for any international educator wanting to develop professional skills. The national organizations mentioned earlier, especially AACRAO and NAFSA, publish fantastic resource books available to member organizations at a discount. Unfortunately, not every institution has a budget that will cover every country and every credential. In fact, those that do are probably the exception rather than the norm. However, for the admissions or credentials professional, sample credentials, workshop materials, conference handouts and electronic information comprise some of the free sources that abound. Even if you are unable to attend a national or regional conference, these organizations often post their handouts online, or you can hunt down the email address of the published presenter and contact them for handouts. Other times, you may find that your school's library has actually purchased some of the AACRAO books. Begin building an electronic file for each coun-

try and add to it whenever you learn new information from mailing lists or education advisors. Make copies of transcripts you receive from countries that fall outside your comfort zone. Subscribe to mailing lists such as the Yahoo group inter-l or electronic newsletters such as those from ECE or WES, and update your country files. Check out the networks on the NAFSA Web site. Many ministry of education Web sites provide extensive information about their education system, institutions and even credentials. Basically, there are numerous ways to expand professional development, from conferences to free resources.

Developing Personal Skills

When thinking about professional development, it may seem inappropriate to discuss personal development, but the two often go hand in hand. Developing personal skills increases job satisfaction, confidence, and leadership skills, all of which enhance professionalism. A variety of measures exist for enhancing personal skills, including campus programming, community programming and campus courses. More often than not, these programs are free or low cost and are definitely worthwhile.

As previously mentioned, campuses often provide professional development through their human resources programming. Many times, HR-sponsored training may be geared less towards the professional and more towards the personal. The types of training will obviously vary based on the institution, but some common themes include conflict resolution, balancing work and family, time management and stress reduction. Topics often closely related to the field of international education include professional networking, internationalization efforts, cross-cultural communication and coalition building. Human resources programs, eager to expand their training and development plan, would love to have suggestions or assistance in creating programs, another effective way to combine personal and professional development. Community programming can also contribute to professional development success.

PUBLIC SPEAKING

College towns and other areas with diverse populations frequently provide excellent occasions for learning new skills. Organizations such as Toastmasters can teach public speaking skills better than any college course. Volunteer opportunities abound in local communities. International student organizations on campus allow for even more ways to expand personal skills. Involve institutions or communities with large groups of nonnative speakers of English as language partners. These are just a few of the ways international educators can use their local communities to enhance personal development.

Toastmasters International is a public speaking and leadership organization with almost a quarter of a million members in more than 90 countries around the world. Most clubs meet weekly to practice public speaking, giving feedback, following rules of order and holding office. Members pay a nominal fee for the workbooks and training materials and can participate in contests at the area, division and district levels. Clubs generally feature between 20 to 30 members to allow for many opportunities to practice speaking skills and getting and giving feedback. In addition to public speaking, communities feature numerous volunteer activities.

VOLUNTEERING

In the arena of international education, volunteering is an important element of professional development. The same holds true for personal development. This can be done around the international student element—airport pickups and drop offs, helping international students move into dorms, assisting with apartment searches, hosting international students during holidays or school closings, arranging play dates for the children of international students, organizing cultural events for spouses, etc. In addition, international populations exist in small and large pockets throughout many communities, and they often need volunteers as well. Film and music festivals, fundraising parties, cultural celebrations, language classes and numerous other activities occur in international districts, and volunteers and participants

are usually welcomed heartily. A good stepping stone into volunteering with international populations can be done through international student organizations.

International student organizations allow students to connect with others from their country or region to create a sense of community and to foster feelings of belonging. These groups help to increase student retention by reducing anxiety and isolation, and building friendships and understanding. International student organizations often arrange airport transportation, apartments, shopping excursions and sometimes even roommates, and the more help they have, the more successful they can be. In addition, they often arrange programs on campus to feature their native dress, food, ceremonies or other cultural aspects; the international educator makes a wonderful campus liaison.

Hundreds of thousands of international students come to the U.S. each year to study English. While they generally receive their formal training in classrooms—in colleges and universities, language centers, churches, libraries or other formats—practice in an informal setting can make a huge difference in their success rates. Volunteering as a language partner enhances an international educator's personal and professional development in several ways. Obviously, the international exposure lends itself to professional development, but that exposure can also enhance the personal. Learning about different cultures and customs, deciphering new accents and looking at language from another perspective all contribute to creating a more fully developed international citizen. In addition, serving as a language partner can enhance the volunteer's own understanding of another language and give them practice as a teacher or mentor, yet again encompassing both the personal and professional.

COLLEGE COURSES

Many educational institutions offer free or low cost courses to enhance personal growth. Increasingly, campuses provide training in technology. Likewise, software training abounds at many institutions. Language lessons, both credit-bearing and conversational, provide wonderful skills. Akin to Toastmasters, many campuses offer lunchtime or classroom public speaking lessons. Writing courses, mini-courses and groups abound in the educational sphere without limitations on context or style. In addition, online campuses like Ed2Go and Free-Ed provide low-cost or free online computer training in a multitude of subjects, ranging from test prep to grant writing, from Microsoft applications to career development and from art appreciation to starting your own business. Clearly, campus courses run the gamut from the fun to the functional.

Technology skills augment any résumé and increase overall job competency. Equally important, however, is the need to increase personal development. Technology, utilized for purely personal reasons, increases the quality of life. Courses that teach or improve technological skills, such as digital photography, Web site design, digital video, blog writing, online investing, basic computer troubleshooting and even basic typing, represent just a fraction of the technology competencies taught on campuses to enhance personal skills. The next step, software training, goes hand in hand.

Software skills can boost personal satisfaction as well as professional development. Like technology, the opportunities for software classes abound on electronic and physical campuses. To the surprise of many, much software can be used for both personal and business uses. Software programs such as Photoshop, Dreamweaver, Quickbooks, and the Microsoft suite constitute just a few of the programs that develop personal and professional abilities. In addition to software, courses that develop writing aptitude increase personal satisfaction as well as marketability.

Language lessons definitely straddle the line between personal and professional. Learning a new language broadens the mind and opens a person up to new ways of thinking. Learning to speak in another tongue also introduces travel and culture in a budget and time friendly way. Language development has been linked with better understanding of other communities while also offering a reexamination of one's own. Courses range from intensive submersion into culture and writing to casual chatting about food and film. Like many of these personal skills, language courses can be found on school campuses, in libraries and churches, in private language training facilities, in social clubs and on the internet. The same holds true for public speaking.

Like the other topics mentioned for personal development, an individual's facility for public speaking can be increased through formal classes on a college or university campus, informal groups such as churches and book clubs and organizations that focus primarily on that art. Thinking specifically about campuses courses, though, even those can vary. Human resource departments may offer public speaking as a professional development tool. International educators can attend college or university classes either as a traditional student or audit the course for the material but receive no grade or credit. Libraries may offer public speaking as an area of interest; the same holds true for professional student associations that offer programming to the public. The campus may also host a speech club (or several) looking to include faculty or staff. Whatever the choice, the chance to improve public speaking is often only a short walk away.

Writing represents one of the easiest personal skills to cultivate; improvement can help people better communicate, organize and advance their ideas. Coherent and clear writing affects people in all facets of their lives. Writing can either enhance or detract from a person's message, thus cultivating this talent offers tremendous rewards. Writing courses, manuals, workshops, clubs and even email lists make it easy to increase proficiency. The same forums available on campus for public speaking may also exist for writing practice. Some campuses also offer writing labs or writing tutors for additional assistance. English departments can often get the budding writer in touch with a writing group or provide prompts for the appropriate competence level. In addition, writing is one of the few skills that lends itself to practice almost anytime and anywhere. To summarize, campus courses offer multitudinous ways to increase personal skills.

As these last few pages have shown, improving personal skills bestows many benefits. Personal development furthers professional development because a more skilled person has greater chances of being offered, and succeeding at, increasingly complex tasks. One often overlooked source for personal development involves utilizing programming from your institution's human resources or training department. The local community, both on and off campus, provides another great outlet for personal development. Campus courses allow for even more training in areas that transcend the personal. All of the methods discussed here emphasize personal and interpersonal abilities, while also positively affecting professional life. Another way to advance professional aptitude is the most fun—training.

Training Opportunities

Training is one of the most important elements of professional development in addition to being the most basic. Methods include intensive programs, organizational conferences, newsletters and mailing lists, etc. In this section, we will discuss some of the most common training methodologies for international admissions and credentials evaluation specialists. AACRAO offers a great deal of training in this field, ranging from conferences to intensive institutes. Similarly, NAFSA provides workshops, seminars and conferences of its own. Both organizations feature constantly evolving training topics as part of their conference sessions. Private evaluation companies also conduct training on best practices and industry basics. World Education Services (WES), Educational Credential Evaluators, Inc. (ECE) and International Education Research Foundation (IERF) are among the most active companies providing this type of training. In addition, government agencies can administer or oversee assistance for the international education community.

AACRAO TRAINING

AACRAO, an organization that focuses many of its energies on admissions topics, assumes many of the responsibilities of training the next generation of cre-

dentials evaluators. Since it does not concern itself with immigration and English-language training, it devotes considerable resources to international credentials. Its two institutes, the Summer Institute for International Admissions and the new Winter Institute on the Evaluation of Transfer Credit from Selected Countries, form the backbone of its programs. The Summer Institute immerses participants in a weeklong workshop focusing on admissions and the most common educational systems sending students to the United States. In a related manner, the Winter Institute spends a few days focusing on transfer credit evaluation and assignment. As mentioned previously, the AACRAO Annual Meeting provides dozens of international admissions/credentials evaluation topics each year. AACRAO also issues books related to specific education systems, handbooks on admissions at various academic levels and guides on diploma mills or other hot topics in the field. In addition, AACRAO publishes the AACRAO Electronic Database for Global Education (EDGE), an online record that encompasses an academic overview, education ladder, placement recommendations and even sample credentials from over 200 countries around the globe. AACRAO's international education committees make every effort to bring training and research to the reach of every international specialist.

NAFSA TRAINING

Likewise, NAFSA trains many international education professionals. NAFSA Trainer Corps members deliver admissions/credentials related training called Core Education Programs (CEP) workshops or foreign credential analysis and the basics of an international admissions office, among other non-admissions topics. NAFSA also holds its own Summer Institute that covers the CEP workshop material as well as professional practice workshops and on-demand training. The annual conference gives international educators time to connect and learn about new topics related to the RAP knowledge community. The Academy for International Education extends the international educator's experience by providing intense training in most areas of international education: recruiting, admissions, education abroad, advising and student programming. NAFSA also co-hosts two intense educational exchange programs that study the educational systems of Germany and Australia, the Baden-Württemberg Seminar and the Australian Higher Education Seminar.

PRIVATE EVALUATION COMPANIES

Private evaluation companies make immense contributions to the field of international education. WES offers a fabulous, free, online grade conversion guide as well as nearly 30 country profiles and country-specific lists of required documents. In addition to evaluation services, they also offer training workshops in credentials evaluation. Their monthly World Education News and Reviews (WENR) electronic newsletter announces updates to international education by region and includes articles specific to credentials evaluation. Educational Credential Evaluators, another highly respected private evaluation company, provides customized, on-demand training in addition to their excellent book series, ECE Presents and ECE Insights. The ECE Newsletter features information on new publications in the field, institutional name changes, ministry of education contact information and other resource updates. IERF also conducts training workshops on theory and practice as they relate to credentials evaluation and stands as a leader in developing international education publications. Their 2004 book, The New Country Index, is an exhaustive list of academic credentials and placement recommendations for 70 of the countries representing the largest pool of international students in North America. In addition to their training programs and extensive publications, representatives from private evaluation companies contribute to the field of international education by serving on committees, teaching workshops and presenting conference sessions at international, national and regional conferences. These organizations increasingly use the Internet to disseminate research material to international educators.

OTHER TRAINING PROGRAMS

Other training exists that focuses on more narrow topics. U.S. Immigration and Customs Enforcement offers immigration training to new and experienced student and scholar advisors. The Fulbright International Education Administrators Program gives participants the chance to truly engage with the educational system, customs and society of specific countries through campus visits, cultural activities and government appointments. The American Council on Education's Center for International Initiatives supports training on internationalizing the campus. These are just a few examples of professional development training available to international educators. Another increasingly important aspect of professional development relates to technology.

Email and Web Based Educational Tools

Technology has changed the face of international education for the better. Without a doubt, the Internet has opened vistas of information. Email, too, has enhanced the way organizations and people communicate and share information. Electronic newsletters have replaced their more costly print counterparts and thus can be sent to more people more often. International educators have embraced advanced technology, such as Webinars, streaming video and blogs for imparting skills and training in a variety of areas. These technologies will only increase in the coming years.

The Internet seems endless with its vast stores of data published and accumulated by millions. With such resources, it is an excellent source for professional development. General professional development skills can be learned through the Web at the sites mentioned earlier as well as others. AACRAO's news Web page, Transcript, features higher education as it relates to industry developments here and abroad as well as government and court proceedings. MIT developed a free online repository of nearly all of its coursework, from mechanical engineering to gender studies, called OpenCourseWare. The Online Education Database's library for online learning links to 200 free online classes from such institutions as Yale, Harvard, Notre Dame and many others. Similarly, the Fulbright Economics Teaching Program partnered with Harvard University and the University of Economics, Ho Chih Minh City, to publish teaching and research material for those working and studying in policy-related fields. The joint program, "What's Up with Culture," by the University of Southern California and the University of the Pacific presents web-based intercultural communication training. Like Web sites, email is also being used as an educational tool for international educators.

EMAIL LISTS

Email has largely replaced postal mail and phone calls as a way of tracking down needed information. An electronic emailing list, often called a listserv, connects international educators around the world in a quick and convenient forum. One of the most popular mailing lists in international education is a Yahoo group called the inter-l, an international education networking environment. The thousands of international members and numerous postings daily about placement recommendations, institutional recognition and immigration concerns make the inter-l a critical tool in the international education arsenal. NAFSA also hosts several email lists under its knowledge communities, and the Admissions and Credentials Evaluation (ACE) Network provides similar support. Local regions may also have their own, more specific mailing lists. Texas admissions and credentials evaluators subscribe to a mailing list called TIES, the Texas International Education Specialists, which allows colleagues to communicate questions and network daily without leaving the office. AMIDEAST also sends information about changes to educational systems and institutions in the Middle East through their own newsletter. Of course, it is also very easy to simply email an educational advisor overseas to research information not easily found. Similar to mailing lists, electronic newsletters convey much needed information to large groups of people in a very efficient manner.

ELECTRONIC NEWSLETTERS

Electronic newsletters, such as the ECE Newsletter, the World Education News and Reviews, and NAFSA wRAP-UP, regularly provide updates and detailed notes about changes in educational systems, *e.g.*, schools losing recognition, new state-approved institutions, upcoming credential changes, etc. The ECE Newsletter features varied information each month, but generally includes information on new publications, Web sites and email addresses of interest, as well as country-specific updates related to universities and their recognition status. World Education News and Reviews, published bimonthly, offers regional news and updates about educational developments and credentials evaluation. The Recruitment, Admissions and Preparation community of NAFSA issues five wRAP-Up newsletters annually with featured credentials evaluations, placement recommendations, explanations of educational systems and other related topics. These newsletters provide necessary and free resource material for professional education.

WEBINARS, PODCASTS, STREAMING VIDEO AND BLOGS

Newer technologies, such as Webinars, podcasts, streaming video and blogs, are also slowly being incorporated into international education professional development. A Webinar or Webcast is an online, or web-based, seminar or conference. The Foreign Policy Research Institute posts its lectures and teacher training materials as Webcasts.

Podcasts refer to downloaded audio or digital media updated automatically through subscriptions when new content gets added. An excellent example of podcasts can be found on the University of Chicago's International and Area Studies Outreach Source (CHIASMOS) Web site, which features hundreds of internationally relevant podcasts. Streaming video means that the viewer does not have to wait for a video to download before watching and, instead, receives electronic media as it arrives. This is becoming increasingly common for video conferencing, lectures and even movies and television shows. The Web site for Boston College's Front Row Magazine offers hundreds of streaming videos on Islam, politics, education and other topics useful for professional development. A blog is a Weblog, or Web site, generally featuring an amalgamation of journal-type updates and may include video, images or sound. Global Voices Online combines podcasts, blogs, video and photography to examine governments, human rights, politics, education and other topics related to international education. All of these elements of technology represent new and diverse training delivery methods. However, there still remain a few aspects of professional development to cover.

Costs and Benefits of Professional Development

After discussing the reasons for professional development, types of professional and personal growth, training and technology, now it is time to consider some key questions. How will you pay for it? How do you get buy-in from your superiors and colleagues to authorize the time and money for professional development? What are you going to do with these skills, really? In addition, what comes after professional development? Answering these questions before you approach your administrators will greatly enhance your chances of success.

OBTAINING FUNDING AND SUPPORT

Funding, or paying for, professional development is obviously a key factor in determining your level of success. Professional development opportunities range in price from free to many thousands of dollars. Clearly, it would not be that difficult to get a manager or director to agree to support professional development activities with limited impact on the budget, but with large quantities of money involved for memberships, conferences, travel, per diems and publications, it becomes easier to dismiss requests for training and professional development funds. Thus, a multi-pronged approach becomes necessary. Many conferences offer newcomer scholarships for first-time attendees. This can be a great

way for new employees to make their first foray into serious, in-depth professional training. Registering early often results in a lowered rate as does membership in the organization. Local and state conferences are generally closer and shorter, thus incurring less expense. Attending for only one day—a day which features the greatest number of relevant sessions—is another, albeit less desirable, way to soften budget constraints. You can alternate conference attendance or industry-specific training with more general professional or personal development using free or low-cost campus and local resources. In order to get buy-in from your institution, develop a two-prong strategy: focus on the direct benefits to the institution and the value for money gained from staff development.

A multitude of reasons exist for attending professional development opportunities, and they offer direct benefits to your institution. Conferences offer discussion of best practices and trends; networking with other international education professionals; opportunities to meet with exhibitors, agents and recruitment institutions; and practical solutions for problems your institution may experience. In-depth training provides a solid foundation for consistent and accurate credentials evaluation skills. Understanding how to use new technology and learning about new publications for recruitment, admissions and evaluation purposes keeps your institution competitive. Failure to follow government regulations for immigration paperwork may endanger your institution's ability to receive international students. Erroneously admitting ill-prepared students can result in lowering the value of your institution's reputation and poor retention. Failing to identify—and determine how to address—new trends early could result in miscommunication, mistakes or unhappy customers.

Plan to maximize the value of your professional development experience by utilizing every networking, training and learning opportunity. Making contacts, collecting free literature, scheduling appointments with institutions for recruitment efforts, gathering handouts for resource libraries, raising institutional questions, meeting with sponsoring agencies, touring immigration facilities and other activities can greatly enhance the value of your attendance at a conference. Present an extensive list of your goals, as well as your intended conference sessions, to your supervisor as soon as the conference program shows up online. As part of your pre-travel plan, schedule a training day for your colleagues on the sessions you attend as a way of spreading the training cost across several employees. Spend your institution's money wisely by showing how much they would lose by not having you attend the conference, training or other professional development event. Prepare a cost-benefit analysis if needed. Emphasize the ways in which the institution directly and indirectly benefits from your increased skills and education.

PERSONAL BENEFITS

Professional development can also benefit you individually. Most immediately, you can commence implementing your new expertise upon your return. In addition, you will practice networking during the event and training once it is complete. This will also help start or augment your resource library. Within your institution, your status may rise by having a robust and cost-effective professional activity under your belt. You will have more resources, including new contacts, on which to draw when facing unusual situations and experience as a recipient of professional material, enabling you to begin the exciting task of writing your own proposals or seeking volunteer activities, which your institution can include among its departmental annual reports. With regular professional development through any of the on- and off-campus, face-to-face or web-based methods discussed here, your résumé will start to look even more impressive. A sample career ladder in an international admissions office might be as follows: admissions officer, credentials evaluator, senior evaluator, process manager, assistant director, associate director, director and then executive director. Regardless of your position, enhancing your professional skills can only serve to improve your standing in the field.

Future Steps

Throughout this chapter, we have discussed numerous aspects of professional development. We began by looking at the varied reasons to further develop professional skills in international education, such as fraud detection, networking, volunteering and experience. We examined many of the more common methods of receiving this professional development through specific organizations, international connections, human resources departments, resource libraries and volunteer activities. We briefly discussed personal development as a way of enhancing professionalism through campus and community programming and classes. Training covered a large section of this chapter since the field provides so many alternatives via national educator organizations, private evaluation companies and even government agencies. Technology relates to professional development by increasing the mediums and delivery methods to include internet, email, newsletters and burgeoning technologies such as Webinars, podcasts, streaming video and blogs. We then followed up by discussing other aspects of professional development such as funding, support and career building. Where do we go from here? One of the great things about international education is that it is constantly evolving making it impossible to know everything. Whenever you reach one milestone, more goals always remain. If you have attended all the workshops and training modules, it is your turn to lead them. Once you start knowing most of the information in conference sessions, you should present that knowledge. If you research the news before it hits your inbox, contribute articles and information to the various newsletters. When you find that you have more answers than questions, it is past time to mentor the next generation while looking ahead to the future.

265

TWENTY-THREE

Envisioning the Future of
Applied
Comparative
Education

2010 AACRAO INTERNATIONAL GUIDE

JOHNNY K. JOHNSON

Professor Emeritus and former Director of International Programs
Monterey Peninsula College

WILLIAM J. PAVER

Director
Foreign Credentials Service of America

Envisioning the Future of Applied Comparative Education

Almost a million people a year need to have their foreign academic credentials evaluated. Yes, that's 1,000,000 foreign credential evaluations completed each and every year. The reasons vary, but include college and university admission, professional licensure, and labor certification. The people who do this work and set the standards often work in obscurity and have almost completely unregulated authority to set standards. Since the standards they employ and the work that they do affects critical moments and opportunities in so many lives, a careful review of how this work is done and who develops placement recommendations for how individual foreign credentials should be evaluated is crucial. This chapter will discuss how this field of applied comparative education came into being and what its future might hold.

Training for ACE Professionals

Training for those practicing applied comparative education can be found at the annual AACRAO and NAFSA conferences and at local and regional conferences of these organizations. Specialized workshops are also offered by AACRAO and some of the larger credential agencies. AACRAO has a vice president for international education on its Board of Directors. This individual also presides over four active committees dedicated to the field, including a publications committee. NAFSA has recently eliminated the admissions section and subsumed its activities into recruitment, admissions, and preparation (RAP). The admissions section (ADSEC) chair used to sit on the Board of Directors of NAFSA but that seat has now been eliminated. A newsletter is still put out by a group of dedicated NAFSA credentials professionals and country profiles are still being developed and published electronically.

Both AACRAO and NAFSA recently supported the decision to eliminate the National Council on the Evaluation of Foreign Educational Credentials (CEC *or* The Council). The Council had reviewed publications and approved placement recommendations throughout its fifty-year history. Several members of The Council had ceased sending representatives prior to the decision to end The Council's existence. Major publications by both organizations had steadily dwindled over the twenty-year period leading up to the decision to end The Council's existence, also contributing to its demise. Currently the only major effort to publish new research on a routine basis is AACRAO's Electronic Database for Global Education (EDGE), which consists of 230 country profiles in its 5,000 pages of content and contains advice on credentials, which is reviewed and approved by a standing committee.

A Brief History

The field of applied comparative education originated in universities in the post-World War II period to deal with an influx of foreign students. In its infancy, it consisted mainly of relatively senior people working in admissions offices at universities. Today, while university-based international admissions offices still play a major role, many universities refer their work out to private international credential evaluation agencies.

The post-World War II United States also began to attract many foreign-trained immigrants seeking work engineers, doctors, nurses, architects, and other professions. Today, the U.S. government issues visas in the tens of thousands to foreign trained individuals who come here to work, conduct research, study, and obtain training.

Clearly the need to evaluate foreign academic coursework extends well past university admissions. This will continue to be a major factor in the future and should expand as our economy becomes more globalized and as more transnational structures develop. The need for competent credentials agencies that employ reasonable standards and are characterized by a commitment to excellence and transparency will continue to grow.

When the National Council on the Evaluation of Foreign Educational Credentials ceased to function in 2006, there was no other widely recognized set of standards available for practitioners. As it had done in 1955 when it created The Council by asking others to join it in its ongoing work, AACRAO addressed this deficiency by developing the Electronic Database for Global Education (EDGE), an online source containing educational profiles of all the countries of the world with information on all their major credentials. The creation of EDGE and the creation by the AACRAO Board of Directors of the International Education Standards Council (IESC) (IESC Charter appended) is the only example of a refereed set of national standards created by an independent, member-based, non-profit higher education organization. Elements of the U.S. government have chosen to utilize EDGE as a referential standard in their work, and many large university systems in the country rely on it daily. A recent article appearing in Benders Immigration Bulletin, "The N'th Degree: Issues and Case Studies in Degree Equivalency: Working with the EDGE Database," documents how the government's use of EDGE as a referential standard affects the work of immigration attorneys as they endeavor to secure visas for their clients (Wada 2010).

What is Needed: Regulation

The major problem facing the field of applied comparative education is the lack of regulation and consistency. A secondary problem, and a direct consequence of the

first, is that anyone can evaluate a foreign credential and write a letter stating their opinion. These twin problems have created a situation where two competent agencies can evaluate the same credential and come to different conclusions (and often do). For the end user, be it a government entity, a university or a state board, this presents a real quandary. Most end users do not have a good idea of how to address it. Given the decentralized nature of the work, and an ongoing dispute within the field as to the nature and use of placement recommendations or comparability statements, the development of a universal referential standard will be elusive but eventually necessary.

Experienced professionals in the field are generally aware that large and well-developed agencies as well as premier universities often evaluate the same credential differently. A good example of this is when one graduate school will admit a candidate with a three-year Indian degree while another will award ninety hours of credit and place an individual in the undergraduate program. Or, a credentials agency will evaluate a secondary credential as a tertiary one and declare that the individual has a bachelor's degree equivalent when in fact most would agree that the credential in question is the equivalent of high school diploma. Further complicating the situation, the agency or individual in question may possess little or no training, retain no professional reputation, and/or be principally interested in the financial aspect of writing such an evaluation. At present there are no consequences for this type of activity, but for the end user this presents a real dilemma.

Many universities and credential evaluation agencies resist the notion of being regulated by a government office or department and wish to retain their independence to evaluate credentials without oversight. In the past, most entities evaluating foreign credentials looked to the placement recommendations reviewed and approved by The Council in developing their own standards for evaluations. Most of the people working in the field got their training through the regional and national meetings of major higher education associations. Today much of the work being done is carried out by credentials agencies and universities who operate without any independent oversight or regulation. While there have been some attempts to verify the competency of the agencies and individuals doing this work, the organizations and methodologies in place are imperfect.

These reviews are not conducted by an independent entity, but are done by other agencies who are evaluating each other and determining who is "qualified" enough to do this work. Consider a situation where Toyota evaluated Ford to determine if they were good enough to make cars and then certified their approval by inclusion in a membership organization. For the field of applied comparative education, this is clearly not the way to determine an objective appraisal of "quality." And what is equally clear is that the field will eventually be called into question because there are no real standards as to who has the proper training and background to do this work.

Furthermore, there are no real guidelines for how a credential should be evaluated. At the very least, a referential standard should be consulted when forming a judgment on how particular credentials should be evaluated. At present the best way to determine if an individual or agency is qualified to do an evaluation continues to be to investigate the training and the background of the evaluators in question; that determination should, at a minimum, be conducted by an independent entity completely free of financial or professional conflicts.

The AACRAO EDGE
(Electronic Database for Global Education)

Elements of the United States Customs and Immigration Service (USCIS) have now adopted EDGE as a referential standard. When USCIS receives a credentials report from one of its agencies stating that the equivalency for a particular foreign degree, the officer at USCIS looks up the degree in EDGE and verifies that this is what EDGE recommends. The officer then approves or declines the petition and moves on.

However, there is a reason that EDGE is a referential database and not an absolute one. A good example is the long running discussion involving how to evaluate three-year bachelor degrees versus four-year degrees. Some universities admit foreign students presenting three-year degrees to their graduate programs. Some credentials agencies state that three-year degrees from India (from certain universities and with good performance) are equivalent to a four-year U.S. bachelors degree. These are reasoned decisions by senior people in the field with plenty of training and background. In such cases it is incumbent upon the admissions officer or credentials agency to provide justification for their decision. Ultimately, it is up to the end user to accept the advice and issue the license, admit the student, or approve the visa. This case also points out the contradictions universities experience when they allow more than one credentials agency to prepare evaluations for the same credential.

Clearly this approach favors those who are well trained and can justify their conclusions. It levels the playing field by eliminating obviously bad evaluations (those that vary widely from the accepted norm) and forces people doing the work to operate transparently and without financial factors driving the evaluation (tailoring evaluations to meet the needs of the client). There currently exist many individuals and agencies working in the field without the proper training and background, and consequently some of the evaluations produced can range from very poor to deliberately misleading. The inherent weaknesses in how the field operates today will eventually become publicly known, and there will be consequences. All it will take is the exposure of some of the worst practices and practitioners, and reform will be mandated by those from outside the profession. At present the relative obscurity of the field accounts for why this has not yet occurred, but relying on that to continue is improbable.

The Role of Technology

The advance of technology, particularly web-based applications, is making the job of research, production of evaluations, and consistency much more manageable. There is no question that much of the work gleaned by previous generations of evaluators from the libraries built largely by AACRAO and NAFSA now readily find that information on the Web. Templates and "one time, many uses" evaluations are now ubiquitous and have reduced workload considerably. Databases such as EDGE, which are created by very high-end and talented professionals, help to resolve difficult credentials and come up with placement recommendations that can now be widely shared. Institutions and agencies that do not have the resources to handle complex credentials now have tools to resolve the most difficult situations they encounter. In the future, we can anticipate that consortiums of institutions and agencies may draw on central data banks of evaluations. Why, for example, would large university systems continue to operate individual foreign credential evaluation offices at each campus? Eventually, cost cutting will lead to the consolidation of offices, and technology will play a big role in helping that to happen. Only agencies and institutions that keep up with technology will be in a strong position in the years ahead.

The Future Role of National Organizations

The major national member-based organizations with interest in this work are AACRAO and NAFSA, and to a lesser extent the Council of Graduate Schools, The College Board, The American Association of Community Colleges (AACC), and the Educational Testing Service (ETS). Of these only AACRAO has a seat on its Board of Directors reserved for someone with direct ties to the field. Training, conference sessions, and workshops will continue to be found at AACRAO and NAFSA and their regional affiliates. Credential evaluation agencies will offer regional training opportunities on a more limited basis.

The publication of books is almost completely moribund and will remain so due to the low numbers of volumes purchased and the expense of publishing them. Electronic books, articles, Web sites, and databases will convey the new research as it is developed. Training, publications, and access to services will become more costly as these organizations recoup their costs. As the field consolidates and the number of highly trained people decline, other venues (small ones) may develop to meet the relatively narrow needs of the professions. Participation in larger organizations will continue, not only because evaluators need access to the resources of larger groups but because, even though their work is relatively unknown, what they do affects many institutions: those enrolling foreign students (a number likely to grow) and government and state agencies (people will be coming from all over the world to work here). Evaluators also need the support of these organizations to help put in place a recognized set of standards and to help develop a mechanism that will require individuals and entities who evaluate foreign credentials to meet a set of minimum professional standards.

Study Abroad

As noted in previous chapters, the number of U.S. students studying abroad is growing rapidly and will continue to do so. Many of these students will be presenting credentials/transcripts from foreign institutions that will need to be combined with their degree plans at their home institutions. Unless good prior planning is involved before a student goes overseas, much of this credit can wind up not meeting degree requirements and subsequently become coursework that has educational merit, but does not allow a student to move closer to fulfilling his or her degree requirements and graduating on time. Evaluating credit for transfer prior to departure, known as a pre-approval process, allows individuals and institutions to accurately assess how credit will be received by the home institution in the United States, and allows for on-time graduation and a reduction in the costs associated with tuition. Universities should look to establish a strong pre-approval process for their students going abroad to study to reduce time to graduation and to lessen tuition costs.

The initial step in the pre-approval process is to determine whether the institution in which the student plans on studying abroad is accredited or credit worthy. An evaluator needs to determine whether the institution is accredited by the country in which the institution is located or if the institution issuing the transcript in question is regionally accredited in the United States. There have been circumstances where programs are set up overseas and credit is "carried" on the transcript of a regionally accredited institution in the United States. Some of these arrangements are now being looked at critically, and institutions should look to their own policies to assess whether they wish to accept such credit for the purposes of transfer. This is an emerging issue which will garner closer scrutiny in the years ahead.

Outsourcing and Consolidation

Over the past twenty years there has been a discernible yet unquantified change in who evaluates foreign credentials. In the 1970s and into the 80s many universities continued to evaluate any foreign credential that came their way. As university admissions officers took on additional responsibilities for the targeted recruitment of their student populations, more attention and resources were dedicated to these activities, and there have been subsequent reductions in support for retaining an in-house international credential evaluation function. While the large university players have generally retained their international admissions office, some smaller institutions' international admissions activities/offices have become reduced in size and are outsourcing this activity to credential agencies. While those institutions enrolling large numbers of students can successfully maintain and operate a profitable international admissions operation, many of the schools running smaller operations cannot really afford to do so. This trend of general outsourcing will continue in the near future and beyond.

Several problems exist with this approach. Not all credential agencies are created equal, and some are vastly more qualified to operate than others. There is no independent national body in place to oversee the agencies that do this work, and therefore, the quality of the work done is quite uneven and can give rise to bad practices, even fraud. Finally, even the good agencies disagree on how to evaluate the same credential. If you are an end user at a regional liberal arts college, you may receive an evaluation report from one agency that tells you that the three-year credential from India (say a B.Com.) is eligible to be considered for graduate studies. At the same time you have another report from another agency for the same student recommending three years of credit and admission as a transfer student. The way to handle this is to establish policies that make sense for your institution, but unfortunately this does not always happen in the day-to-day world of university admissions.

Three-Year Versus Four-Year Degrees

Much time and discussion has gone into understanding how three-year degrees should be evaluated, and the current discussions of the Bologna process have helped to frame the central question: exactly how well prepared are persons presenting a three-year Bologna degree for graduate study in the United States? A further question involves what to do with the Indian three-year degrees which are seen much more widely in the United States. How are the quantitative and qualitative factors broken out in making a distinction? What role does institutional policy play in all of this?

In the Fall 2009 issue of *College and University* [85(2)] an article was devoted to the Bologna Process and AACRAO EDGE deliberations regarding this subject. This article is highly recommended for a further understanding of this issue.

Conclusions

CONTINUED GROWTH IN DEMAND FOR APPLIED COMPARATIVE EDUCATION

Currently, one million people a year require foreign credential evaluations. This is important work that affects many people, both those seeking evaluations and those representing institutions and government bodies in admissions offices, study abroad offices, registrar's offices, and international education offices. The pacing of the outsourcing of work to credentials agencies will continue to grow, albeit not dramatically, as larger institutions that evaluate foreign credentials will continue to handle things in-house. As a result, experts in the field will continue to require training opportunities and the building of structures to ensure proper regulation of the field.

The movement within the European Union to provide a common academic transcript as a means of facilitating the movement of students and professionals from country to country will create additional demand for evaluations should these students wish to study in the United States. The more detailed and extensive the information provided on a standardized EU transcript, the greater the need will be to distill that information to manageable portions.

THE EFFECTS OF TECHNOLOGY ON THE FIELD

The "Golden Days" of abundant funding for publications and a fully-funded National Council are long gone, and new structures and opportunities need to be sought out. The AACRAO Electronic Database for Global Education (EDGE) is an extremely useful tool and contains straightforward and well organized information on credentials from over 230 countries. Never before has so much thoroughly vetted information on foreign educational systems (over 5,000 pages) been available in one place. The AACRAO team and the leadership that helped put it together are to be commended.

THE EFFECTS OF INCREASED DEMAND FOR STUDY ABROAD

More U.S. students than ever before are studying abroad. In fact, there has been a 25 percent increase in the number of Americans going abroad since the terrible events of September 11, 2001. This welcome increase in the number of students going abroad and learning about other cultures will also increase the demand for evaluation of foreign educational credentials. In addition, the increase in short-term study abroad and in the number

of countries where students choose to study will also increase the demand for interpretation of foreign educational credentials in U.S. terms. Study abroad will continue to grow vigorously, and resources must be developed to make this a smooth transition for students going overseas. Research on the best practices involved and utilized in the pre-approval process should be developed and published.

THE NEED FOR REGULATION

Busy university administrators and faculty members, licensing boards, and government agencies responsible for immigration, visas, and labor certification will increasingly require the summarizing of essential bits of information. Whether this work will be done by private credential evaluation services, professional associations, or some government entity remains to be seen. Some combination of these, such as a government or professional association oversight to ensure consistency and minimal standards, is the probable outcome for the future (witness the health insurance debate of 2010). Indeed, it is time for the field of applied comparative education to seek out truly independent and trusted organizations to provide regulation for the industry. Other approaches currently in place are inadequate to the task at hand and transparently lack the ability to bring meaningful reform and good practices nationwide.

Universities will continue to outsource credential evaluation, and general interest in the field from senior management—in both academic institutions and professional organizations representing higher education—will continue to wane. Whether the credential evaluation agencies will assume greater control over the process of evaluation and the setting of standards seems unlikely. Recent problems in student financial aid and study abroad have led to legislation which limits abuses in these fields. Do private credential evaluation agencies possess enough enlightened self-interest to reform, set, and follow standards before state or federal government does it for them?

THREE VERSUS FOUR-YEAR DEGREES

For the past several years there has been much discussion about how to evaluate three-year versus four-year degrees. In essence the question is can a three-year degree be called comparable to a U.S. bachelors degree? For credential evaluation professionals much of the concern surrounding the Bologna process has been associated with this particular issue. In the United States, for the most part, this involves who has access to U.S. graduate schools but resolving this question also has important implications for the issuance of visas. There will be circumstances where a three-year degree will yield access to graduate level studies in the United States, though these will be the exception and not the rule. Exceptions will be found mostly in business schools, a few graduate programs and via recommendations from some credentials agencies. However most practitioners will continue to look to the placement recommendations developed in the past by the Council and in the present by the AACRAO EDGE system in formulating how to evaluate these credentials. This discussion will continue and will remain unresolved for the near future. No overall consensus among U.S. evaluators on how to resolve this issue exists at this point. Other higher education associations, particularly The Council of Graduate Schools, could play a major role in shaping this issue.

Appendix A:
Resource Organizations, Agencies and Institutions

PEGGY BELL HENDRICKSON

Alliance for International Educational and Cultural Exchange
1776 Massachusetts Avenue, NW, Suite 620
Washington, DC 20036-1912
Telephone: (202) 293-6141
Fax: (202) 293-6144
www.alliance-exchange.org

America-Mideast Educational and Training Services, Inc. (AMIDEAST)
1730 M Street, NW, Suite 1100
Washington, DC 20036-4505
Tel: (202) 776-9600
Fax: (202) 776-7000
Email: inquiries@amideast.org
www.amideast.org

American Association of Collegiate Registrars and Admissions Officers (AACRAO) International Education Services
One Dupont Circle, NW, Suite 520
Washington, DC 20036
Tel: (202) 293-9161
Fax: (202) 872-8857
Email: oies@aacrao.org
www.aacrao.org

American Association of Community Colleges (AACC)
One Dupont Circle, NW, Suite 410
Washington, DC 20036
Tel: (202) 728-0200
Fax: (202) 833-2467
www.aacc.nche.edu

American Association of State Colleges and Universities (AASCU)
1307 New York Avenue, NW
Washington, D.C. 20005
Tel: (202) 293-7070
Fax: (202) 296-5819
Email: info@aascu.org
www.aascu.org

American Council on Education (ACE)
One Dupont Circle, NW
Washington, D.C. 20036-1193
Tel: (202) 939-9300
Fax: (202) 833-4760
Email: cii@ace.nche.edu
www.acenet.edu

American Institute for Foreign Study (AIFS)
River Plaza, 9 West Broad Street
Stamford, CT 06902
Tel: (203) 399-5000
Fax: (203) 399-5590
Email: info@aifs.com
www.aifs.org

Association of American Colleges and Universities (AACU)
1818 R Street, NW
Washington, DC 20009
Tel: (202) 387-3760
Fax: (202) 265-9532
www.aacu.org

Association of Canadian Community Colleges (ACCC)
Suite 200-1223
rue Michael Street Nord/North
Ottawa, Ontario K1J 7T2
Canada
Tel: (613) 746-2222
Fax: (613) 746-6721
Email: info@accc.ca
www.accc.ca

Association of International Education Administrators (AIEA)
AIEA Secretariat
Duke University, Campus Box 90404
Durham, NC USA 27708-0404
Tel: (919) 668-1928
Fax: (919) 684-8749
Email: aiea@duke.edu
www.aieaworld.org

Association of International Credential Evaluators (AICE)
P.O. Box 6756
Beverly Hills, CA 90212
Tel: (310) 550-3305
Fax: (310) 275-1606
Email: info@aice-eval.org
www.aice-eval.org

Association of Universities and Colleges of Canada (AUCC)
350 Albert Street, Suite 600
Ottawa, Ontario K1R 1B1
Canada
Tel: (613) 563-1236
Fax: (613) 563-9745
Email: info@aucc.ca
www.aucc.ca/index.html

British Council
Tel: +44 (0) 161 957 7755
Fax: +44 (0) 161 957 7762
Email: general.enquiries@britishcouncil.org
www.britishcouncil.org

Canadian Bureau for International Education (CBIE)
220 Laurier West, Suite 1550
Ottawa, ON K1P 5Z9
Canada
Tel: (613) 237-4820
Fax: (613) 237-1073
Email: info@cbie.ca
http://cbie.ca

The College Board
45 Columbus Avenue
New York, NY 10023
Tel: (212) 713-8000
www.collegeboard.org

Commission on Graduates of Foreign Nursing Schools (CGFNS)
3600 Market Street, Suite 400
Philadelphia, PA 19104-2651
Tel: (215) 222-8454
Fax: (215) 662-0425
Email: info@cgfns.org
www.cgfns.org

Council for Higher Education Accreditation (CHEA)
One Dupont Circle NW, Suite 510
Washington DC 20036-1135
Tel: (202) 955-6126
Fax: (202) 955-6129
Email: chea@chea.org
www.chea.org

Council of Graduate Schools (CGS)
One Dupont Circle, NW, Suite 230
Washington, DC 20036
Tel: (202) 223-3791
Fax: (202) 331-7157
Email: general_inquiries@cgs.nche.edu
www.cgsnet.org

Council on International Educational Exchange (CIEE)
300 Fore Street
Portland, ME 04101
Tel: (207) 553-4000
Fax: (207) 553-4299
Email: contact@ciee.org
www.ciee.org

Council for International Exchange of Scholars (CIES)
3007 Tilden Street, NW, Suite 5L
Washington, DC 20008-3009
Tel: (202) 686-4000
Fax: (202) 362-3442
Email: apprequest@cies.iie.org
www.cies.org

Educational Credentials Evaluators (ECE)
PO Box 514070
Milwaukee, WI 53203-3470
Tel: (414) 289-3400
Email: eval@ece.org
www.ece.org

EducationUSA
U.S. Department of State, Bureau of Educational and Cultural Affairs
www.educationusa.state.gov

EDUCAUSE
1150 18th Street, NW, Suite 1010
Washington, DC 20036
Tel: (202) 872-4200
Fax: (202) 872-4318
Email: info@educause.edu
www.educause.edu

Educational Testing Service (ETS)
Rosedale Road
Princeton, NJ 08541
Tel: (609) 921-9000
Fax: (609) 734-5410
Email: etsinfo@ets.org
www.ets.org

ERIC—Clearinghouse on Higher Education
655 15th St. NW, Suite 500
Washington, DC 20036
Tel: (800) 538-3742
www.eric.ed.gov

European Association for International Education (EAIE)
PO Box 11189
1001 BT Amsterdam, The Netherlands
Tel: +31-20-344 5100
Fax: +31-20-344 5119
Email: eaie@eaie.nl
www.eaie.org

Foreign Policy Research Institute (FPRI)
1528 Walnut St., Suite 610
Philadelphia, PA 19102
Tel: (215) 732-3774
Fax: (215) 732-4401
Email: fpri@fpri.org
www.fpri.org

The Fulbright Program
Email: fulbright@state.gov
http://fulbright.state.gov

Graduate Management Admission Council (GMAC)
1600 Tysons Blvd., Suite 1400
McLean, VA 22102 USA
Tel: (703) 749-0131
Fax: (703) 749-0169
www.gmac.com

International Education and Research Network (iEARN)
475 Riverside Drive, Suite 450
New York, NY 10115
Phone: 212-870-2693
Fax: 212-870-2672
Email: iearn@us.iearn.org
www.iearn.org

International Educational Research Foundation (IERF)
Post Office Box 3665
Culver City, CA 90231
Phone: (310) 258-9451
Fax: (310) 342-7086
www.ierf.org

International English Language Testing System (IELTS)
825 Colorado Boulevard, Suite 112
Los Angeles, CA 90041
Tel: (323) 255-2771
www.ielt.org

International Research & Exchanges Board (IREX)
2121 K Street, NW, Suite 700
Washington, DC 20037
Tel: (202) 628-8188
Fax: (202) 628-8189
Email: irex@irex.org
www.irex.org

Institute of International Education (IIE)
809 United Nations Plaza
New York, NY 10017
Tel: (212) 883-8200
Fax: (212) 984-5452
Email: info@iie.org
www.iie.org

LASPAU: Academic and Professional Programs for the Americas
25 Mount Auburn Street
Cambridge, MA 02138-6095
Tel: (617) 495-5255
Fax: (617) 495-8990
Email: laspau-webmaster@calists.harvard.edu
www.laspau.harvard.edu

Linden Educational Services
917 Duke Street
Alexandria, VA 22314
Tel: (703) 683-0164
Fax: (703) 683-0210
Email: linden@lindentours.com
www.lindentours.com

**NAFSA: Association of
International Educators**
1307 New York Avenue, NW, Eighth Floor
Washington, DC 20005-4701
Tel: (202) 737-3699
Fax: (202) 737-3657
Email: inbox@nafsa.org
www.nafsa.org

**National Association of Graduate
Admissions Professionals (NAGAP)**
PO Box 14605
Lenexa, KS 66285-4605
Tel: (913) 895-4616
Fax: (913) 895-4652
Email: info@nagap.org
www.nagap.org

**National Association of Credential
Evaluators (NACES)**
Email: info@naces.org
www.naces.org

**National Association of Independent
Colleges and Universities (NAICU)**
1025 Connecticut Ave., NW, Suite 700
Washington, DC 20036
Tel: (202) 785-8866
Fax: (202) 835-0003
www.naicu.edu

**National Collegiate Athletic
Association (NCAA)**
700 W. Washington Street
P.O. Box 6222
Indianapolis, Indiana 46206-6222
Tel: (317) 917-6222
Fax: (317) 917-6888
www.ncaa.org

**NASPA: Student Affairs Administrators
in Higher Education**
1875 Connecticut Avenue, NW, Suite 418
Washington, DC 20009
Tel: (202) 265-7500
Fax: 202) 797-1157
www.naspa.org

Oregon Office of Degree Authorization
1500 Valley River Drive, Suite 100
Eugene, OR 97401
Tel: (541) 687-7452
www.osac.state.or.us/oda

U.S. Department of Education
400 Maryland Avenue, SW, 7E-247
Washington, DC 20202
Tel: 1-800-USA-LEARN
Email: CustomerService@inet.ed.gov
www.ed.gov

World Education Services (WES)
Bowling Green Station
PO Box 5087
New York, NY 10274-508
Tel: (212) 966-6311
Fax: (212) 739-6100
Email: wenr@wes.org
www.wes.org

Appendix B:
Publications and Other Useful Resources

PEGGY BELL HENDRICKSON

PUBLICATIONS

GENERAL

American Association of Collegiate Registrars and Admissions Officers (AACRAO). 2009. *AACRAO Electronic Database for Global Education (EDGE).* http://aacraoedge.aacrao.org/register/.

———. 1988. *International Academic Credentials Handbook, Volume I.* Washington, DC: AACRAO.

———. 1989. *International Academic Credentials Handbook, Volume II.* Washington, DC: AACRAO.

———. 1992. *International Academic Credentials Handbook, Volume III.* Washington, DC: AACRAO.

———. 1996. *Handbook for the Admission of International Students to Elementary and Secondary Schools in the United States.* Washington, DC: AACRAO.

———. 2003. *Foreign Educational Credentials Required.* Washington, DC: AACRAO.

———. 2003. *The AACRAO International Graduate Admissions Guide.* Washington, DC: AACRAO.

———. 2006. *Guide to Bogus Institutions and Documents.* Washington, DC: AACRAO.

———. 2008. *The Impact of Bologna and Three-Year Degrees on U.S. Admissions: A Focus on Europe, Australia, and the United Kingdom.* Washington, DC: AACRAO.

Aldrich-Langen, Caroline. 1993. *Understanding the Admissions Process in U.S. Higher Education—A Case Study Approach.* Washington, DC: World Education Series/Projects for International Education Research (PIER).

Association of African Universities. 2007. *Guide to Higher Education in Africa, 4th Edition.* Accra, Ghana: Association of African Universities and International Association of Universities.

Association of Commonwealth Universities. 2008. *Commonwealth Universities Yearbook 2008,* 82nd edition. London, England: Association of Commonwealth Universities.

Bear, John and Ezell, Allen. 2005. *Degree Mills: The Billion-Dollar Industry That Has Sold More Than a Million Fake Degrees.* Amherst, NY: Prometheus Books.

Beeson, Christopher W. 2002. *The Immigration and Naturalization Service.* Washington, DC: AACRAO.

Caplan, Bram and Teter, Wesley. 2008. *From Reykjavik to Vladivostok: Student Advising Trends from EducationUSA.* Washington, DC: EducationUSA.

Cook, Rebecca M. 2005. *Affordable Resources for International Credential Evaluation.* Milwaukee, WI: Educational Credential Evaluators, Inc.

Cook, Rebecca M. 2005. *The Dilemma of Forgery: Altered Documents in an International Context.* Milwaukee, WI: Educational Credential Evaluators, Inc.

Ezell, Allen. 2007. *Accreditation Mills.* Washington, DC: AACRAO.

———. 2008. *Counterfeit Diplomas and Transcripts.* Washington, DC: AACRAO.

Feagles, Shelly. 1999. *A Guide to Educational Systems around the World.* Washington, DC: NAFSA.

Frey, James S. 2003. *Credit Practices in the United States and Suggestions for Determining U.S. Credit Equivalents for Credit Systems Used in Other Countries.* Milwaukee, WI: Educational Credential Evaluators, Inc.

———. 2003. *Grading Practices in the United States and Suggestions for Determining U.S. Grade Equivalents for Grading Systems Used in Other Countries.* Milwaukee, WI: Educational Credential Evaluators, Inc.

Higher Education Directory. 2008. Reston, VA: Higher Education Publications.

International Association of Universities. 2006. *World List of Universities and Other Institutions of Higher Education, 25th edition.* Paris, France: International Association of Universities.

———. 2008. *International Handbook of Universities, 20th edition.* Paris, France: International Association of Universities.

———. 2008. *World Higher Education Database, 10th edition.* New York, NY: Palgrave Macmillan's Global Academic Publishing.

The International Credential Assessment Service (ICAS) of Canada Handbook Volume I. Guelph, ON: International Credential Assessment Service of Canada.

International Education Research Foundation. 2004. *The New Country Index: Making Sense of International Credentials.* Culver City, CA: International Education Research Foundation.

NAFSA. *NAFSA Adviser's Manual Online.* www.nafsa.org/publication.sec/working_with_international/nafsa_adviser_s_manual/.

O'Hara, Marie, Raftus, Karen and Stedman, Joann. 2000. *Guide to International Student Recruitment.* Washington, DC: NAFSA.

Popovych, Erika. 1995. *Newly Independent States and the Baltic Republics: A Directory of Institutions in Armenia, Azerbaijan, Belarus, Estonia, Georgia, Kazakhstan,*

Kyrgyzstan, Latvia, Lithuania, Moldova, Russian Federation, Tajikistan, Turkmenistan, Ukraine, Uzbekistan. Washington, DC: World Education Series/Projects for International Education Research.

Teferra, Dantew and Altbach, Philip G. 2003. *African Higher Education: An International Reference Handbook.* Bloomington, IN: Indiana University Press.

REGIONS

Levin-Stankevich, Brian and Popovych, Erika. 1992. *The Soviet System of Education.* Washington, DC: World Education Series/Projects for International Education Research

Marcus, Jane. 1996. *Central America Update.* Washington, DC: World Education Series/Projects for International Education Research.

Sweeney, Leo J. and Woolston, Valerie. 1986. *The Admission and Placement of Students from Bangladesh, India, Pakistan, and Sri Lanka.* Washington, DC:

World Education Series/Projects for International Education Research.

World Education Series/PIER. 1984. *The Admission and Placement of Students from Bahrain, Oman, Qatar, United Arab Emirates, and Yemen Arab Republic.* Washington, DC: World Education Series/Projects for International Education Research.

———. 1987. *Admissions and Placement of Students from Central America: Belize, Costa Rica, El Salvador, Guatemala, Honduras, Nicaragua, Panama.* Washington, DC: World Education Series/Projects for International Education Research.

COUNTRIES

Albania

Koenig, Ann. 1993. *Albania: An Overview of the Educational System of Albania.* Milwaukee, WI: Educational Credential Evaluators, Inc.

Argentina

Australian Education International. 2006. *Argentina,* Australian Education International Country Education Profiles (CEP) online subscription service. http://aei.gov.au/AEI/CEP/Default.htm.

Armenia

Australian Education International. 2005. *Armenia.* Australian Education International CEP online subscription service. http://aei.gov.au/AEI/CEP/Default.htm.

Australia

AACRAO International Education Services. 2004. *Australia: Education and Training.* Washington, DC: AACRAO.

Australian Education International. 2008. *Australia.* Australian Education International CEP online subscription service. http://aei.gov.au/AEI/CEP/Default.htm.

Austria

Australian Education International. 1992. *Austria.* Australian Education International CEP online subscription service. http://aei.gov.au/AEI/CEP/Default.htm.

Azerbaijan

Australian Education International. 2005. *Azerbaijan.* Australian Education Inter-

national CEP online subscription service. http://aei.gov.au/AEI/CEP/Default.htm.

Bahrain

World Education Series/PIER. 1984. *Bahrain: The Admission and Placement of Students from Bahrain, Oman, Qatar, United Arab Emirates, and Yemen Arab Republic.* Washington, DC: World Education Series/Projects for International Education Research.

Bangladesh

Australian Education International. 2007. *Bangladesh.* Australian Education International CEP online subscription service. http://aei.gov.au/AEI/CEP/Default.htm.

Belarus

Australian Education International. 2005. *Belarus.* Australian Education International CEP online subscription service. http://aei.gov.au/AEI/CEP/Default.htm.

Belgium

AACRAO. 1996. *Belgium: Handbook for the Admission of International Students to Elementary and Secondary Schools in the United States.* Washington, DC: AACRAO.

Australian Education International. 2005. *Belgium.* Australian Education International CEP online subscription service. http://aei.gov.au/AEI/CEP/Default.htm.

Bolivia

Australian Education International. 2007. *Bolivia.* Australian Education International

CEP online subscription service. http://aei.gov.au/AEI/CEP/Default.htm.

Bosnia and Herzegovina

Australian Education International. 2008. *Bosnia and Herzegovina.* Australian Education International CEP online subscription service. http://aei.gov.au/AEI/CEP/Default.htm.

Botswana

Australian Education International. 2005. *Botswana.* Australian Education International CEP online subscription service. http://aei.gov.au/AEI/CEP/Default.htm.

Brazil

AACRAO International Education Services. 2004. *Brazil: A Country Study on the Education System of Brazil and Guide to the Academic Placement of Students in Education Institutions in the United States.* Washington, DC: AACRAO.

Australian Education International. 2005. *Brazil.* Australian Education International CEP online subscription service. http://aei.gov.au/AEI/CEP/Default.htm.

Brunei Darussalam

Australian Education International. 2005. *Brunei Darussalam.* Australian Education International CEP online subscription service. http://aei.gov.au/AEI/CEP/Default.htm.

Bulgaria

Aldrich, Caroline. 1996. *Bulgaria: A Workshop Report on the Educational System* and *Guide to the Academic Placement of Students in Educational Institutions in the United States.* Washington, DC: World Education Series/Projects for International Education Research.

Australian Education International. 2006. *Bulgaria.* Australian Education International CEP online subscription service. http://aei.gov.au/AEI/CEP/Default.htm.

Cambodia

Australian Education International. 2008. *Cambodia.* Australian Education International CEP online subscription service. http://aei.gov.au/AEI/CEP/Default.htm.

Cameroon

Saidi, Jasmin. 1995. *Cameroon: Country Guide.* Washington, DC: AACRAO.

Canada

Association of Universities and Colleges. 2008. *Directory of Canadian Universities.* Ottowa, Ontario: Association of Universities and Colleges of Canada.

Australian Education International. 2008. *Canada.* Australian Education International CEP online subscription service. http://aei.gov.au/AEI/CEP/Default.htm.

Cape Verde

Sevigny, Joseph A. 1995. *Cape Verde: Country Guide.* Washington, DC: AACRAO.

Central African Republic

Bretherick, Dona. 1995. *Central African Republic: Country Guide.* Washington, DC: AACRAO.

Chad

Sevigny, Joseph A. 1995. *Chad: Country Guide.* Washington, DC: AACRAO.

Chile

Australian Education International. 2005. *Chile.* Australian Education International CEP online subscription service. http://aei.gov.au/AEI/CEP/Default.htm.

China

Australian Education International. 2007. *China.* Australian Education International CEP online subscription service. http://aei.gov.au/AEI/CEP/Default.htm.

Feagles, Shelley. 1992. *A Guide to Evaluating Educational Credentials from China.* Milwaukee, WI: Educational Credential Evaluators, Inc.

Higher Education Press. 2004. *Chinese Universities and Colleges, 4th edition.* Higher Education Press.

Surowski, David. 2000. *The People's Republic of China: A Workshop Report on the Education System of The People's Republic of China and Guide to the Academic Placement of Students in Education Institutions in the United States.* Washington, DC: World Education Series/Projects for International Education Research.

Colombia

AACRAO. 1996. *Colombia: Handbook for the Admission of International Students to Elementary and Secondary Schools in the United States.* Washington, DC: AACRAO.

Australian Education International. 2008. *Colombia.* Australian Education International CEP online subscription service. http://aei.gov.au/AEI/CEP/Default.htm.

Congo

Sevigny, Joseph A. 1996. *Congo: Country Guide.* Washington, DC: AACRAO.

———. 1996. *Democratic Republic of Congo: Country Guide.* Washington, DC: AACRAO.

Cook Islands

Australian Education International. 2007. *Cook Islands.* Australian Education International CEP online subscription service. http://aei.gov.au/AEI/CEP/Default.htm.

Costa Rica

Australian Education International. 1993. *Costa Rica.* Australian Education International CEP online subscription service. http://aei.gov.au/AEI/CEP/Default.htm.

Croatia

Australian Education International. 2008. *Croatia.* Australian Education International CEP online subscription service. http://aei.gov.au/AEI/CEP/Default.htm.

Cuba

Australian Education International. 2005. *Cuba.* Australian Education International CEP online subscription service. http://aei.gov.au/AEI/CEP/Default.htm.

Czech and Slovak Federal Republic

Australian Education International. 2008. *Czech Republic.* Australian Education International CEP online subscription service. http://aei.gov.au/AEI/CEP/Default.htm.

———. 2005. *Czech and Slovak Federal Republic.* Australian Education International CEP online subscription service. http://aei.gov.au/AEI/CEP/Default.htm.

———. 2008. *Slovenia.* Australian Education International CEP online subscription service. http://aei.gov.au/AEI/CEP/Default.htm.

Denmark

Australian Education International. 2005. *Denmark.* Australian Education International CEP online subscription service. http://aei.gov.au/AEI/CEP/Default.htm.

Dickey, Karlene and Woolston, Valerie. 1995. *Denmark.* Washington, DC: World Education Series/Projects for International Education Research.

Dominican Republic

AACRAO. 1996. *Dominican Republic: Handbook for the Admission of International Students to Elementary and Secondary Schools in the United States.* Washington, DC: AACRAO.

Sellew, Kathleen T. 1987. *Dominican Republic.* Washington, DC: World Education Series/Projects for International Education Research.

Ecuador

Forbes, Michele M. *Ecuador: Country Guide,* Washington, DC: AACRAO.

Egypt

AACRAO. 1996. *Egypt: Handbook for the Admission of International Students to Elementary and Secondary Schools in the United States.* Washington, DC: AACRAO.

Australian Education International. 2005. *Egypt.* Australian Education International CEP online subscription service. http://aei.gov.au/AEI/CEP/Default.htm.

El Salvador

Australian Education International, 2005. *El Salvador.* Australian Education International CEP online subscription service. http://aei.gov.au/AEI/CEP/Default.htm.

Estonia

Australian Education International. 2005. *Estonia*. Australian Education International CEP online subscription service. http://aei.gov.au/AEI/CEP/Default.htm.

Ethiopia

Australian Education International. 2005. *Ethiopia*. Australian Education International CEP online subscription service. http://aei.gov.au/AEI/CEP/Default.htm.

Fiji

Australian Education International. 2005. *Fiji*. Australian Education International CEP online subscription service. http://aei.gov.au/AEI/CEP/Default.htm.

Finland

Australian Education International. 2005. *Finland*. Australian Education International CEP online subscription service. http://aei.gov.au/AEI/CEP/Default.htm.

Warren, Kenneth. 1999. *Finland*. Milwaukee, WI: Educational Credential Evaluators, Inc.

France

AACRAO. 1996. *Handbook for the Admission of International Students to Elementary and Secondary Schools in the United States: France*. Washington, DC: AACRAO.

Australian Education International. 2007. *France*. Australian Education International CEP online subscription service. http://aei.gov.au/AEI/CEP/Default.htm.

Jahn, Linda and Trayte, Kathleen. 2007. The Educational System of France. Washington, DC: AACRAO.

Gabon

Sowa, Mary Beth. 2000. *Gabon: Country Guide*. Washington, DC: AACRAO.

Gambia

Sowa, Mary Beth. 2000. *Gambia: Country Guide*. Washington, DC: AACRAO.

Georgia

Australian Education International. 2005. *Georgia*. Australian Education International CEP online subscription service. http://aei.gov.au/AEI/CEP/Default.htm.

Germany

AACRAO. 1996. *Germany: Handbook for the Admission of International Students to Elementary and Secondary Schools in the United States.* Washington, DC: AACRAO.

Australian Education International. 2007. *Germany*. Australian Education International CEP online subscription service. http://aei.gov.au/AEI/CEP/Default.htm.

Lukas, Karen. 1991. *The Educational System of the Former German Democratic Republic*. Washington, DC: World Education Series/Projects for International Education Research.

Porter, Georgeanne B. 1986. *Federal Republic of Germany*. Washington, DC: World Education Series/Projects for International Education Research.

Ghana

Australian Education International. 2005. *Ghana*. Australian Education International CEP online subscription service. http://aei.gov.au/AEI/CEP/Default.htm.

Greece

AACRAO. 1996. *Greece: Handbook for the Admission of International Students to Elementary and Secondary Schools in the United States*. Washington, DC: AACRAO.

Australian Education International. 2005. *Greece*. Australian Education International CEP online subscription service. http://aei.gov.au/AEI/CEP/Default.htm.

Guatemala

Australian Education International. 2005. *Guatemala*. Australian Education International CEP online subscription service. http://aei.gov.au/AEI/CEP/Default.htm.

Guinea

Sowa, Mary Beth. 2000. *Guinea: Country Guide*. Washington, DC: AACRAO.

Haiti

AACRAO. 1996. *Haiti: Handbook for the Admission of International Students to Elementary and Secondary Schools in the United States*. Washington, DC: AACRAO.

Honduras

Australian Education International. 2005. *Honduras*. Australian Education International CEP online subscription service. http://aei.gov.au/AEI/CEP/Default.htm.

Hong Kong

Australian Education International. 2008. *Hong Kong*. Australian Education International CEP online subscription service. http://aei.gov.au/AEI/CEP/Default.htm.

Hungary

Australian Education International. 2005. *Hungary*. Australian Education International CEP online subscription service. http://aei.gov.au/AEI/CEP/Default.htm.

India

Association of Indian Universities. 2006. *India: Universities Handbook, 31st edition*. Delhi, India: Association of Indian Universities.

Australian Education International. 2007. *India*. Australian Education International CEP online subscription service. http://aei.gov.au/AEI/CEP/Default.htm.

Kallur, Ravi and Sweeney, Leo J. 1998. *India: A Special Report on the Higher Education System and Guide to the Academic Placement of Students in the United States*. Washington, DC: World Education Series/Projects for International Education Research.

Indonesia

Australian Education International. 2005. *Indonesia*. Australian Education International CEP online subscription service. http://aei.gov.au/AEI/CEP/Default.htm.

Chamberlain, Jerry, Gaylord, Wendy and Johnson, Karin. 1993. *Indonesia*. Washington, DC: World Education Series/Projects for International Education Research.

Iran

Australian Education International. 2007. *Iran*. Australian Education International CEP online subscription service. http://aei.gov.au/AEI/CEP/Default.htm.

Iraq

AACRAO. 1996. *Iraq: Handbook for the Admission of International Students to Elementary and Secondary Schools in the United States.* Washington, DC: AACRAO.

Australian Education International. 2005. *Iraq.* Australian Education International CEP online subscription service. http://aei.gov.au/AEI/CEP/Default.htm.

Frey, James S. 1988. *Iraq.* Washington, DC: World Education Series/Projects for International Education Research.

Israel

Australian Education International. 2005. *Israel.* Australian Education International CEP online subscription service. http://aei.gov.au/AEI/CEP/Default.htm.

Fletcher, Ann. 1993. *Higher Education in Israel.* Washington, DC: World Education Series/Projects for International Education Research.

Italy

AACRAO. 1996. *Italy: Handbook for the Admission of International Students to Elementary and Secondary Schools in the United States.* Washington, DC: AACRAO.

Australian Education International. 2009. *Italy.* Australian Education International CEP online subscription service. http://aei.gov.au/AEI/CEP/Default.htm.

Zanetti, Kristin. 1996. *The Educational System Italy.* Milwaukee, WI: Educational Credential Evaluators, Inc.

Japan

AACRAO. 1996. *Japan: Handbook for the Admission of International Students to Elementary and Secondary Schools in the United States.* Washington, DC: AACRAO.

Association of International Education, Japan. 2001. *Japanese Colleges and Universities, 3rd edition.* Association of International Education, Japan.

———. 2006. *Japan.* Australian Education International CEP online subscription service. http://aei.gov.au/AEI/CEP/Default.htm.

Mashiko, Ellen E. 1989. *Japan.* Washington, DC: World Education Series/Projects for International Education Research.

Jordan

Australian Education International. 2005. *Jordan.* Australian Education International CEP online subscription service. http://aei.gov.au/AEI/CEP/Default.htm.

Kazakhstan

Australian Education International. 2005. *Kazakhstan.* Australian Education International CEP online subscription service. http://aei.gov.au/AEI/CEP/Default.htm.

Kenya

Australian Education International. 2005. *Kenya.* Australian Education International CEP online subscription service. http://aei.gov.au/AEI/CEP/Default.htm.

Meyers, James. 1993. *The Educational System of Kenya.* Milwaukee, WI: Educational Credential Evaluatiors, Inc.

Kiribati

Australian Education International. 2007. *Kiribati.* Australian Education International CEP online subscription service. http://aei.gov.au/AEI/CEP/Default.htm.

South Korea

Australian Education International. 2007. *South Korea.* Australian Education International CEP online subscription service. http://aei.gov.au/AEI/CEP/Default.htm.

Kosovo

Australian Education International. 2008. *Kosovo.* Australian Education International CEP online subscription service. http://aei.gov.au/AEI/CEP/Default.htm.

Kuwait

Australian Education International. 2008. *Kuwait.* Australian Education International CEP online subscription service. http://aei.gov.au/AEI/CEP/Default.htm.

Kyrgyzstan

AACRAO International Education Services. 2003. *The Educational System of Kyrgyzstan.* Washington, DC: AACRAO.

Australian Education International. 2005. *Kyrgyzstan.* Australian Education International CEP online subscription service. http://aei.gov.au/AEI/CEP/Default.htm.

Latvia

Australian Education International. 2005. *Latvia.* Australian Education International CEP online subscription service. http://aei.gov.au/AEI/CEP/Default.htm.

Lebanon

Australian Education International. 2008. *Lebanon.* Australian Education International CEP online subscription service. http://aei.gov.au/AEI/CEP/Default.htm.

Libya

Australian Education International. 2005. *Libya.* Australian Education International CEP online subscription service. http://aei.gov.au/AEI/CEP/Default.htm.

Lithuania

Australian Education International. 2005. *Lithuania.* Australian Education International CEP online subscription service. http://aei.gov.au/AEI/CEP/Default.htm.

Macau

Australian Education International. 2006. *Macau.* Australian Education International CEP online subscription service. http://aei.gov.au/AEI/CEP/Default.htm.

Macedonia

Australian Education International. 2008. *Macedonia.* Australian Education International CEP online subscription service. http://aei.gov.au/AEI/CEP/Default.htm.

Malawi

Australian Education International. 2005. *Malawi.* Australian Education International CEP online subscription service. http://aei.gov.au/AEI/CEP/Default.htm.

Niesen, Karen L. and Onaga, Christine. 2000. *Malawi: Country Guide.* Washington, DC: AACRAO.

Malaysia

AACRAO. 1996. *Malaysia: Handbook for the Admission of International Students to Elementary and Secondary Schools in the United States.* Washington, DC: AACRAO.

Australian Education International. 2008. *Malaysia.* Australian Education International CEP online subscription service. http://aei.gov.au/AEI/CEP/Default.htm.

Stedman, Joann. 1986. *Malaysia*. Washington, DC: World Education Series/Projects for International Education Research.

Malta

Australian Education International. 2005. *Malta*. Australian Education International CEP online subscription service. http://aei.gov.au/AEI/CEP/Default.htm.

Mauritania

Trayte, Kathleen. 2000. *Mauritania: Country Guide*. Washington, DC: AACRAO.

Mauritius

Australian Education International. 2008. *Mauritius*. Australian Education International CEP online subscription service. http://aei.gov.au/AEI/CEP/Default.htm.

Mexico

Australian Education International. 2007. *Mexico*. Australian Education International CEP online subscription service. http://aei.gov.au/AEI/CEP/Default.htm.
Villa, Kitty M. 1982. *Mexico*. Washington, DC: World Education Series/Projects for International Education Research.

Moldova

Australian Education International. 2005. *Moldova*. Australian Education International CEP online subscription service. http://aei.gov.au/AEI/CEP/Default.htm.

Mongolia

Australian Education International. 2007. *Mongolia*. Australian Education International CEP online subscription service. http://aei.gov.au/AEI/CEP/Default.htm.
Sevigny, Joseph A. 2000. *Mozambique: Country Guide*. Washington, DC: AACRAO.

Montenegro

Australian Education International. 2008. *Montenegro*. Australian Education International CEP online subscription service. http://aei.gov.au/AEI/CEP/Default.htm.

Myanmar

Australian Education International. 2008. *Myanmar*. Australian Education International CEP online subscription service. http://aei.gov.au/AEI/CEP/Default.htm.

Niesen, Karen L.D. *Myanmar: Country Guide*. Washington, DC: AACRAO.

Nepal

Australian Education International. 2007. *Nepal*. Australian Education International CEP online subscription service. http://aei.gov.au/AEI/CEP/Default.htm.

The Netherlands

Australian Education International. 2008. *Netherlands*. Australian Education International CEP online subscription service. http://aei.gov.au/AEI/CEP/Default.htm.
Schuler, Peter. 1984. *The Netherlands*. Washington, DC: World Education Series/Projects for International Education Research.

New Zealand

Australian Education International. 2007. *New Zealand*. Australian Education International CEP online subscription service. http://aei.gov.au/AEI/CEP/Default.htm.
Kennedy, Patrick J. 1981. *New Zealand*. Washington, DC: World Education Series/Projects for International Education Research.

Niger

Salonga, Lydia C. 1996. *Niger: Country Guide*. Washington, DC: AACRAO.

Nigeria

Australian Education International. 2005. *Nigeria*. Australian Education International CEP online subscription service. http://aei.gov.au/AEI/CEP/Default.htm.

Norway

Australian Education International. 2008. *Norway*. Australian Education International CEP online subscription service. http://aei.gov.au/AEI/CEP/Default.htm.
Dickey, Karlene N. 1994. *Norway*. Washington, DC: World Education Series/Projects for International Education Research.

Oman

Australian Education International. 2007. *Oman*. Australian Education International CEP online subscription service. http://aei.gov.au/AEI/CEP/Default.htm.

Pacific Islands

Carpenter, Ken. 1996. *Pacific Islands: Country Guide*. Washington, DC: AACRAO.

Pakistan

Australian Education International. 2007. *Pakistan*. Australian Education International CEP online subscription service. http://aei.gov.au/AEI/CEP/Default.htm.

Palestinian National Authority

Australian Education International. 2005. *Palestinian National Authority*. Australian Education International CEP online subscription service. http://aei.gov.au/AEI/CEP/Default.htm.

Papua New Guinea

Australian Education International. 2007. *Papua New Guinea*. Australian Education International CEP online subscription service. http://aei.gov.au/AEI/CEP/Default.htm.

Peru

Australian Education International. 2008. *Peru*. Australian Education International CEP online subscription service. http://aei.gov.au/AEI/CEP/Default.htm.
Gray, Colleen. 1983. *Peru*. Washington, DC: World Education Series/Projects for International Education Research.

The Philippines

Australian Education International. 2006. *Philippines*. Australian Education International CEP online subscription service. http://aei.gov.au/AEI/CEP/Default.htm.
Vorderstrasse, Jason. 2001. *The Philippines: A Workshop Report on the Education System of the Philippines and Guide to the Academic Placement of Students in Education Institutions in the United States*. Washington, DC: World Education Series/Projects for International Education Research.
Warren, Karen. 2000. *Philippines Workshop Report*. Washington, DC: World Education Series/Projects for International Education Research.

Poland

Australian Education International. 2005. *Poland*. Australian Education International CEP online subscription service. http://aei.gov.au/AEI/CEP/Default.htm.
Devlin, Edward, Lockyear, Frederick E. and Silny, Joseph. 1992. *The Admission and Placement of Students from the Republic of Poland*. Washington, DC:

World Education Series/Projects for International Education Research.

Portugal

Australian Education International. 2006. *Portugal*. Australian Education International CEP online subscription service. http://aei.gov.au/AEI/CEP/Default.htm.

Romania

Alisauskas, Arunus. 2000. *Romania: A Workshop Report on the Educational System and Guide to the Academic Placement of Students in Educational Institutions in the United States*. Washington, DC: World Education Series/Projects for International Education Research.

Australian Education International. 2005. *Romania*. Australian Education International CEP online subscription service. http://aei.gov.au/AEI/CEP/Default.htm.

Russian Federation

AACRAO World Education Series. 2008. *Education System of the Russian Federation*. Washington, DC: AACRAO.

Australian Education International. 2005. *Russian Federation*. Australian Education International CEP online subscription service. http://aei.gov.au/AEI/CEP/Default.htm.

Drewitz, Majka. 2005. *Evaluation Tools for Russian Credentials*. Milwaukee, WI: Educational Credential Evaluators, Inc.

Rwanda

Sevigny, Joseph A. *Country Guide: Rwanda*. Washington, DC: AACRAO.

Samoa

Australian Education International. 2007. *Samoa*. Australian Education International CEP online subscription service. http://aei.gov.au/AEI/CEP/Default.htm.

Saudi Arabia

AACRAO. 1996. *Saudi Arabia: Handbook for the Admission of International Students to Elementary and Secondary Schools in the United States*. Washington, DC: AACRAO.

Australian Education International. 2007. *Saudi Arabia*. Australian Education International CEP online subscription service. http://aei.gov.au/AEI/CEP/Default.htm.

Serbia

Australian Education International. 2008. *Serbia*. Australian Education International CEP online subscription service. http://aei.gov.au/AEI/CEP/Default.htm.

Seychelles

Trayte, Kathleen. *Country Guide: Seychelles*. Washington, DC: AACRAO.

Sierra Leone

Australian Education International. 2005. *Sierra Leone*. Australian Education International CEP online subscription service. http://aei.gov.au/AEI/CEP/Default.htm.

Singapore

Australian Education International. 2008. *Singapore*. Australian Education International CEP online subscription service. http://aei.gov.au/AEI/CEP/Default.htm.

Solomon Islands

Australian Education International. 2006. *Solomon Islands*. Australian Education International CEP online subscription service. http://aei.gov.au/AEI/CEP/Default.htm.

South Africa

AACRAO. 1996. *Handbook for the Admission of International Students to Elementary and Secondary Schools in the United States: South Africa*. Washington, DC: AACRAO.

Australian Education International. 2005. *South Africa*. Australian Education International CEP online subscription service. http://aei.gov.au/AEI/CEP/Default.htm.

Spain

Australian Education International. 2005. *Spain*. Australian Education International CEP online subscription service. http://aei.gov.au/AEI/CEP/Default.htm.

Bachman, Jane, McCarty, Maxine and Mihalyi, David. 1997. *The Educational System of Spain*. Milwaukee, WI: Educational Credential Evaluators, Inc.

Sri Lanka

Australian Education International. 2008. *Sri Lanka*. Australian Education International CEP online subscription service. http://aei.gov.au/AEI/CEP/Default.htm.

Sudan

Australian Education International. 2007. *Sudan*. Australian Education International CEP online subscription service. http://aei.gov.au/AEI/CEP/Default.htm.

Sweden

Australian Education International. 2005. *Sweden*. Australian Education International CEP online subscription service. http://aei.gov.au/AEI/CEP/Default.htm.

Dickey, Karlene and Zanotti, Kathleen. 1995. *Sweden*. Washington, DC: World Education Series/Projects for International Education Research.

Switzerland

Australian Education International. 2008. *Switzerland*. Australian Education International CEP online subscription service. http://aei.gov.au/AEI/CEP/Default.htm.

Dickey, Karlene and Lukas, Karen. 1991. *Swiss Higher Schools of Engineering and Swiss Higher Schools of Economics and Business Administration*. Washington, DC: World Education Series/Projects for International Education Research.

Syria

AACRAO. 1996. *Handbook for the Admission of International Students to Elementary and Secondary Schools in the United States: Syria*. Washington, DC: AACRAO.

Australian Education International. 2005. *Syria*. Australian Education International CEP online subscription service. http://aei.gov.au/AEI/CEP/Default.htm.

Taiwan

AACRAO. 1996. *Taiwan: Handbook for the Admission of International Students to Elementary and Secondary Schools in the United States*. Washington, DC: AACRAO.

Australian Education International. 2007. *Taiwan*. Australian Education International CEP online subscription service. http://aei.gov.au/AEI/CEP/Default.htm.

Hu, Julie and Zhou, Muriel. 2004. *A Country Study on the Education System of Taiwan and Guide to the Academic Placement of Students in Education Institutions in the United States*. Washington, DC: AACRAO.

Tajikistan

Australian Education International. 2005. *Tajikistan*. Australian Education International CEP online subscription service. http://aei.gov.au/AEI/CEP/Default.htm.

Tanzania

Australian Education International. 2005. *Tanzania*. Australian Education International CEP online subscription service. http://aei.gov.au/AEI/CEP/Default.htm.

Bretherick, Dona. 1996. *Country Guide: Tanzania*. Washington, DC: AACRAO.

Australian Education International. 2005. *Thailand*. Australian Education International CEP online subscription service. http://aei.gov.au/AEI/CEP/Default.htm.

Thailand

Conquest, Fay and Katz, Nancy. 2000. *Thailand*. Washington, DC: World Education Series/Projects for International Education Research.

Tonga

Australian Education International. 2005. *Tonga*. Australian Education International CEP online subscription service. http://aei.gov.au/AEI/CEP/Default.htm.

Tunisia

Trayte, Kathleen. 2000. *Tunisia*. Washington, DC: AACRAO.

Wenger, Margaret. 2002. *The Educational System of Tunisia*. Milwaukee, WI: Educational Credential Evaluators, Inc.

Turkey

Australian Education International. 2005. *Turkey*. Australian Education International CEP online subscription service. http://aei.gov.au/AEI/CEP/Default.htm.

Frey, James. 1992. *The Educational System of Turkey*. Milwaukee, WI: Educational Credential Evaluators, Inc.

———. 2004. *Turkey: Update on Education 1997–2004*. Milwaukee, WI: Educational Credential Evaluators, Inc.

Turkmenistan

Australian Education International. 2005. *Turkmenistan*. Australian Education International CEP online subscription service. http://aei.gov.au/AEI/CEP/Default.htm.

Uganda

Australian Education International. 2005. *Uganda*. Australian Education International CEP online subscription service. http://aei.gov.au/AEI/CEP/Default.htm.

Ukraine

Australian Education International. 2008. *Ukraine*. Australian Education International CEP online subscription service. http://aei.gov.au/AEI/CEP/Default.htm.

United Arab Emirates

Australian Education International. 2005. *United Arab Emirates*. Australian Education International. http://aei.gov.au/AEI/CEP/Default.htm.

United Kingdom

AACRAO. 2006. *The Educational System of the United Kingdom*. Washington, DC: AACRAO.

2008. *British Qualifications: A Complete Guide to Professional, Vocational and Academic Qualifications in the UK*, 38th edition. London: Kogan Page.

Australian Education International. 2006. *Ireland*. Australian Education International CEP online subscription service. http://aei.gov.au/AEI/CEP/Default.htm.

———. 2006. *United Kingdom*. Australian Education International CEP online subscription service. http://aei.gov.au/AEI/CEP/Default.htm.

United States of America

2009. *Accredited Institutions of Postsecondary Education: 2009–2010*. Washington, DC: American Council on Education.

Australian Education International. 2007. *United States of America*. Australian Education International CEP online subscription service. http://aei.gov.au/AEI/CEP/Default.htm.

Uruguay

Australian Education International. 2005. *Uruguay*. Australian Education International CEP online subscription service. http://aei.gov.au/AEI/CEP/Default.htm.

Uzbekistan

Australian Education International. 2005. *Uzbekistan*. Australian Education International CEP online subscription service. http://aei.gov.au/AEI/CEP/Default.htm.

Venezuela

AACRAO. 1996. *Handbook for the Admission of International Students to Elementary and Secondary Schools in the United States: Venezuela*. Washington, DC: AACRAO.

Australian Education International. 2006. *Venezuela*. Australian Education International CEP online subscription service. http://aei.gov.au/AEI/CEP/Default.htm.

Vietnam

Australian Education International. 2006. *Vietnam*. Australian Education International CEP online subscription service. http://aei.gov.au/AEI/CEP/Default.htm.

Dean, Michael. 1998. *Vietnam*. Washington, DC: World Education Series/Projects for International Education Research.

Feagles, Shelley M. 2008. *Tools for Evaluating Educational Documents from Vietnam*. Milwaukee, WI: Educational Credential Evaluators, Inc.

Zaire

Sevigny, Joseph A. 1996. *Country Guide: Zaire*. Washington, DC: AACRAO.

Zambia

Australian Education International. 2005. *Zambia*. Australian Education International CEP online subscription service. http://aei.gov.au/AEI/CEP/Default.htm.

O'Neill, Holly A. 1996. *Country Guide: Zambia*. Washington, DC: AACRAO.

Zimbabwe

Australian Education International. 2008. *Zimbabwe*. Australian Education International CEP online subscription service. http://aei.gov.au/AEI/CEP/Default.htm.

WEB SITES

Association of African Universities. www.aau.org/membership/fullmembers.htm.

Bologna Secretariat. 2009. Participating Countries and Organizations. www.ond.vlaanderen.be/hogeronderwijs/bologna/pcao/.

European National Information Centre and National Academic Recognition Information Centre (ENIC-NARIC). www.enic-naric.net.

Eurydice. The Information Network on Education in Europe (formerly Socrates). www.eurydice.org.

Fulbright Country Pages. www.cies.org/country.

International Association of Universities. Education Systems and List of Universities. www.unesco.org/iau/onlinedatabases/index.html .

International Network for Higher Education in Africa. Country Higher Education Profiles. www.bc.edu/bc_org/avp/soe/cihe/inhea/profiles.htm.

International Student Exchange Programs Country Handbooks. www.isep.org/students/placed/country_handbooks.asp.

Michigan State University. African Studies Center: Search African Higher Education Institutions. http://africa.msu.edu/AUP/search-form.php.

OSEAS-Europe Fact Sheet for Higher Education. www.bibl.u-szeged.hu/oseas/edsystems.html.

Overseas Advisers and U.S. Admissions Connection Link Project (OSEAS). Information on Education Systems around the World. www.bibl.u-szeged.hu/oseas_adsec/sources.htm.

Trans-European Mobility Scheme for University Studies (TEMPUS). http://ec.europa.eu/education/external-relation-programmes/doc70_en.htm.

UNESCO-CEPES. Monographs on Higher Education. www.cepes.ro/publications.

UNESCO International Bureau of Education. Country Dossiers. www.ibe.unesco.org/countries/countrydossiers.htm.

World Data on Education. International Bureau of Education—United Nations Educational, Scientific, and Cultural Organization (IBE-UNESCO). http://nt5.scbbs.com/cgi-bin/om_isapi.dll?clientID=275562&depth=3&infobase=iwde.nfo&softpage=PL_tocframe

World Education Services Canada. World Education Profiles. www.wes.org/ca/wedb/ecountrylist.htm.

NEWSLETTERS AND MAILING LISTS

AACRAO List-servs
www.aacrao.org/useful_links/listserv.cfm

AACRAO Transcript
www.aacrao.org/transcript

Association of African Universities e-Courier
www.aau.org/e-courier

Australian Government Higher Education 2020
www.dest.gov.au/sectors/higher_education/publications_resources/2020_newsletter/default.htm

British Council
www.magnetmail.net/actions/subscription_form_british.cfm

Chronicle of Higher Education
http://chronicle.com/section/Home/5

Comparative and International Education Society
www.cies.us/newsletter.htm

DAAD—German Academic Exchange Service
www.daad.org/?p=46367#newsletters

Diploma Mills News
http://diplomamillnews.blogspot.com

Educational Credential Evaluators
www.ece.org/main/content=Newsletter&SubSite=2&LeftNav=7

European Association for International Education
www.eaie.org/networking/eaiel.asp

Inside Higher Ed
www.insidehighered.com/news

Inter-L Yahoo Group
http://groups.yahoo.com/group/inter-l

International Association of Universities E-Bulletin
www.unesco.org/iau

International Higher Education: the Quarterly Publication of the CIHE
www.bc.edu/bc_org/avp/soe/cihe/newsletter

International Research and Exchanges Board
www.irex.org/newsroom/irex-news.asp

Institute of International Education (IIE) Interactive
http://iienetwork.org/?p=27503

NAFSA wRAP-Up
www.nafsa.org/knowledge_community_network.sec/recruitment_admissions/admissions_and_credential/practice_resources_19/admissions_wrap-up_newsletter

Not-So-Foreign
www.higher-edge.com/inst/publications.php

UNESCO Education Newsletter EduInfo
http://portal.unesco.org/education

World Education News and Reviews
www.wes.org/ewenr/09jan/index.asp

Appendix C:
Bill of Rights and Responsibilities for International Students and Institutions

AACRAO, DECEMBER 1996

PREAMBLE

In response to a growing need for policy guidance on issues related to the delivery of programs and services to international students, the American Association of Collegiate Registrars and Admissions Officers (AACRAO), with guidance from members of the international education community, has developed this Bill of Rights and Responsibilities for International Students and Institutions (Bill of Rights). As signatories to the Bill of Rights, we reserve the right to display the official logo signifying our support of the principles and practices articulated herein.

DEFINITIONS

* An *international student* is defined as any person engaging in learning outside of his or her country of citizenship.

* An *institution* is defined as any institution or entity providing information, facilitating the enrollment of or providing learning opportunities to international students or scholars.

* The *international community* is defined as a complex system of educational entities, government agencies, private organizations, regulatory bodies and individuals delivering education programs and services

ARTICLE I: Individual Rights of the International Student

SECTION 1

International students have the right to know who the provider of educational services is and all of the provider's affiliations.

SECTION 2

International students have the right to a clear explanation from the institution to which they are applying of the admissions process and documentation necessary to complete their admissions dossiers.

SECTION 3

International students have the right to a clear and complete explanation and description of the academic course offerings and the approximate time normally required to complete an intended program from the institution to which they are applying.

SECTION 4

International students have the right to receive a clear and accurate account of all costs for the academic year or a reasonable estimation of the full cost of their educational program. This should be explained in application material sent to them by the institutions to which they are applying. International students also have the right to a clear and detailed explanation of costs for services provided by placement agencies or other third parties assisting them in the admissions process. Such service costs should be readily distinguishable from the standard costs associated with a course of study at the students' intended institutions.

SECTION 5

International students have the right to know what personal information is collected about them, why it is being collected and how they may review their files and correct any errors. International students should have assurance that personal information about them may be used only by those persons with a legitimate right to know.

SECTION 6

International students have the right to have their applications for admission and their prior learning experiences evaluated by admissions officers or credential evalua-tors trained to evaluate international applications and learning.

SECTION 7

International students have the right to a clear explanation from their home institution of whether, or the extent to which, course work at their host institution may be transferable to their program of study at their home institution.

SECTION 8

International students have the right to services and information that support their unique needs as international students, such as counseling on immigration regula-tions, cultural adjustment, orienta-tion to the host institution, and information on insurance and taxes.

SECTION 9

International students have the right to have their language abilities assessed to determine if their skills are sufficient to enable them to ben-efit from the host institution's aca-demic course offerings.

SECTION 10

International students have a right to a clear and complete explanation of all legal requirements governing their enrollment, including how to maintain their student status.

SECTION 11

International students have owner-ship rights over their intellectual works unless the works are subject to specific published institutional policies to the contrary or owner-ship rights are relinquished by the students.

ARTICLE II: Individual Responsibilities of the International Student

SECTION 1

International students shall be hon-est in their representations to insti-tutions, government entities and others in the international educa-tion community. International stu-dents shall abide by the host institutions' honor systems. Fraud or misrepresentation of achieve-ments are valid reason for expulsion from the institution.

SECTION 2

International students shall recog-nize, honor and properly attribute the intellectual property of others.

SECTION 3

International students shall adhere to the laws, rules and regulations of the host nation and institution.

ARTICLE III: Rights of Educational Institutions

SECTION 1

Educational institutions have the right to establish appropriate admissions criteria and deadlines consistent with their educational programs.

SECTION 2

Educational institutions have the right to establish appropriate and realistic deadlines for completion of the international student's program.

SECTION 3

Educational institutions have the right to deny admission or continuing enrollment if evidence proves fraud or lack of achievement by the international student.

SECTION 4

Educational institutions have the right to be informed if an international student is being assisted in admission by a placement agency or other third party.

ARTICLE IV: Responsibilities of the Educational Institution

SECTION 1

Educational institutions claiming an affiliation with another institution shall explain to students the nature of their affiliation, particularly as it might relate to the recognition of academic credentials. Similarly, the institution's official recognition or accreditation shall be disclosed to students.

SECTION 2

Educational institutions shall provide students with a clear explanation of their admissions process and what documentation is necessary to complete the students' admissions dossiers.

SECTION 3

Educational institutions shall provide students with a clear and complete explanation and description of the academic course offerings and the approximate time normally required to complete the intended program.

SECTION 4

Educational institutions shall provide students and their financial sponsors with accurate information about all reasonable costs for the academic year or an estimation of the full cost of their educational program. This information should appear in literature provided to prospective students with application materials. Placement agencies or other third parties assisting students in the admissions process shall provide students with a clear and detailed explanation of the costs associated with these services. These service costs should be readily distinguishable from the standard costs associated with a course of study at the intended institution.

SECTION 5

Educational institutions, upon request of the student, shall let the student know what personal information is collected about him or her, why it is being collected and how the student may review the file and correct any errors. Institutions shall treat all files on students as confidential, examining or disclosing the contents only when authorized by the owner of the information, approved by the appropriate institutional official on a need-to-know basis, or as required by law. Institutions shall develop, implement, and maintain security procedures to insure the integrity of their files.

SECTION 6

Educational institutions shall ensure that students' applications for admission and their prior learning experiences are evaluated by admissions officers and/or credential evaluators trained to evaluate international applications and learning.

SECTION 7

Educational institutions considered home institutions shall provide clear explanations as to whether, or the extent to which, students' course work may be transferable to their programs of study in their home countries.

SECTION 8

Educational institutions shall provide services and information that support the unique needs of international students, such as immigration regulations, cultural adjustment advising, orientation, insurance, and tax information.

SECTION 9

Educational institutions shall assess whether international applicants possess sufficient command of the language of the host country to ensure that students will benefit from the academic course offerings. If the institution lacks proficiency programs to remedy an applicant's language deficiency, it shall not admit the applicant until he or she shows evidence of facility in the host language.

SECTION 10

Educational institutions shall inform international students and their financial sponsors of all legal requirements governing the students' enrollment.

PERMISSION: Permission is hereby given to make and distribute copies of the Bill of Rights and Responsibilities for International Students and Institutions for non-profit purposes on condition that the Bill of Rights or any publication in which it appears is attributed to the American Association of Collegiate Registrars and Admissions Officers. Please forward a copy of the publication in which the Bill of Rights appears to AACRAO, One Dupont Circle, NW, Suite 520 Washington, DC 20036-1135.

INFORMATION: Questions or comments regarding the Bill of Rights and Responsibilities for International Students and Institutions should be addressed to AACRAO at the above address or voice: (202) 293-9161 or Fax: (202) 872-8857.

References

2009-10 Almanac. Chronicle of Higher Education, Volume LV, Number 1.

Academic and Language Students: 8 C.F.R. 214.2(f). Retrieved February 16, 2009 from U.S. Immigration and Customs Enforcement at <www.ice.gov/sevis/regs/8cfr214_2f.htm>.

Albrecht, T.J. 2007. *Challenges and Service Needs of Undocumented Mexican Undergraduate Students: Students' Voices and Administrators' Perspectives.* Doctoral dissertation, The University of Texas at Austin, Austin. ProQuest Digital Dissertations, AAT 3290814.

Anderson, L. 2009. To friend or not to friend? College admissions in the age of Facebook. *USAToday.com.* September 18.

Baxton, M., J.K. Johnson, G. Nathanson, W. Paver and R. Watkins. 2009. Understanding the bologna process for admissions officers. *College and University.* 85(2).

Bhandari, R. and P. Chow. 2008. *Open Doors : Report on International Education Exchange.* New York: Institute of International Education.

———. 2009. *Open Doors 2009: Report on educational exchange.* New York: Institute of International Education.

Bhandari, R. and S. Laughin. 2009. *Higher Education on the Move: New Developments in Global Mobility.* New York: AIFS Foundation & Institute of International Education.

Bohm, A., T. Davis, D. Meares, and D. Pearce. 2002. *Global Student Mobility 2025: Forecast of the Demand for International Higher Education.* Sydney, Australia: IDP Education Pty Ltd.

Bonfiglio, R. 2007. Enough to e-mail from colleges! *The Chronicle of Higher Education.* 53(34): B28.

Britz, J.D. 1998. Maguire reviews the past, forecasts the future. *The Lawlor Review.* VI (3): Fall. Minneapolis, MN.

Brockington, J, W. Hoffa, and P. Martin. 2005. *Guide to Education Abroad for Advisers and Administrators, 3rd Edition.* New York: NAFSA: Association of International Educators.

Brown, H.A., and P.D. Syverson. 2004. *Findings from U.S. Graduate Schools on International Graduate Student Admissions Trends.* Retrieved from the Council of Graduate Schools <www.cgsnet.org/portals/0/pdf/R_intladmit04_II.pdf>.

Council of Graduate Schools. 2008. *Global Perspective on Graduate Education, Proceedings of the Strategic Leaders Global Summit on Graduate Education.*

Curtis, S., S. Dunnett, C. Perdreau, W. Weiner, and J. Williams. 2005. *Internationalizing the Campus 2005.* Washington DC: NAFSA. Retrieved May 19, 2010 from <www.nafsa.org/_/File/_/itc2005.pdf>.

Destination Indiana. Retrieved May 6, 2010 from <http://fadams.iweb.bsu.edu>.

Dilenschneider, R.L., and J. Salak. 2003. Do ethical communicators finish first? Walking the straight and narrow information path. *Communication World.* 20(4). Retrieved from EBSCOhost database on May 13, 2009.

Eckel, P.D., and J.E. King. 2004. *An Overview of Higher Education in the United States: Diversity, Access, and the Role of the Marketplace.* Washington, D.C.: American Council on Education.

Educational Testing Service. 2008. *Our Heritage.* Retrieved December 29, 2008, from: <www.ets.org/portal/site/ets/menuitem.22f30af61d34e9c39a77b13bc3921509/?vgnextoid=a1e65784623f4010VgnVCM10000022f95190RCRD>.

———. 2010. *For Test Takers: TOEFL® Internet-Based Test (iBT).* Available at: <www.ets.org/portal/site/ets/menuitem.1488512ecfd5b8849a77b13bc3921509/?vgnextoid=fdd8af5e44df4010VgnVCM10000022f95190RCRD&vgnextchannel=7929d898c84f4010VgnVCM10000022f95190RCRD>.

Electronic Code of Federal Regulations. Retrieved February 2, 2009 from: <http://ecfr.gpoaccess.gov/cgi/t/text/textidx?c=ecfr&tpl= %2Findex.tpl>.

Ellison, P. 2009. Interview by author. Buffalo, NY. Telephone. Jan 28 and Feb. 2.

ETS. *See* Educational Testing Service.

Florida, R. 2007. *The Flight of the Creative Class: The New Global Competition for Talent.* Harper Collins Business.

Fosnocht, D.J. 2007. *NAFSA Advisor's Manual* (desk edition). Washington D.C: NAFSA.

Fratt, L. 2006. Text messaging: The newest recruitment innovation. *University Business.* May.

Frey, J. 2003. Basic principles of international educational credential evaluation. *EAIE Forum.*

Friedman, T.L. 2007. *The World is Flat: A Brief History of the Twenty-First Century.* New York: Farrar, Straus & Giroux.

Graddol, D. 2006. *English Next: Why Global English Might Mean the End of 'English as a Foreign Language'.* Retrieved December 29, 2008, from: <www.britishcouncil.org/learning-research -english-next.pdf>.

Gullahorn, J.T., and J.E. Gullahorn. 1963. An extension of the U curve hypothesis. *Journal of Social Issues.* 19(3): 33–47.

Gutierrez, R., and R. Bhandari. 2009. *The Value of International Education to U.S. Business and Industry Leaders: Key Findings from a Survey of CEOs* (an IIE briefing paper). New York: Institute of International Education.

Henderson, S.E. 2001. On the brink of a profession. In *Strategic Enrollment Management Revolution,* edited by J. Black. Washington, DC: AACRAO.

Hoefer M., N. Rytina, and B. Baker. 2008. *Estimates of the Unauthorized Immigrant Population Residing in the United States: January 2007.* Department of Homeland Security, Office of Immigration Statistics. Retrieved from <www.dhs.gov/xlibrary/assets/statistics/publications/ois_ill_pe_2007.pdf>.

Hossler, D., J.P. Bean & Associates. 1990. *The Strategic Management of College Enrollments.* San Francisco: Jossey-Bass, Inc.

IIE. *See* Institute of International Education.

Institute of International Education. 2008a. *International Students on U.S. Campuses at All-Time High.* November 17. Retrieved April 2, 2009 from: <http://opendoors.iienetwork.org/?p=131590>.

———. 2008b. Top 40 host community colleges. *Open Doors 2008: Report on International Educational Exchange.* Retrieved April 20, 2009 from: <http://opendoors.iienetwork.org/page/136334/>.

———. 2009a. *Open Doors 2009: Report on Educational Exchange.* New York: Institute of International Education.

———. 2009b. *Funding for United States Study.* Retrieved February 4, 2009, from: <www.fundingusstudy.org>.

———. 2010. Meeting America's global education challenge. *Study Abroad White Papers.* Available at: <www.iie.org/en/Research-and-Publications/Research-Projects/Study-Abroad-Capacity-Research-Initiative>.

Kaptein, M., L. Huberts, S. Avelino, and K. Lasthuizen. 2005. Demonstrating ethical leadership by measuring ethics. *Public Integrity* 7(4): 299–311. Retrieved from EBSCOhost database on May 13, 2009.

Lauren, B. 2008. *The College Admissions Officers' Guide.* Washington, DC: AACRAO.

Light, R.L., M. Xu, and J. Mossop. 1987. English proficiency and academic performance of international students. *TESOL Quarterly.* 21(2): 251–261. Retrieved December 19, 2008, from: <www.jstor.org/pss/3586734>.

Lipson, C. 2008. *Succeeding as an International Student in the United States and Canada.* Chicago and London: The University of Chicago Press.

Maguire, J. 1976. To the organized go the students. *Bridge Magazine.* XXXIX(I) Fall.

McKeon, D.W. 2008. *TOEFL Score Interpretation.* Retrieved December 29, 2008 from: <www.grads.vt.edu/igss/faculty_staff/toefl_interp.html>.

NACES. 2010. *General Guiding Principles of Good Practice for Educational Credential Evaluation.* National Association of Credential Evaluation Services. Retrieved June 4, 2010 from: <www.naces.org/codeofgoodpractice.html>.

NAFSA. See NAFSA: Association of International Educators.

NAFSA: Association of International Educators. 2009. *NAFSA's Intercultural Activity Toolkit.* Retrieved February 12, 2009 from: <www.nafsa.org/knowledge_community_network.sec/teaching_learning_and/intercultural_communications/practice_resources/orientation_programs/intercultural_activity_1>.

———. 2009a. *The Economic Benefits of International Education to the United States: A Statistical Analysis, 2008–2009.* Washington, DC: NAFSA.

———. 2009b. *NAFSA's Statement of Ethics.* Retrieved February 12, 2009 from: <www.nafsa.org/about.sec/governance_leadership/ethics_standards/nafsa_s_code_of_ethics>.

Noronha, A. 2004. How competent employees transform a company. *IT People.* June 28. Available at: <www.expressitpeople.com/20040628/management1.shtml>.

Obst, D., and M. Kuder. 2009. *Joint and Dual Degree Programs: An Emerging Model for Transatlantic Exchange.* New York: Freie Universitat Berlin & Institute of International Education.

Olivas, M. 2008. The DREAM Act and in-state tuition for undocumented students. In *The College Admission Officer's Guide,* edited by B. Lauren. Washington, DC: AACRAO.

Passel, J.S. 2006. *Size and Characteristics of the Unauthorized Migrant Population in the U.S.: Estimates Based on the March 2005 Current Population Survey.* March 7. Retrieved 3/9/2006 from <http://pewhispanic.org/files/reports/61.pdf>.

Powers, E. 2007. The community college role in developing countries. *Inside Higher Education.* August 10. Retrieved April 2, 2009 from: <www.insidehighered.com/news/2007/08/10/ccabroad>.

Press, L., W. Foster, P. Wolcott, and W. McHenry. 2003. The Internet in India and China. *Information Technologies and International Development.* 1(1): 41–60.

Raby, R.L. 2008. Expanding education abroad at U.S. community colleges. *Meeting America's Global Education Challenge.* Issue 3. September. Retrieved May 19, 2010 from Institute of International Education at <www.iiebooks.org/isnu3exedaba.html>.

Rincon, A. 2008. Undocumented immigrants and higher education. *Si Se Puede!* LFB Scholarly Publishing.

Sevigny, J. 2001. *The AACRAO International Guide: A Resource for International Education Professionals.* Washington, DC: AACRAO.

The Forum on Education Abroad. 2008. *Standards of Good Practice for Education Abroad.* Accessed June 10, 2010 from <www.forumea.org/documents/ForumEAStandardsGoodPrctMarch2008.pdf>.

The Linguist: The Power of Language. The importance of TOEIC, TOEFL, and IELTS. Retrieved December 16, 2008, from: <www.thelinguist.com/en/en/library/item/20614/>.

Triandis, H.C. 1989. Cross-cultural studies of individualism and collectivism. In *Nebraska Symposium of Motivation,* edited by J. Berman. Lincoln, NE: University of Nebraska Press.

U.S. Citizenship and Immigration Services. 2009. *Immigration and Naturalization Act.* Retrieved February 4. 2009 from <www.uscis.gov>.

U.S. Department of Education and Office of Postsecondary Education. 2005. *The Handbook for Campus Crime Reporting.* Available at <www2.ed.gov/admins/lead/safety/campus.html#handbook>.

U.S. Department of Education. 2010. *Structure of the U.S. Education System: Credit Systems.* U.S. Network for Education Information. Retrieved June 4, 2010 from: <www2.ed.gov/about/offices/list/ous/international/usnei/us/edlite-evaluation.html>.

U.S. Department of State, Bureau of Educational and Cultural Affairs, EducationUSA. 2009. *Finance Your Studies.* Retrieved January 30, 2009 from: <www.education-usa.info/pages/students/finance.php>.

U.S. Department of State, Bureau of Consular Affairs. 2009. *Exchange Visitors (J) Visas.* Retrieved February 4, 2009 from: <http://travel.state.gov/visa/temp/types/types_1267.html#12>.

U.S. Journal of Academics. 2009. *Scholarships to Study in the USA.* Retrieved January 30, 2009 from: <www.usjournal.com/en/students/info/finaid.html>.

UNESCO. 2008. *Global Education Digest 2008: Comparing Education Statistics Across the World.* Montreal, Canada: UNESCO Institute for Statistics.

Vancouver English Centre Inc. 2010. *TOEFL Equivalency Table.* Retrieved May 25, 2010 from: <http://secure.vec.bc.ca/toefl-equivalency-table.cfm>.

Vinke, A.A., and W.M.G. Jochems. 1993. English proficiency and academic success in international postgraduate education. *Higher Education.* 26(3): 275–285. Retrieved December 16, 2008, from: <www.springerlink.com/content/h7544285x382u356/>.

Wada, R. 2010. The n'th degree—Issues and case studies in degree equivalency: Working with the EDGE Database. *Bender's Immigration Bulletin.* May 15. Available at: <archive.fcsa.biz/docs/15BIB_Wada.pdf>.

Wickersham, M.E. 2009. Leading by example: High ethical expectations foster trust in schools. *American School Board Journal.* 196(3): 20. Retrieved from EBSCOhost database on May 13, 2009.